Reconstructing the Cold War

Reconstructing the Cold War

The Early Years, 1945–1958

TED HOPF

OXFORD
UNIVERSITY PRESS

OXFORD
UNIVERSITY PRESS

Oxford University Press is a department of the University of Oxford.
It furthers the University's objective of excellence in research, scholarship,
and education by publishing worldwide.

Oxford   New York
Auckland   Cape Town   Dar es Salaam   Hong Kong   Karachi
Kuala Lumpur   Madrid   Melbourne   Mexico City   Nairobi
New Delhi   Shanghai   Taipei   Toronto

With offices in
Argentina   Austria   Brazil   Chile   Czech Republic   France   Greece
Guatemala   Hungary   Italy   Japan   Poland   Portugal   Singapore
South Korea   Switzerland   Thailand   Turkey   Ukraine   Vietnam

Oxford is a registered trade mark of Oxford University Press
in the UK and certain other countries.

Published in the United States of America by
Oxford University Press
198 Madison Avenue, New York, NY 10016

© Oxford University Press 2012

First issued as an Oxford University Press paperback, 2014.

All rights reserved. No part of this publication may be reproduced, stored in a retrieval system, or transmitted,
in any form or by any means, without the prior permission in writing of Oxford University Press, or as expressly permitted by
law, by license, or under terms agreed with the appropriate reproduction rights organization.
Inquiries concerning reproduction outside the scope of the above should be sent to the Rights Department,
Oxford University Press, at the address above.

You must not circulate this work in any other form
and you must impose this same condition on any acquirer.

Library of Congress Cataloging-in-Publication Data
Hopf, Ted, 1959–
Reconstructing the Cold War : the early years, 1945–1958 / Ted Hopf.
pages ; cm
Includes bibliographical references and index.
ISBN 978-0-19-985848-4 (hardback : alkaline paper); 978-0-19-937976-7 (paperback : alk. paper)
1. Soviet Union—Foreign relations—1945–1991. 2. Cold War.
3. Social change—Soviet Union. 4. Group identity—Soviet Union. I. Title.
DK268.5.H67   2012
327.47009′04—dc23   2011047116

CONTENTS

Preface vii

1. Introduction 3

2. Stalinism after the War: A Discourse of Danger, 1945–53 29

3. Stalin's Foreign Policy: The Discourse of Danger Abroad, 1945–53 72

4. The Thaw at Home, 1953–58 143

5. The Thaw Abroad, 1953–58 198

6. Conclusions 254

References 269
Index 291

PREFACE

There are many reasons to revisit the Cold War. The first is its remarkably misleading name. The Cold War was anything but cold for the almost 20 million people who lost their lives during the postwar conflict between the Soviet Union and the United States from 1945 and 1991. It has been said that victors write the history. In this case, the very naming of the conflict erases what it meant for most of the rest of the world. While the United States and Soviet Union lost fewer than 100,000 men and women in combat during the so-called Cold War, these losses are dwarfed by the millions who died in Vietnam, Angola, Afghanistan, Honduras, Mozambique, Somalia, Kampuchea, and elsewhere, as the two superpowers acted out their competition in arenas where they could plausibly avoid directly fighting each other. One purpose of this book is to remind readers that the "long peace" and the era of "bipolar stability" remarked by historians and political scientists only mask how dangerous and bloody and hot the Cold War really was for much of the rest of the world, especially the decolonizing world.

The political science subfield of international relations (IR) theory also needs a book on the Cold War. In particular, social constructivism should provide an account of the Cold War based on the identity relations of the Soviet Union and its allies and enemies around the world. Systemic IR theories, such as neorealism or systemic constructivism, are not aimed, or able, to do more than explain why there was conflict between the Soviet Union and the United States after World War II. And historians, for the most part, concentrate on providing compelling accounts of particular events and relationships during the Cold War. What I offer here fills the middle-range theoretical void left by systemic IR theories and Cold War historians. Through societal constructivism, I offer explanations for Soviet relations with both individual countries, but also for entire regions, such as Eastern Europe, or categories, such as the decolonizing world, and over some significant period of time.

This book has a history of its own. After finishing a book that applied constructivism to Soviet foreign relations in 1955 and Russian foreign relations in 1999, I was asked by Ron Suny to write a chapter for a volume he was editing, *The Cambridge History of Modern Russia*. In that chapter I both tried to account for the entire postwar period of Soviet foreign policy until its collapse in 1991, and also attempted to add institutions to my societal constructivist argument. I did this in response to many well-placed criticisms of constructivist work, including my own. In arguing that particular discourses of identity inform a state's interests in other states, we had not developed convincing arguments for why one discourse rather than another ended up the dominant one infusing the state's conceptions of its own interests. In this book, I suggest that domestic institutions, as sites for alternative discourses of identity, help address these criticisms.

Having written the chapter for Ron Suny's volume, I realized that what I really needed to do was write a book on the entire Cold War, applying societal constructivism and institutions to its entire sweep. Several years into the project I realized that I already had written far too many words, and was only approaching 1958. So, this book is just volume I in a prospective three-volume constructivist account of the Cold War. The second volume will bring the Cold War up to Gorbachev's assumption of leadership in 1985, and the third volume will deal with the six years that ended the Cold War.

In a project of this size and duration, I have relied on many colleagues, institutions, and friends. The place that has been my most faithful companion is the Mershon Center of International Security at Ohio State University. Not only has it been my research home for the last 12 years, but it has responded generously to my requests for financing trips to archives in Moscow, as well as meetings at which I presented pieces of the book as it unfolded. This book would have taken even longer had it not been for the release time from courses provided by the Center over the years. In addition, the Mershon Center itself, through its broad and deep multi-disciplinary interpretation of the concept of security, has provided a rich intellectual home in which my ideas have fermented for some time. I would especially like to thank Richard Herrmann for his years of support as director of the Mershon Center, as well as to note my appreciation of his superb performance as director of the Center for the last eight years. While I would like to thank two Mershon colleagues, Robert McMahon and Carole Fink, for commenting on the manuscript, I would also like to note that many Mershon associates have contributed over the years to my thinking in conversations about everything but the Cold War. I am grateful to Dorothy Noyes, Alexander Wendt, Allan Silverman, Gerry Hudson, Peter Gries, Brian Pollins, Markus Kornprobst, David Hoffmann, Chad Alger, Jacques Hymans, and Andrew Ross. In addition, I have been blessed with an extraordinarily talented cohort of graduate students in political science. While only a few—Jim Delaet, Dane Imerman, Caleb Gallemore, Richard Arnold, and Srdjan Vucetic—worked directly on this book, many others, in class and out, continually educated me about social theory and international relations. They enriched my understanding of both, directed me to literature of which I was not aware, and convinced me to change my views on much of what I had read. I am deeply appreciative to all of them for their many keen insights. Special thanks goes to Suzanna Dunbar whose last minute editing made the final manuscript possible. Finally, I would like to thank David McBride and Marc Schneider at Oxford University Press for their attention and advice during the development and production of this manuscript, Michele Bowman for her truly superior copyediting, and Mary Hashman for the index.

I am also deeply grateful to the Davis Center for Russian and Eurasian Studies for inviting me to spend my sabbatical year, 2006–07, there. In particular, I wish to thank Tim Colton, Yoi Herrera, Lis Tarlow, and Nira Gautam for making that time possible and most productive. During those nine months I depended on Mark Kramer's incomparable reserve of knowledge of the Soviet archives. Mark has given me advice on researching the Cold War for the last 15 years, and this book would be hard to imagine without his abiding generosity and continual stream of comments and advice.

Mark Kramer is a member of another extraordinary institution whose members I have learned from for the last 15 years. PONARS, or the Program on New Approaches to Russian Security, was created by Celeste Wallander in 1995 and is now under the leadership of Henry Hale and Cory Welt. By now a network of almost 100 scholars from around the world who specialize in Eurasian security studies, understood most broadly and deeply, PONARS has been a constant source of information, good advice, and meetings of incomparable value.

I am also very grateful to Matthew Evangelista and Jeffrey Checkel, my two anonymous reviewers at Oxford University Press, who revealed their identities to me, no doubt fearing I was not going to follow their many useful pieces of advice. I hope I have done enough to justify them outing themselves.

Over the years I have also received penetrating and timely advice from Iver Neumann, Peter Katzenstein, Jim Richter, Ned Lebow, and Iain Johnston.

Kavita Baireddy, a software engineer by trade, read the introduction and conclusion, and deemed the book readable by an audience beyond IR faculty and graduate students. That was perhaps the most encouraging commentary of all.

This book is dedicated to the 20 million who died in the not-so cold Cold War.

Reconstructing the Cold War

1

Introduction

In June 1947, US Secretary of State George Marshall announced a European Recovery Plan (the "Marshall Plan") for all European countries. Soviet foreign minister Viacheslav Molotov attended the initial meetings on the Marshall Plan in Paris in July. Indeed, Moscow initially encouraged its east European allies to attend the meeting. Within days, however, this $15 billion economic aid package provoked the Soviet Union to embark on the Stalinization of Eastern Europe, the wholesale replication of the Soviet political and economic system, replete with arrests, purges, show trials, collectivization of agriculture and expropriation of property owners. To ensure greater obedience among its communist allies, Moscow resurrected the Communist International (Comintern), this time as the Cominform, in September 1947. Why was the Marshall Plan considered so much more threatening in Moscow than the Truman Doctrine which had been announced in March 1947? After all, this was a commitment by the US to provide military support to Turkey and Greece as part of a global commitment against communist expansion. It was one of the initial linchpins of the new US strategy of containment.

On March 27, 1948, Moscow announced that Yugoslavia, its most powerful military ally in Eastern Europe, was a threat to socialism and "requested" that all its other socialist allies in Eastern Europe sever all economic, military, and political ties with Belgrade. Just months before, as a consequence of the Marshall Plan, the Cominform had just evaluated all the Soviet Union's East European allies for ideological rectitude. Yugoslavia was judged to be the most advanced on the path to Soviet-style socialism. Moreover, Yugoslavians themselves were understood as "little Slavic brothers" of the elder Russian brother in Moscow. Nevertheless, the Soviet Union withdrew its advisers and began formulating plans for Yugoslavian prime minister Josip Broz Tito's overthrow and assassination. How is it possible that Moscow would make an enemy of one of its closest allies just weeks after Belgium, France, Luxembourg, the Netherlands, and the United Kingdom signed a defense alliance, the Brussels Pact? This West European predecessor to NATO was the first alliance among

West European countries not explicitly directed against Germany. Meanwhile, just three months later, Moscow blockaded Berlin, necessitating the Berlin airlift. Why would any great power get rid of one of its strongest allies just when the danger posed by its primary opponent has reached unprecedented heights, and it is about to launch the riskiest foreign policy venture since the end of World War II?

In July 1955, a Soviet delegation led by Communist Party General Secretary Nikita Khrushchev went to Belgrade to apologize to Tito and effect a rapprochement between the two countries. While Khrushchev blamed Stalin, and still more, Lavrentii Beria, for excommunicating Yugoslavia from the socialist bloc, the Soviet Union found itself admitting that it had made a monumental error. Its apologies made the Yugoslavian model of socialism, or Titoism, a legitimized alternative to its own Soviet model of socialism for all its East European allies. This was done in the wake of a marked reduction in tensions between the Soviet Union and the West. The first postwar meeting of the leaders of the four wartime allies was to be held in Geneva a couple of weeks later; the war in Korea had ended two years before; the French colonial war in Vietnam was ended by the 1954 Geneva Accords; and the great powers had agreed to a neutral and united Austria. Why would the Soviet Union choose to make its Yugoslav enemy into its friend at a time when its alliance was far less urgent? If anything, the Soviet Union needed Yugoslavia as an ally far less in 1955 than it did in 1948. Moreover, the reconciliation with Tito emboldened other East European communist reformers to pursue more "national" roads to socialism themselves, eventuating in the Hungarian revolution the following year, and the Soviet military suppression of that rebellion.

In February 1950, the Soviet Union and the People's Republic of China signed a Treaty of Friendship and Cooperation that cemented a military alliance between the two largest countries in the world. But parts of this treaty clearly subordinated China to the Soviet Union. Moscow was granted military basing and transit rights, exclusive control over certain strategic Chinese natural resources, privileged participation in joint-stock companies, and control over China's railroads in Manchuria. With Stalin's death in 1953, and Khrushchev's increasing de-Stalinization of Soviet domestic and foreign policy, Sino-Soviet relations improved, as Khrushchev revised the offensive elements of the Treaty in China's favor. But beginning in 1956, after Khrushchev's secret speech to the Twentieth Party Congress in which he denounced Stalin, and later in 1958, at which time Mao announced China's Great Leap Forward, the alliance between Moscow and Beijing began to deteriorate, verging on open hostility. Just as the Soviet Union was de-Stalinizing, China was re-Stalinizing. How is it possible that the Soviet Union allowed, or even facilitated, the dissolution of its single most important strategic alliance in the world?

In February 1950, the Vietnamese communist leader Ho Chi Minh was permitted to come to Moscow only if he came in secret. Meetings with him were not allowed to be held in the Kremlin but were shunted off to the trade union hall, and he was told to not deal with Moscow directly, but work through Beijing. In fact, in 1949, Stalin had anointed China as the leader of the national liberation movement in Asia, effectively outsourcing that part of the world revolutionary alliance to Beijing, reserving for Moscow revolutionary responsibilities in developed capitalist states. And yet in December 1955, Khrushchev, Malenkov, and other Soviet leaders spent almost a month touring India, Burma, and Afghanistan, declaring them potential allies against imperialism. What could possibly account for Soviet rejection of an alliance against imperialism with the Vietnamese national liberation hero Ho Chi Minh in 1950, but an enthusiastic recruitment of allies from among "bourgeois nationalists" just five years later? Why would the Soviet Union pursue detente with the United States, creating the "spirit of Geneva" in 1955, while simultaneously opening up an entirely new front in the Cold War in the decolonizing world?

These are apparently hard Cold War puzzles for a single approach to solve. Probably most confounded is realism, as the Soviet Union created enemies where there were friends, and declined to make friends with those who wished to ally with it. Even common sense would suggest a great power should not be driving potential friends away, or allowing its closest and most powerful allies to become enemies.

One might take the opposite approach, and resolve these contradictions by invoking personalities. Stalin accounts for the postwar anomalies of fearing the Marshall Plan more than the Truman Doctrine, excommunicating Tito in the face of a growing imperialist threat in the West, and rejecting overtures from potential allies in the newly decolonizing world, a part of the globe seething with anti-imperialist sentiment. And Khrushchev accounts for reversing these self-defeating policies. But why would Khrushchev drive China away, then? Or adopt policies that caused rebellions in East Germany, Poland, and Hungary? Moreover, it was not Khrushchev who first proposed the de-Stalinization of Soviet foreign policy after Stalin's death, but Lavrentii Beria, Stalin's secret police chief.

I offer an explanation for these puzzles, and others, in this book. It is an approach called "societal constructivism." It argues that how the Soviet Union understood itself at home explains how it related to other states abroad. By Soviet Union, I do not mean just Soviet elites, though of course they matter in the last instance. No, it is mass public understandings of what it means to be Soviet, to be socialist, that animates societal constructivism. What accounts for the seemingly strange twists and turns in Soviet foreign policy from 1945 to 1958 can be explained by paying attention to discourses of Soviet identity that are present in novels and films, not just in party circulars and Politburo meeting minutes. In short, a Stalinist discourse of danger accounts for Stalin's mixture of policies in the world; a post-Stalinist discourse of difference explains the new mixture of policies one sees under Khrushchev.

What seemed dangerous under Stalin—allowing Tito's Yugoslavia to be considered socialist, for example—became permissible difference under Stalin's successors. Who seemed unreliable lackeys of imperialism under Stalin—such as Nehru's India—became possible allies against imperialism according to a discourse of Soviet identity that permitted a wider understanding of socialism. While the discourse of difference initially liberated China from its subordinate position in the Stalinist hierarchy of Soviet-led socialist development, its growing rejection of Stalinist orthodoxy ran head-on into Mao's growing adoption of the same, realized in 1958 by the Great Leap Forward. The discourse of difference, therefore, both produced allies, and destroyed alliances. This is something that neither realism, nor "great men" theories can adequately apprehend. Societal constructivism proves necessary.

This book covers the origins and early years of the Cold War, and hence supplies an answer to the question of what "caused" the Cold War, as well as shaped its early trajectory in various parts of the world. I claim that societal constructivism can provide an account for a broad array of Soviet relationships with countries around the world, including China, eastern Europe, the decolonizing world, and the United States.

This is not a book about Soviet foreign policy, strictly speaking. It is about Soviet relations with an array of states, but not about particular Soviet foreign policy decisions with respect to any of them. The constructivist account here is a "mid-range" theory; that is, it cannot generalize to the degree a systemic theory would, but it is also not limited to the explanation of individual foreign policy choices. It is a theory that explains medium-term relationships in world politics.

Constructivisms: Systemic, Norm-Centric, and Societal

Before differentiation must come definition. What is constructivism? In short, constructivism is a theory of reality, or an ontology. There are three main theories of reality: objective, subjective, and intersubjective. Objective reality is the reality that exists independent of our perceptions of it. So, for example, everything around you, including your own body, is objective reality, and if you were not perceiving it, it would still be there. The second reality is subjective reality, that is, your interpretation of objective reality, the meaning you give to what you perceive—your perception of your body as overweight, for example. These are obviously two very important realities, but constructivism assumes that the reality that matters the most in the social and political world is intersubjective reality, that is, the reality that you and I, and perhaps millions more, agree on as existing. So, for example, your perception of your body as overweight is not subjective at all, as what counts as overweight is a social construction, a norm created by society, advertisers, gymnasium chains, fashion magazines, and medical associations and insurance companies. Other examples would be how a man wears pants rather than a skirt because of an intersubjective reality of masculinity; how a piece of furniture becomes a table rather than an ironing board because of an agreed collective meaning; or how a country is deemed democratic rather than authoritarian, and another state becomes a threatening foe rather than a friendly ally.

From the constructivist perspective, all reality, including objective reality, must be interpreted to be meaningful. And, unlike those who believe in the subjective world, constructivists argue that these interpretations and meanings that we come up with to make sense of the objective world are themselves social products. They come from one's society, workplace, school, family, or subway ride. As we will see, this means that the objects of the constructivist's theoretical attention are the social identities that are constructed in society. This means a constructivist concentrates on the intersubjective realities that dominate in any given state and society.

And these intersubjective realities often come in the form of discourses, or a collection of practices and texts, written, spoken, or just done or performed, that define an actor's position or role within some intersubjective community. For example, a discourse of the nation daily defines who is inside, and who is outside, the national community. Your body image might be governed by a discourse on gender, such that a little paunch for a man signifies wealth, while for a woman it might signify obesity.

An extremely favorable example to objectivists, the atomic bomb, demonstrates the relevance of constructivism. If the objectivists are right, they definitely should be right when it comes to the atomic bomb. What has more self-evident material power than an atomic explosion? What objective reality is more likely to speak for itself, without interpretation? What happened after Hiroshima and Nagasaki demonstrates that even atomic bombs don't speak for themselves. After the bombings, two intersubjective communities of interpretation quickly formed. The first thought that they had just witnessed a more efficient way of fighting a conventional war. The second believed they had just witnessed the end to conventional war, that atomic weapons could only be used for mutual deterrence.

Social Identity Construction

The concept that does most of the work for constructivism is social identity: how you understand yourself in relationship to others.[1] And this social identity is constructed through one's daily interactions not just with other people, but also with ideas, landscapes, art, music, television, cinema, etc. What it means to be a woman is not concocted by an individual mind out of the material available at birth. Instead, a female identity is constructed through both primary socialization within the family and through the quotidian social practices that constitute everyday life.[2] These discourses of national, ethnic, racial, sexual, class, religious, and other identities operate like social structures in that they privilege some identities over others, thus making more probable one configuration of identities in society over others.

Relationality implies the existence of multiple identities for any actor. There is no such thing as the United States, or France, or the Soviet Union. Instead there is only a US identity in relationship to France, to the Soviet Union, to Egypt, etc. Any state has multiple identities, and these identities are social products. According to systemic constructivism, these identities are mostly formed during interaction between states—between the United States and the Soviet Union, for example. According to the societal constructivism applied in this book, these identities are also generated at home, in domestic societies.

How do mundane, taken-for-granted daily practices re/produce structures of identity? When a white woman walking down the street shifts her handbag away from an oncoming pair of African-American men, she is both agent and object. She is an agent in two ways. First, she has chosen to move her purse. But second, she has inadvertently reproduced the particular discourse on racial identity that identifies African-American men as potential dangers. Meanwhile, she is also an object to the extent that her actions are partly the product of the predominant discourse on race in America. Her almost automatic response to approaching

---

[1] This is conventional wisdom among constructivists and rests on decades of research in experimental social psychology. See, for example, Iver Neumann, "Self and Other in International Relations," *European Journal of International Relations* 2, no. 2 (1996): 139–74; and Michael Barnett, "The Israeli Identity and the Peace Process: Re/creating the Un/thinkable," in *Identity and Foreign Policy in the Middle East*, ed. Shibley Telhami and Michael Barnett (Ithaca: Cornell University Press, 2002), 58–87. Rationalist accounts of states that assume fixed identities, independent of context and interaction with particular other states, disregard this body of empirical work.

[2] Peter L. Berger and Thomas Luckmann, *The Social Construction of Reality* (New York: Anchor, 1966).

black men is not only her choice, but is also the output of a social text that writes her as white, and so a potential target.[3]

One reason identities are so powerful as a producer of feelings, perceptions, and understandings is that they are cognitively necessary to ensure a predictable social environment. If it were impossible to categorize the external world, one could not go on in that world. Each experience would be *sui generis*, and not only would anarchy reign, but individual mental disorder and a true absence of social order would predominate.[4] Already in infancy, humans formulate categories to go on in the world. The human need to understand and to be understood, combined with limited cognitive resources, results in identities emerging as shortcuts to bounding probable ideas, reactions, and practices toward categorized others.[5] These are the human needs for "ontological security," or the certainty that you and others are meaningfully the same from one day, or year, to the next.[6]

Constructivists do not regard social identity as merely a political constraint for governing elites, that is, a source of costs if challenged or violated, and electoral or selectoral rewards if supported or unleashed.[7] Such a conceptualization would ignore society's agency in the construction of a state's identity. What is central is the constitutive aspect of a social identity, that is, the role it plays in constituting the imaginable understandings of the self, in relationship to significant others. In this way domestic identities perform social cognitive functions: They help delimit the representations available to elites.

Identities also constitute interests. Identities, as social structures, make possible some views of other states, and make improbable other views of these states. In this way, identities make more likely some interests in other states, and at the

---

[3] It is sad to report that studies have shown white Americans experience anxiety and fear at the mere sight of an African-American male, before thinking, and even if deliberately thinking anti-racist thoughts. This shows the power of socialization by the predominant discourse of race in the United States. Allen J. Hart et al., "Differential Response in the Human Amygdala to Racial Outgroup vs. Ingroup Face Stimuli," *NeuroReport* 11: no. 11 (August 2000): 2351–55.

[4] As we know from laboratory experiments, animals lose their hair and eat off their own limbs when exposed to random reinforcement.

[5] Alfred Schutz, *Collected Papers* (The Hague: M. Nijhoff, 1973), 237.

[6] Jonathan Turner, *A Theory of Social Interaction* (Stanford: Stanford University Press, 1988), 51 and 164; and Anthony Giddens, *Modernity and Self-Identity* (Stanford: Stanford University Press, 1991), esp. 35–63. See Jennifer Mitzen, "Ontological Security in World Politics," *European Journal of International Relations* 12, no. 3 (2006): 341–70, for an application of this concept in IR theory.

[7] Richard Price, "Reversing the Gun Sights: Transnational Civil Society Targets Land Mines," *International Organization* 52, no. 3 (1998): 631; Martha Finnemore and Kathryn Sikkink, "International Norm Dynamics and Political Change," *International Organization* 52, no. 4 (Autumn 1998): 903; and Maja Zehfuss, "Constructivism and Identity: A Dangerous Liaison," *European Journal of International Relations* 7, no. 3 (2001): 316 and 332–38.

same time make other interests less probable. For example, French interests in Francophone Africa are plausibly the product of a French identity relationship with these countries that includes the French language, a colonial past, and shared French civilization. The United States could never have interests in Francophone Africa of that type, much as France could never have the relationships with Britain or Israel that emerge from US identity.

Systemic Constructivism

Since Alexander Wendt's articulation of a structural constructivist alternative to Waltz's structural realism, constructivist scholarship has roughly divided into two streams of scholarship. Systemic constructivism has developed theoretical accounts of international politics at the global level of intersubjective structure.[8] A second body of scholarship has concentrated on why states do and do not adhere to particular norms of conduct in international affairs.[9] What is mostly missing from social constructivism, paradoxically enough, is society. This is not to say that constructivists have ignored domestic actors. But on the whole, constructivists have conceptualized social actors as either part of the state or legislature, or as interest groups or social movements trying to influence the state to adopt a particular norm.[10] The broader public has been mostly ignored.[11]

---

[8] Alexander Wendt, *Social Theory of International Politics* (Cambridge: Cambridge University Press, 1999); Christian Reus-Smit, "The Constitutional Structure of International Society and the Nature of Fundamental Institutions," *International Organization* 51, no. 4 (1997): 555–90; and Brian Frederking, "Constructing Post-Cold War Collective Security," *American Political Science Review* 97, no. 3 (2003): 363–78.

[9] Martha Finnemore, *National Interests in International Society* (Ithaca: Cornell University Press, 1996); Kathryn Sikkink, "Human Rights, Principled Issue-Networks, and Sovereignty in Latin America," *International Organization* 47, no. 3 (1993): 411–41; Margaret Keck and Kathryn Sikkink, *Activists Beyond Borders: Advocacy Networks in International Relations* (Ithaca: Cornell University Press, 1998); Nina Tannenwald, "The Nuclear Taboo: The United States and the Normal Basis of Nuclear Non-Use," *International Organization* 53, no. 3 (1999): 433–68; Audie Klotz, "Norms Reconstituting Interests: Global Racial Equality and US Sanctions Against South Africa," *International Organization* 49, no. 3 (1995): 451–78; Jeffrey Checkel, "Why Comply? Social Learning and European Identity Change," *International Organization* 55, no. 3 (2001): 553–88; and Price, "Reversing the Gun Sights."

[10] Jutta Weldes, *Constructing National Interests: The United States and the Cuban Missile Crisis* (Minneapolis: University of Minnesota Press, 1999); Elizabeth Kier, *Imagining War* (Princeton: Princeton University Press 1997); Tannenwald, "Nuclear Taboo"; Keck and Sikkink, *Activists Beyond Borders*; and Finnemore, *National Interests*.

[11] For notable exceptions, see Peter Katzenstein, *Cultural Norms and National Security: Police and Military in Postwar Japan* (Ithaca: Cornell University Press, 1996); Thomas U. Berger, *Cultures of Antimilitarism: National Security in Germany and Japan* (Baltimore: Johns Hopkins University Press, 1998); and Rodney Bruce Hall, *National Collective Identity: Social Constructs and International Systems* (Cambridge: Cambridge University Press, 1999).

Systemic constructivism is as unsuited to explain Soviet relations with other states during the Cold War as any other systemic theory would be. It is just too blunt an instrument whose theoretical sights are set on characterizing the entire system of world politics, not bilateral or even multilateral relationships among states.[12] Like neorealism, systemic constructivism is not intended to explain the Cold War. Another neorealist theory, balance of threat theory, is more suited to such an account, but tellingly only by abandoning neorealism's structural and objectivist hard core.[13] Instead of hypothesizing that states balance against objective power, as Waltzian neorealism claims, Walt argues that states balance against power they perceive as subjectively threatening.[14] But Walt does not theorize how a state becomes subjectively threatening. That is a job for societal constructivism, because systemic constructivism cannot capture something as fine-grained as the identity relations between two states.[15]

Systemic constructivism was born in opposition to structural realism.[16] The transformative logic of Wendt's systemic constructivism works through the move from one international systemic culture to another, from a Hobbesian world of unrestrained enmity to a Lockean world of limited rivalry to a Kantian one of collective amity.[17] These three systemic cultures yield three roles for states: revisionist, status quo, and collectivist.[18] Revisionist states in a Hobbesian world do not recognize the right of other states to exist, and so the norm of sovereignty is no constraint on the use of violence to achieve one's ends. Status quo states in a Lockean world do recognize the sovereign rights of other states, and so while war is possible, it is not waged for unlimited aims. Finally, collectivist states in a Kantian world already understand other states as part of themselves; the use of violence becomes unthinkable in the pursuit of one's aims. While a powerful heuristic for understanding international politics at the systemic level, Wendt's three possible worlds are problematic.

---

[12] Although the latter may serve as empirical evidence to confirm or disconfirm the claims that are being made about the character of world politics in general. While Kenneth Waltz, for example, is correct to argue a systemic theory, such as neorealism, does not explain foreign policy, it is also true that great power foreign policies are evidence that may count for or against a systemic theory's claims.

[13] Kenneth A. Waltz, "Evaluating Theories," *American Political Science Review* 91, no. 4 (1997): 916.

[14] Stephen M. Walt, *The Origins of Alliances* (Ithaca: Cornell University Press, 1987).

[15] Peter J. Katzenstein, "Introduction: Alternative Perspectives on National Security," in *The Culture of National Security: Norms and Identity in World Politics* (New York: Columbia University Press, 1996), 27–28; and Mlada Bukovansky, "The Altered State and the State of Nature: The French Revolution and International Politics," *Review of International Studies* 25, no. 2 (1999): 201–03.

[16] Yale Ferguson and Richard Mansbach, *Polities: Authority, Identities, and Change* (Columbia: University of South Carolina Press, 1996); Wendt, *Social Theory*; and Hall, *National Collective Identity*, 12–14.

[17] Wendt, *Social Theory*, 259–308.

[18] Ibid., 247–285.

First, cultures are not discrete, but continuous. The level of cooperation among states is underpredicted by not recognizing that there is identification in another state in the space between Lockean and Kantian worlds. In a continuum of identification, states may partially identify with other states before they reach a Kantian world of sublimation of self into Other. The latter is sufficient for cooperation, but not necessary.[19] This focus on collective identity is misleading in its emphasis on the need for cooperating states to have similar or even identical domestic orders.[20] This also theoretically precludes much cooperation that may occur among states that are not at all identical, but secure in that very difference.[21]

Second, multiple international cultures exist in the world at any one time, with none being clearly controlling. Wendt's paradigmatic example of a predominant culture is the "cultural structure of the Cold War."[22] But there was far greater variation within the Cold War than any structural account could accommodate. There was a great deal of cooperation on nuclear arms control, an ultimate commitment to the status quo in Europe, and a sanguinary acting-out of the enmity in the decolonizing world. No single culture can account for all this variety.

Third, each state is in a different culture with different states. For example, South Africa in the 1970s could have been in a Hobbesian relationship with Angola, a Kantian one with Rhodesia, and a Lockean one with Great Britain. Finally, different cultures may prevail within relationships between the same two states. In the example above, South Africa and Angola were in a Hobbesian world militarily, but a Lockean one when it came to managing the world's diamond supplies.[23] The latter observation implies that different issue areas of world politics, say trade and military competition, may be located in different cultures between the same pair of states.[24]

---

[19] Karl Deutsch, *Political Community and the North Atlantic Area* (Princeton: Princeton University Press, 1957); and Emanuel Adler and Michael Barnett, "Security Communities in Theoretical Perspective," in *Security Communities*, ed. Emanuel Adler and Michael Barnett (Cambridge: Cambridge University Press, 1998), 3–28.

[20] Adler and Barnett, "Security Communities," 36.

[21] Andrew Hurrell, "An Emerging Security Community in South America?" in *Security Communities*, ed. Adler and Barnett, 256; and Iurii Lotman and Boris Uspenskii, "Binary Models in the Dynamics of Russian Culture to the End of the Eighteenth Century," in *The Semiotics of Russian Cultural History*, ed. Alexander D. and Alice Stone Nakhimosvsky (Ithaca: Cornell University Press, 1985), 30–66.

[22] Wendt, *Social Theory*, 109; and Alexander Wendt, "Collective Identity Formation and the International State," *American Political Science Review* 88, no. 2 (1994): 384–96.

[23] Deborah Spar, *The Cooperative Edge: The Internal Politics of International Cartels* (Ithaca: Cornell University Press, 1994), 39–87. See also Alison Brysk, Craig Parsons, and Wayne Sandholtz, "After Empire: National Identity and Post Colonial Families of Nations," *European Journal of International Relations* 8, no. 2 (2002): 267–305.

[24] David A. Lake, "The New Sovereignty in International Relations," *International Studies Review* 5, no. 3 (2003), esp. 308–15; and Ferguson and Mansbach, *Polities*, 15.

These four points reduce to one general observation: Systemic constructivism is too blunt a theoretical instrument to account for significant variations that exist within any global culture of anarchy. To shed light on these requires a social constructivism that includes society.

The failure to include the domestic face of the state has been one of the most frequent criticisms of all systemic theories.[25] But the bracketing of the domestic for constructivists is especially pernicious. Wendt's revisionist, status quo, and collectivist states are "pre-social" and "exogenously given," a critique lodged against neorealism by its constructivist critics. The identity of the state is placed "outside analysis."[26] Bill McSweeney has observed that "this is to postulate a logical barrier between domestic and systemic which is familiar in neorealist literature, but cannot be justified within a sociological account of the process of state identity-formation."[27]

But Wendt needs the domestic identity terrain to make his theory work. He gets his theory off the ground by describing a theoretical encounter between alter and ego.[28] In this initial meeting, neither has any information about the other, but must choose how to act: advance, retreat, brandish weapons, disarm, or attack. Once ego chooses, alter interprets the meaning of the action as threatening or not, and responds itself. But how does ego choose among the possible options open to her? Why does alter understand her actions one way, and not another? The answer is that that ego and alter, though not socialized to each other, are socialized with respect to their own societies. They are not in a state of nature at all, but are already cognitively and socially equipped to choose an action from among many, and interpret the action of others in particular ways. They already have relevant intersubjective realities that exist independently of interaction with each other.

---

[25] James March and John P. Olsen, "The Institutional Dynamics of International Political Orders," *International Organization* 52, no. 4 (1998): 945; Helen Milner, *Interests, Institutions, and Information: Domestic Politics and International Relations*, (Princeton: Princeton University Press, 1997), 254; Helen Milner, "Rationalizing Politics: The Emerging Synthesis of International, American, and Comparative Politics," *International Organization* 52, no. 4 (1998): 759; and Robert O. Keohane, *International Institutions and State Power* (Boulder: Westview Press, 1989), 60.

[26] Richard Rorty has termed this move "social naturalism." *Philosophy and the Mirror of Nature* (Princeton: Princeton University Press, 1979). See, specifically on Wendt, Steve Smith, "Wendt's World," *Review of International Studies* 26, no. 1 (2000): 161; Lars-Erik Cederman and Christopher Daase, "Endogenizing Corporate Identities: The Next Step in Constructivist IR Theory," *European Journal of International Relations* 9, no. 1 (2003): 6–11; Hidemi Suganami, "On Wendt's Philosophy: A Critique," *Review of International Studies* 28, no. 1 (2002): 36; Naeem Inayatullah and David L. Blaney, "Knowing Encounters: Beyond Parochialism in International Relations Theory," in *The Return of Culture and Identity to IR Theory*, ed. Yosef Lapid and Friedrich Kratochwil (Boulder: Lynne Rienner, 1996), esp. 71–74; and Zehfuss, "Constructivism and Identity," esp. 316–27.

[27] Bill McSweeney, *Security, Identity, and Interests: A Sociology of International Relations* (Cambridge: Cambridge University Press, 1999), 128.

[28] Alexander Wendt, "Anarchy is What States Make of It," *International Organization* 46, no. 2 (1992): esp. 404–05.

Inayatullah and Blaney write that "the changing structure of meanings [between states] is not the result simply of cultural interaction *after* first contact. Rather, each culture brings to the interactions images of itself and others that are prefigured by myths, texts, and traditions. In this sense there is no such thing as 'first contact.'"[29] Wendt, stylizing the encounter of Montezuma with Spanish conquistadores, admits that "many representations were conceivable, and no doubt the one he chose—that they were gods—drew on the discursive materials available to him."[30] It is the latter that systemic constructivism ignores. Wendt has acknowledged repeatedly and explicitly the theoretical costs of bracketing society, suggesting that "the principal determinants of [how states define their identities and interests] lie in domestic politics."[31] This is what societal constructivism promises to restore.

The inclusion of the domestic construction of state identity does not inevitably entail a reductionist international relations (IR) theory. This would be true only if one stipulated that a state's identity was the cause of a state's foreign policy, independent of its interactions with other states. Instead, societal constructivism assumes that a state's identity cannot be constructed at home alone. It is meaningful only in relationship to other states. As James Fearon has pointed out, systemic theories may focus on any properties of the units that are relational, in this case, identity.[32]

Indeed, one of the most promising aspects of a discursive conceptualization of identity is that it is seamless: It assumes no boundary between meanings within and outside the state's official borders. The assumption that meaningful Others exist both at home and abroad differentiates a societal constructivist account of the domestic from those that assume primacy for either.

Norm-centric Constructivism

Perhaps the most prolific empirical work in constructivism has been on norms—what I call here norm-centric constructivism.[33] While it has gone beyond systemic constructivism to engage some domestic determinants of norm adoption by states,

---

[29] Inayatullah and Blaney, "Knowing Encounters," 82. See also Roxanne Lynn Doty, "Aporia: A Critical Exploration of the Agent-Structure Problematique in International Relations Theory," *European Journal of International Relations* 3, no. 3 (1997), esp. 379–83.

[30] Wendt, *Social Theory*, 56.

[31] Ibid., 11–28; and Wendt, "Anarchy," 423. Quote is from Wendt, "Levels of Analysis vs. Agents and Structures: Part III," *Review of International Studies* 18 (1991): 184.

[32] James Fearon, "Bargaining, Enforcement, and International Cooperation," *International Organization* 52, no. 3 (Spring 1998): 297.

[33] See sources in note 9.

its focus is too narrow to answer questions of threat and interest generation more broadly construed, and its treatment of domestic society rarely goes deep enough to be appropriately regarded as societal.

By concentrating on when states do and do not adopt a particular norm, it focuses on a particular decision, and not on an explication of the state's identity beyond that particular choice. This "weak cognitivist" approach of looking at the "normative and causal beliefs that decision makers hold" does not reconstruct the intersubjective context which made possible the particular understanding of that norm such that it could be adopted by a decision maker.[34] Ruggie has noted that constructivists overall are not "beginning with the actual social construction of meanings and significance from the ground up."[35] At best, norm-centric constructivists describe the politics surrounding the contestation of a norm, the struggle among branches of government, bureaucracies, and interest groups, but do not delve into the social construction of these norms in society.[36] Without a thick social narrative, a constructivist account reduces to the choice or rejection of a norm by a decision maker, rather than a social account of the configurations of intersubjective meanings that made possible the very imaginability of these choices. Some have criticized constructivists for failing to offer some account of the origins of norms.[37] A thick and deep social account might speak to this theoretical lacuna. Finnemore acknowledges that more research needs to be done on "localized social understandings" if we are ever to know "which norms matter as well as how, where, and why they matter."[38]

But why any particular normative position would resonate in a wider society remains an unasked and unanswered question. What is missing is what Jeffrey Checkel has called the "cultural match" between an international norm and

---

[34] Andreas Hasenclever, Peter Mayer, and Volker Rittberger, *Theories of International Regimes* (Cambridge: Cambridge University Press, 1998), 136.

[35] John G. Ruggie, "What Makes the World Hang Together?" *International Organization* 52, no. 4 (1998): 876.

[36] William Bloom, *Personal Identity, National Identity and International Relations* (Cambridge: Cambridge University Press, 1990), 78. For example, in *Cultures of Insecurity: States, Communities, and the Production of Danger*, ed. Jutta Weldes et al., (Minneapolis: University of Minnesota Press, 1999), only one out of the 12 empirical chapters (Bellinger on Trieste) goes beyond the production of identity at the official state level. The "communities" referred to in the title of the volume are those intersubjective collectivities produced by interstate interaction, not interaction between states and their societies.

[37] Paul Kowert and Jeffrey Legro, "Norms, Identity, and their Limits: A Theoretical Reprise," in *The Culture of National Security: Norms and Identity in World Politics*, ed. Peter J. Katzenstein (New York: Columbia University Press, 1996), 451–97; and Ann Florini, "The Evolution of International Norms," *International Studies Quarterly* 40, no. 3 (1996): 363–89.

[38] Finnemore, *National Interests*, 145 and 130. See also Thomas Risse, "Constructivism and International Institutions: Toward Conversations Across Paradigms," in *Political Science: The State of the Discipline*, ed. Ira Katznelson and Helen Milner (New York: Norton, 2002), 610–13.

domestic understandings of self.[39] This intersubjective reality is what social constructivism is designed to empirically recover and theorize.[40] But norm-centric constructivism is more about what Rogers Smith has termed "political construction" than "social construction." Political construction is concerned with the "high politics of law-making [and] organized political movements," as opposed to "culture, language, discourses, social groups, religious affiliations, economic interests, territoriality, folkways, [and] unconscious norms."[41]

Societal Constructivism

Societal constructivism fills the void between systemic and norm-centric constructivisms. It is more precise and determinant than systemic constructivism, and is able to furnish understandings of non-trivial foreign policy and strategic decisions by states. It is also more generalizable, and more generalizing, than norm-centric constructivism. By establishing what a state's identity is within a particular bounded context, it implies the kind of identity relations we can expect that states would have with a bounded collection of others across some medium range of time. This is not possible to accomplish if one limits one's constructivist account to a particular norm, or to a particular institution within a state. The Cold War can be explained through the identity relations the Soviet Union has with other states.

Other scholars have used a constructivist approach to link the identity of states to foreign policy and international relations.[42] Jutta Weldes makes the boundaries of this task clear: "Meanings . . . for states are necessarily the meanings . . . for . . . individuals who act in the name of the state. . . . And these . . . officials do not approach international politics with a blank slate onto which meanings are

---

[39] Jeffrey Checkel, "Norms, Institutions, and National Identity in Contemporary Europe," *International Studies Quarterly* 43, no. 1 (1999): 83–114. See also Andrew P. Cortell and James W. Davis Jr., "Understanding the Domestic Impact of International Norms: A Research Agenda," *International Studies Review* 2, no. 1 (2000): 73–76; Theo Farrell, "Transnational Norms and Military Development: Constructing Ireland's Professional Army," *European Journal of International Relations* 7, no. 1 (March 2001): esp. 71–81; Mark Laffey and Jutta Weldes, "Beyond Belief: Ideas and Symbolic Technologies in the Study of International Relations," *European Journal of International Relations* 3, no. 2 (1997), 202–03; and Amitav Acharya, "How Ideas Spread: Whose Norms Matter?" *International Organization* 58 (2004): 239–75.

[40] Barnett, "Israeli Identity," esp. 72–79.

[41] Rogers M. Smith, *Stories of Peoplehood: The Politics and Morals of Political Membership* (Cambridge: Cambridge University Press, 2003), 38.

[42] For example, Katzenstein, *Cultural Norms*; Reus-Smit, "Constitutional Structure"; Ruggie, "What Makes the World Hang Together"; Hall, *National Collective Identity*; and Neumann, "Self and Other."

written as a result of interactions among states.... Their appreciation of the world, of international politics, and of the place of their states within the international system, is necessarily rooted in collective meanings already produced, at least in part, in domestic political and cultural contexts."[43] The job of societal constructivists is to find out what is on the slate that decision makers are bringing with them in their interaction with external Others. Just as Wendt explores the issue of systemic "cognitive structures," we need to pay as much attention to their domestic variants.[44]

Critics have rightly complained that constructivist scholars have not convincingly demonstrated why one particular discourse of identity is chosen by elites over other competing identities. As Peter Hall put it in the context of comparative political economy, "there must be vehicles for the creation and transmission of political culture; and cultural analysis must say more about those vehicles."[45] I would like to address this issue by quickly reviewing the "liberal" approach to this problem and suggesting how the addition of the concept of institutions to societal constructivism might address it. In short, how does what goes on within a state affect world politics?

Societal Constructivism and Liberalism

Let's start with the most explicitly domestic theory of IR: liberalism. In "Taking Preferences Seriously," Andrew Moravcsik made state interests a centerpiece of liberal theorizing. In elaborating the core assumptions of liberal IR theory, Moravcsik writes that "the fundamental actors in international politics are individuals and private groups."[46] This runs contrary to social constructivism's intersubjectivist ontology and structuralist understanding of social identity. It is unlikely that constructivism would ever have a "fundamental actor," but if it did, it could not be an individual or private group. There is no such thing as a private identity in constructivism. The individualism at the heart of liberalism is contradicted by the social structures of constructivism.

Liberalism's second assumption, according to Moravcsik, is that the state always represents just a subset of domestic society when defining state preferences in world politics. Given that there are always competing discourses of identity in any country, a societal constructivist would definitely agree that the

---

[43] Weldes, *Constructing National Interests*, 9.

[44] Friedrich V. Kratochwil, "Constructing a New Orthodoxy? Wendt's 'Social Theory of International Politics' and the Constructivist Challenge," *Millennium* 29, no. 1 (2000): 83.

[45] Peter A. Hall, *Governing the Economy* (Cambridge, UK: Polity Press, 1986), 9.

[46] Andrew Moravcsik, "Taking Preferences Seriously: A Liberal Theory of International Politics," *International Organization* 51, no. 4 (1997), 516.

state only reflects some subset, as Moravcsik argues. The difference is between whether the state reflects or represents these interests. The latter requires a conscious choice to advance the interests of some, rather than others. Societal constructivism can accommodate such an instrumentalist view of how identity works, but cannot privilege it at the expense of a social structure of identity working its way through simple cognitive availability as a way of understanding oneself and one's national identity.

In the version of liberalism closest to constructivism, what Moravcsik terms "ideational liberalism," the central assumption is that identities matter if they concern "the scope and nature of public goods provision," goods such as "national unity, legitimate political institutions, and socioeconomic regulation."[47] This kind of theoretical preloading is anathema to constructivism which makes no assumption about the content or substance of identities and their relevance. It is impossible to know in advance whether relevant national identities are infused with religious, ethnic, and civilizational content, or the kind of reasoning Moravcsik specifies. That said, a societal constructivist would completely agree that "the configuration of domestic social identities and values" are "a basic determinant of state preferences and, therefore, of interstate conflict and cooperation."[48]

Societal constructivism does not share liberal theory's assumption that rationality entails stable preferences. Because identity relations are always being constructed in relationship to Others abroad and at home, their consequent preferences are always being constructed as well. Just because most of these relations are very stable (and so preferences remain mostly stable over the short or medium term) does not at all mean that they cannot change. Moreover, according to constructivist logic, a state's preferences will likely vary across different relationships with other states. While liberal theory calls a violation of its rationality assumption the "strategic situation lead[ing] to a variation in state preferences," constructivism would deem such an outcome a vindication of its theoretical expectations about how identities and interests are mutually constituted.[49]

One fundamental principal of liberalism, its "bottom-up view of politics," is shared by societal constructivism.[50] Both expect that domestic society will affect how elites go about their pursuit of state interests. But constructivism would put as much stress on the socialization of elites by society as on society's exertion of political pressures on elites. Liberalism tends to privilege electoral and interest

---

[47] Ibid., 515 and 524.
[48] Ibid., 525.
[49] Ibid., 542.
[50] Ibid., 517.

group politics as the transmission belts between society and the state, while societal constructivism privileges the social identity structures in society in which elites have been brought up and educated. Both could be said to realize that international politics begin at home.

Louis Althusser argued that ideological "action can never be purely instrumental; the men who would use an ideology purely as a ... tool, find that they have been caught by it, implicated by it, just when they are using it and believe themselves to be absolute masters of it."[51] Discourses of identity act similarly. Even when politicians try to fashion a state's identity, hoping to appeal to some s/electorate in doing so, they are already under the power of the already existing social identity terrain. If they formulate an identity that does not resonate with what is already the lived daily experience of the audience population, they will hardly succeed in their aims.

Prime ministers, presidents, foreign ministers, defense secretaries, and secretaries of states are all social products. They are all constrained by the social cognitive structure within which they are situated and the dominant discourse of state identity they daily and practically experience. Any prime minister is constrained by the dominant discourse of her society. When interacting with foreign leaders, she brings along these understandings of her country in relation to that other state, part of the world, or issue area. This claim assumes that the dominant discourse trumps her own idiosyncratic beliefs, the organizational cultures and identities of the foreign policy and military institutions of the government, and the identities that are generated by the interaction between her state and other states.[52]

A critical question is how or why does a particular discourse of national identity get empowered. It would be mistaken to stop with the most obvious answer, viz., that a s/electorate chooses its ruling elite based on the attractiveness or resonance of its discourse. While this might well happen, much more likely is that s/electors are choosing their elites based on a myriad of factors, only one of which might be national identity. For example, in 2000, George

---

[51] Louis Althusser, *For Marx* (New York: Pantheon, 1969), 234–35.

[52] For evidence of this type of discursive relationship in migration policy, see Kirsten Hill Maher, "Who Has a Right to Rights," in *Globalization and Human Rights*, ed. Alison Brysk (Berkeley: University of California Press, 2002), esp. 26–36; and Leo Chavez, *Covering Immigration* (Los Angeles: University of California Press, 2001). In domestic policy choices, see Jan Jenson, "Gender and Reproduction: Or, Babies and the State," *Studies in Political Economy* 20, no. 1 (1986): 9–46; Ann Shola Orloff, "Motherhood, Work, and Welfare in the United States, Britain, Canada, and Australia," in *State/Culture: State-Formation after the Cultural Turn*, ed. George Steinmetz (Ithaca: Cornell University Press, 1999), 321–54; Nancy Fraser, "Women, Welfare, and the Politics of Need Interpretation," *Hypatia: A Journal of Feminist Philosophy* 2, no. 1 (1987): 103–21; and George Steinmetz, *Regulating the Social: The Welfare State and Local Politics in Imperial Germany* (Princeton: Princeton University Press, 1997).

W. Bush became the president of the United States based on his position on many different issues.[53] But few voted for a US foreign policy, especially in the Middle East, and more especially with regard to Israel, that was informed by a US Christian Zionist identity.[54] This is why our attention should turn toward societal discourses of identity, as they might be empowered without anyone explicitly lobbying for them.

Societies also have the power of practice. Just by going on in their daily lives their members reproduce social identities with which the state must reckon. Social constructivism foregrounds the dead hand of mundane naturalizing daily practices and habits that constitute intersubjective reality. As Habermas wrote, "[C]ommunicative daily practice is embedded in a sea of cultural taking for grantedness, that is, of consensual certainties."[55] It is in this ocean of naturalized normality that identities are produced and reproduced most of the time. Society exercises a kind of power whose full extent even its bearers are unconscious of wielding. This kind of power of "common sense has been largely ignored" by scholars of IR.[56]

Societal Constructivism and Institutions

Liberalism rightly stresses that institutional configurations within countries affect which parts of society are reflected in state preferences.[57] The more open and democratic the governing institutions, the more of society's identities and values will be represented by the state. The more closed and authoritarian these institutions, the more the state will represent a narrower range of society and

---

[53] And because the US Supreme Court had a 5–4 conservative majority.

[54] On discourses of US identity and US foreign policy in the Middle East, see Melani McAlister, *Epic Encounters: Culture, Media, and U.S. Interests in the Middle East Since 1945* (Berkeley: University of California Press, 2001).

[55] Juergen Habermas, "Replik auf Einwande," in Habermas, *Vorstudien und Ergaenzungen zur Theorie des kommunikativen Handelns* (Frankfurt am Main: Suhrkamp, 1995), 553. Quoted in Thomas Risse, "Let's Argue!: Communicative Action in World Politics," *International Organization* 54, no. 1 (2000): 17. On habit and identity, see Giddens, *Modernity*, esp. 39–43; McSweeney, *Security, Identity, and Interests*, 154–58; and Herbert Simon, *Administrative Behavior* (New York: Macmillan, 1947), esp. 88–90.

[56] Jennifer Milliken, "The Study of Discourse in International Relations: A Critique of Research and Methods," *European Journal of International Relations* 5, no. 2 (1999): 238. On renewed attention to non-reflective practices and habits in international politics, see Vincent Pouliot, "The Logic of Practicality," *International Organization* 62, no. 2 (2008): 257–88; and Ted Hopf, "The Logic of Habit in International Relations," *European Journal of International Relations* 16, no. 4 (December 2010): 539–61.

[57] Moravcsik, "Taking Preferences Seriously," 530.

instead will advance the interests of its ruling elites. What is missing here, however, is the recognition that society has its own institutions and the state's institutions may be used by society for its own ends. In other words, societal discourses of identity, even if unrepresented, or even repressed, by the state, may be sustained institutionally, and so retain the possibility of being empowered by the state at a later time. These societal institutions include religious communities, trade unions, professional associations, and families.

This is not to say that those elites in control of the state do not have great institutional power vis-a-vis the population. I agree with liberalism's view of the state as an institutional resource to be captured, rather than as an autonomous actor itself.[58] Depending on the institutional arrangements in a polity, elites exercise more or less control over public education, the media, religion, and laws governing daily life. But, as Poulantzas observed, "[I]nstitutions of the state do not, strictly speaking, have any power" in and of themselves.[59] Their power, instead, derives from dominant societal discourses of identity. As instruments of the state, institutions are replete with potential power over society, but since their content emanates from society, institutional exercises of power reproduce and enact dominant societal discourse as much as shape and counteract it.

Institutional arrangements help determine which discourses get empowered, how relatively powerful the dominant discourse is, and how enduring a dominant discourse is once institutionalized within the state. For example, having regular elections provides at least the possibility that different discourses will come to power in a particular state, such that the identity relations of that state with others will not be fixed. States with less centralized control over the media, education, religion, and law- and regulation-making in general are likely to experience more variability in which discourse of identity is empowered by the state. States approaching the autocratic are more likely to establish strong control over any potentially competing institutions within the state, for example, the foreign or defense or education ministries, such that a single dominant identity is likely to prevail across bureaucracies and issue areas.

In addition, as noted above, society has institutions, too. While the state is propagating one national identity through its control of the public education system, military training, and official media, an array of churches, mosques, and temples are propagating a variety of religious identities; local media are advancing particular ethnic identities; specialized journals are promoting various class, sexual, and gender identities; and opposition political parties are advancing discourses of national identity that frontally challenge the predominant

---

[58] Ibid., 518.
[59] Nicos Poulantzas, *Political Power and Social Classes* (London: New Left Books, 1975), X n. 115.

one being pushed by the state. Or, at least, this is one possible way in which the domestic politics of identity may work.

If constructivists can show that a particular discourse of identity has been reproduced in various sites within the state and society and then comes to power when a previous discourse has been discredited or abandoned, then constructivism could claim to have "endogenized" the sources of change within a particular state and society. Endogenization in this case means not resorting to exogenous shocks, like revolutions, great depressions, or war to explain why one discourse replaces another, but instead demonstrating that an alternative discourse was in existence all along, although in institutions that had theretofore not been empowered by the ruling elites of the state.

One of the foundational texts of constructivist IR used such a technique, and its revival here can be put to good use. Kathryn Sikkink concluded her comparative constructivist study of Brazilian and Argentinean economic development strategies by observing that "powerful individuals are important for the adoption of ideas, but if these ideas do not find institutional homes, they will not be able to sustain themselves over the long term."[60] Sikkink found that the "developmentalist" program of economic development endured in Brazil because it found an institutional home within the Brazilian federal bureaucracy, but did not in Argentina because that collection of ideas had no such refuge in Buenos Aires.[61]

In the Soviet case, discourses of Soviet identity that were repressed by Stalin found homes in various institutions: the Union of Writers, the editorial boards of journals such as *Novyi Mir/New World*, academic faculties at universities, ministries within the Soviet government, such as the State Council on Religious Cults, informal *kruzhki*/circles of the intelligentsia, and elsewhere. All these institutions were financed and supported by the Soviet party and state because they were deemed necessary for the Stalinist project. But at the same time, they became refuges for understandings of the Soviet Union that were contrary to Stalinist understandings. While necessarily kept mostly below the radar during Stalin's reign, for fear of repression or worse, they immediately surfaced as anti-Stalinist alternatives once Stalin died in March 1953. In a sense they became *the* alternative collection of understandings of Soviet identity available to the post-Stalin ruling elite. As we will see, they were quickly empowered by the most unlikely of reformers, the secret police chief Lavrentii Beria. Institutions, like

---

[60] Kathryn Sikkink, *Ideas and Institutions: Developmentalism in Brazil and Argentina* (Ithaca: Cornell University Press, 1991), 248.

[61] Ibid., 22–24. See also Peter Hall, *Governing the Economy*; and G. John Ikenberry, David A. Lake, and Michael Mastanduno, eds. *The State and American Foreign Economic Policy* (Ithaca: Cornell University Press, 1988).

societal constructivism more generally, both stress how collectively held ideas can account for policy outcomes independent of any particular leader.[62]

My use of institutions here is not the only way in which institutions might be integrated into constructivist IR theory. In fact, what I am using here is probably the most simple and commonsensical version. Social constructivism as a theory of international politics can be regarded as an institutionalist theory. Because it assumes that it is the intersubjective world that matters most, as opposed to the objective or subjective world, it assumes that collective structures of meaning, or institutions, are a central focus of concern. Often these institutions are conceptualized as discourses of identity, as is the case in this book.

Discourses themselves are institutions. A discourse of the nation daily defines who is inside, and who is outside, the national community. This discourse operates like an institution insofar as it daily guides, implicitly and explicitly, each actor's sense of herself as a member of that community, or as an outsider looking in. "Institutions are therefore *constitutive* of actors as well as vice versa."[63] In fact, one of the underlying assumptions of this book is that every Soviet, whether within the political elite or a worker on the Moscow metro, both creates and recreates that discourse of Soviet identity every day through her daily practices, while simultaneously being formed by that same discourse. What I am doing in this book is assessing how this predominant discourse influences Soviet elite understandings of the outside world. While this predominant discourse is institutionalized at the highest levels of the state and party, and ramified throughout Soviet society in the education system, party meetings at the workplace, in daily newspapers, and in a range of cultural productions, understandings of Soviet identity that challenge the predominant discourse also have their own institutional resources. In that sense, institutionalized discourses are themselves located in institutions.

Sources and Methods

Societal constructivism hypothesizes that the identities that are being generated in society as a whole inform elite understandings of national identity. These understandings of what the Soviet Union is, for example, are what informs a

---

[62] On the institutionalization of human rights norms, for example, see Thomas Risse and Kathryn Sikkink, "The Socialization of International Human Rights Norms into Domestic Practices," in eds. Thomas Risse, Stephen C. Ropp, and Kathryn Sikkink, *The Power of Human Rights* (Cambridge: Cambridge University Press, 1999), 17.

[63] Robert O. Keohane, "International Institutions: Two Approaches," *International Studies Quarterly* 32 (1988): 382.

political elite's understanding of other states. There is an interaction, a mutually constitutive relationship, between what an elite understands about her own country and what she understands about some particular other. These understandings establish an identity relationship between the two states. And this relationship implies policy choices toward that country, from the broadest distinction between enmity and amity, to more specific policies such as political support or military aid.

To assess the argument in this book we need to establish three large empirical findings. The methodology used is comparative case study analysis with process tracing of the hypothesized causal links between discourses, perceptions, and behavior.[64] The first empirical task is to find out how Soviets understood themselves from 1945 to 1958. What was their intersubjective world? How did they think of themselves as Soviet? What was Soviet? What was the Soviet Union? The second is to find out what the official predominant Soviet discourse of identity was in that period. What we are trying to assess is whether society's intersubjective world is reflected in the predominant official discourse.

These discourses of identity are the "causes" that societal constructivism hypothesizes will influence Soviet relations with other states. To establish this link, we must have access to archival evidence on Soviet foreign policy decision-making in the two periods. For the first period, we assess whether the predominant discourse affects how Stalin, Molotov, and a few others understood other states in the world. The societal constructivist approach would be disconfirmed if we found out that Soviet foreign policy elites understood the outside world in terms that did not appear in the discourse of Soviet identity at home.

During the second period, from 1953 to 1958, we investigate whether the changes observed in Soviet relations with the world are based on the societal discourses of identity repressed during the Stalinist period. Finally, we examine primary source material on Soviet foreign policy decision-making to see whether societal sources of Soviet identity can account for the changes and continuities in Soviet foreign relations after Stalin's death.

[64] On comparative case study method and process-tracing, see Alexander L. George, "Case Studies and Theory Development: The Method of Structured, Focused Comparison," in *Diplomatic History: New Approaches*, ed. Paul Gordon Lauren (New York: Free Press, 1979); Alexander L. George, "The Causal Nexus Between Cognitive Beliefs and Decision-Making Behavior: The 'Operational Code' Belief System," in *Psychological Models in International Politics*, ed. Lawrence S. Falkowski (Boulder: Westview Press, 1979), 95–124; Alexander L. George and Andrew Bennett, *Case Studies and Theory Development in the Social Sciences* (Cambridge: MIT, 2005); Alexander L. George and Timothy J. McKeown, "Case Studies and Theories of Organizational Decision Making," *Advances in Information Processing in Organizations* 2 (1985); and John Gerring, *Case Study Research: Principles and Practices* (New York: Cambridge University Press, 2007), 21–58. For a previous use of this method in linking Soviet discourses of identity with foreign policy outcomes, see Hopf, *Social Construction of International Politics*.

In this work, I rely on a sample of texts to reconstruct the intersubjective reality of Soviets in Moscow from 1945 to 1958. The sampling strategy is driven by theoretical concerns. First, there are going to be three large collections of documents to construct: the intersubjective world of the most average Soviet citizens, the predominant official discourse of Soviet identity, and the identities used by Soviet decision-makers when making their foreign policy choices. The latter must be kept separate from the two previous collections as much as is possible, so as to avoid reading the outcomes back onto the collection of the previous texts, which are the independent variables of this study.

We need to realize that the Soviet Union presents some unique features when trying to assess the merits of societal constructivism. On the one hand, it is a least likely, or crucially hard, case, in Eckstein's terms.[65] Who would think that the public, especially under Stalin, and even under Khrushchev, would have any influence on Soviet foreign policy? In that sense, any evidence that societal understandings of Soviet identity find their way into Soviet elite decision-making is a striking confirmation of the theoretical approach. On the other hand, what makes the Soviet Union a hard case also makes it a tractable, if not easy, case. Authoritarian regimes of the Soviet-type established unusually strict control over the official production of ideology, and so, determining the predominant official discourse on Soviet national identity is much easier than, say, finding the official predominant American national identity in the United States.

While we cannot, strictly speaking, be ethnographers in the Soviet past, we can take advantage of a peculiar feature of Soviet political reality: The elite, in scrupulously guarding against any violations of the official Soviet national identity project, continually policed the artistic and cultural productions of Soviet authors, playwrights, and cinematographers. In so doing, they constantly identified those works which potentially threatened the official project, and the features they found threatening. In this way, Soviet ideological minders acted like research assistants for this book. They have helped give me at least a partial sample of the societal discourse of identity that politically mattered in the period.

The second part of that sample relies on contemporary accounts, memoirs, and later secondary accounts of which movies were most well-attended, which novels and plays were most popular, and which journals were most read. What we end up with for the sample of texts that represent societal understandings of national identity are novels, movies, mass newspapers, and specialized publications.

---

[65] For a discussion of critical cases, see Harry Eckstein, "Case Study and Theory in Political Science," in *Handbook of Political Science*, vol. 7, ed. Fred L. Greenstein and Nelson W. Polsby (Reading, MA: Addison-Wesley, 1975), 79–137.

The objective is to have both a sample of that which was most read or watched, as well as a variety across genres of media.

I chose to sample both *Pravda* and *Kommunist* as public official party sources. *Krasnaia Zvezda*, an official publication of the Soviet military, was chosen to assess whether there was a military point of view on Soviet identity. I reviewed the journal *Sovetskaia Etnografiia* to see how Soviet ethnographers, anthropologists, and historians understood Soviet identity in their work. For an official take on culture, I sampled *Literaturnaia Gazeta*. I will leave the list of novels and other cultural productions to the ensuing chapters.

One common methodological approach I used in all my discourse analysis of texts, with the partial exception of the Soviet ethnographic work, was to read articles that had nothing to do with identity. If we are trying to get at the lived, intersubjective world of Soviet citizens, then what they understand about identity should be evident when they are not talking about it. It should just come up incidentally, in asides, as taken for granted knowledge.

Discourses are both constraints and opportunities. On the one hand, they bound what is readily imaginable and thinkable to those who operate within them. On the other hand, to the extent they are recognized as legitimizing ways of talking about and acting on the social world, they become instruments to be used against others with whom one is struggling for power and advantage. Similarly, failure to use the appropriate discursive devices discredits or devalues one's arguments and actions, reducing one's social or cultural capital accordingly. In some sense a predominant discourse is political and cultural currency that determines the kinds of representations of identity that will, minimally, make sense and be intelligible to others, and/or more ambitiously, empower one to discredit and delegitimize the positions of others who find themselves being read out of the legitimizing discourse.

One can imagine a variety of relationships between a predominant discourse propagated by the state, or in this case, the party and the state, and societal challengers. First the predominant discourse may be *imposed* upon a resistant collection of societal self-understandings. To the extent this occurs in the Stalinist period, we should expect the predominant discourse to "win," mostly by intimidating challengers, who fear costly punishments, into silence, not by dint of compelling argumentation. But the mere fact of the existence of these challengers bears noting, as these are the discourses whose emergence should not at all surprise us once the institutional constraints are lifted—in this case, at Stalin's death.

Second, the predominant discourse might be *reinforced* by societal self-understandings, such that the state's efforts resonate with discourses of the Soviet self already widely and deeply understood and practiced in Soviet society. In this case, we should expect such discursive constructions to simply continue beyond Stalin's death.

Third, the predominant discourse might be *infused* by societal discursive content, i.e, how the society understands itself provides the substance of the identities one finds in the predominant discourse. The assumption here is that no matter who the leader, she is a social product, too, and therefore is a carrier of societal discourses of identity. This relationship is the one of maximal societal power.

Fourth, the predominant discourse might be *competed against* by counter-hegemonic societal discourses. This would manifest itself in an ongoing struggle between official representations of the Soviet self and its challengers, with neither able to drive the other from the field of discursive play. We would expect that these challengers would be potential candidates for elevation to official status once the predominant discourse's primary institutionalization, in the person of Stalin, passes from the scene.

Finally, the predominant discourse might be *circumvented* if societal understandings of Soviet identity are simply outside the gaze of the state and party, that is, take forms that are not relevant to the predominant discourse's rendition of the Soviet self. These orthogonal identities should also simply continue to operate after Stalin's death.

Another way of arraying these discursive principles is in terms of degrees of agency associated with each instance, and the relative agency of state and society, broadly construed. Imposing a discourse implies a great deal of agency for the state. Having a predominant discourse be reinforced by societal identities implies a kind of co-agency between the state and society. Infusion of the predominant discourse with societal content shows a great deal of societal agency. Competition between the predominant discourse and societal challengers shows contested agency. Circumvention of the predominant discourse by daily social practices in society implies independent agencies for both state and society.

Finally, I spent a great deal of time in Russian archives. There were two primary aims. The first was to reconstruct the official discourse of Soviet identity from the officials themselves, as well as to find out what societal discourses were found challenging to that predominant understanding. The second, and last stage of the project, was to assess the influence of societal discourses of identity on Soviet foreign policy decision-making.

One is right to be skeptical about the ability to pull off what has been described above. But I have one methodological advantage that constructivists are often charged with lacking: a falsifiable argument with variables that vary. If societal constructivism is wrong, we will not find the elements of societal discourse I recover in novels and plays in Soviet foreign policy decision-making. And indeed, to foreshadow, one of the Soviet Union's most important identities, that of great power, is absent from societal discourses, and so, societal constructivism is disconfirmed in that instance.

What to Expect

The plan of the book is straightforward. In chapter 2, I present my findings on the identity landscape of Moscow from the end of World War II to Stalin's death. This chapter establishes both the predominant official discourse of Soviet identity and its potential societal challengers. In chapter 3, I assess the ability of societal constructivism to explain a host of Soviet relationships with the external world, which includes China, eastern Europe, Yugoslavia, and the West. In chapter 4, I describe the official and societal discourses of Soviet identity from 1953 until 1958. The critical issue is how much the official discourse under Khrushchev owes to the anti-Stalinist societal challengers of the previous period. In chapter 5, I once again assess how much the societal discourse of Soviet identity informs Soviet foreign relations with China, Yugoslavia, Hungary, Poland, eastern Europe, the developing world, and the West. In the conclusion, I summarize the findings of the book and try to answer some of the eternal questions of the Cold War based on those findings.

2

Stalinism after the War

A Discourse of Danger, 1945–53

Stalin, along with Mao and Hitler, is often identified as one of the most heinous characters of the twentieth century. He was responsible for the deaths of millions after coming to power in 1928, whether through the collateral damage of famines during collectivization, or the imprisonment and execution of 80 percent of the country's political and military elite in the years leading up to World War II. After the defeat of Hitler's armies in the war, the Soviet people expected that there would be a reduction in the level of daily repression, more breathing room for personal, if not public, freedom. Their expectations were never met, although the first year or so after the war did see some respite from the years of terror before the war. And the level of executions never matched those seen during the worst of Stalinism in the 1930s.

This light historical background is necessary in order to judge the promise of societal constructivism. Since it postulates that there will be discourses of identity contrary to those propagated by the state, postwar Stalinism is an especially hard case in which societal constructivism can demonstrate its potential. As we will see, however, such societal discourses did in fact exist under Stalinism, and their survival helps to explain what happens in the Soviet Union, and in its foreign relations, after Stalin's death in March 1953. This goes to show that even one of the more totalitarian projects cannot snuff out every challenging thought, and even the most totalizing discourse has holes, inconsistencies, ambiguities, and slippages. I hope to demonstrate that although there was definitely a predominant Stalinist discourse of Soviet identity after the war, there were also counter-hegemonic understandings of Soviet identity. While the latter did not cohere into a systematic anti-Stalinist discourse, they did offer daily challenges to the predominant and officially authorized Soviet identity. Moreover, and most significantly, the new Soviet discourse of identity during the post-Stalinist Thaw was made up of the fragmented societal discourse repressed under Stalin.

Discourses, understood as a collection of texts and social practices that reproduce a particular identity, do not float freely, but rather, are empowered by institutions.[1] The most important institution in this period was Stalin himself, and the party apparatus and governing machinery used to reproduce Stalinism. But, as I show below, anti-Stalinist understandings of Soviet identity were also institutionalized, and so were empowered to resist. Being so secured against elimination, these understandings flourished as what we now call "de-Stalinization."

The bulk of this chapter is spent describing and analyzing the predominant discourse of Soviet identity and its relationships to various challengers. To summarize most briefly, the predominant discourse was one of danger, binarization, dichotomization, infallibility, typicality, paternalism, and hierarchy. Its substantive core was defined by modernity, the Russian nation, and fear of its external Western Other. I offer some ideas about how these discourses were institutionalized and how they worked in the Soviet context, both as instruments wielded by actors in struggles with each other, and as social structures constraining these very actors. I conclude with some implications for Soviet identity relations with other states in the world.

Institutional Context

Soviet identity, official and otherwise, was promulgated and practiced in a variety of social milieux. Cinema, newspapers, magazines, and novels were the most widely consumed media after the war.[2] The content of films, articles, and books was the object of struggle between the many institutions and resources of Stalinism and the more diffuse sites of resistance to that Stalinist Soviet identity.

Stalin and Stalinism

Stalin was an institution unto himself. By arrogating so much power to himself, he need only make a negative comment about some policy to set in motion the entire machinery of the state, party, and police apparatus. Most often, his subordinates, fearful of the consequences of not fulfilling even his implicit wishes,

---

[1] Discourses themselves may be usefully understood as institutions, at least as defined by new institutionalists as expectations of normatively prescribed and proscribed actions.

[2] There were only 10,000 televisions in the Soviet Union in 1950. Aleksandr A. Danilov and Aleksandr V. Pyzhikov, *Rozhdenie Sverkhderzhavy: SSSR v Pervye Poslevoennye Gody* (Moscow: ROSSPEN, 2001), 193.

implemented his hints, let alone directives, as comprehensively as could be imagined. His subordinates would carry notebooks, hoping to write down Stalin's orders and intimations, fearing to miss some command, even if only subtly implied.[3] For example, Stalin wanted Konstantin Simonov, a most popular writer and high-ranking figure in Soviet letters, to write a play about Soviet scientists giving away secrets to imperialist intelligence agents, a cultural production to accompany his anti-kowtowing campaign. The latter was part of Stalin's efforts to simultaneously make Russia into the Soviet nation, and make the Soviet nation superior in all respects to the West. Upon reading the subsequent manuscript, Stalin only corrected the ending, allowing the repentant chemist Trubnikov to remain working in the laboratory, despite his betrayal of Soviet science to the West. The play, *Chuzhaia Ten*, or *Someone Else's Shadow*, was considered for a Stalin Prize in 1949. At the meeting of the selection committee, the play was attacked for its excessive indulgence toward Trubnikov. He should have been arrested and sent to the camps, the writers said, trying to insure themselves against Stalin's expected reaction. Simonov retrospectively mused that little did they know, Stalin had authorized the deviance they were now competing with each other to punish.[4]

Why Stalin's subordinates might overfulfill any of his wishes is exemplified by the "Banana Affair," recounted in the memoirs of Presidium member Anastas Mikoian. In late summer 1951 Mikoian and his wife were vacationing in Sukhumi, a Black Sea resort town in Georgia. Once or twice a week, Mikoian would visit Stalin, who was resting at Novyi Afon. Once at dinner, at four o'clock in the morning, they brought out bananas. Stalin loved bananas. After the war he proposed importing bananas to the largest Soviet cities. But this morning he asked why the bananas were so green. He asked why, when he (Mikoian) was Minister of Foreign Trade, the bananas were yellow, but now with Mikhail Menshikov, the foreign trade minister at the time, they are green. Mikoian went home to sleep. But upon waking up around noon, he called Moscow to inquire about the unripe bananas. But Lavrentii Beria, Presidium member and secret police chief, anticipating Stalin's concerns, had already called Moscow, as Stalin had called him at six o'clock in the morning, instructing him to get to the bottom of the affair. In November, after some futile resistance from Mikoian, Stalin had Menshikov fired.[5]

---

[3] Kees Boterbloem, *The Life and Times of Andrei Zhdanov, 1896–1948* (Montreal: McGill-Queen's University Press, 2004), 257; and Dmitrii T. Shepilov, "Politicheskii Arkhiv XX Veka. Vospominaniia," *Voprosy Istorii* (March 1998): 17.

[4] Konstantin Simonov, *Glazami Cheloveka Moego Pokoleniia: Razmyshleniia o I. V. Staline* (Moscow: Kniga, 1990), 123–37.

[5] Anastas Mikoyan, *Tak Bylo: Razmyshleniia o Minuvshem* (Moscow: Vagrius, 1999), 529–33.

The point here, from the discursive point of view, is that Stalin's own personal wishes concerning what Soviet identity should be, enjoyed not only the institutional resources of the state and party, but also the reflexive overfulfillment by often fearful associates and subordinates. The results were efforts to propagate a Soviet identity that exaggerated Stalin's own personal proclivities.[6]

Another additional institutional feature of Stalinism was the systematic treatment of information in a particularly biased fashion. The predominant discourse of danger frequently identified various threats to Soviet identity. Soon on the heels of such an identification followed a reflexive discovery, at every level of Soviet society, of precisely these kinds of threats. Their revelation was duly reported up the chain of responsibility, as well as the actions taken to counter them. In this way threats and deviants were continually being revealed and overcome. Simultaneously, of course, the discourse took on a life of its own, often completely independently of the non/existence of any particular threats or deviants.

Stalin himself was sometimes not the most intolerant defender of the predominant discourse of danger that he himself authored. Instead, it seems that his subordinates, terrified at the prospect of violating some ambiguous boundary, overcompensated in the direction of greater orthodoxy than even the patriarch endorsed. All officials beneath Stalin had to guess what his preference might be on any particular issue. Prudence dictated erring on the side of exaggerating danger, not experimenting with deviation.

Not so long after Mikhail Zoshchenko had been expelled from the Union of Soviet Writers, for example, Stalin approved Simonov's request to publish Zoshchenko's "Partisan Stories," in *Novyi Mir*, the "thick" journal of literature that was highly prized by Soviet readers. At this May 1947 meeting, Stalin said in general that "editors should publish, and then he and Andrei Zhdanov would read" the articles.[7] This must have been a terrifying thought for any editor at the time. The next year, Simonov recalled that Stalin had defended Vera Panova's novel *Kruzhilikha* from critics during the May 1948 meeting on Stalin Prizes. When her characterization of Uzdechkin, the factory party chairman, was declaimed, Stalin replied, "But we have such Uzdechkins," implying that one need not show infallible atypical characters all the time. But just how often remained a dangerous question to answer.[8]

---

[6] On the phenomenon of "over-insurance," see Dmitri T. Shepilov, "Politicheskii Arkhiv XX Veka. Vospominaniia," *Voprosy Istorii* (June 1998): 34.

[7] Simonov, *Glazami Cheloveka*, 121. From the end of the war until his death in 1948, Zhdanov was Stalin's enforcer of cultural orthodoxy. "Zhdanovshchina" was the term given to harsh repression of deviations from cultural orthodoxy in the period.

[8] Simonov, *Glazami Cheloveka*, 121; Dmitrii T. Shepilov, "Politicheskii Arkhiv XX Veka. Vospominaniia," *Voprosy Istorii* (May 1998): 22.

Stalin also defended Ilya Ehrenburg's 1948 novel, *The Storm*, in which there were scenes of retreat in the early months of World War II, unheroic Soviet citizens, ironicization of Germans as the Soviets' one-time "eternal friends," a detailed description of the massacre of Jews at Babi Yar, as well as a very favorable and lengthy characterization of France, where half the action takes place. The Stalin Prize committee only recommended it receive a "second class" because the novel had been nominated, so Stalin must have approved its appearance on the list. But Stalin, at the May 1948 meeting, asked "Why not give it the first prize?" That settled it.[9]

In early 1949, the Soviet press began to "out" Jewish authors, publishing their Jewish surnames alongside their Slavic pseudonyms. This "anti-cosmopolitan" campaign petered out soon thereafter. Ehrenburg recalled that Aleksandr Fadeev, at the time general secretary of the Union of Writers (UW), told him that Stalin had authorized the anti-cosmopolitan campaign in the press but personally ended the practice of outing Jewish writers. Stalin told the editors in a March 1949 meeting, "Comrades, the divulging of literary pseudonyms is inadmissible, it smells of anti-Semitism."[10]

At the March 1950 Stalin Prize meeting, Fadeev argued against awarding a prize to Antonina Koptiaeva's *Ivan Ivanovich*, but Stalin defended it, including the love triangle, saying, "It happens in real life, doesn't it?" Stalin also excused writers who were not party members, claiming that Lenin's slogan "Out with the Non-Party Writers!" was issued when the Bolsheviks were in opposition, not when "we answer for all of society, for the bloc of communists and non-party people." Then he noted that "they want all heroes to be positive . . . [b]ut this is stupid, simply stupid."[11]

In his last meeting with Stalin in March 1952, Simonov recalls Stalin again defending difference: "Playwrights think they are banned from writing about negative phenomena. Critics demand the ideal life from them. . . . They say we have no bastards, but we do. Not showing them sins against the truth. . . . There are conflicts in life. Plays must show them. . . ."

The Cinema

Films, books, and journals were the most important sources of media consumption. But the Soviet film industry was cowed into submission under Stalin after the war. While Hollywood was making 400 to 500 films a year and 200 to 300

---

[9] Simonov, *Glazami Cheloveka*, 140–41.

[10] Ilya Ehrenburg, *Post-War Years, 1945–1954*, trans. Tatiana Shebunina (Cleveland: The World Publishing Company, 1967), 133.

[11] Simonov, *Glazami Cheloveka*, 203–04.

films were being produced in Japan and India, the Soviet Union produced all of 183 films in the eight years between 1945 and 1953. And these numbers exaggerate what was really going on, as so many films were just the videotaping of plays, operas, and ballets being performed on stage. On the other hand, the films that were made enjoyed mass audiences.[12]

Two semi-documentary films appeared in 1949, *The Fall of Berlin* and *The Battle of Stalingrad*, which were widely distributed and enthusiastically received. Students and workers were brought to theatres en masse to watch them.[13] *Kuban Cossacks* was the most popular of all postwar films, remarkable for the extraordinarily rosy picture of rural life in southern Russia at a time of famine and repression.[14]

For both material and political reasons, what appeared in Soviet films was far more strictly controlled from the start than what appeared on stages or pages. Simonov and others recall that Stalin personally loved film, thought cinema the single most important cultural instrument of the state, and considered himself an expert, both aesthetically and politically, on their contents. While he often deferred to others' judgments on literature, he rarely listened to others' evaluations of film.

Moreover, because of the relatively large production costs, number of required workers, and demand on scarce supplies of resources, the screenplays and scripts for films were closely monitored from the very beginning, as well as outtakes from ongoing production, let alone final cuts.[15]

The production of *Far From Moscow* received the attention at the very highest levels. Based on Vasilii Azhaev's best-selling 1949 Stalin Prize-winning novel of the same name, the film version won its own Stalin Prize in 1951. Leonid Ilyichev, editor of *Izvestiia* and head of the Central Committee (CC) Propaganda and Agitation (Agitprop) Department; Vladimir Ermilov, editor of *Literaturnaia Gazeta (LG)*; Leonid Leonov, member of the Supreme Soviet, Presidium of the Writers' Union, author of *Russian Forest*; Aleksei Surkov, Writers' Union Secretary; Ivan Bolshakov, Minister of Cinematography; and others along with Azhaev and the film's production staff met in June 1949 to fashion the script.[16]

---

[12] Peter Kenez, *Cinema and Soviet Society, 1917–1953* (Cambridge: Cambridge University Press, 1992), 210–11.

[13] Ibid., 228.

[14] Elena Iu. Zubkova, *Russia After the War: Hopes, Illusions, and Disappointments, 1945–1957* (Armonk: M.E. Sharpe, 1998), 35.

[15] Simonov, *Glazami Cheloveka*, 157–64.

[16] Thomas Lahusen, *How Life Writes the Book: Real Socialism and Socialist Realism in Stalin's Russia* (Ithaca: Cornell University Press, 1997), 185.

Institutional Carriers of anti-Stalinist Identities

Oppositional understandings of what it meant to be Soviet had institutional resources of their own. While they were of course much weaker than that of the Stalinist party apparatus and government bureaucracy, which extended from the capital to every village, township, school, and workplace, they existed, and challenged, this dominance. And even if no challenge was mounted, these institutions provided homes for contrary views that, although not publicly expressed, survived until the institutional terrain shifted at Stalin's death. It is important to highlight here the fact that much creative work was subject only to post-publication review by the most orthodox organs of the Stalinist regime. Therefore, much counter-hegemonic discourse made it to the broadest reading public. And this under one of the most authoritarian regimes in history.

Creative Unions

The unions of musicians, artists, and writers carved out a zone of some autonomy between themselves and Stalin's regime.[17] This is reflected in, if nothing else, the continual attacks on the plays, poems, operas, films, and novels that these cultural figures produced. While censorship of course operated, not only through the Main Administration for Preserving State and Military Secrets in the Press (Glavlit), but also through the CC Ideology, Culture, and Agitprop Departments, all layers of party organizations, and through self-censorship, editors and writers still published works in which the predominant discourse was ignored or challenged.

Editorial Boards

The party continually reshuffled editorial boards and created institutions to monitor, rectify, and compete with the institutions and works of the creative intelligentsia. For example, in April 1946, the CC Agitprop Department created a new journal, *Kultura and Zhizn* (*Culture and Life*), in which it could publish official critiques of deviant works. Along with an August 1946 CC resolution condemning the literary journals *Leningrad* and *Zvezda,* the CC appointed new editorial boards. Aleksandr Egolin, the new editor of *Zvezda* was simultaneously deputy head of the Agitprop Committee.[18]

---

[17] Vera Tolz, "'Cultural Bosses' as Patrons and Clients: The Functioning of the Soviet Creative Unions in the Postwar Period," *Contemporary European History* 11, no. 1 (2002): 99.

[18] Denis L. Babichenko, *Pisateli I Tsenzory: Sovetskaia Literatura 1940–x Godov pod Politicheskim Kontrolem TsK* (Moscow: Rossiia Molodaia, 1994), 117–36.

Scientific Intelligentsia

The power of one counter-hegemonic institution, the Soviet Academy of Sciences, was evident in the debates over genetics launched by Trofim Lysenko in 1947–48. Trying to take advantage of the anti-kowtowing campaign launched with the Kliueva-Roskin affair, Lysenko and his followers accused their detractors of worshiping bourgeois science.[19] They managed to carry on this campaign in mass publications such as *Pravda* and *Literaturnaia Gazeta*, but they had much less influence over how science itself was carried out in the period. The Academy of Sciences held conferences at which Lysenko's work was refuted in dozens of papers that presented empirical results countering his claims that intra-species competition does not occur. The result was an official public discourse endorsing Lysenkoist Soviet patriotism, and official backing for anti-Lysenkoist science within scientific institutions, such as the Academy. Not until July 1948, when Stalin himself came down on the side of Lysenko, did the Academy's institutional power become moot. Although, even after this most authoritative endorsement, hundreds of Soviet scientists quietly continued research yielding results that contradicted Lysenko's claims.[20]

Research institutes held the required party meetings in the fall of 1948, and reported to the Central Committee in Moscow of their successful purging and re-education of cadres in the desired patriotic direction against Western genetics, but then proceeded to pursue the same research as they had previously. One strategy was to loudly dismiss a deviant "Morganist" whom the institution already knew had been purged by the central party authorities. Moreover, such deviants, often purged from high administrative positions, found themselves ending up in research positions instead. These were considered demotions, and so, punishment had been meted out to these kowtowers. Taking advantage of the predominant discourse that privileged the "Center" in Moscow from the "periphery," that is, all of the Soviet Union which was not Moscow, institutes "exiled" purged deviants to provincial branches outside Moscow and Leningrad. Some of those sacrificed had multiple positions in different institutions, so they could be purged multiple times, counting in each institution's report to the center, or, alternatively, they could be purged from one institution and could easily keep a position elsewhere.

Some institutions concentrated on the party's demand that deviants be "re-educated," thereby defying the party's demands that particular researchers be

---

[19] The Kliueva-Roskin affair involved accusations of the two oncologists of leaking the results of their cancer research to Western agents.

[20] Nikolai Krementsov, *Stalinist Science* (Princeton: Princeton University Press, 1997), 149–83, 227–53.

fired. Institutions also made very loud announcements of their restructuring of editorial boards and policies at their main popular journals. While doing this, or not, they simultaneously continued publishing "deviant" research on genetics in their limited circulation professional specialized journals. Research programs were also declared changed "in accordance with Michurinist doctrine," but often all this meant was adding this exact phrase, or "on the basis of Lysenko's theory," to a title attached to research already under way.[21] Formulaic "forewords" and "afterwords" were added to articles, whose substantive content went unaltered.[22]

Soviet physicists, both more numerous (more than 600 versus 100 or so geneticists) and more concentrated institutionally in Moscow State University's Institute of Physics and the Soviet Academy of Sciences, and involved in the production of the atom bomb, avoided accusations of deviance altogether. The March 1949 meeting intended by party ideologues and their "scientists" to bring Lysenkoism to physics, and prepared for months with 42 dress rehearsals, was cancelled, apparently at the orders of Beria himself.[23]

The Culture Market

The unchallenged position of the dominant discourse was also in conflict with a most unlikely institution: the Soviet market for cultural products. Publishing houses and film studios constantly vied for resources from the state and party coffers: salaries, positions, vacations, buildings, paper, office equipment, etc. Of course one should bear in mind that many of the resources were fungible in the exchange economy: A ton of paper could be traded for a bus, for instance.

The unpalatable fact was that deviant art paid. The Western films that were part of the cache of films taken back to Moscow from Germany after the war earned money for the film industry. In March 1949, Minister of Cinematography Ivan Bolshakov appealed to Viacheslav Molotov, Presidium member and foreign minister, to speed up the CC's decision about the 50 trophy films he had recommended for distribution around the country. He wrote Molotov that further delay "will lead to the nonfulfillment of the plan for revenues. . . ." A compromise was reached in late April 1949. Six films were shown, but they were edited by the CC Agitprop Department, which provided each film with

---

[21] Lysenko was an avowed adherent of Vladimir Michurin, a Soviet biologist who stressed the ability of plants to acquire heritable characteristics from their environments.

[22] Krementsov, *Stalinist Science*, 239–48. A common phenomenon throughout the postwar period, at least, was the public reproduction of the predominant discourse, if only to provide oneself enough credit with relevant authorities, or power, to pursue one's private life. Alexei Yurchak, *Everything was Forever, Until it was No More: The Last Soviet Generation* (Princeton: Princeton University Press, 2006).

[23] Krementsov, *Stalinist Science*, 277–79.

an introductory gloss and suitably doctored subtitles.[24] In 1947, *Girl of My Dreams*, starring Hungarian actress Marika Rokk, made five times more per showing than the year's biggest overall moneymaker, Boris Barnet's wartime thriller, *Secret Agent's Feat*. In 1949, German trophy films accounted for 94 percent of all box office receipts in the Soviet Union.[25]

Defending the Rights of Religious Believers

This idea is probably more shocking even than the effects of the culture market, but two Soviet institutions, the State Council for Russian Orthodox Church Affairs and the State Council on the Affairs of Religious Cults, both frequently acted to defend the rights of believers, or their religious identities, we might say, against the far more powerful instruments of the party that were propagating the predominant discourse of atheistic modernity.

In the face of the state and party's official commitment to atheism, the leadership of these two State Councils repeatedly and consistently advocated for the construction of more churches, mosques, and synagogues, for more religious publications, and for observation of the constitutional protection of believers. Moreover, they frequently succeeded in getting local party officials reprimanded for unauthorized anti-religious conduct, such as closing of places of worship, plundering of church property, and the erection of arbitrary administrative barriers in the way of practicing a religion.

Two broad conclusions suggest themselves from this discussion of institutions in the postwar Soviet Union. First, what Stalin paid attention to resulted in not only its institutional reproduction in the most powerful institutions of all, the party and state apparatus, but its over-production, such that Stalin himself at times had to intervene to restrain his over-zealous agents. Second, despite this dramatic concentration of institutional power, there were significant institutional homes throughout the period in which challenges to the predominant discourse could maintain themselves, offer some limited resistance, and most importantly, survive to fight another day.

A writer or playwright could accumulate capital by producing works that propagated the predominant discourse and then carefully convert that accumulated capital into space to produce works that challenged it. This was made possible by

---

[24] Kirill M. Anderson, ed., *Kremlevskii Kinoteatr, 1928–1953: Dokumenty* (Moscow: ROSSPEN, 2005), 831–39.

[25] Shepilov noted in his memoirs the pernicious effects of the market on Soviet cinema after the war. Shepilov, "Politicheskii Arkhiv XX Veka. Vospominaniia," *Voprosy Istorii* (May 1998): 25; Julian Graffy, "Cinema," in *Russian Cultural Studies: An Introduction*, ed. Catriona Kelly and David Shepherd (Oxford: Oxford University Press, 1998), 181.

the presence of the counter-hegemonic institutional possibilities elaborated above. It was also made possible by the room for interpretation necessarily left by the party when issuing directives concerning what was permissible, or not, in the realm of representations of Soviet identity. One could not possibly know for sure what was being prohibited by the vague, abstract terms used by the Central Committee.

One common disciplinary form under Stalinism was the exemplary ostracism or shot across the bow. So, particular journals such as *Zvezda* and *Leningrad*, particular authors like Anna Akhmatova and Mikhail Zoshchenko, and particular films such as *Big Life* and *Ivan the Terrible II*, were singled out for comprehensive criticism.[26] They were depicted as rife with an array of particular vices that violated the desired predominant Soviet identity, but interpretation of what these vices might end up being in subsequent works was left up to the authors and writers themselves. At this point, the twin logics of over-insurance and slippage appeared. Some writers chose to become more Stalinist than Stalin; others chose to try to find niches in the discursive armor where they could continue to explore just where the limits of counter-hegemonic discourse might have lain, at some risk to themselves, of course. Counter-hegemonic possibilities were further enabled by the fact that so many works were subjected only to post-publication or post-performance verification by the minders of the predominant discourse.

Postwar Uncertainty, 1945–47

For a year or so after the war, the orthodox Stalinist version of Soviet identity was not firmly established. There seemed to be room for competing visions of the Soviet Union, within narrow limits, of course. There was competition among different understandings of the Soviet Union. This ended by 1947 with the firm imposition of the predominant Stalinist discourse of Soviet identity onto Soviet society. Even so, as has been noted, opposition continued throughout the period, even if only from positions of weakness.

A very short window of opportunity for discursive pluralism existed from August 1945 to August 1946, from the end of the war to the CC promulgations that marked the beginning of the *Zhdanovshchina* in cultural affairs. The Interior Ministry's Special Commission issued 27,000 indictments in 1945, only 8,000

---

[26] Peter Kenez and David Shepherd, "'Revolutionary' Models for High Literature: Resisting Poetics," in *Russian Cultural Studies: An Introduction*, ed. Catroina Kelly and David Shepherd (Oxford: Oxford University Press, 1998), 50; Elena Iu. Zubkova, "Fenomen 'Mestnogo Natsionalizma:' 'Estonskoe Delo' 1949–1952 Godov v Kontekste Sovetizatsii Baltii," *Otechestvennaia Istoriia* (May 2001): 90–91.

in 1946, but 38,000 in 1949.[27] Richard Stites writes that "all sources attest to the relative loosening of intellectual and creative controls in the years of the German occupation."[28] This relative tolerance for difference would last months or, at most, a couple of years.[29] Manifestations were found in culture and religious practice, and in Stalin's own words.

In December 1943, the April 1932 CC resolution "On Restructuring Literary and Arts Organizations" was repealed; in April 1946, Dmitrii Polikarpov was removed as head of the Writers' Union, and Fedor Panferov's article "O cherepakh i cherepushkakh" appeared in the normally orthodox literary journal *Oktiabr*.[30] In his piece, Panferov criticized editors and "ignorant unqualified literary bureaucrats" for demanding the "varnishing of reality" by, for example, showing the war as the "victorious march of our Red Army accompanied by cheering, singing, and dancing." If such bureaucrats were at work in factories or farms hindering progress, "they would be immediately removed." The literary minders treat writers like "infants," he added.[31] In the memo from CC Agitprop Department head Georgii Aleksandrov to Zhdanov criticizing this article, Panferov is taken to task for not even pointing out that the Red Army's retreat "exhausted the enemy." But, significantly, this article was published, and then criticized in other journals, but was neither forbidden nor censored in the first place.[32]

From October 1945 to January 1948, the number of Orthodox churches increased by almost 40 percent, from 10,300 to 14,100. Each reopening was a huge public event. In Kirov, for example, more than 15,000 people came from as far as 100 kilometers away to celebrate the occasion. In 1946 and 1947 education for priests resumed with the opening of pre-revolutionary seminaries.[33] While about 2,000 titles of anti-religious literature were published per year from 1918 to 1941, none was published from 1945 to 1947. Meanwhile, church weddings and

---

[27] Vladislav M. Zubok, *A Failed Empire: The Soviet Union in the Cold War from Stalin to Gorbachev* (Chapel Hill: University of North Carolina Press, 2009), 55.

[28] Richard Stites, *Russian Popular Culture: Entertainment and Society since 1990* (Cambridge: Cambridge University Press, 1992), 5.

[29] Werner G. Hahn, *Postwar Soviet Politics: The Fall of Zhdanov and the Defeat of Moderation, 1946–1953* (Ithaca: Cornell University Press, 1982), 67; Zubkova, "Fenomen 'Mestnogo Natsionalizma,'" 89.

[30] Under Khrushchev, Polikarpov would become an orthodox head of the CC Science and Culture Department.

[31] The battle against infantilization by the predominant discourse will carry on through Khrushchev's period in power.

[32] Denis L. Babichenko, ed., *Literaturnyi Front: Istoriia Politicheskoi Tsenzury, 1932–1946 gg. Sbornik Dokumentov* (Moscow: Entsiklopediia Rossiiskikh Dereven, 1994), 189–91.

[33] Aleksandr A. Danilov and Aleksandr V. Pyzhikov, *Rozhdenie Sverkhderzhavy: SSSR v Pervye Poslevoennye Gody* (Moscow: ROSSPEN, 2001), 181–86.

baptisms grew dramatically.³⁴ The increased official tolerance for Orthodoxy was a response to the dramatic increase in religious practice seen during, and especially after, the war, given postwar material hardships.³⁵ In 1947, religious calendars were allowed for Estonian and Latvian Lutherans, and for Muslims in 1944, albeit with both Soviet and religious holidays displayed.³⁶

At the March 14, 1946, CC meeting, it was decided to replace commissariats with ministries. Stalin introduced the move, arguing socialism in the Soviet Union was more secure than ever. "Commissars reflect a period of an unsettled/ [*neustoiavshiisia*] system, of the civil war, of the revolutionary breakthrough. This period has passed." He goes on to draw lessons from the victory in the war, saying it has "shown that our social system sits very strongly . . . [and it has] entered into our daily life/[*byt*] . . . and become our flesh and blood. . . ." Because of the greater stability of the system, Stalin concludes that "the people will understand the change."³⁷ The issue of how secure the Soviet Union is, and how irreversible socialism is, is a continuing critical point of disagreement between the emergent Stalinist discourse of danger and its opponents.

"Real" Dangers

The short 12 months of official Soviet ambivalence toward the content of an orthodox Soviet identity appeared to rest, in part at least, on confidence that the war had proven that socialism was secure at home. The August 1946 turn toward a predominant discourse of danger rested on the notion that socialism was not secure at home, after all. In this section, I highlight some of the objective sources of threat to the Soviet project that contributed to the discourse of danger that soon emerged.

I include this section for at least two reasons. First, Stalin is often described as an insane paranoiac. This might be true, but it might also be true that any prudent General Secretary in the Soviet Union at the time would have had serious fears for the future of socialism. Second, it is important to highlight the world of "brute" facts that are subject to social construction, as they provide an objective, material baseline that can be traced over the subsequent years of this study.

Real dangers existed for Stalin and socialism in the Soviet Union after the war. In tapes made by the secret police in hopes of gathering compromising material

---

³⁴ Tatiana A. Chumachenko, *Church and State in Soviet Russia: Russian Orthodoxy from World War II to the Khrushchev Years* (Armonk, New York: M. E. Sharpe, 2002), 67–85.

³⁵ Zubkova, *Russia After the War*, 69.

³⁶ RGANI f5 op16 d642, 67–69.

³⁷ RGANI f2 op1 d7, 22–23.

(*kompromat*) on wartime hero Marshal Georgii Zhukov in December 1946, the following dialogue was recorded among Lieutenant General Gordov, former commander of the Volga military district and Hero of the Soviet Union; his wife; and his deputy, Major General Rybalchenko: "I say now I am convinced if they got rid of the *kolkhozes* (collective farms), tomorrow there would be order, there would be a market, and therefore, there would be everything. Let people live, they have the right to live, they won this life, they defended it!" Gordov replied, "We need real democracy." "Precisely, pure, real democracy...," answered Rybalchenko.[38]

As Elena Zubkova's comprehensive review of archival materials shows, dangerous rumors were widespread in the years after the war. It was expected that the *kolkhozes* would be disbanded, either voluntarily, or under threat of force from Britain and the United States.[39] The miserable conditions on *kolkhozes* generated more than 93,000 complaints just to the Council of Ministers from peasants in the three years from 1947 to 1950.[40] In the summer of 1945 there were demonstrations at defense plants in pursuit of better living conditions.[41]

There was good reason to fear peasant opposition to collective farms, and so to socialism: the widespread famine after the war. Two million died of hunger and hunger-related diseases in 1946–48.[42] The famine was so bad that private plots were officially sanctioned after the war. Nineteen million Soviets had such plots after the war, 1.2 million in and around Moscow alone.[43] Immediately after the war there was no soap and no winter clothing. Many local party committees cancelled outdoor parades for the November 1946 celebrations of the revolution, fearing people didn't have the clothing to survive the cold.[44]

In addition to the desperate material conditions, there was sporadic guerilla warfare against the government going on in western Ukraine, Belarus, and the Baltic republics throughout Stalin's rule.[45] In a June 1946 report to Stalin from Ministry of Internal Affairs (MVD) Chief Sergei Kruglov, it was stated that

---

[38] Rudolph G. Pikhoia, *Sovetskii Soiuz: Istoriia Vlasti, 1945–1991* (Novosibirsk: Sibirskii Khonograf, 2000), 39–40.

[39] Elena Iu. Zubkova, "Stalin i Obshchestvennoe Mnenie v SSSR, 1945–1953," in *Stalinskoe Desiatiletie Kholodnoi Voiny: Fakty i Gipotezy*, ed. I. V. Gaiduk, N. I. Yegorova and A. O. Chubarian (Moscow: Nauka, 1999), 152–54.

[40] Elena Iu. Zubkova, "Mir Mnenii Sovetskogo Cheloveka. 1945–1948 Gody," *Otechestvennaia Istoriia* 3 (1998): 32.

[41] Zubkova, *Russia After the War*, 37.

[42] Ibid., 47; and Jeffrey Brooks, *Thank You, Comrade Stalin! Soviet Public Culture from Revolution to Cold War* (Princeton: Princeton University Press, 2000), 196.

[43] Stephen Lovell, *Summerfolk: A History of the Dacha, 1710–2000* (Ithaca: Cornell University Press, 2003), 163–66.

[44] Zubkova, *Russia After the War*, 36.

[45] Amir Weiner, *Making Sense of the War: The Second World War and the Fate of the Bolshevik Revolution* (Princeton: Princeton University Press, 2001), 180–81.

hundreds of rebels had been killed in these recently acquired Soviet territories, and 1,000 arrested.[46] Western governments, especially the United States and Britain, airdropped weapons and equipment to these fighters.[47]

An additional danger was posed by the fact that those who had fought in the war had been exposed to the more economically prosperous parts of Europe. After the war, a constant question on official forms, passports, employment books, school registrations, and Komsomol and party applications was whether or not one had been on occupied territory.[48] Over five million Soviet citizens returned home after the war, almost two million prisoners of war and 3.5 million civilian slave laborers. Almost all had their party memberships revoked.[49] It was feared that these returnees had been exposed to a different system, and so could imagine an alternative to the especially miserable Soviet reality that existed after the war.

Stalin's interpretation of these events put the danger in the predominant discourse of danger. At his dacha in December 1952, Stalin told the assembled Presidium members, "[T]he more success we have, the more our enemies will try to harm us. Our people have forgotten this under the influence of our great success; there has been complacency, heedlessness, and conceit...."[50] In other words, the stronger the Soviet Union, the more successful its socialist construction, the more insecure the Soviet Union, the more dangerous its enemies.

The Predominant Discourse of Soviet Identity

In Table 2.1 I present the elements that constituted the predominant discourse of Stalinist Soviet identity, and its relationship to its challengers.

Table 2.1 has three parts. Part A lists the ways in which the predominant discourse and its challengers *relate* to each other, and the general way in which the discourses are arranged with regard to each other and with respect to the major themes of Soviet identity that emerge from the texts in this period. Part B shows areas of agreement between the official and societal discourses when it comes to understanding the Soviet Union as modern. Part C details how the Russian nation is treated in the predominant discourse, a rendering with which Russian

---

[46] Kees Boterbloem, *The Life and Times of Andrei Zhdanov, 1896–1948* (Montreal: McGill-Queen's University Press, 2004), 280, 479 n. 177.
[47] Peter Grose, *Operation Rollback* (Boston: Houghton Mifflin, 2000).
[48] Brooks, *Thank You, Comrade Stalin!*, 197.
[49] Zubkova, *Russia After the War*, 105; and Zubkova, "Mir Mnenii Sovetskogo Cheloveka," 102.
[50] Pikhoia, *Sovietski Soiuz*, 65.

Table 2.1 **Discourses of Soviet Identity**

Part A. Points of Contestation

Predominant Discourse of Danger	Societal Discourse of Difference
Optimistic	Realistic
Infallible	Fallible
Conflictual	Contradictory
Clear	Ambiguous
Literal	Abstract
Dichotomous	Continuous
Public	Private
Collective	Individual
Unique	Normal
Childlike	Adult
Insecure	Secure
Dangerous	Different

Part B. Points of Agreement between the Discourses of Danger and Difference

What's Modern?	What's Pre-Modern?
Urban	Rural
Center	Periphery
Russian	Non-Russian
Moscow	Outside Moscow
Russia	Central Asia and the North
Vanguard	Masses
Developed	Underdeveloped

(continued)

Table 2.1 (Continued)

Part C. Russia: The Taken for Granted Soviet Nation
Atop the Hierarchy of Development
Modern
Vanguard
Elder Brother
Non-Russian Others
Post-Bourgeois Nation
Orthodox

societal discourse, if not all non-Russian, is in agreement. The table's contents risk giving the false impression that each of these dozens of elements is operating independently of the others. Instead, these elements are continually related to each other, informing how the predominant discourse of Soviet identity is constructed, and how it relates to its societal counterpart.

Part A lists the many elements of Soviet identity in which the two discourses, official and societal, are in conflict. The official discourse maintains a constant optimism about Soviet reality, declaiming its challenger's realistic portrayal of reality as misleadingly concentrating on non-representative parts of that reality, flaws that will be overcome in any case. The "HyperOfficial" discourse of *lakirovanie*, or varnishing, which is borne of the institution of overinsurance described above, serves the important purpose of showing the boundary of the absurd, that is, claims that idealized reality has already been achieved, a position even rejected by the orthodox official discourse.

The predominant discourse treats the Soviet project as infallible, as incapable of making any serious errors, given its objective and scientific foundations. Challengers maintain that the Soviet project can make mistakes and still be Soviet. Official discourse acknowledges that conflict still exists in Soviet society, but holds that it is aberrational and is being overcome. The challenger suggests that there are more fundamental and widespread conflicts, or contradictions, in Soviet society that may be overcome, but only if attention is paid to them. Meanwhile, the discourse of *beskonfliktnost*, or lack of conflict, claims that there is no meaningful conflict left in Soviet society, and so should not even be mentioned.

Official discourse treats Soviet reality as clearly delineated into official categories of analysis. Challengers expect ambiguity in these categories, such that much of reality does not fit so neatly. Official discourse demands literal representations of reality, so that possible alternative interpretations of it may be reduced to a minimum. Challengers are comfortable with abstract depictions of reality, allowing individual Soviets to have many different understandings and still remain Soviet.

Official discourse understands being Soviet in a zero-sum manner: Either one is, or one is not, Soviet. There are no exceptions. Challengers treat being Soviet as a continuum, so that someone may be more or less Soviet, but still Soviet. Predominant discourse maximizes the public sphere of discourse, claiming that being Soviet requires the sacrifice of one's private pursuits and concerns. One is always in public. Challengers suggest that a Soviet may have a large and inviolable private sphere without doing any harm to the Soviet project. Official discourse privileges the collective Soviet project. Societal discourse finds room for the individual.

Official discourse treats the Soviet Union as a unique and extraordinary project, apart from and in a hostile relationship with, the West, while the societal discourse understands many aspects of being Soviet as creating commonality with other peoples in the world, especially in the West. Official discourse maintains that the Soviet project is always at risk of degenerating into its bourgeois past. Societal understandings represent the Soviet project as fundamentally secure. Official discourse treats all deviations as potentially dangerous. Anti-Stalinist challengers treat deviations as harmless differences.

Official discourse is paternalistic, treating Soviets as children who require guidance to become real Soviets. Its HyperOfficial boundary treats Soviets as permanent infants, unable to make any but the most trivial choices without guidance from above. Societal discourse treats Soviets as adults capable of making choices that maintain a Soviet identity.

In Parts B and C are the elements of Soviet identity that are mostly shared by society and the state. Soviet identity is "unanimously" understood as modern and urban, positioned against a pre-modern rural periphery that the Center will ultimately bring to modernity.[51] And this Center is Russian, as opposed to non-Russian, peoples; Russia, as opposed to non-Russian republics; and Moscow, as opposed to any other city. This modern, urban, developed, Russian, and Muscovite Center is the vanguard of Soviet identity for all pre-modern and undeveloped masses who will be led into modernity by that vanguard in Moscow.

[51] The counter-hegemonic discourse here is in the periphery itself. Because I concentrate on foreign policy in this volume, I concentrate on discourses of the Soviet self that predominate in Moscow, not in Kiev, let alone in the many non-Russian territories of the Soviet Union. To the extent these counter-hegemonic discourses matter, they will appear in the societal discourses available in Moscow. This is not to say that these peripheral discourses do not matter; they surely do. It would be hard to explain the collapse of the Soviet Union in the 1980s without exploring them. But I am not trying to explain that.

The Russian nation has a particularly paradoxical place in the predominant discourse of Soviet identity. On the one hand, the modern Soviet identity is supposed to transcend any ethnonational identity. On the other hand, the Russian nation was the Soviet nation in this period, both implicitly as a taken for granted background condition for societal discourse, as well as explicitly, as proclaimed by Stalin himself. The Russian nation was understood as the modern vanguard for all others, sitting atop a hierarchy of non-Russian nations. The Russian nation was understood as their elder brother, teaching them how to become Soviet. It is significant that Russian nationalism was never understood as the dangerous bourgeois variety, unlike its non-Russian variants. In addition, Russian identification with the Orthodox religion was never treated as stimulating dangerous Russian nationalism, unlike Tajik Muslims, Russian Jews, or Lithuanian Catholics, all of whose religions were understood as constitutive of anti-Soviet nationalism.

If societal constructivism's insights are correct, then elements of the societal discourse on Soviet identity should appear after Stalin's death in the new predominant discourse of Soviet identity.

To summarize most grossly, the predominant discourse constructs the Soviet Union and the ideal Soviet as a modern, implicitly Russian man atop a hierarchy and at the center identified against pre-modern non-Russians at home, and a dangerous Western world abroad. Because the discourse has binarized the world into Us and Them, danger is found in only the slightest of differences from oneself. There is no tolerable or innocuous level of difference. What follows is an elaboration of this stripped down version of the predominant Soviet self under Stalin. I begin with the more substantive themes of the Russian nation, religion, the external Other, and modernity.

The Russian Nation

> Comrades! Allow me to make still another final toast. I would like to raise a toast to the health of our Soviet people, and first of all, the Russian people. I drink, first of all, to the health of the Russian people because it is the most outstanding nation among all nations in the Soviet Union. I raise a toast to the health of the Russian people because it earned in this war general recognition as the leading force of the Soviet Union among all other peoples of our country. I raise a toast to the health of the Russian people not only because it is the leading people, but also because it has a clear mind, resolute character, and patience. Our government made more than a few mistakes; we had desperate moments in 1941–42 when our army retreated, when it abandoned our villages and cities in Ukraine, Belarus, Moldavia, Leningrad oblast, the

Baltic, and Karelo-Finnish Republic, because there was no other way out. A different people could have said to the Government: you have not justified our expectations, get out, we will put in a different government which will conclude peace with Germany and guarantee us quiet. But the Russian people did not do this, for they believed in the correctness of the policy of its Government and sacrificed in order to secure the rout of Germany. And this trust of the Russian people in the Soviet government turned out to be the decisive force which secured the historic victory over the enemy of mankind—over fascism.

Thank them, the Russian people, for the trust!

To the health of the Russian people!

Josef Stalin, 24 May 1945[52]

One of the most taken for granted elements of Soviet identity was the Russian nation. While perhaps no statement of Stalin has been more often quoted to attest to the official ideology of Russian nationalism adopted during the war, the argument here is that official benediction of the Russian nation as the Soviet nation resonated deeply and broadly with societal understandings of the nation, too, at least among the three-quarters of the population that was Russian, but also, too, among many non-Russian elites. As Brandenberger concluded, "[C]onflation of the terms 'Russian' and 'Soviet' became routine during the late 1940s and early 1950. . . . Publishing, theater, opera, radio, film, and museum exhibitions . . . refer[red] to the Russian national past and a [R]ussocentric reading of the recent war experience."[53]

Many events marked the official glorification of the Russian nation, from its commencement at war's end to its fading out in early 1949. The public spectacle accompanying Moscow's 800th anniversary officially proclaimed what was already well understood.[54] As part of these celebrations in September 1947, a statue of Moscow's founder, Iurii Dolgorukii, was erected just behind the Institute of Marx, Engels, and Lenin on Gorky Street, replacing an obelisk devoted to the Bolshevik Revolution.[55] The Soviet Academy of Sciences had opened a Slavic Studies section just months before. Brandenberger's examination of postwar Soviet party and public education led him to conclude that its curriculum turned Soviet patriotism into "little more than discourse on Russian national

---

[52] Quoted in Evgenii Dobrenko, *Metafora Vlasti: Literatura Stalinskoi Epokhi v Istoricheskom Osvshchenii* (Munich: Verlag Otto Sagner, 1993), 368–69.

[53] David Brandenberger, *National Bolshevism*, 192, 224; and Dobrenko, *Metafora Vlasti*, 364–81.

[54] Dobrenko, *Metafora Vlasti*, 371.

[55] Brandenberger, "Stalin's Last Crime?" 216–17.

pride." If anything, Soviet public schools and party instructors, due to their very poor education in Marxism-Leninism-Stalinism, tended to default to what they knew: Russian history and its centrality to all Soviet reality.[56]

In this sense, official Soviet discourse glorifying the Russian nation fell on very fertile commonsensical and societal soil.[57] Surveys of Soviet readers showed that they preferred the Russian classics of Tolstoi, Pushkin, and Lermontov to the Soviet writers Gorkii and Sholokhov, let alone to contemporary Soviet writers, still less any non-Russians. These findings were replicated, as well, in the 1950–51 Harvard émigré interview project. Moreover, secret police files on private conversations, and the texts of private diaries, correspondence, and memoirs all show how deeply and matter-of-factly Russian national identity was embedded in the taken for granted everyday world.[58] Infinite daily practices of average Soviets reproduced a Russian national identity, not least of course being the use of the Russian language in daily life and in interaction with party and state officials. Official tour guides in the Kremlin referred to "our tsars."[59]

The Russian nation was understood to be more modern and developed, an older brother for non-Russian nations, a vanguard for those less advanced peoples constituting the USSR.[60] At the official level, non-Russians participated in their own subordination and peripheralization with regard to their "older Russian brothers." For example, on the fifth anniversary of Stalin's postwar toast, *Literaturnaia Gazeta (LG)* ran a front-page headline, "On our older brother, the Russian people," below which Zvenki, Yakuts, Tatars, Chuvashis, Nanaitsy, and Bashkirs wrote sentiments reducible to the following words of Rasul Gamzatov, from Daghestan: "At work, you are our teacher, in struggle our defender, when necessary you help and correct. For this thank you, thank you."

Virtually simultaneously with Stalin's toast, CC Agitprop Secretary Georgii Aleksandrov gave a speech declaring that all histories of non-Russians are "only intelligible in relation to the history of others, above all else, Russians."[61] Russian history was to be the history through which the experiences of all others should be understood. In the official history propagated after the war, the Russian nation was at the apex of modern development in the Soviet Union, and at the center of the socialist project with underdeveloped peripheries aspiring to

---

[56] This is a good example of the "slippage" that occurs in efforts to deploy discursive power coherently.

[57] Brandenberger, *National Bolshevism*, 198–213.

[58] Ibid., 218, 226–39.

[59] Milovan Djilas, *Conversations with Stalin* (New York: Harcourt, Brace & World, 1962), 165.

[60] Ilya Prizel, *National Identity and Foreign Policy: Nationalism and Leadership in Poland, Russia, and Ukraine* (Cambridge: Cambridge University Press, 1998), 189–90.

[61] Brandenberger, *National Bolshevism*, 184–85.

become Russia. By 1948, Russia's imperial rule over Central Asia, the Caucasus, and the "little peoples" of the North and East, was officially typified as that of modernizing benevolence, rather than oppressive exploitation.[62]

The flip side of this exaltation of Russia's centrality was the derogation of non-Russian histories. In 1947, for example, the Armenian CC attacked Armenian "nationalist" historians for claiming medieval Armenia experienced a "golden age" before it had contact with Russia. The official history of Belorussia was taken to task for claiming that Aleksandr Nevskii, not Prince Vladimir Polotskii, had defeated the Teutonic hordes.[63] All national "golden ages" were officially reinterpreted to begin for non-Russian peoples only after the revolution "led by the Russian proletariat"; silver ages were the time surrounding "joining" Russia.[64]

All non-Russian manifestations of national identity were condemned as "bourgeois nationalism," implying the danger of class deviance. The affair began with a series of attacks in *Pravda* in June and July 1951 against "nationalistic" Ukrainian literature.[65] In December 1951 Estonian party officials were reprimanded for this sin, and the Mingrelian Affair was launched in 1951–52 against Georgian nationalism.[66] Tajik communists were disciplined for "bourgeois nationalism," one manifestation of which were their continuing complaints that Samarkand and Bukhara, ancient Tajik cities, had ended up in Uzbekistan.[67]

At the 19th Party Congress in October 1952, 23 speeches attacked "bourgeois nationalism," primarily of the Mingrelian kind, with a few anti-cosmopolitan gestures.[68] But only Lavrentii Beria attacked "great Russian chauvinism" and the tsarist oppression of non-Russians.[69]

Reflecting the tension in official discourse between privileging the Russian nation and declaring an identity that transcended nation, or perhaps just lip service to official ideology, were official recognitions that local nations had the right to develop, too. Along with widespread condemnation of manifestations of nationalism among non-Russian nations was the recognition that these nations were too often denied the capacity to develop as nations. For example, in reports

---

[62] Yuri Slezkine, *Arctic Mirrors: Russia and the Small Peoples of the North* (Ithaca: Cornell University Press, 1994).

[63] David Brandenberger, *National Bolshevism*, 188–90.

[64] Dobrenko, *Metafora Vlasti*, 378.

[65] Hahn, *Postwar Soviet Politics*, 149.

[66] Zubkova, "Fenomen 'Mestnogo Natsionalizma,'" 89–102.

[67] RGANI f5 op16 d582, 42–44.

[68] Cosmopolitanism was a code word signifying unpatriotic Jewish identification with Jews beyond Soviet borders.

[69] Amy Knight, *Beria: Stalin's First Lieutenant* (Princeton: Princeton University Press, 1993), 165.

from Uzbekistan to the CC Agitprop Department in Moscow, the local Uzbek party was directed to end its "neglectful attitude" toward the development of local Uzbek culture. There were not enough Uzbek directors in Tashkent theaters and cinemas. Of 250 graduates from the conservatory since 1940, only 19 had been Uzbek, and not a single violinist or pianist.[70]

But Russia was not only the apogee and core of modernity within the Soviet Union; historically it had been at the forefront of global civilization, technology, and science. At a week-long conference held at the Academy of Sciences in January 1949, speakers recalled how, despite imperialist lies to the contrary, Russian inventors had been responsible for the steam engine, light bulb, airplane, radio, etc. These claims were widely circulated.[71] In his February 1951 comments to CC Presidium member Georgi Malenkov on the screenplay for *Admiral Ushakov*, Minister of Cinematography Ivan Bolshakov considered the film's release most opportune, as Ushkaov had taught British Admiral Horatio Nelson of Battle of Trafalgar fame everything he knew about naval warfare.[72] The Russian nation benefitted greatly from the campaign against Western influence and kowtowing to the West launched in 1946.

In this period, the Russian nation was not only understood with regard to its less developed little brothers or dangerous Western Others. It was also understood with regard to Soviet Jews. I think the evidence overall supports Brandenberger's conclusion: "It may be more productive to view this [postwar Soviet] antisemitism as a reflection of a broader postwar atmosphere of extreme Russocentrism and xenophobia in Soviet society rather than as an isolated travesty of justice committed against a single minority group."[73] The anti-Semitic campaigns also reveal complicated relationships between mass understandings of the Russian nation and Jews, official versions of Soviet supranationalism, and the Stalinist institution of anti-Semitic "affairs."

In fact, it took almost two years to get the official Stalinist anti-Semitic campaign off the ground. In October 1946, the Ministry of State Security (MGB) sent the CC a memo titled "On the nationalistic manifestations of certain workers of the Jewish Antifascist Committee." The same month CC Secretary Aleksei Kuznetsov requested that the question of nationalistic and religious tendencies of Jewish literature be discussed at a CC Secretariat meeting.[74] A month later, CC Secretary Mikhail Suslov sent a similar memo to Stalin himself. But in April 1947, CC Agitprop Department Head Georgii Aleksandrov concluded

---

[70] RGANI f5 op16 d582, 31–32, February 27, 1953.
[71] Brooks, *Thank You, Comrade Stalin!*, 214; and Dobrenko, *Metafora Vlasti*, 388.
[72] Anderson, *Kremlevskii Kinoteatr*, 859–62.
[73] Brandenberger, "Stalin's Last Crime?" 204.
[74] Danilov and Pyzhikov, *Rozhdenie Svekhderzhavy*, 167.

that Jewish literature overall was "penetrated by the ideas of Soviet patriotism and bears an optimistic character." He recommended to Andrei Zhdanov that the CC need not discuss the question of the state of Soviet Jewish literature "at this time."[75] The official discourse of supranational Soviet patriotism could be a weapon in the defense of those accused of nationalism.

The murder of Solomon Mikhoels on January 13, 1948, former chairman of the Jewish Anti-Fascist Committee, was used as a pretext to begin the purge of Jews from state and party institutions, social organizations, editorial boards, and the MGB.[76] In March 1948 the MGB accused Mikhoels and others of anti-Soviet nationalism, linking them to treasonous contacts with Western intelligence agencies.

In November, the Jewish Anti-Fascist Committee was officially dissolved and in January 1949, the arrests began.[77] A CC resolution of February 3, 1949, dissolved the official associations of Jewish writers and the Jewish literary almanacs in Moscow and Kiev. In early 1949, the Soviet press began to "out" Jewish authors, publishing their Jewish surnames alongside their Slavic pseudonyms.[78] In October 1950, Suslov ordered the Bolshoi Theater to stop preparations for Camille Saint-Saens's opera, *Samson and Delilah*, on the grounds that it depicted too many episodes from Jewish life in the Bible.[79] Less trivially, by 1952, 110 people had been arrested, and 10 executed.[80]

Beginning in 1949, as well, the party began to count Jews in various institutions. In an October 1950 memo from Iurii Zhdanov, the late Andrei Zhdanov's son and head of the CC Science and Higher Education Department, the "predominance of Jews among theoretical physicists" was documented. Russians, for example, were only 20 percent of laboratory leaders. There were no Russians at all in Lev Landau's theoretical physics graduate student seminar. Jews were almost 80 percent of the leadership of the Institute of Physical Chemistry, and all the theorists were Jews. Thirty-seven of 42 doctoral dissertations defended from 1943 to 1949 in physical chemistry were Jewish. And so on in the optics laboratory, and

---

[75] Gennadii Kostyrchenko, *Gosudarstvennyi Antisemitizm v SSSR, 1938–1953: Dokumenty* (Moscow: Materik, 2005), 96–97.

[76] Kostyrchenko, *Gosudarstvennyi Antisemitizm*, 110–19; Zubkova, *Russia after the War*, 136; Brooks, *Thank You*, 215; Rubenstein, *Tangled Loyalties*, 255–57; and Dobrenko, *Metafora Vlasti*, 337–64.

[77] For text of MGB report to the CC on the Jewish Antifascist Committee, see Kostyrchenko, *Gosudarstvenni Antisemitizm v SSR*, 120–30.

[78] Ehrenburg, *Post-War Years, 1945–1954*, 133.

[79] Kostyrchenko, *Gosudarstvennyi Antisemitizm v SSSR*, 330–31.

[80] Aleksandr N. Iakovlev, ed., *Reabilitatsiia: Politicheskie Protsessy 30-50-x godov* (Moscow: Izdatelstvo Politicheskoi Literatury, 1991), 323–26; and Fedor D. Volkov, *Vzlet i Padenie Stalina* (Moscow: Spektr, 1992), 279.

institutes of economics and geography. In May 1952 a comprehensive "Table of the Dynamics of the Quantitative Representation of Bureaucrats of Jewish Origin in the Soviet Nomenklatura in 1945–52" was prepared for the CC. Many of the entries were marked with an exclamation point or two. For example, 12 percent of the leading cadres of central institutions and ministries are Jewish! and 11 percent of the directing cadres of the central press are Jewish!![81] From May to July 1952, the trials associated with the Anti-Fascist Committee were held.

The last official anti-Semitic campaign began with a January 13, 1953, *Pravda* article about the Doctors' Plot, a conspiracy of elite physicians to murder high party officials, the majority of whose participants "belonged to an international Jewish organization called Joint."[82] The affair's careful preparation is reflected by the fact that the Glavlit chairman, Konstantin Omelchenko, sent a memo the very same day outlining which books needed to be removed from libraries and stores because they included articles by, or photos of, one or more of the identified doctors.[83]

Mass publications began to publish openly anti-Semitic attacks. In the February 12, 1953, issue of *Komsomolskaia Pravda*, for example, a typical Jew is described as having "a long, fleshy nose, puffy lips, small ratlike eyes. . . . He only comes to life when he tells how he bought gold and hid diamonds." The satirical magazine *Krokodil* ran caricatures easily mistaken for Nazi cartoons.[84] Only a month before the launch of the Doctors' Plot, at a meeting at his dacha, Stalin had declared that "any Jewish nationalist is an agent of American intelligence. Jewish nationalists think that the United States has saved their nation. . . . They consider themselves obliged to Americans."[85] Here is a direct connection between the dangerous deviance of domestic ethnonational identifications and the foreign imperialist threat.

It would seem from a broad range of testimony that the official discourse of anti-Semitism launched in 1949 resonated broadly and deeply with mass public antipathy toward Jews.[86] The famous Soviet Jewish director Mikhail Romm recalled that in 1944 an idea for "Russfilm" came up. This project would have allowed the Slavic directors Ivan Pyrev, Grigorii Aleksandrov, Sergei Gerasimov, Igor Savchenko, Boris Babochkin, and Mikhail Zharov to move to Moscow and work, while leaving Jewish directors Romm, Sergei

---

[81] Kostyrchenko, *Gosudarstvenni Antisemitizm v SSR*, 351–57.
[82] American Jewish Joint Distribution Committee; and Zubkova, *Russia After the War*, 136.
[83] RGANI f5 op16 d635, 15–16.
[84] Amir Weiner, *Making Sense of the War*, 199.
[85] Pikhoia, *Sovetskii Soiuz*, 60.
[86] For copies of hundreds of documents from the Soviet archives attesting to anti-Semitism from daily life to CC resolutions, see Kostyrchenko, *Gosudarstvenni Antisemitizm v SSSR*.

Eisenstein, Iuli Raizman, and Grigorii Roshal to run studios in Tashkent and Almaty.[87] There were also widespread anti-Jewish pogroms in Ukraine in 1944–45.[88] One could say that the official "sowing of anti-Semitism relied on thoroughly cultivated daily anti-Semitism."[89]

One public discourse after the war was that Jews had not participated in the war; they had been "Tashkent partisans," or among those who had been evacuated from the front to the Uzbek capital. In fact, 161,000 Jews had won military awards, the fourth largest group after Russians, Ukrainians, and Belarussians, while Jews were only the ninth largest nationality in the 1939 census.[90] Given the privileged position of "frontoviki" in official Soviet discourse, this was just one more way of denying Jews their positions in the Soviet project.

Vsevolod Kochetov's popular 1952 novel, *Zhurbiny*, described the villain, Veniamin Semenovich, a Jew who had avoided the front, coming up against Skobelev, another shirker. But the latter redeems himself by publicly slapping Semenovich. While the party committee condemns Skobelev's "primitive" use of violence, they privately reassure Skobelev that "such people deserve a slap in the face." Weiner concludes that "in a polity that identified sacrifice on the battlefield as a sign of true patriotism, exclusion from the myth of war amounted to exclusion from the Soviet family."[91]

It seems that the other part of official discourse, that of a supranational modern Soviet identity, was reflected in official treatment of Jews in Ukraine after the war that was far more tolerant than popular sentiments. The party punished many who committed anti-Semitic acts during the war, and reinstated many to party membership who had assisted Jews at the time.[92] Ludmilla Alexeyeva describes a similar dynamic while a student at Moscow State University shortly after the anti-cosmopolitan campaign began in early 1949. A fellow student, who would call for the strangulation of "fucking kikes" while walking the hallways of the university, initiated a campaign against a Professor Atzarkin. Instead of supporting his charges, the local Komsomol officially reprimanded the student for anti-Semitism, noting that the party was against cosmopolitans, not Jews.[93] In an analysis of Soviet censorship of literature in the period, Ermolaev finds that the

---

[87] Kenez, *Cinema and Soviet Society*, 221.

[88] Weiner, *Making Sense of the War*, 192.

[89] Dobrenko, *Metafora Vlasti*, 344.

[90] Weiner, *Making Sense of the War*, 216–19.

[91] In the same year, Ivan Goncharov's popular novel, *Fregat Pallada*, was republished, this time with long anti-Semitic sections. Weiner, *Making Sense of the War*, 196, 230–32.

[92] Ibid., 114–22.

[93] Ludmilla Alexeyeva and Paul Goldberg, *The Thaw Generation: Coming of Age in the Post-Stalin Era* (Boston: Little, Brown and Company, 1990), 44.

pejorative Russian word for Jew, "yid," is systematically removed from the 1953 edition of Mikhail Sholokhov's *Quiet Don*, the 1951 edition of Aleksandr Fadeev's *The Rout*, and even in the twenty-volume edition of Anton Chekhov's correspondence published from 1944 to 1951.[94]

In an officially commissioned full-page letter to *Pravda* in September 1948, Ilya Ehrenburg defended the patriotism of Soviet Jews and accused their detractors of being "obscurantists concocting cock and bull stories" since the Middle Ages. He wrote that only anti-Semitism brings Jews together across national boundaries and quoted Stalin's definition of anti-Semitism as "an extreme form of racial chauvinism, a most dangerous vestige of cannibalism."[95] Ehrenburg here invoked the second strand of official Soviet discourse: supranationalist modernity, as uttered by Stalin himself.

As in the postwar period, grass roots anti-Semitism seemed to significantly outstrip its official variety after the January 1953 launching of the "Doctors' Plot." Once unleashed at the official level, it became difficult for local party officials to control its more popular manifestations. Violence erupted against Jews, and anti-Semitic pamphlets were distributed. The party had to convene meetings on the "friendship of peoples," reminding people that not all Jews were murderers. Not only did average Soviet citizens avoid their Jewish physicians; many came forward and claimed Jewish doctors had tried to poison their children.[96] Yakov Rapoport recalls in his memoirs how widespread anti-Semitism was in Moscow at the time of his arrest in early 1953.[97] After the woman who had purportedly unmasked the Jewish murderers was awarded an "Order of Labor," letters poured into Soviet newspapers praising this "Russian woman, this true Russian soul," etc.[98]

In a rare sample of public opinion after the Doctors' Plot was publicized, the Central Committee Agitprop Department collected 92 letters to the editor from *Pravda, Izvestiia, Komsomolskaia Pravda, Trud,* and *Meditsinskii Rabochii*.[99] Of these 92 letters, eight singled out Jews as the enemy, five defended Jews as a people, but 79, or almost 90 percent, did not mention Jews at all. Though not particularly numerous, the letters attacking Jews were especially vicious and violent. I quote some of them in some detail to give the flavor of the moment:

---

[94] Herman Ermolaev, *Censorship in Soviet Literature: 1917–1991* (Lanham, MD: Rowman & Littlefield, 1997), 114–15.
[95] Ehrenburg, *Post-War Years, 1945–1954*, 125–27.
[96] Weiner, *Making Sense of the War*, 216–19; and Ehrenburg, *Post-War Years, 1945–1954*, 298.
[97] Yakov Rapoport, *The Doctors' Plot of 1953* (Cambridge: Harvard University Press, 1991).
[98] Ehrenburg, *Post-War Years, 1945–1954*, 299.
[99] RGANI f5 op16 d 602, 11–43.

> I am a simple worker and not an anti-Semite, but I say frankly, it is high time to drive out all Jews from medical institutions, pharmacies, hospitals, rest homes, and sanitoria.... These are people who didn't fight in the war, but love to live in butter... All work in warm places: medicine, science, art, literature, commerce. Here it is easy to earn big money. In a word, one must purge these people.
>
> I never was a nationalist or anti-Semite; I am a Soviet citizen. I fought at the front with Georgians, Uzbeks, and Kazakhs, but no Jews. Those bastards sat in the rear.... But they were the first to return to Moscow.... Isn't it time to resolve the Jewish question by removing them from all the big cities to Birobidzhan? Let the bastards live there.[100]
>
> "Let them mine coal.... Let them work like Russians work."

Of course, we know nothing about the sampling strategy used by the editors of these journals in choosing what to pass along to CC Secretary Nikolai Mikhailov and so cannot say this is a representative poll of Soviets. If it were, however, it would mean that while only a small percentage of Soviets understood Jews as the despicable Other, this understanding was demonstrably hateful and terrifying to any Jew.

In a similarly vexed sample, this time of overheard conversations among soldiers and sailors in Moscow, reported by MGB counter-intelligence officers to their chief, Semyon Ignatiev, and through him, to Presidium members Georgii Malenkov, Nikolai Bulganin, Beria, and Khrushchev on March 5, 1953, of 29 recorded comments, five attributed Stalin's reported illness to Jewish doctors. They went on to recommend deportation of Soviet Jews to Palestine, or worse.[101]

But the official discourse of Soviet supranationalism was present, as well. Ilya Ehrenburg was one of the few Soviets, let alone Soviet Jews, to swim against the anti-Semitic tide that gathered over the last months of Stalin's rule. A Central Committee functionary had asked that three out of 115 surnames be deleted from his most recent book, *Second Day*: Kronberg, Kahn, and Kaplan. Ehrenburg sent a letter directly to Suslov in January 1953, arguing that in the Soviet Union "national origins cannot be seen as a vice or as an occasion for singling anyone out."[102] Suslov agreed, and the novel was published without the deletions.[103] Once again, instrumental use of the Soviet discourse of supranationalism was employed.

---

[100] Birobidzhan is the eastern Siberian autonomous republic set aside for Jewish settlement.

[101] Vladimir. A. Kozlov, ed., *Neizvestnaia Rossiia: XX Vek*, vol. II (Moscow: Istoricheskoe Nasledie, 1992), 253–58.

[102] RGANI f5 op17 d392, 136–38, 161–63.

[103] *Kultura I Vlast ot Stalina do Gorbacheva. Apparat TsK KPSS I Kultura 1953–1957. Dokumenty* (Moscow: ROSSPEN, 2001), 19; and Ehrenburg, *Post-War Years, 1945–1954*, 237.

Religion: Relative Orthodox Privilege

Similar to the Russian nation, religion should have been identified as anathema to the modern Soviet project in official discourse. Instead, Russian Orthodoxy, like the Russian nation, benefited from the same "invisible whiteness" that characterizes contemporary European and North American societies. Moreover, it had an institutional defender in the State Council for the Affairs of the Russian Orthodox Church (CAROC). Meanwhile, other religions, in particular Judaism and Islam, but also Catholicism and Lutheranism, as they were associated with the evil of bourgeois nationalism, were treated as pre-modern dangers.

Religious identities are pre-modern vestiges of a feudal past in official Soviet discourse. That said, given the abiding predominance of the Russian nation as the not so implicit Soviet nation, Russian Orthodoxy remained in the background as the most tolerated of religions. Unlike Islam and Judaism, which were frequently associated with the development of pernicious national identities, Orthodoxy was never connected to the undesirable propagation of a Russian national identity. As Zubkova, perhaps exaggeratedly, observes, "While Soviet policies changed toward the Russian Orthodox Church (ROC) after World War II, no such changes occurred for other religions."[104]

I say exaggerated because there were not infrequent cases of the Council on Affairs of Religious Cults (CARC) effectively intervening on behalf of believers. For example, in 1947, religious calendars were allowed for Estonian and Latvian Lutherans, albeit with both Soviet and religious holidays displayed. Soviet Moslems had been granted the same privilege in 1944. Permission for their publication was granted anew in 1953.[105] Moreover, it was not uncommon for local party officials to be reprimanded for "administrativnost" in their approach to local religious groups, that is, unauthorized administrative abuse of local believers. So the Borislavskii city soviet chairman, or gorispolkom, Gordienko, was officially rebuked for demanding that the local Baptist minister give him the names and autobiographies of all his followers, under threat of expulsion from the town. Importantly, it was the CARC that intervened on behalf of the Baptist parishioners, sending on their complaints to the CC Agitprop Department.[106]

It is interesting that local party officials, and often elements of the local party aktiv and average Soviet citizens enforced the predominant discourse of atheism against the societal discourse of private religious identity. Meanwhile, two state institutions, the two Councils on Orthodoxy and Cults, were charged with vindicating the rights granted in the Soviet Constitution to religious believers.

---

[104] Zubkova, *Russia After the War*, 215 n. 1.
[105] RGANI f5 op16 d642 67–69.
[106] RGANI f5 op16 d642, 71–73.

The Russian Orthodox Church, and Orthodox religious identity, was institutionally empowered by the CAROC, headed since its founding in September 1943 by Georgii Karpov, who was simultaneously a NKVD/KGB officer. It is evidence of the privileged position of the Russian nation and its religion that all other religions—Islam and Judaism, most significantly—were under the jurisdiction of the CARC.[107] Karpov enjoyed genuinely warm relations with the Orthodox Patriarch Aleksei. Karpov's Council was in constant battle with the avowed official discourse of atheism, and its most enthusiastic proponents, local party officials.

Apparently, things were going so well for Orthodoxy that an October 1947 Central Committee report criticized the work of the Council. In February 1948, Karpov met with Kliment Voroshilov, the Politburo member responsible for overseeing the Council. Voroshilov reassured him that the Council's job was not to create anti-religious propaganda; leave that to the party. Throughout 1948, local party officials and the CC Agitprop Department, chaired by Suslov, rejected Council requests for any leniency toward religious practice.[108] In 1947–48, only 49 churches were reopened, and from 1948 to 1950, 31 Orthodox monasteries were closed.[109]

In October 1948, permission was withdrawn for the opening of 18 churches that year. That year there had been over 3,000 petitions to open churches; 28 were opened. In 1949, there were 2,300 requests, in 1950, 1,100, in 1951, 700, in 1952, 800. Of the nearly 5,000 requests, zero were granted. Meanwhile 300 Orthodox churches were closed or demolished.[110]

As the raw statistics reported above show, official discourse had brought any further religious revival after the war to a halt by 1948. Nevertheless, Karpov went on defending the constitutionally protected rights of the believers who remained. It was his institutional mandate to represent grievances of believers against the party and the state, and he continually followed this charge.

Meanwhile, Jewish religious identity was conflated with bourgeois nationalism, or still worse, cosmopolitanism, or a transnational connection with Jews elsewhere in the world, including the new state of Israel. In Ukraine, at least, local police and party officials condemned Jewish commemorations of the Holocaust in 1945–46, treating them as religious meetings with nationalist content.[111] In an April 1949 report on the practice of Judaism more generally, the

---

[107] It would be helpful to my story if the word "kult" had the same pejorative connotations in Russian that it has in English. This is, however, not the case, at least to my knowledge.

[108] Chumachenko, *Church and State*, 89–94.

[109] Zubkova, *Russia After the War*, 78.

[110] Chumachenko, *Church and State*, 100–21.

[111] Weiner, *Making Sense of the War*, 214.

chairman of the CARC, Ivan Polianskii, began his memo to Georgii Malenkov by stipulating that "the activities of synagogues, as before, are distinguished by great liveliness and are maintained not only, or not so much, by religious motives of believers, as by dissatisfied actions of nationalistic clerics...." The nationalistic identities of Jews reached the point where the leader of the Jewish community in Uzhgorod, Ukraine, told his parishioners they should ask the Soviet government to allow them to form military units to go fight on Israel's behalf. While Karpov would defend the rights of Orthodox believers against illegal repression by local party officials, Polianskii, on the contrary, reported local party officials who illegally allowed Jews to hold services in private apartments, or still worse, built new synagogues without permission from the Council.[112]

In general, we may conclude that the societal discourse of religious identity reinforced the predominant discourse of the Russian nation but was in conflict with the predominant discourse that associated the practice of Islam, Judaism, Catholicism, and Lutheranism with the dangers of bourgeois nationalism.

The External Western Other

Discourses of Soviet, or any other, identity are not made in vacuums, isolated from the world by political boundaries. While one should not assume the external world plays an important role in constructing such an identity, let alone assume which significant others in the world do the constituting, one should expect the mutual constitution of identities with external Others. In the Soviet case in this period, the West was a very significant other for both the predominant discourse of Soviet identity and its societal challenger. Indeed, they were in uneasy contradiction with each other.

Relations to an external other raised the issue of Soviet normalcy or uniqueness. To the extent the Soviet Union could even be compared to some other country, or region, or history, or idea external to itself, it shared enough in common to sustain that kind of discussion. But a truly unique Soviet Union, such as the one that denied a "common human" science, instead claiming there to be a Soviet science based on class principles, or a Russian history based on uniquely Russian experiences, the external Other was something axiomatically to be ignored or feared. Isolation from the threatening influence was recommended. Uniqueness entailed insecurity, fear in the face of a contaminating possibility.

Stalin told Boris Likharev, editor of the literary journal *Leningrad*, in August 1946, that "you go on tiptoe in front of foreign writers.... You encourage these groveling feelings. This is a big sin.... You instill a feeling that we are second-rank

---

[112] Kostyrchenko, *Gosudarstvenni Antisemitizm v SSR*, 265–69.

people, and they are of the first rank. We are pupils, they are teachers. This is wrong."[113] The hierarchy here is all wrong; the West cannot possibly be above the Soviet Union and Russia. Russia cannot be anyone's periphery or subordinate.

There was a very close connection between the centrality of the Russian nation in Soviet identity and the official fear of external influence on that identity. In accusing Ukrainian authors of nationalism for "overlooking the relationship between Russian and Ukrainian literatures," they were additionally condemned for thereby "exaggerating the influence of Western European literature."[114] As Ermolaev concluded in his analysis of censorship in the period, "[R]ehabilitation of the Russian past and the praise of everything Soviet proceeded parallel with the denigration of the West...."[115] There was a dichotomous relationship between the West and Russia in official Soviet discourse.

On January 26, 1946, Stalin awarded Sergei Eisenstein's film, *Ivan the Terrible, Part One,* the Stalin Prize, First Class. Just a week later, Eisenstein collapsed with a heart attack at the awards banquet for the film. He was in the hospital during the meeting of the committee reviewing the second installment of the film. In August, Stalin previewed it, and announced that "it wasn't a film, but some kind of nightmare." In his February 1947 meeting with Eisenstein to discuss how to remake *Ivan the Terrible II*, Stalin told him that "the wisdom of Ivan the Terrible was that he stood on a national point of view and did not allow foreigners into the country."[116] Being Soviet meant being national, which in the context of the simultaneous exaltation of the Russian nation, meant being a Russian nationalist. Stalin opined that "Peter I was a great leader, but he too liberally related to foreigners, opened the gates to foreigners too much, allowed foreign influence, and the Germanization of Russia. Catherine allowed still more. And was Alexander I's court really Russian? Or Nicholas I's? No. They were German courts."[117] It is significant, as well, in this discussion of Eisenstein's second installment that while Zhdanov criticized the film for its constant display of Orthodox religious ceremonies, Stalin did not object to this tacit identification of the Russian nation with the Russian Orthodox Church.[118]

---

[113] Evgenii Gromov, *Stalin: Vlast i Iskusstvo* (Moscow: Respublika, 1998), 387; and Babichenko, *Literaturnyi Front*, 197–209.

[114] Brandenberger, *National Bolshevism*, 190.

[115] Ermolaev, *Censorship in Soviet Literature*, 106.

[116] Maureen Perrie, *The Cult of Ivan the Terrible in Stalin's Russia* (Hampshire: Palgrave, 2001), 102–05, 169–78; and Gromov, *Stalin: Vlast I Isskusstvo*, 373–75.

[117] Quoted in Grigorii B. Mariamov, *Kremlevskii Tsenzor: Stalin Smotrit Kino* (Moscow: Kinotsentr, 1992), 85.

[118] Boterbloem, *The Life and Times of Andrei Zhdanov*, 299.

In February 1947, the Soviet government banned marriages between Soviet citizens and foreigners, including those from eastern Europe.[119] In August 1947 the Council of Ministers ordered increased police vigilance in 12 Soviet cities chosen on the basis of how much contact their citizens had with foreign visitors.[120] The same year the Moscow Museum of New Western Art was closed, and no Western art was exhibited in the Soviet Union until after Stalin's death.[121] Ludmilla Alexyeva woke up one day and found out that French bread had become "urban" bread at Moscow bakeries.[122] The jamming of Voice of America (VOA) and British Broadcasting Company (BBC) broadcasts began in 1948–49. In 1949, the journal *Znamia* debuted a new section, "Through our own eyes," written by Soviets who had been abroad. For months followed testimonials to the poor, wretched, and inhuman conditions prevailing in the United States, France, Britain, and the West more generally.

The official turn against identifying the Soviet Union or the Russian nation in relationship to a Western, or European, Other is manifested in two contributions to *Voprosy Istorii* by Professor M. Tikhomirov just five months apart in 1947. In April, Tikhomirov criticized a book by Dmitrii Likhachev for excessively glorifying Russian culture. Tikhomirov asked, "Does love for one's own Homeland really have to be tied up with running down the *chuzhoi*/the other? Had the author, even for a minute, compared the rich cities of medieval Italy with Moscow in the fourteenth or fifteenth centuries, he couldn't have insisted on the superiority of Muscovite culture over Florentine in this epoch." Tikhomirov had a change of heart by September, where in the lead article in the same journal he asserted the superiority of Russian over Florentine architecture.

What had happened in between was the "Professors' Affair" of June 1947 launched against the oncologists Nina Kliueva and Grigorii Roskin for allegedly allowing their anticancer drug to be given to American spies.[123] A month before the "Professors' Affair" was launched, Stalin declared at a meeting with

---

[119] Tatiana A. Pokivailova, "Moskva i Ustanovlenie monopolii Kompartii na Informatsiiu na Rubezhe 40-50-x godov," in *Moskva i Vostochnaia Evropa. Stanovlenie politicheskikh rezhimov sovetskogo tipa (1949–1953). Ocherki istorii*, ed. Tatiana V. Volokitina et al. (Moscow: ROSSPEN, 2002), 421.

[120] Anatolii M. Beda, *Sovetskaia Politicheskaia Kultura Cherez Prizma MVD* (Moscow: Mosgorarkhiv, 2002), 34.

[121] Antoine Baudin, "'Why is Soviet Painting Hidden from Us?' Zhdanov Art and its International Relations and Fallout, 1947–53," in *Socialist Realism Without Shores*, ed. Thomas Lahusen and Evgeny Dobrenko (Durham: Duke University Press, 1997), 230–31.

[122] Alexeyeva, *The Thaw Generation*, 38. Any resemblance to the renaming of French fries as "freedom fries" in the US Congress cafeterias after French refusal to join the US adventure in Iraq in 2003 is completely coincidental.

[123] Zubkova, *Russia After the War*, 119; Krementsov, *Stalinist Science*, 131–36; and Boterbloem, *The Life and Times of Andrei Zhdanov*, 293–97.

the writers Konstantin Simonov, Aleksandr Fadeev, and Boris Gorbatov that "Soviet patriotism" should be a primary theme for writers because "our average intelligentsia has an unjustified admiration for foreign culture.... First the Germans under Peter, then the French." Stalin then gave Fadeev a folder on Kliueva and Roskin.[124] Fadeev read the letter the CC was to send to party organizations. In it a straight line was drawn from insufficient admiration for the Soviet Union and the Russian nation to susceptibility to recruitment by imperialist intelligence agencies.[125] As Molotov, Malenkov, and Zhdanov summarized the situation in a September 1947 memo to Stalin, "[S]ervility before the West ... is a serious danger to the Soviet state since agents of international reaction try to use people infected by a feeling of servility before bourgeois culture...."[126]

In late March 1947 "honor courts" were established in government ministries to instill "the spirit of Soviet patriotism and devotion to Soviet state interests." The very first trial was that of Kliueva and Roskin, held in June before 1,000 people and lasting for three days. A "closed letter" defining the affair's significance for the party's battle against undue deference to the West was circulated to 9,600 party leaders in July. In September the party launched a public campaign for "Soviet patriotism."[127]

Fear of the Western Other was tied to fear about the effects returnees from the war were having on the security of the Soviet project. While it would be easy to attribute this fear to one man's paranoia, Stalin's views were not merely personal, but were part of the official understanding of the threat emanating from the appearance of millions who had experienced an alternative reality. Twenty years after the fact, Dmitrii Shepilov, writing about the end of the war, and on his way to becoming Suslov's deputy in the CC Agitprop Department, recalled that "our people want to live well now. Millions were abroad, in many countries. They saw not only bad, but also some things that compelled them to ponder things. But much of what they saw was interpreted in their heads inaccurately and one-sidedly. But one way or another, people want to enjoy the fruits of their victories; they want to live better: to have good apartments (they saw what these are in the West), to eat well, to dress well. And we are obliged to give people all this." Here we see both the predominant discourse of the dangerous Western Other, and the patronizing attitude toward the Soviet masses, their portrayal as unable to understand reality accurately.

---

[124] Simonov, *Glazami Cheloveka*, 111–15; and Gromov, *Stalin: Vlast I Isskusstvo*, 403.

[125] Iurii S. Aksenov, "Poslevoennyi Stalinizm: Udar po Intelligentsii," *Kentavr* (October–December 1991), 82.

[126] RGASPI f82 op2 d159, 77–79.

[127] Krementsov, *Stalinist Science*, 136–43.

Shepilov went on to infer that "apolitical and non-ideological sentiments are dangerous for the fate of our country." That is, the public sphere must be maximally expanded; otherwise, the socialist project may fail. Shepilov recalled that such feelings were tangible at that time. "In literature, theater and film some kind of rot appeared. These feelings became still more dangerous when combined with servility before the West: 'Oh, the West!,' Oh, democracy!,' 'What literature!,' 'What garbage cans on the streets!'"[128]

The predominant discourse and its affiliated campaigns confronted a societal discourse of identification with the West. As was the case in the anti-cosmopolitan campaign and the doctors' plot, a notable contrarian voice was that of Ehrenburg, who, in a series of articles in *Izvestiia* in the summer of 1946 concluded from his May 1946 trip to the United States that "we have much to learn from American writers and American architects, and even, despite the appalling vulgarity of the average production, from their film directors."[129] Writing in *Novoe Vremia/New Times* in November 1947, Ehrenburg, in direct contradiction of what was said just days before on Red Square by Molotov at the celebrations of the 30th anniversary of the Bolshevik Revolution, asserted, "It is impossible to fawn upon Shakespeare or Rembrandt, because bowing before them cannot humiliate the idolizer."[130] Ehrenburg's works in general were larded with frequent and alluring descriptions of life in the West. Vasily Aksyonov recalls that Ehrenburg's writings were "windows on the West" for millions of his readers.[131] But the same could be said for the countless asides made in other Soviet publications, as well as the background settings in the many Western movies circulating in the postwar Soviet Union.

Unlike the official Soviet discourse that condemned Soviet and Russian identification with the West in general, Ehrenburg distinguished between Russia's more natural affinity with Europe and its fundamental differences with the United States. In an August 1947 article, he wrote that "to speak of West European culture as separate from Russia, or of Russian culture as separate from Western Europe is ignorant.... We have learned from them and they from us. Modern European and American literature is unthinkable without the classical Russian novel, modern art without the work of nineteenth century French painters...."[132]

---

[128] Shepilov, "Politicheskii Arkhiv XX Veka. Vospominaniia," *Voprosy Istorii* (May 1998), 11.

[129] Ehrenburg, *Post-War Years*, 61.

[130] Ilya Ehrenburg, "Zashchitniki Kultury," *Novoe Vremia* 46 (1947): 8.

[131] Joshua Rubenstein, *Tangled Loyalties: The Life and Times of Ilya Ehrenburg* (New York: Basic 1996), 249.

[132] Ehrenburg, *Post-War Years, 1945–1954*, 109.

Meanwhile, a more important breach in the campaign against identifying with the West was made by early postwar reliance on films captured from Germany during the war. In part a product of the demands of the marketplace, and in part a consequence of meager postwar Soviet film production, cinemas' repertoires were dominated by old Soviet films from the 1930s and European and American "trophy" films from Germany. From March to September 1946, for example, Dom Kino, the main movie palace in Moscow, showed 60 foreign films. It even aired a foreign film on the fifth anniversary of Germany's invasion in June 1941. *Sun Valley Serenade* and *Girl of My Dreams* were especially popular. Bulat Okudzhava recalls that the star of the latter Hungarian film, Marika Rokk, was wildly popular in Tbilisi, with people humming the soundtrack, discussing it, and lining up again and again to see it.[133]

One of the underlying reasons for official condemnation of Evgenii Varga's 1946 book, *Changes in the Economy of Capitalism as a Result of the Second World War* was that the author observed that capitalists had adopted some of socialism's advantages of planning and state intervention. This made the West more like the Soviet Union, and hence less threatening than the predominant discourse allowed.[134]

Finally, the discourse of Russian superiority over the West had instrumental value to the likes of the charlatan of Soviet science, Trofim Lysenko. In August 1948, Lysenko defended his peculiar take on genetics by claiming his detractors relied on Western biology, agronomy, and genetics, rather than on Russian achievements.[135] The defense of Soviet/Russian science had precious little to do with science, but "the *image* of Soviet science and the Soviet scientist," that is, what it meant to be Soviet.[136]

In sum, the predominant Soviet discourse of Western danger and Soviet Russian superiority was in direct conflict with a societal discourse of identification with the West, with the European roots of Russia.

The Soviet Union: A Most Modern Project

In both official and societal discourses, being Soviet was being modern. Moving from the village to the city, from the farm to the factory, from manual labor to machines, abandoning an ethnonational identity for a supranational Soviet one,

---

[133] Kenez, *Cinema and Soviet Society*, 213–14.

[134] Hahn, *Postwar Soviet Politics*, 84–93.

[135] Brooks, *Thank You, Comrade Stalin!*, 213; Krementsov, *Stalinist Science*, 179–83; and Dmitrii T. Shepilov, "Politicheskii Arkhiv XX Veka. Vospominaniia," *Voprosy Istorii* (June 1998): 5–11.

[136] Krementsov, *Stalinist Science*, 275.

forsaking superstition and religion for science and atheism, were all part of the new modern Soviet citizen.

There was a constant axis in Soviet discourse: the center versus the periphery. Modernity was in the center; pre-modernity in the periphery. Operating across different identities, Russia was the center to the non-Russian periphery. Moscow was the center of Russia not only to its rural reaches, but even to other cities, such as Leningrad or Kiev. Urban areas were centers to their rural peripheries. This way of thinking was both officially expressed and popularly taken for granted. In a jocular moment meeting with Stalin, Fadeev reported that he had managed to send about 100 writers around the country to observe Soviet "reality," but only "average" writers. Stalin asked ironically why, "krupnyi" (big/famous) writers didn't want to go? Fadeev responded that it was hard to get them moving.[137] In Pyrev's 1947 film, *Tale of the Siberian Land*, Moscow was "the center of centers, ultimately taming and subordinating Siberian nature."[138] Intelligentsia unlucky enough to not be in Moscow or Leningrad frequently complained to the party and government about the unfair allocation of resources.[139]

Most peripheral of all in the Soviet Union were the peoples of Central Asia, and the "North," which was construed as Siberia and the Arctic. These peoples were considered pre-modern and most in need of the Soviet, Russian, Muscovite vanguard center to eliminate their "old, backward, stagnant way of life."[140] In Vasilii Azhaev's 1949 novel, *Far from Moscow*, one of the main themes was the development of indigenous peoples in the Far East. Local Nanai, for example, are depicted as leaping "from the Stone Age straight into our Soviet age," laughing in "a childlike way."[141] Peripheral peoples were at the bottom of a hierarchy whose apex was a benevolent Russian father in modern Moscow who thankfully is willing to help them climb the ladder to mature modernity.

Failure to depict Soviet reality as sufficiently modern was punished by those guarding the boundaries of official Soviet discourse. In the August 1946 CC resolution "On the Journals *Zvezda* and *Leningrad*," which launched the *Zhdanovshchina* in cultural matters, Zoshchenko's works were condemned for "slanderously presenting Soviets as primitive, uncultured, stupid, and with philistine tastes and morals."[142] In the September 1946 CC resolution condemning the film *The Big Life*, what was singled out was its focus on the pre-modern in

---

[137] Simonov, *Glazami Cheloveka*, 110–11.

[138] Emma Widdis, "Russia as Space," in *National Identity in Russian Culture*, ed. Simon Franklin and Emma Widdis (Cambridge: Cambridge University Press, 2004), 46.

[139] Tolz, "'Cultural Bosses,'" 96.

[140] Slezkine, *Arctic Mirrors*, 313.

[141] Lahusen, *Real Socialism*, 106.

[142] Gromov, *Stalin: Vlast I Isskusstvo*, 390.

the contemporary Soviet Union. The postwar reconstruction of Don basin coal mines was "depicted as if it were done with manual labor and old technology.... It is absurd and outrageous to depict the promotion of backward and uncultured people to leading posts as positive when Soviet power has created its own intelligentsia."[143] Katerina Clark writes that one of the major themes in postwar Soviet novels was a "new stress on kultura/culture, which in Russia was understood as what happens when a peasant moves from a wooden hut ... in favor of a more urban and Western way of life."[144]

Discursive Elements and Danger

Thus far, I have elaborated four main substantive elements in discourses of Soviet identity under Stalin. But as important is how predominant and societal discourses differentially treated these substantive elements. These differences are in Part A of Table 1.2. I could apply each of the dozen differences to each of the four substantive themes, but it would rapidly become repetitive and mechanical. That said, it should be borne in mind the myriad complicated ways in which these four themes were daily arranged and positioned vis-à-vis each other and with regard to the dozen differentiating elements. To illustrate, I will use a variety of empirical examples.

Let's begin with the predominant discourse's paternalism. In her analysis of postwar "middlebrow" fiction, Vera Dunham concluded that the theme of the family came to overshadow all others, in particular the relationship between parents and children.[145] In analyzing postwar cinema, Hans Gunther concludes that the "most amply developed Soviet myth is the myth of the Great Family." It extended the features of the "natural family onto the entire society." Peculiarly, sons always remained sons, never maturing, eternally infantilized by their parents, and of course, the party and the state.[146] Gunther reminds us that in the popular postwar Soviet film *The Oath* (1946) Stalin is portrayed as the father of the Soviet Union. In *The Fall of Berlin* (1949) Stalin is literally the father, as he blesses the marriage of the two heroes while standing on the ruins of Berlin.[147]

---

[143] A. S. Kiselev, ed., *Moskva Poslevoennaia 1945/47* (Moscow: MOSGOARKhIV, 2000), 763–64.

[144] Katerina Clark, *The Soviet Novel: History as Ritual*, 3rd ed. (Bloomington: Indiana University Press, 2000), 197.

[145] Vera S. Dunham, *In Stalin's Time: Middleclass Values in Soviet Fiction* (Durham: Duke University Press, 1990), 91.

[146] Hans Gunther, "Wise Father Stalin and his Family in Soviet Cinema," in *Socialist Realism Without Shores*, ed. Thomas Lahusen and Evgeny Dobrenko (Durham: Duke University Press, 1997), 178; and Leonid Heller, "A World of Prettiness: Socialist Realism between Modernism and Postmodernism," in *Socialist Realism Without Shores*, ed. Thomas Lahusen and Evgeny Dobrenko (Durham: Duke University Press, 1997), 65.

[147] Gunther, "Wise Father Stalin," 183–87.

One extremely popular novel, and Stalin Prize winner of 1946, was Fadeev's *Molodaia Gvardiia*, or *Young Guard*. Fadeev had spent months researching the young partisans of Krasnodon, including reading three volumes of Komsomol documents and diaries, and interviewing surviving guerilla fighters.[148] In a bizarre and instructive twist, Stalin commanded the novel be rewritten *after* it was already awarded the Stalin Prize, an illustrative case of the very good commanded to become perfect. Stalin had concluded that the "images of the older generation, the underground Bolshevik 'fathers' had been poorly elaborated and the political maturity of the younger generation, Oleg Koshevoi and others, the 'children', had been overestimated."[149] Fadeev spent five years revising the novel, correcting its exaltation of the "exploits of the sons, but neglect[ing] to tell the pivotal role of the fathers." Clark concludes that the 1951 edition is "almost perfectly transparent, lacking impurities.... The [young] hero is assisted by an older and more conscious figure who has made a successful quest before him.... The initiate is young and maturing."[150]

The young, the peripheral, the pre-modern, the non-Russian, all must be protected from dangerous influences, especially from the West. The Soviet project is so insecure that its vulnerable elements must be defended against exposure to deviations from the predominant understanding of Soviet identity. Stalin told the Yugoslav communist Milovan Djilas over dinner in May 1948 that Dostoevsky was "a great writer and a great reactionary. We are not publishing him because he is a bad influence on the young people."[151] In the CC Resolution "On *Zvezda* and *Leningrad*," it was asked, "What are the errors of the editors" of these two journals? "They forgot that our journals are a powerful instrument of the Soviet state in bringing up the Soviet people, especially our youth.... The Soviet system cannot tolerate bringing them up in a spirit of indifference ... and lack of ideology."[152]

Additional danger is to be found in ambiguity, in gray areas, in continua, in unclear representations of the Soviet project. Ideally, there should be no question who are the good and bad Soviets. But the presentation of good Soviets, without any flaws, or the Soviet good life, without any problems, was too ridiculous even for the guardians of orthodoxy. Clark describes postwar Soviet novels analyzing how the already good becomes perfect.[153] Taken too far, the

---

[148] *Rossiiskii Illiuzion*, (Moscow: Materik, 2003), 255; and Harold Swayze, *Political Control of Literature in the USSR, 1946–1959* (Cambridge: Harvard University Press, 1962), 44–46.

[149] Shepilov, "Politicheskii Arkhiv XX Veka. Vospominaniia," *Voprosi Istorii* (June 1998): 44.

[150] Clark, *The Soviet Novel*, 161–70.

[151] Djilas, *Conversations with Stalin*, 157.

[152] Kiselev, *Moskva Poslevoennaia*, 765.

[153] Clark, *The Soviet Novel*, 202–03.

deviation of *beskonfliktnost* appears, viz., the presentation of reality as if there is no conflict between the old and the new, just some tidying up around the edges. More threatening antagonisms had to be presented than that. Related to this excessive infallibility was the sin of *lakirovanie*, or the "laquering," varnishing, or prettifying of reality. Even Andrei Zhdanov noted, at the March 1947 discussion of Stalin Prizes for movies, that prior films such as *Traktoristy*, had too many kolkhoz chairpersons with motorcycles and dinners "we don't have even in the Council of Ministers."[154]

The problem with ambiguity is that it permits of multiple interpretations. This helps account for the official fear and ridicule of abstraction in art in general. When Vladimir Kemenov edited the official volume *Bourgeois Art and Aesthetics* (1951), examples of modern art were not even permitted to be illustrated, as they were deemed "indescribable."[155] Vasilii Grossman's treatment of the battle of Stalingrad, "For a Just Cause," appeared in *Novyi Mir* in July 1952 and was roundly criticized for its lack of an obvious hero. *NM*'s editorial board officially apologized for publishing it just days before Stalin, and the campaign against the work, died. Reflective of the institutionalized over-implementation of Stalin's presumed preferences, and the post-Stalin emergence of tolerated difference, was Fadeev's public apology for attacking the novel in the first place.[156]

Shepilov recalls the personal danger incurred if one raised any questions about a policy after Stalin had decided the issue. Instead of being regarded as a reasonable concern for the effectiveness of the given policy, "it was immediately qualified as 'wavering in implementation of the general line of the party,' (in one's party record was a special paragraph: had there been waverings in implementing the general line of the party?) or as 'indulgence' of Trotskyism or Right Opportunism with all the ensuing consequences."[157]

Included in an infallible Soviet identity was the assumption that flaws and mistakes are minor and exceptional aberrations in the process of being overcome. Their elimination and avoidance are inevitable. How to do this was laid out in the lead editorial in *Pravda* in April 1952: "Expose and mercilessly criticize vestiges of capitalism and manifestations of political indifference, bureaucratism, stagnation, servility, vainglory, arrogance, conceit, graft, unconscientious attitude toward duties, and a heedless attitude toward socialist property. Expose all

---

[154] Kirill M. Anderson, *Kremlevskii Kinoteatr*, 797.

[155] Baudin, "Zhdanov Art," 232.

[156] Edith Rogovin Frankel, *Novy Mir: A Case Study in the Politics of Literature, 1952–1958* (Cambridge: Cambridge University Press, 1981), 5–12.

[157] Shepilov, "Politicheskii Arkhiv XX Veka. Vospominaniia," *Voprosi Istorii* (June 1998): 36.

that is *backward* ... and help *the new* to triumph." What is exposed must be exceptions that prove the general rule of Soviet modernity.

The predominant discourse left little room for private life, that is, a space where one could be who one was without worrying about acting out the Soviet model. As Katerina Clark has concluded, "Many of the questions that most preoccupied 1940s society centered around the relationship between the individual, private world, and public life and duties."[158] The struggle here was between those who wished to carve out some private personal space where one could manifest an individual personality or self without fear of the predominant discourse demanding adherence to its idealized qualities.

In Zhdanov's notes for his August 16, 1946, talk before the Leningrad writers' meeting, he wrote that "nonideological people want to deprive our art of its sense and purpose, to take away from art its transforming role, turning it into an end in itself or an amusement."[159] In the CC Resolution on *Leningrad* and *Zvezda*, Anna Akhmatova was identified as a "typical representative of empty, unideological/ [*bezideinoi*] poetry," that is, work that deals with the personal, rather than the public.[160] The September 1946 CC Resolution criticized *The Big Life* for its excessive attention to the private lives of its characters, rather than to their public roles and party activities.[161] The film director Vsevolod Pudovkin, by eliminating those kinds of scenes from his first version of *Admiral Nakhimov*, received a Stalin Prize.

The official elimination of the private and the personal is linked to the issue of the relative insecurity of the Soviet project, and the danger of ambiguities in public texts, ambiguities that can only lead average Soviets to come up with their own individualized interpretations of what they might mean. But alternative meanings are precisely what must be reduced to the barest minimum. There needs to be a single authoritative interpretation of what it is to be Soviet.

The film *The Big Life* was criticized for showing individual miners taking matters of reconstruction into their own hands in the Don basin after the war, instead of being led by party and state collectives.[162] Stalin commanded that Fadeev rewrite *Young Guard*, a 1946 Stalin Prize winner, in part in order to increase the role of the party in organizing partisan resistance, at the expense of individual efforts.[163]

If one had to pick a single underlying attitude in the predominant discourse that places it in clearest opposition to societal discourse, it would be fear—fear

---

[158] Clark, *The Soviet Novel*, 208.
[159] Babichenko, *Literaturnyi Front*, 229.
[160] Gromov, *Stalin: Vlast I Isskusstvo*, 391.
[161] Kenez, *Cinema*, 216.
[162] For the text of the CC resolution on the film, see Kiselev, *Moskva Poslevoennaia*, 763–64.
[163] Clark, *The Soviet Novel*, 162.

that the Soviet project was vulnerable to being overthrown. Associated with this fear was the demand that Soviet reality be presented optimistically, that state and party decisions be presented as scientifically unassailable, that the public sphere be maximally expanded and purged of any sources of misunderstanding or individualized interpretations of reality. Meanwhile societal discourse, reflecting certainty in the security of the Soviet project, welcomed critical depictions of Soviet failings, greater room for private life, greater tolerance for deviations from the Soviet ideal, and broader definitions of what would fall under the rubric of a genuine Soviet identity.

The Predominant Discourse of Soviet Identity and Soviet Relations with Other States

If the predominant discourse of Soviet identity actually determined Soviet identity relations with other states in the world, there are many testable propositions that follow.

First, and most straightforward, hostile relations motivated by fear and danger should characterize relations with the West, with the United States and Europe.

The implicit Russian nation should imply closer relations with Slavic states than with non-Slavic ones, with one critical stipulation. These non-Slavic states will be subordinated to the superior, more modern, vanguard in Moscow. To the extent they deviate from their Slavic older brother, they will be treated as dangerous.

The modern Soviet Union will understand the rest of the world hierarchically. There will be pre-modern and modern areas of the world. The former may become modern, but only under the tutelage of the Soviet vanguard in Moscow.

Overarching all of this are such discursive elements as the dichotomization and binarization of identity relations between the Soviet Union and its Others. To remain nonthreatening to Soviet identity, one must either be Soviet, or be becoming Soviet under the close patronage of Moscow. This implies that vast areas of the world are automatically consigned to enemy status, rather than simply neutral or meaningless.

If we turn now to particular countries or collections of countries in the world, we can hypothesize about Soviet relations with the West, China, Eastern Europe, and the decolonizing world.

As I intimated above, we should expect Soviet relations with the United States and Europe to be marked by hostility and fear. Soviet relations with China should be complicated. On the one hand, understanding China through a Russian national identity should evoke images of the Russian imperial past, and a subordinated China, and still more, given Russia's position atop a hierarchy of modernity, and as vanguard for the less-developed, such as China. On the other hand China is on its way to becoming the Soviet Union, a modern socialist state. Relations will be close to the extent China subordinates itself to the Soviet Center in Moscow.

Eastern Europe is also a region of subordination, where deviation from the Soviet model of development will be understood as dangerous deviation, not permissible difference. As in the case of China, the Soviet vanguard should be directing domestic developments in Eastern Europe. Finally, it might be expected that Slavic states including Yugoslavia, Poland, Czechoslovakia, and Bulgaria will be understood differently, as members of an ethnonational fraternity, with Russia as their elder brother.

Because of the dichotomization of the world into us and them, the decolonizing world will be understood, at best, as irrelevant, at worst, as potentially threatening, and certainly as no potential collection of allies. Only those decolonizing states committed to becoming the Soviet Union in detail, should be deemed sufficiently similar to warrant being trusted as allies.

In addition, there is the issue of periodization here. Since I argue that Soviet identity was one of uncertainty and tolerance for ambiguity, at least until the summer of 1946, we should expect that the effects of the identity dynamics sketched out above will not be apparent until after this date.

The "causal" sequence we should expect to uncover if my theoretical approach is correct should be the following: Predominant Discourse of Soviet Identity → Soviet Understanding of Significant External Others Through that Discourse → Soviet Relations with Those Significant External Others Consistent with that Understanding.

For example, Soviet rejection of the Marshall Plan in July 1947 should be *preceded* by both a predominant discourse of Soviet identity that characterizes the West as threatening, and by a discursive construction of the West during elite discussions that reflects that prior understanding. In other words, the policy outcome that we are trying to establish as parasitic on prevailing identity relations must in fact occur after such identity relations have been established as prevailing.

3

Stalin's Foreign Policy

The Discourse of Danger Abroad, 1945–53

Stalin presents a real challenge to any brand of structural theory, a challenge which societal constructivism handles, if imperfectly. Some societal understandings of the Soviet Union that appeared in chapter 2 are fully embodied by Stalin, Molotov, and other Soviet foreign policy decision-makers when making foreign policy choices after the war. Since they are so widely shared in Soviet society, they are likely understandings of the Soviet Union that Stalin, Molotov, and other Soviet elites were socialized into earlier in their lives, and not products of the predominant official discourse.

A number of the hypotheses raised in chapter 2 are confirmed empirically by the archival records of this period. The ambiguous period marked in Soviet society after the war until 1946 is reflected in Soviet foreign relations in the same period. The intolerance of difference that follows, its treatment as dangerous deviation that threatened the very continuation of the Soviet project, is also well-reflected in the Stalinization of Eastern Europe from 1947 to 1953. Fear and intolerance of difference from the Soviet model is also manifested in Soviet indifference to the possibility of allying with revolutionary movements in the decolonizing world. Finally, understandings of China in the period as an under-developed, pre-modern periphery, on its way to becoming the Soviet Union echoes a vanguard Soviet identity atop the hierarchy of socialist development in the world.

Identity relations don't seem to help as much in understanding Soviet support for the Korean War. That choice is hard to explain from any general theoretical perspective, other than one that foregrounds Stalin's own authority and agency in making Soviet foreign policy during the period.

This chapter is divided into two parts, the first dealing with the period of relative Soviet tolerance of difference at home, reflected in a more tolerant foreign policy abroad. The second part reflects the triumph of the discourse of danger at home, and its projection onto Soviet relations with Eastern Europe, Yugoslavia,

East Germany, China, the Third World, and the United States. Besides telling the story of these events based on the latest primary documentation available, I point out both the limits and rewards of paying attention to the elements of Soviet identity elaborated in the previous chapter.

Part One. Stalin's Tolerance of Difference: Soviet Foreign Policy before the Cold War, 1945–47

Stalin's tolerance of difference perhaps most graphically manifested itself in relations with the Soviet Union's Eastern European allies after the war.[1] In this period, while ensuring that pro-Moscow communists were in power in these countries, Soviet leaders frequently reined in those allies who, like many officials around Stalin, tried to anticipate the leader's wishes by rushing ahead with the Stalinization of their countries. Stalin personally recommended the maintenance of coalition governments, or popular or national fronts, in Eastern Europe, often against the more sectarian and reckless wishes of the latter's communist politicians.

For example, in July 1945 Stalin told the Bulgarian Communist Party to not remove the Agrarian Party from its government. After the London Council of Foreign Ministers (CFM) meeting in September–October 1945, Stalin called on Georgii Dimitrov, first secretary of the Bulgarian communist party, to recruit two opposition party members to the government, to satisfy American and British demands.[2] He complied. In June 1946, Stalin advised that the Bulgarian communist party maintain its "fatherland front" for the upcoming elections, of course, assuming "everything necessary" is done so the communists win. After winning the elections, Andrei Zhdanov told his Bulgarian communist allies to avoid "dizziness from success," and maintain the Fatherland Front, of course, on terms favorable to communists.[3]

---

[1] Zbigniew Brzezinski, in his splendid book *Unity and Disunity in the Soviet Bloc*, periodized Soviet rule in Eastern Europe in this fashion, too, basing his arguments mostly on open party documents. More recently, scholars who have used archival materials have reached the same conclusion. For example, Elena Iu. Zubkova, "The Rivalry with Malenkov," in *Nikita Khrushchev*, ed. William Taubman, Sergei Khrushchev, and Abbott Gleason (New Haven: Yale University Press, 2000), 196; and Iurii P. Bokarev, "Eshche Raz ob Otnoshenii SSSR k Planu Marshalla," *Otechestvennaia Istoriia* 1 (2005): 88.

[2] For the sake of simplification, I refer to all Eastern European parties as communist parties, rather than differentiating between the Socialist United Party of Germany (the result of the merger of socialists and communists in April 1946), Hungarian Socialist Workers' Party, the Polish Workers' Party, and so on.

[3] Georgi Dimitrov, *The Diary of Georgi Dimitrov, 1933–1949* (New Haven: Yale University Press, 2003), 375, 393, 405. The phrase "dizziness from success" comes from Stalin's March 1930 front page *Pravda* editorial designed to put an end to the excesses of forced collectivization, as its level of arbitrary violence even exceeded Stalin's expectations and desires.

While the popular front in Bulgaria did not result in any electoral threat to communist rule, circumstances were different in Hungary, where the Smallholders Party won the majority of votes in the October 1945 Budapest assembly elections, contrary to Matias Rakosi's assurances to Kliment Voroshilov, the Soviet chairman of the Allied Control Commission (ACC) for Hungary.[4] The November 1945 parliamentary elections saw the Smallholders Party win an absolute majority of 57 percent, while the Hungarian Communist Party and Socialist Party won 15 percent each, the National Peasants Party 5 percent, and the Bourgeois Democratic Party, less than 1 percent. Soviet advice was to get the Hungarian communists to form a national front with as many of the least anti-Soviet parties as they could.[5]

In Voroshilov's report to Stalin and Molotov in Moscow about the campaign, he complained that the Hungarian communists, including Rakosi, behaved and spoke too radically, their "leftist sentiments" driving the farmers away.[6] In post-election advice from Stalin to Hungarian communists, he suggested the latter accept 3 of 14 seats, but insist on the Ministry of the Interior over the Ministry of Finance. The communist Laszlo Rajk became Hungary's new interior minister.[7] This was and would be a common pattern in Stalin's recommendations: In coalition governments, make sure you have control over the "power ministries:" the police, interior ministry, armed forces, intelligence agencies, and so forth.[8]

While in general Stalin and the Soviet foreign policy establishment consistently recommended moderate tactics to their Eastern European communist

---

[4] Rakosi was the general secretary of the Hungarian communist party.

[5] Bela Zhelitski, "Postwar Hungary, 1944–1946," in *The Establishment of Communist Regimes in Eastern Europe, 1944–1949*, ed. Norman Naimark and Leonid Gibianskii (Boulder: Westview Press, 1997), 78.

[6] Volokitina et al., *Vostochnaia Evropa v Dokumentakh Rossiiskikh Arkhivov, 1944–1953 gg., Tom I, 1944-48*, (Moscow: Sibirskii Khronograf, 1997), 271. A word about the references: Many of my citations are to collections of Soviet archival materials collected by Russian academics in large edited volumes. These are mostly from the Archive of Russian Ministry of Foreign Affairs. As far as I can tell, based on other compilations of archival materials by Russian scholars, the transcripts of memoranda, conversations, etc., are mostly verbatim. Of course, any materials I have reviewed myself are cited as such by the name of archive, the fond, the opus, the delo, and the page numbers. The most important compilations of foreign ministry documents used here are those of Gibianskii, Kynin, Ledovskii, Murashko, and Volokitina. Fortunately, these Russian scholars, and others, continue to produce work based on archives often inaccessible to foreign scholars.

[7] Volokitina et al., *Vostochnaia Evropa v Dokumentakh Rossiiskikh Arkhivov, 1944-1953 gg., Tom I, 1944-48*, (Moscow: Sibirskii Khronograf, 1997), 290–91.

[8] On the Czechoslovakian case, see Igor Lukes, "The Czech Road to Communism," in *The Establishment of Communist Regimes in Eastern Europe 1944–1949*, ed. Normal Naimark and Leonid Gibianskii (Boulder: Westview Press, 1997), 252–58; on Yugoslavia, see Christopher Andrew and Vasili Mitrokhin, *The Sword and the Shield: The Mitrokhin Archive and the Secret History of the KGB* (New York: Basic Books, 1999), 355–56.

allies, at least one figure did not concur. The Bulgarian communist Georgii Dimitrov, general secretary of the Communist International (Comintern) from 1934 to its dissolution in 1943, but after the war a Soviet Central Committee International Information Department (CC IID) head, was just as militant as other Eastern European communists who had to be restrained.[9]

On May 10, 1945, Wladyslaw Gomulka, at the time a deputy prime minister in the Polish government, was summoned to the CC IID to report on the situation in Poland. He was severely criticized by Dimitrov for being too timid. After Gomulka explained that his party tells the peasantry that it is against collectivization of private farms, Dimitrov asked, "[W]hat if someone wants to enter a collective farm? What then? You are against the introduction of collective farms by force, but what if someone wants it?" Gomulka answered defensively that such situations didn't exist yet. When Gomulka spoke of resistance in the countryside to collectivization, Dimitrov suggested, "This means you have not smashed their faces enough. You're the ruling party after all." Gomulka: "No, comrade Dimitrov, we couldn't do this because we don't want a fratricidal war." Dimitrov: "Without conflict, nothing will happen, you need to purge...." To Gomulka's statement that the Polish government wouldn't "go for concentration camps or mass arrests," Dimitrov answered, "This is right, but you cannot get along without concentration camps." Gomulka reassured him that "we have one."[10]

It should be added here that, given the peculiar way in which Soviet alliance relations operated with its Eastern European allies, Dimitrov had allies in the Polish party leadership, and could expect to receive some support from them for his more militant positions, even if Stalin opposed him.[11]

Five days later, in a letter to Stalin, Gomulka assured him that the Polish Workers' Party leadership agreed with Stalin about the need to oppose sectarianism, and the "mechanical transfer of... the Soviet model, without consideration of the specific features of Poland." Gomulka went on to promise land reform, free retail trade of agricultural products in cities, and the release from prison of those arrested without sufficient evidence of a crime.[12] Six months later, Stalin agreed with Gomulka's proposal to free up the agricultural market,

---

[9] The CC IID was created in July 1944 but was replaced by the CC Foreign Policy Department (CC FPD) in December 1945, a month after Dimitrov returned to Bulgaria.

[10] Gennadii Bordiugov and Gennadi Matveev, eds., *SSSR-Polsha: Mekhanizmy Podchinennia,1944–1949 gg.* (Moscow: AIRO-XX, 1995), 105–22.

[11] I. S. Yazhborovskaia, "Vovlechenie Polshi v Stalinskuiu Blokovuiu Politiju: Problemy i Metody Davleniia na Plskoe Rukovodstvo. 1940-e gody," in *Stalin i Kholodnaia Voina*, ed. A. O. Chubarian (Moscow: In-t vseobshchei istorii RAN, 1997), 92–93.

[12] Bordiugov, *SSSR-Polsha*, 122–39.

get rid of state-controlled bread rationing, and accept loans from the United States and Britain.[13]

One principle of identity that made this encouragement of coalitions possible in this period was Stalin's rejection of binarization and dichotomization in favor of multiplicity and continua. Instead of the world being black and white (either you are with us or against us), Stalin told Polish socialist leaders visiting Moscow in August 1946 that "the sharp border which existed earlier between communists and socialists is gradually eroding. For example, the merging of the communist and social-democratic parties in Germany."[14]

A crucial feature of Stalinist tolerance in this exchange is the acknowledgement, or even encouragement, of Eastern European communists to take into account their peculiar national characteristics, the unique contexts in which they have to operate, and the necessary differences they will have to have from the Soviet model, and from the historical Soviet experience of becoming socialist.

Stalin explicitly differentiated the Polish path to socialism from the one pursued in Russia and the Soviet Union in a May 1946 meeting with Polish President Boleslaw Bierut in Moscow. Stalin explained:

> in Poland there is no dictatorship of the proletariat, and no need for one.... We had strong enemies, we had to topple three pillars—the czar, the landlords, and a relatively strong class of Russian capitalists.... We needed coercion, a dictatorship. You have a completely different situation. Your capitalists and landlords have so seriously compromised themselves with the Germans that you crushed them with no great effort.... Undoubtedly, the Red Army also helped remove them from Poland.... You are getting closer to socialism without any need for a dictatorship of the proletariat or the Soviet system.... Lenin permitted the possibility of socialism by using the institutions of a bourgeois democratic system, such as parliament.... It is sufficient for you to reduce prices and give people more consumer goods and the situation will stabilize.... You will get closer to socialism without a bloody struggle....

Stalin went on to distinguish between those against whom "you spare nothing to do away with," viz., the armed resistance, and those legal parties, such as that of

---

[13] Volokitina et al., *Vostochnaia Evropa*, 301–02. For similar moderating advice to Rumania's communist party chief Gheorghe Gheorgiu-Dej on issues of nationalization of industry and freedom for the opposition press, see *Tri Vizita A. Ia, Vyshinskogo v Bukharest, 1944–1946: Dokumenty Rossiiskikh Arkhivov* (Moscow: ROSSPEN, 1998). In February 1947, Stalin urged Dej to accept US offers of wheat and corn. Volokitina et al., *Vostochnaia Evropa*, 568.

[14] Volokitina et al., *Vostochnaia Evropa*, 511.

Mikolayczyk, whom you can repress, but not destroy.[15] Stalin further advised not to move against the Catholic Church, as it "can all the same be in coalition with you...."[16] In his November 1946 meeting with the Polish party aktiv, Gomulka repeated Stalin's analysis in order to justify Poland's "peaceful path" to socialism.[17]

The period after the war was also marked by both explicit and implicit references to the Russian nation as part of the Soviet self. At a meeting with the CC IID in the autumn of 1945, Stalin said that Slavic peoples had been especially victimized by Germany in the past, but now "an emerging alliance of these Slavic peoples will once and for all resist German aggression...."[18] Soviet diplomats evaluated the March 1947 treaty between Poland and Czechoslovakia as "strengthening the unity of Slavic peoples" against Germany.[19] In agreeing with Tito's territorial ambitions in the Balkans during a May 1946 meeting in Moscow, Molotov noted that Thessaloniki is an "old Slavic city," and Yugoslavia needs an outlet to the Aegean Sea.[20] In October 1946, Suslov objected to a Hungarian communist party suggestion to convene a meeting of Danube River basin communist parties in Budapest, because its "successes in socialist construction were less significant than in the Slavic countries" of Yugoslavia and Bulgaria.[21]

Rarely, the obvious anti-Marxist nature of privileging the Russian nation was so explicit it provoked some critical response. A Slavic Congress was planned to meet in Prague in April, and then June, 1948. Its postponement until after Stalin's death was in no small part due to the unusual recognition of the contradictions posed by an ethnonational Slavic identity and a supranational Soviet socialist one. In discussing the upcoming congress with its organizing committee, including

---

[15] Stalin made a similar point about the harder Soviet road to Czechoslovakia's Klement Gottwald in the summer of 1946. Galina P. Murashko and Albina F. Noskova, "Sovetskii faktor v poslevoennoi Vostochnoi evrope (1945–1948)," in *Sovetskaia Vneshniaia Politika v Gody "Kholodnoi Voiny" (1945–1985)*, ed. L. N. Nezhinskii, (Moscow: Mezhdunarodnye otnosheniia, 1995), 90. Stanislaw Mikolayczyk was prime minister of the Polish government in exile in London during the war.

[16] Volokitina et al., *Vostochnaia Evropa*, 443–60. Tatiana V. Volokitina, "Stalin i Smena Strategicheskogo Kursa Kremlia v Kontse 40-x Godov: ot Kompromissov k Konfrontatsii," in *Stalinskoe Desiatiletie Kholodnoi Voiny: Fakty i Gipotezy*, ed. I. V. Gaiduk, N. I. Yegorova and A. O. Chubarian (Moscow: Nauka, 1999), 14; Tatiana V. Volokitina, "Nakanune: Novye Realii v mezhdunarodnykh Otnosheniiakh na kontinente v kontse 40-x godov i Otvet Moskvy," in *Moskva i Vostochnaia Evropa. Stanovlenie politicheskikh rezhimov sovetskogo tipa (1949–1953), Ocherki istorii*, ed. Tatiana V. Volokitina et al. (Moscow: ROSSPEN, 2002), 36–38.

[17] Grant M. Adibekov, *Kominform i Poslevoennaia Evropa, 1947–1956* (Moscow: Rossiia Molodaia, 1994), 93.

[18] Volokitina, "Nakanune," 31.

[19] Volokitina et al., *Vostochnaia Evropa*, 586.

[20] Leonid Ia. Gibianskii, "Poslednii Vizit I. Broza Tito k I. V. Stalinu," *Istoricheskii Arkhiv* 2 (1993): 27.

[21] Leonid Ia. Gibianskii, "Kak Voznik Kominform. Po Novym Arkhivnym Materialam," *Novaia i Noveishaia Istoriia* 4 (1993): 137; and Adibekov, *Kominform I Poslevoennaia Evropa*, 23.

Suslov and Shepilov, Zhdanov said he was "categorically against" discussing the economic construction of "Slavic countries" because "the very question is artificial and unscientific." He asked, "Where is the Marxist approach here? Is there even a gram of Marxism?" He went on to object to any ethnographic discussion of "Slavic peoples," fearing that such "questions as whether Galician Ukrainians are closer to Great Russians or to Western Slavs" will come up, as will "conversations about little brothers." Zhdanov clearly recognized the political costs of projecting the predominant discourse of Russian identity beyond Soviet borders.[22]

Both Soviets and those with whom they interacted off-handedly referred to Soviets as Russians. Stalin, in conversation with Polish socialists in Moscow, said, "As far as Lenin is concerned, and us, his Russian students, we always stand for the independence of any country...."[23] In a March 1948 meeting with the East German communist leadership in Moscow, Stalin asked whether Grotewolhl knew "how much the Russians take every year in reparations in millions of marks or dollars."[24] This kind of matter of fact slip of the tongue precisely replicates what was occurring in Soviet novels and daily conversations at the time.

If we recall from chapter 2, the predominant discourse about the superiority and centrality of the Russian nation did not adopt an anti-Semitic character until 1948–49. Indeed, two highly-placed efforts by the MGB in October 1946 and Suslov a month later, got nowhere. It is noteworthy, therefore, that anti-Semitism in Eastern European allies that manifested itself prior to the official campaigns in the Soviet Union were also criticized by Stalin himself. In particular, in February 1947, during a meeting with Rumania's communist leader Gheorgiu-Dej, Stalin asked him whether it was true that they "would like only Rumanians to be in the party," and added that if true, the party "would become a racialist party, not a class one. If it acquires a racial character, the party will inevitably die."[25] A week later, just before Dej's departure, Stalin told him he was dissatisfied with Dej's candor about the "nationalistic deviation" within the Rumanian communist party, and reminded him he needed to "value and promote good workers independent of

---

[22] M. Iu. Dostal, "Zapis Besedy A. A. Zhdanova s Organizatorami Kongressa Uchenykh-Slavistov, Mart 1948 g.," *Istoricheskii Arkhiv* 5 (2001): 3–10.

[23] And in conversation with German leaders in January 1947, Stalin substituted Russian for Soviet. Georgii P. Kynin and Johan P. Laufer, "Vvedenie: Politika SSSR po Germanskomu Voprosu (6 oktiabria 1946 g.—15 iiuniia 1948 g.)," in *SSSR I Germanskii Vopros*, vol. III (Moscow: Mezhdunarodnye Otnosheniia, 2003), 261; and Volokitina et al., *Vostochnaia Evropa*, 512.

[24] "Za Sovetami v Kreml: Zapis Besedy I. V. Stalina s Rukovoditeliami SEPG. Mart 1948 g.," *Istoricheskii Arkhiv* 2 (2002): 23.

[25] Volokitina et al., *Vostochnaia Evropa*, 565.

whether they are Rumanians, Jews, or Hungarians. In Russia also there was a strong anti-Semitic movement, stronger than in Rumania. . . . However, Bolsheviks didn't cede their positions on the national question." Stalin warned that "if the Rumanian communist party will be racial, it will die, for racism leads to fascism."[26]

Another area in which Stalin initially tolerated difference was in his not infrequent insistence that Eastern European communists were Soviet equals, not Moscow's subordinates. For example, in April 1946, after a long "report" by Hungary's prime minister, Nad Ferents, Stalin said that Ferents was not obliged to give a "report," since the Soviet government saw Hungary as an independent country, and therefore the Soviet government considered what the prime minister just said to be a "communication/soobshchenie," and thanked him for it.[27]

Stalin's tolerance for difference in these initial months after the war extended to the encouragement of productive relations with imperialist powers. For example, in Stalin's last meeting with Tito in May 1946, Stalin encouraged Yugoslavia to "allow other Powers into the Yugoslav economy," and Tito agreed.[28] In meetings with Polish and Czechoslovakian communists, Stalin advised them to have "good diplomatic relations with the United States, Britain, and France, as well as the Soviet Union."[29]

In the first 18 months after the war, it appears that Stalin expected and hoped that the United States, Soviet Union, and, much less so, and less and less, Britain, would manage world, especially European, affairs. One sees a mixture of mostly restraint, but some cautious probing, in these first 18 to 24 months after the war.

There is much evidence that Stalin expected long-term cooperation with the United States after the war.[30] In a June 1945 meeting in Moscow with representatives of the Polish provisional government, Stalin said, "Poland should have alliances with several big states. Poland needs alliances with Western states, with Great Britain, France, and friendly relations with America." This collection of security guarantees was aimed against what Stalin expected to be a revived German threat which he suggested might appear within six years.[31] It appears so long as Western states aimed their alliances against Germany, Stalin was satisfied. For

---

[26] Ibid., 582.
[27] Ibid., 408.
[28] Gibianskii, "Kak Voznik Kominform," 21.
[29] Volokitina, "Stalin i Smena Stratigicheskogo Kursa Kremlina," 12–13.
[30] Cold War historians who also have concluded that early postwar Soviet expectations entailed continuing cooperation include Campbell Craig and Sergey Radchenko, *The Atomic Bomb and the Origins of the Cold War* (New Haven: Yale University Press, 2008), 98.
[31] Stalin told Tito in April 1945 that Germany would "re-establish its power" in 12 to 15 years. Volokitina, "Nakanune," 31, 35.

example, the March 1947 English-French treaty was positively evaluated by the Soviets because of its explicit identification of Germany as the target of mutual assistance.[32]

Even after Winston Churchill's bellicose Fulton, Missouri speech describing an "iron curtain" descending across Europe, Stalin's reply published in the March 14, 1946, *Pravda* was critical primarily of Churchill's efforts to "sow seeds of discord among the allied states and complicate their cooperation."[33] In conversation with the then Czechoslovakian Foreign Minister Hubert Ripka on March 28, Molotov said he didn't think the tense situation would get worse. "We are not on the offensive, and if our Western friends don't launch any new attacks on us, the situation can normalize itself."[34] On May 24, 1946, Stalin told visiting Polish president Bierut that "no kind of war is now possible. Neither we, nor the Anglo-Americans can now start a war. We have all had enough of war. Furthermore, there is no point to a war. We are not getting ready to attack England and America, and they will not risk it. No kind of war is possible for at least 20 years.... Churchill's speech is blackmail aimed at bullying us.... But if you don't intimidate yourself, they will make noise and more noise and then calm down."[35] Stalin repeated his arguments to Zhdanov in September, adding that conflict between American and English imperialists was far more likely.[36] In his speech on the 29th anniversary of the Bolshevik Revolution in November, Zhdanov still called for the possibility of continued cooperation among allies in the coalition against Hitler.

Underlying Stalin's expectation of continued collaboration with the allies after the war was his Leninist belief that inter-imperialist contradictions would eventually lead to a new war among them, most likely between Britain and the United States. Zubok and Pleshakov write that "Stalin went to his grave believing that war between the US and its European allies was the most likely outcome, more so than between the US and Soviet Union."[37] And why not? Had not the last world war vindicated Lenin's theory of imperialism? Germany, Britain, and France in Europe, the United States and Japan in Asia had all gone to war over

---

[32] N. I. Yegorova, "NATO i Evropeiskaia Bezopasnost: Vospriiatie Sovetskogo Rukovodstva," in *Stalin i Kholodnaia Voina*, ed. A. O. Chubarian (Moscow: In-t vseobshchei istorii RAN, 1997), 296.

[33] It bears noting however, given Stalin's warning to Gheorgiu-Dej about the road to fascism originating with racism, that Stalin also warned that Churchill's appeal to "English-speaking nations" was also racist. I thank Matthew Evangelista for bringing this parallel to my attention.

[34] Volokitina et al., *Vostochnaia Evropa*, 397.

[35] Ibid., 456–61.

[36] Dimitrov, *The Diary of Georgi Dimitrov*, 415.

[37] Vladislav Zubok and Constantine Pleshakov, *Inside the Kremlin's Cold War* (Cambridge: Harvard University Press, 1996), 73–74.

conflicts of colonial interests. Had not these inter-imperialist contradictions overcome or transcended any threat emanating from the socialist project in the Soviet Union? On the other hand, if the Soviet Union could ally with the United States and Britain against Hitler, why not against Hitler's successors, who Stalin believed would inevitably arise and seek revenge?

But early postwar Soviet foreign policy wasn't without its cautious probing of what the postwar settlement might bring one of its primary victors. Among these tests of Western forbearance we could include material support for Greek communists in their civil war. In late November 1945, Molotov approved the provision of 100,000 tons of Soviet grain to the Greek resistance, to be funneled through Bulgaria. On the other hand, just three months later, Molotov indirectly recommended the Greek resistance not prepare for an armed uprising against the monarchy.[38] During their January 1946 visit to Moscow, Greek communists were not even permitted to meet with Stalin or Molotov, and had to meet with lesser Soviet officials, not in the Kremlin, but at the trade union headquarters.[39] Although the Soviets approved the Greek communist establishment of a provisional government in December 1947, neither Moscow, nor Belgrade, nor anyone else, recognized it.[40] In February 1948, Stalin told Yugoslav and Bulgarian leaders that he was "beginning to have doubts about a victory by the partisans." He concluded that "of course Greek partisans should be supported, but what is lacking in the correlation of forces cannot be made up for by proclamations . . . We need a rational calculation of forces. . . ."[41] Even so, it was not until May 1949 that Moscow ordered the closure of the Greek-Albanian border for military aid to the Greek resistance and got Albanian agreement to disarm and intern any Democratic Army of Greece fighters and officers on its territory.[42]

By May 1945 it was clear that Soviets were thinking of prolonging their occupation of northern Iran in order to extract the same oil concessions from Tehran in the north that Britain enjoyed in the south. In January 1946 Iran took the issue before the United Nations (UN). In April, Iran and the Soviet Union agreed to link the Soviet withdrawal to the creation of a joint oil concession. By

---

[38] Dimitrov, *The Diary of Georgi Dimitrov*, 396.

[39] Artiom A. Ulunian, "The Soviet Union and 'the Greek Question,' 1946–53: Problems and Appraisals," in *The Soviet Union and Europe in the Cold War, 1943–53*, ed. Francesca Gori and Silvio Pons (New York: St. Martin's Press, 1996), 145.

[40] Vojtech Mastny, *The Cold War and Soviet Insecurity* (New York: Oxford University Press, 1996), 35.

[41] Gibianskii, Leonid Ia., "Na Poroge Pervogo Raskola v 'Sotsialisticheskom Lagere,'" *Istoricheskii Arkhiv* 4 (1997): 99–100.

[42] Tatiana V. Volokitina et al., eds., *Vostochnaia Evropa v Dokumentakh Rossiiskikh Arkhivov, 1944–1953 gg., Tom II, 1949–1953* (Moscow: Sibirskii Khronograf, 1998), 82–83.

May, the Soviet Union effected its withdrawal. In November Iranian government forces began an offensive in southern Azerbaijan and northern Kurdistan. By spring 1947, they had imprisoned the leaders of the national liberation movements (NLMs) created in Moscow, and Mustafa Barzani, leader of the Kurds, had fled to Moscow.[43] but the Iranian parliament rejected the agreement in the autumn of 1947, leaving the Soviet Union with nothing for its efforts, other than a closer relationship between Washington and Tehran.[44]

Whether genuine or not, Stalin expressed a great deal of fear of the United States and the West during this period, constantly advising Soviet allies to behave more moderately or more covertly, and frequently invoking the threat of provoking the United States and its allies in order to justify his refusal to take some actions to expand communist influence somewhere. So, Stalin advised the Bulgarian communist leadership during a September 1946 visit to Moscow to create a Labor Party, not a Workers' or Communist party, as it will "help you internationally," that is, not make the United States as suspicious. At the same meeting, Stalin refused to provide Soviet military instructors for the Bulgarian army, suggesting "enemies will make good use of it."[45]

In a November 1945 meeting with Gomulka, Stalin advised the Polish party to not invite Soviet CPSU representatives to the Polish party congress, "so enemies cannot say that the congress occurs under the control of the CPSU...." Stalin also advised Gomulka to not postpone parliamentary elections, but hold them by the spring of 1946, to "avoid international complications."[46]

In explaining his retreat from Iran, Stalin wrote to the Democratic Party of Azerbaijan leader, Said Jafar Pishevari, that "we couldn't leave our armed forces in Iran primarily because ... England and America would say to us that if Soviet forces can remain in Iran, why can't English forces remain in Egypt, Syria, Indonesia and Greece, and American forces in China, Iceland, Denmark, etc...."[47] It bears stressing that during Soviet bargaining with Iran over trading Soviet withdrawal for rights to oil concessions, the Iranian Tudeh/Communist Party was pressing for permission to mount an armed rebellion against the government in Teheran, promising that "short and easy victory" that clients of great powers are seemingly always pledging in order to garner support from their patrons.[48]

---

[43] Barzani's son Massoud was holding on to power in Iraqi Kurdistan as of 2011. Iurii Zhukov, *Stalin: Tainy Vlasti* (Moscow: Vagrius, 2005), 403.

[44] Nataliia I. Egorova, "'Iranskii Krizis' 1945–1946gg. Po Rassekrechennym Arkhivnym Dokumentam," *Novaia i Noveishaia Istoriia* 3 (1994): 24–42.

[45] Dimitrov, *The Diary of Georgi Dimitrov*, 413–14.

[46] Volokitina et al., *Vostochnaia Evropa*, 302–03.

[47] Egorova, "Inranskii Krizis," 40; and Westad, *The Global Cold War* (Cambridge: Cambridge University Press, 2005), 63.

[48] Westad, *The Global Cold War*, 61.

Soviets also rejected Greek communist party participation in the founding meetings of the Cominform in September 1947, arguing that "it would discredit the Greek party, as if they were taking orders..." from Moscow.[49]

The overall picture of postwar Soviet foreign policy tracks in general terms with the domestic identity topography prevailing in Moscow at the same time. Just as there is uncertainty and contestation at home about how dangerous deviations from the Soviet model are, there is the same ambiguity and temporizing abroad, especially evident in Eastern Europe. The taken for granted quality of the Russian nation as the surrogate nation for the Soviet Union is also apparent in Soviet interactions with its western neighbors. Relations with the West were also under development, not yet fixed in a Cold War binary of mutual enmity.

Part Two: The Discourse of Danger: Stalin's Cold War, 1947–53

As the discourse of danger became the official Soviet discourse in the Soviet Union, its effects were most immediately, dramatically, and deeply felt in Eastern Europe, where Soviet allies found themselves subjected to an ever-escalating program of Stalinization, culminating in mass purges of their parties, and ritualized show trials often ending in the executions of those accused. This turn toward orthodoxy made Yugoslavia's independence anathema, and made the United States and the West into mortal enemies. Soviet actions in Eastern Europe and Germany helped the United States and the West decide on creating a separate Germany. Stalinist orthodoxy, however, also made the decolonizing world irrelevant to Soviet interests. The successful communist revolution in China gave the Soviet Union an ally in the Far East, one eager to assume the role as vanguard for revolutionary movements there. Its first role was in the Korean War.

A. The Stalinization of Eastern Europe, 1947–53

I think that Rajk must be executed, since people will not understand any other sentence for him. (Stalin to Rakosi, September 1949)

The growing intolerance of difference at home was increasingly projected onto Eastern Europe, with the partial exception of eastern Germany. Not only is this projection of Soviet identity true as a general statement, but remarkably precise details of the Stalinization of Eastern Europe follow closely after whatever turning of the screw had recently occurred in Moscow. This shows how

---
[49] Gibianskii, "Kak Voznik Kominform," 143.

desperately insecure Stalin was about any "identity gap" that might emerge between the socialist countries of Eastern Europe and the model of socialism in the Soviet Union.

What counts as a threat to Soviet identity at home became what Soviets looked for in their Eastern European allies as threats to the socialist projects there. Soviets at every level simply could not escape their own domestic categorizations of danger. Moreover, they followed, temporally speaking, their emergence in the Soviet Union as threats, thereby supporting the hypothesis that Soviet identity, and dangers to it, imply how identity relations unfold with the external world, in this case some of Moscow's very closest others in the world.

Soviet fears of Eastern Europe slipping out of its grasp and into the American orbit were reinforced by knowledge that initial public support for Moscow and the Red Army as liberators had turned to resentment and anxiety, and still worse, positive attitudes toward the United States. In essence, there was a race between initial gratitude toward Moscow for liberating them from Nazi Germany and continued fear of Germany and growing fear of Moscow and displeasure with occupation and subordination. Especially in Poland and Czechoslovakia in the first two years after the war the Soviet Union was regarded as a protector against Germany.[50]

As early as May 1947, a turn toward greater orthodoxy was marked in Soviet leaders' conversations with Eastern European leaders. Hungary's Rakosi was told by Molotov to "intensify the class struggle."[51] Gomulka was criticized for his idea of a "Polish national path" to socialism. At the founding meeting of the Cominform in September 1947, all such national paths to socialism were condemned.[52] On March 18, 1948, Yugoslavia was condemned for nationalist deviations; on 24 March, Hungary, and then on April 5, Poland and Czechoslovakia were accused of the same heresy. While the general charge linked the erroneous choice of a national path to servility before the West, anti-Sovietism, and hence danger to socialism in these countries and to relations with Moscow, each long memorandum produced in the CC FPD and sent to Suslov revealed evidence of deviation particular to each country.

In the case of Hungary, for example, the party was accused of not transferring German property to the Soviets, of permitting the publication of *Games of the Underground World*, a 1946 book in which Soviet soldiers were depicted as "wild men and tyrants," of not showing enough Soviet films and too many American and English films, of publishing too much Western literature and philosophy in journals, and of not deleting entries for the "disgraced" Zoshchenko and Akhmatova

---

[50] Murashko and Noskova, "Sovetskii faktor," 74–77.
[51] Volokitina, "Stalin i Smena Stratigicheskogo Kursa Kremlina," 17.
[52] Volokitina et al., *Moskva i Vostochnaia Evropa*, 46–48.

from the "Bibliography of Russian Literature."[53] The Hungarian CC Secretary, Jozsef Revai, was taken to task for "bourgeois nationalism" for being "silent about Soviet achievements" in a speech in which he correctly said, "we learn from Soviet culture; we consider it a model, but we don't copy it." Not copying, while not extolling, equaled danger in the minds of Soviet representatives in Budapest.[54]

Czechoslovakia's main errors were its "orientation on a peaceful path to socialism without victims or class struggle, parliamentary illusions, an accommodationist stance toward "backward nationalistic elements" in society and toward capitalism in the countryside. Stalin's portentous speech from the 1930s was quoted, "On Rightist Deviation," in which he laid out the starkest of binary choices: "Either the Marxist theory of class struggle or the theory of accepting the right of capitalists in socialism. Either the irreconcilable contradiction of class interests or the theory of harmony of class interests. One of the two." Of course, the report was criticizing many of the policies that Stalin himself had encouraged Czechoslovakian and other communists to adopt during the 1945–47 period of ambivalence toward difference in the Soviet Union.[55] Czechoslovakia was further criticized for its "liberal-pacifistic" attitude toward "leaders of bourgeois parties," having permitted some 8,000 to emigrate by August 1948, rather than arresting them and "conducting big political trials which would have unmasked them as enemies."[56] Soviet warnings had their effects. By November 1948, 600,000 Czechoslovak party members had been verified; 75,000 were arrested or expelled from the party.[57]

Along with East Germany, Poland was the last and least Sovietized of Moscow's Eastern European allies. For example, throughout 1947 Soviet MGB officers were being recalled from Poland, at Poland's request. Stalin and Bulganin also agreed in 1947 to remove all Soviet military officers from Poland by 1951,

---

[53] Volokitina et al., *Vostochnaia Evropa*, 802–05; and Pokivailova, "Moskva i Ustanovlenie Monopolii," 322.

[54] Volokitina et al., *Vostochnaia Evropa v Dokumentakh Rossiiskikh Arkhivov, 1944–1953 gg. Tom II*, 766–67.

[55] The report "On Certain Errors of the Czechoslovakian Communist Party," is in RTsKhIDNI f17 op128 d1162, 44–73. A CC FPD report made similar charges against Czechoslovakian communists in the autumn of 1948. Galina P. Murashko and Albina F. Noskova, "Repressii Kak Element Vnutripartiinoi Borby Za Vlast," in *Moskva i Vostochnaia Evropa. Stanovlenie politicheskikh rezhimov sovetskogo tipa (1949–1953). Ocherki istorii*, ed. Tatiana V. Volokitina et al. (Moscow: ROSSPEN, 2002), 512.

[56] Murashko and Noskova, "Repressii Kak Element Vnutripartiinoi," 443.

[57] Tatiana V. Volokitina, "Istochniki Formirovaniia Partiino-Gosudarstvennoi nomenklatury—Novogo Praviashchego Sloia," in *Moskva i Vostochnaia Evropa. Stanovlenie politicheskikh rezhimov sovetskogo tipa (1949–1953) Ocherki istorii*, ed. Tatiana V. Volokitina et al. (Moscow: ROSSPEN, 2002), 156–57.

and in 1948 agreed to withdraw advisers from the security ministries. All these Soviet withdrawals were suspended after Gomulka's removal from the Polish leadership in September 1948.[58]

More dramatically, at the founding meeting of the Cominform in September 1947, Gomulka alone objected to the "coordinating" functions of the new organization, having been told by Stalin in person just a month before that it would only be a body for the exchange of information. According to Jakub Berman, a Polish Politburo member at the time, the rest of the Polish delegation had to plead with Gomulka not to vote against the very creation of the Cominform. They did succeed in getting its headquarters, planned for Warsaw, moved to Belgrade, fearing its location's effects on a loan being negotiated with the United States at the time.[59]

By March 1948, the Soviet ambassador to Poland, Viktor Lebedev, reported to Molotov that the Polish party was split between "Gomulka who is infected with Polish chauvinism and Hilary Minc who was in Moscow during the war and is pro-Moscow." He characterized the Gomulka group as having stayed in Poland "and headed the communist anti-Hitler underground," while Minc, Jakub Berman, and Roman Zambrowski only returned to Poland after Soviet liberation. The Gomulka circle considers itself to be "real Poles," not "Moscow agents." The Minc circle, on the other hand, is "a Jewish group." Lebedev's recommendation was to disempower Gomulka by surrounding him with pro-Moscow party leaders.[60] In June, Berman told the Soviet embassy in Warsaw that he and his comrades were doing everything they could to "save Gomulka as leader of the party," that is, convince him to accept the new orthodoxy being promulgated from Moscow.[61]

The Central Committee report "On the Anti-Marxist Ideological Positions of the Leadership of the Polish Workers' Party," dated April 5, 1948, foregrounded Poland's anti-Russian nationalism, Gomulka's failure to pay public tribute to the role of the Red Army in liberating Poland, insufficient militance in collectivizing the countryside, hence preserving capitalist positions there, and the continued toleration of the vast influence of the Catholic Church.[62]

---

[58] Galina P. Murahsko and Albina F. Noskova, "Institut Sovetskikh Sovetnikov v Stranakh Regiona: Tseli, Zadachi, Rezultaty," in *Moskva i Vostochnaia Evropa. Stanovlenie politicheskikh rezhimov sovetskogo tipa (1949–1953). Ocherki istorii*, ed. Tatiana V. Volokitina et al. (Moscow: ROSSPEN, 2002), 606.

[59] Gibianskii, Leonid Ia., "Problemy Mezhdunarodno-Politicheskogo Strukturirovaniia Vostochnoi Evropy v Period Formirovaniia Sovetskogo Bloka v 1940-e Gody," in *Kholodnaia Voina: Novye Podkhody, Novye Dokumenty*, ed. M. M. Narinskii (Moscow: Institute of General History, 1995), 121; and Teresa Toranska, *"Them:" Stalin's Polish Puppets* (New York: Harper & Row, 1987), 282–84.

[60] Volokitina et al., *Vostochnaia Evropa*, 830; Murashko and Noskova, "Repressii Kak Element Vnutripartiinoi," 505–06.

[61] Volokitina et al., *Vostochnaia Evropa*, 900.

[62] This report is in RTsKhIDNI f17 op128 d1161, 2–19.

In August 1948, Boleslaw Bierut met with Stalin in Moscow where they formulated the main accusations for the "Gomulka Affair" to be used at the upcoming Polish CC plenum. These included an accommodating stance toward Tito, "rightist nationalist deviation," and "distrust for the Soviet Union." In his futile defense at the plenum, Gomulka continued to cite Stalin's previous, and by now repudiated, approval of "national paths to socialism" in Eastern Europe.[63] On December 16, Molotov advised the Polish leadership to remove Gomulka from the Politburo, but leave him on the Central Committee.[64]

By July 1949, Ambassador Lebedev could report progress: Collective farms had begun to appear since April; kowtowing before everything coming from the West had begun to decline; Lysenkoism was making its way among Polish biologists and geneticists; and an offensive was being prepared against the Catholic church.[65] But his guarded optimism was short-lived. By February 1950 he was complaining to the Soviet leadership about Polish suspicions of the Soviet-born Polish Defense Minister Marshal Konstantin Rokossovsky and Poland's slow pace of collectivization, "interpreting as they wish" Stalin's former counsels of moderation. The Polish leadership also failed to take its November 1949 "vigilance plenum" seriously. Indeed, after that plenum, Minc had the nerve to warn against extremes, "so we don't have a Yezhovshchina"—a reference to the bloody purges under Stalin in 1937–38. Stalin circled this word in blue pencil on his copy of the memo.[66]

At the plenum, Bierut, influenced by the Rajk Affair in Hungary, warned of penetration by Tito's agents, but blamed it all conveniently on the ousted Gomulka.[67] Gomulka was arrested in August 1951, but the wheels of injustice in Poland moved so slowly that Stalin's death came before Gomulka's execution.[68]

A revealing exception to accelerated Stalinization was Albania. Albania earned this exemption by being lower on the hierarchy of modernity than any other Eastern European country. In his March 1949 conversation with the visiting Albanian leader Enver Hoxa, Stalin, noting Albania's backwardness, advised him not to rush with collectivization and criticized his appropriation of commercial

---

[63] Murashko and Noskova, "Repressii Kak Element Vnutripartiinoi," 508–09.

[64] Volokitina et al., *Vostochnaia Evropa*, 932–44.

[65] Bordiugov, *SSSR-Polsha*, 341–48.

[66] Volokitina et al., *Vostochnaia Evropa v Dokumentakh Rossiiskikh Arkhivov, 1944–1953 gg. Tom II*, 311–15.

[67] Volokitina, "Istochniki Formirovaniia Partiino-Gosudarstvennoi Nomenklatury," 124.

[68] For what it is worth, Edward Ochab, a Polish CC Secretary at the time, has said that Poles dragged their feet on Gomulka's trial, despite being pressed by Soviet leaders, and especially Beria, to accelerate the proceedings. Toranska, *Them*, 49–50.

bourgeois property. "Albanians shouldn't copy what happened in Russia. . . . They should consider local peculiarities. . . ."[69] Relative backwardness, as in the Soviet Union itself, justified local or national roads to socialism, deviance that was not dangerous, but just unavoidable, given one's place on the lower rungs of development.

Reports from Eastern Europe warned of servility before the West after the campaign against it had been launched in the Soviet Union in 1946–47. In a June 1947 report to the Soviet leadership from the CC FPD, the analyst P. Guliaev warned that "market servility before Americans is especially prevalent among the middle classes in Czechoslovakia." Moreover, more than 5,000 foreign students are studying here, and a similar number of Czechoslovak students are abroad. Dozens of Czechoslovakian professors are invited to England, the United States, and France. Bookstores are filled with foreign literature.[70] The problem is that "to a great degree the influence of so-called 'Western culture' in different areas of science, culture and art is still preserved in Poland and Czechoslovakia." The danger lies in "Western propaganda finding fertile soil in Eastern Europe" because of the intelligentsia's "spirit of admiration for the West and hostility for Soviet culture."[71] Even Red Cross workers giving tuberculosis vaccinations to Slovakian school children were accused of espionage by the Soviet ambassador in October 1949.[72] Reporting on their May 1949 tour of Eastern Europe, Soviet analysts from the CC FPD wrote that "the influence of the West isn't being controlled" by the parties in Bulgaria, Hungary, Romania, Poland, and Czechoslovakia.

A July 1948 report from a political section chief of the Red Army in Poland to V. G. Grigorian, deputy head of the CC Propaganda and Agitation (Agitprop) Department in Moscow, contained complaints about the number of American films being shown in Poland: "There are days when in all the theaters only American films are shown." In general, Soviet films are shown "in the worst theaters, Americans in the best." American films are even shown in Polish military officers' clubs. There are still Young Men's Christian Associations in 16 big Polish cities.[73]

---

[69] Stalin repeated this moderating advice to Hoxa in April 1951. Volokitina et al., *Vostochnaia Evropa v Dokumentakh Rossiiskikh Arkhivov, 1944–1953 gg. Tom II*, 504; Tatiana V. Volokitina et al., eds., *Sovetskii Faktor v Vostochnoi Evrope, 1944–1953*, vol. 2, 1949–1953 (Moscow: ROSSPEN, 2002), 70–73.

[70] RTsKhIDNI, f17 op128 d1083, 213–21.

[71] From a March 21, 1949, memo from the head of the MFA's Fourth European Department, S. P. Kirsanov, quoted in Pokivailova, "Moskva i Ustanovlenie monopolii Kompartii na Informatsiiu na Rubezhe 40-50-x godov," 329–30.

[72] Volokitina et al., *Sovetskii Faktor v Vostochnoi Evrope*, 191.

[73] Bordiugov, *SSSR-Polsha*, 255–57.

"The average Warsaw citizen jokes that the US Embassy has more cars than the biggest firms in Poland. You can meet cars with US flags on any street."[74]

Over a year after Stalin had launched the anti-cosmopolitan campaign in the Soviet Union, Soviets in Poland complained that the article hadn't been republished by a single Polish paper. When it finally appeared in April 1949, there was no cosmopolitanism in Poland exposed, but just an abstract discussion. This was because, the Sovinformburo analyst concluded, the Polish CC Press Department "still indulges bourgeois cosmopolitans and Anglo-Saxonophiles who use Polish newspapers and publishers to propagandize the superiority of Anglo-American science and culture." He concluded that despite the September 1948 plenum [which ousted Gomulka], "rightist opportunist tendencies in the party are still strong. . . ."[75] Only in June 1949 did the Union of Polish Artists declare "socialist realism" to be the privileged form of art in Poland.[76] Ambassador Lebedev reported to Stalin in June 1950 about the Polish intelligentsia's "recognition of no authorities other than Americans, French, and English . . . [with] the overwhelming majority still being captivated by Anglo-American ideas."[77]

The Soviet campaign against Western influence had some effect. According to Goban-Klas, only one American film was shown in Poland from 1949 to 1958.[78] By June 1952 the Soviet embassy could report that in Poland 48 percent of films being shown in Poland were Soviet, 38 percent Polish and other people's democracies, and 14 percent progressive films from capitalist countries, mostly France and Italy. By July 1949, the Soviet Union was requesting the closure of all Western cultural and information centers in Eastern Europe.

If one were to read the correspondence between Moscow's leadership and any allied capital in Eastern Europe, one could easily mistake it for exchanges

---

[74] April 9, 1949, report from TASS correspondent in Warsaw NG Pantiukhin to Stalin and Molotov. In Bordiugov, *SSSR-Polsha*, 282. It should be noted that most Soviets who travelled abroad in this, and subsequent, periods were either required to submit reports about their trips, who they met, the conversations they had, etc., or felt a strong normative constraint to so report. This should be kept in mind when one encounters charges of some Soviet journalist being a spy or intelligence agent. They all more or less were providing intelligence, but could hardly be considered intelligence agents in the sense of CIA operative or KGB mole.

[75] Asked almost 40 years later whether there was a struggle with cosmopolitanism in Poland, Berman answered, "Yes, there was, because copying the model of the Soviet Union was obligatory in every sphere." His older brother, Adolph, emigrated to Israel in 1950. Toranska, *Them*, 320–22; and Bordiugov, *SSSR-Polsha*, 292–304.

[76] Baudin, "Zhdanov Art," 234.

[77] Volokitina et al., *Vostochnaia Evropa v Dokumentakh Rossiiskikh Arkhivov, 1944–1953 gg. Tom II*, 343.

[78] Tomasz Goban-Klas and Pal Kolsto, "Eastern European Mass Media: The Soviet Role," in *The Soviet Union in Eastern Europe, 1945–89*, ed. Odd Arne Westad, Sven Holtsmark, and Iver B. Neumann (London: St. Martin's Press, 1994), 110–36, 133.

between Moscow and any oblast in the Soviet Union.[79] The taken for granted hierarchy in the relationship was palpable. In a February 1950 conversation Hungary's Rakosi had with a Soviet MGB adviser in Budapest, he "stressed repeatedly that Hungary is a small country, no bigger than Moscow oblast, and he is only 'an obkom secretary.'"[80] This is precisely the identity relations Moscow understood as both natural and desirable.

The growth of the institutions of repression in the region also reflected the new discourse of danger applied to Eastern Europe. For example, Polish internal security forces grew from 21,000 to 33,000 from 1948 to 1953, and Czechoslovakian forces from 3,000 to 11,000. Eastern European interior ministry officers began to enroll in Soviet MGB and MVD schools.[81] The number of sentences for political crimes in Bulgaria increased from 134 in 1948 to nearly 1,500 in 1951, in Czechoslovakia from 1,600 in 1949 to 16,000 in 1950. The courts averaged over 250 death sentences per year.[82] In Hungary alone, from 1950 to 1953 650,000 people were investigated by the security organs, and 400,000 were penalized in some fashion.[83] In Rumania, 200,000 members were expelled from the party between 1948 and 1951, 20 percent of its total membership. After its May 1952 plenum, another 200,000 were purged.[84]

Institutions of domestic repression aimed at danger at home were soon matched by a build-up of Eastern European military power aimed at defending socialism from dangers abroad. The Soviets deployed an additional 80,000 men to their forces in Germany between 1949 and 1950. The Czechoslovakian army grew from 180,000 to 400,000. In Moscow in January 1951, Eastern European communist leaders were requested to increase their defense spending. Even the Polish defense minister, Rokossovsky, claimed Soviet targets for spending couldn't be reached until 1956. The other defense ministers agreed. By 1953, Eastern European armies numbered one million.[85]

If, prior to 1947, Stalin advised Eastern European allies to develop good relations with the West, thereafter, and especially after the confusion surrounding

---

[79] Pokivailova, "Moskva i Ustanovlenie Monopolii," 325–31. An oblast is the Soviet unit of goverance beneath the republic. A raion, or district, is beneath the oblast. There were "oblast committee/ obkom" and "district committee/raikom" party secretaries heading these political jurisdictions. A city (gorod) committee is a gorkom.

[80] Volokitina et al., *Sovetskii Faktor v Vostochnoi Evrope*, 259.

[81] Galina P. Murashko and Albina F. Noskova, "Repressii—Instrument Podavleniia Politicheskoi Oppozitsii," in *Moskva i Vostochnaia Evropa. Stanovlenie politicheskikh rezhimov sovetskogo tipa (1949–1953). Ocherki istorii*, ed. Tatiana V. Volokitina et al. (Moscow: ROSSPEN, 2002), 430–34.

[82] Volokotina et al., *Moskva i Vostochnaia Evropa*, 286.

[83] Murashko and Noskova, "Repressii," 447.

[84] Volokitina et al., *Moskva i Vostochnaia Evropa*, 142–49.

[85] David Holloway, *Stalin and the Bomb* (New Haven: Yale University Press, 1994), 240, 287; Yoram Gorlizki and Oleg Khlevniuk, *Cold Peace: Stalin and the Soviet Ruling Circle, 1945–1953* (New York: Oxford University Press, 2004), 98–100; and Toranska, *Them*, 46–47.

responses to the Marshall Plan, these allies asked Moscow's advice and approval for every foreign policy decision imaginable. Illustrative in this regard are the minutes of the Rumanian ambassador G. Valdescu-Rakoas's meeting with deputy minister of foreign affairs Valerian Zorin in March 1949. Over the course of the meeting, the ambassador asked Zorin for the "Soviet attitude" toward Rumanian participation in the following meetings: International Organization of Health Care; Congress of Engineers in Cairo; Congress of Veterinarians in London; Congress on Forestry in Helsinki; International Exhibit of Philately in Belgium; Milk Congress in Stockholm; a Stockholm sports festival; International Congress of Meteorologists; a musical competition in Belgium; the International Congress of Jurists on Human Rights in Prague (here Zorin noted that the Soviet Union wouldn't be attending); and the Congress of Criminology in Paris (here Zorin said no). Besides the last two, Zorin responded that each state could decide for itself. The Ambassador was clearly anxious about the granted autonomy as he continued to try to feel out Zorin about Soviet preferences.[86] The fear and anxiety felt by those working with Stalin, the incentive to overfulfill his slightest intimations is tangible as well in exchanges between Eastern European allies and Soviet representatives at all levels.

Some of the most gruesome evidence of the relationship between Soviet domestic identity and its policy in Eastern Europe was the deep Soviet concern over the precise details of the many political show trials conducted in Eastern Europe beginning in 1949.

In May of that year, Hungarian Foreign Minister Laszlo Rajk was arrested. In late June, MGB Lt. General M. I. Belkin arrived from Moscow with his investigative team. Belkin reported to Moscow that excessive torture had been used, resulting in "confusing testimony." Belkin, in consultation with Hungarian party general secretary Rakosi, changed the direction of the affair from simple nationalism and Trotskyism, to the more directly dangerous Titoism and US imperialism. Rajk's purported espionage was associated with his stay in French prisons, again reinforcing the danger of exposure to the West. Stalin himself confirmed the text of the accusations against Rajk in an August meeting with Rakosi in Moscow. The September trial was covered extensively in the Soviet press, showing average Soviets how easily one could slip from nationalism and servility before the West to betrayal of the motherland and service as an agent of imperialism. On September 14, Rakosi sent Stalin a letter informing him of seven death sentences to be issued based on the trials. Stalin replied a week later: "I think that Rajk must be executed, since people will not understand any

---

[86] Volokitina et al., *Sovetskii Faktor v Vostochnoi Evrope*, 57–61.

other sentence for him."[87] The conduct and substance of the affairs were so carefully controlled from Moscow that when Soviet advisers in Hungary complained to Rakosi about flaws in the case he replied that "he doesn't attach special significance to this because the texts will be transferred to Moscow where there are specialist-jurists, in particular comrade Vyshinsky...," who will put things in order.[88]

As was argued in chapter 2, Stalin followed a strategy of "exemplary" punishment of selected individuals or groups to mark in bold letters the ever-narrowing boundaries of permissible difference. This perhaps explains one of the rare moments of Soviet restraint toward Eastern European purges in the period. In September 1951 the Soviet ambassador to Hungary, Evgenii Kiselev, told the Hungarian leadership that it was a mistake to purge technical workers, such as engineers, en masse, "indiscriminately considering them potential enemies" of the People's Republic of Hungary. Such a strategy, Kiselev advised, would only alienate many who could "honestly serve" the country.[89] Rakosi apparently didn't listen to Kiselev, for a year later Kiselev complained to then foreign minister Vyshinsky that "too many cases are being sent to the procurator. In 1951 there were 362,000, and police organs dealt with another 500,000+. As the facts show, many of them have no serious basis and they were thrown out by the procurator." He concluded, as he had over a year before, that such "mass charges can only negatively affect the mood of the population."[90]

In September 1949 the Soviet leadership instructed its Bulgarian allies to make "connections with Tito" the decisive direction in investigating the Kostov affair. The indictment itself was drawn up in Russian by Soviet advisers and then translated into Bulgarian. In December Traicho Kostov, former president of the Council of Ministers, was sentenced to death and Vulko Chervenkov, General Secretary Dimitrov's successor since July 1949, cabled Stalin for any revisions to the sentence. Stalin offered none.[91]

The "Slansky Affair" in Czechoslovakia had its roots in Hungary's Rajk Affair. As Murashko has concluded, "In order to appear worthy in the eyes of Moscow,

---

[87] Murashko and Noskova, "Institut Sovetskikh Sovetnikov," 522–27; Bela I. Zhelitski, "Arest Raika. Smena Kontseptsii 'Dela,'" *Novaia i Noveishaia Istoriia* 3 (2001): 166–78; and Volokotina et al., *Moskva i Vostochnaia Evropa*, 108–09.

[88] Murashenko and Noskova, "Institut Sovetskikh Sovetnikov," 621.

[89] Volokitina et al., *Vostochnaia Evropa v Dokumentakh Rossiiskikh Arkhivov, 1944–1953 gg. Tom II*, 604.

[90] Ibid., 853–54.

[91] Murashko and Noskova, "Repressii Kak Element Vnutripartiinoi,"518–519; Danilov and Pyzhikov, *Rozhdenie Svekhderzhavy*, 54; and Volokitina et al., *Vostochnaia Evropa v Dokumentakh Rossiiskikh Arkhivov, 1944–1953 gg. Tom II*, 263.

the Czechoslovakian Communist Party leadership needed a public trial with the unmasking of at least one plot against the new system...."[92] Even after requesting Stalin send MGB agents secretly to help him investigate the Rajk Affair's implications for Czechoslovakia, Klement Gottwald, party chairman, still told his MGB advisers in Prague on September 27, 1949, that he didn't think the "Anglo-American spy network had grown to the size of that revealed in Hungary." He insisted "there is no Rajk" in the Czechoslovakian government. But his MGB advisers reported to Moscow that local security forces were not finding enough intelligence agents—"for five months they haven't uncovered a single affair of foreign intelligence agents." Gottwald ultimately gave in to Soviet pressure and held the demanded CC meeting "on revolutionary vigilance" in Feburary 1950, his report having been prepared on the basis of direct instructions from Stalin himself.[93] He then agreed to remove Vladimir Clementis, his foreign minister, on March 18, 1950.[94]

The Slansky Affair proved more complicated than those of Kostov, Rajk, or Clementis because Rudolf Slansky was a Moscow Communist who enjoyed the trust of many in the Soviet CC FPD, for whom he had served as an agent in Czechoslovakia for the past seven years. On July 20, 1951, Stalin telegrammed Gottwald to say the materials on Slansky weren't sufficient, and Gottwald agreed. Four days later, however, Stalin recommended replacing Slansky as general secretary of the party, and agreed to Gottwald's suggestion to move him to the Council of Ministers. Slansky was arrested in November 1951, charged with consorting with Tito, advocating a "special Czechoslovakian path" to socialism, restoration of capitalism, and its consequent subordination to "English and American imperialists." In the intervening year, the new charge of Zionism was hung on Slansky, linking him with American intelligence through Jewish nationalist groups. Of the 14 defendants in the Slansky affair, 11 were Jewish. A year later, Slansky and 11 others were sentenced to death.[95]

---

[92] Murashko and Noskova, "Repressii Kak Element Vnutripartiinoi," 450.

[93] In 1949–50, all Eastern European parties held plena on "revolutionary vigilance" to discuss the dangers revealed by the Rajk, Tito, Kostov and Gomulka affairs, and their connections to Anglo-American intelligence. Pokivailova, "Moskva i Ustanovlenie Monopolii," 331.

[94] Murashko and Noskova, "Repressii Kak Element Vnutripartiinoi," 532–33; Murashenko and Noskova, "Institut Sovetskikh Sovetnikov," 622–27; Volokitina et al., *Vostochnaia Evropa v Dokumentakh Rossiiskikh Arkhivov, 1944–1953 gg. Tom II*, 159–60; and Volokitina et al., *Sovetskii Faktor v Vostochnoi Evrope*, 285–90.

[95] Murashko and Noskova, "Repressii Kak Element Vnutripartiinoi," 555–62; Volokitina et al., *Vostochnaia Evropa v Dokumentakh Rossiiskikh Arkhivov, 1944–1953 gg. Tom II*, 166, 841; and Raymond Taras, "Gomulka's 'Rightist-Nationalist Deviation,' The Postwar Jewish Communists, and the Stalinist Reaction in Poland, 1945–1950," *Nationalities Papers* 22, no. 1 (1994): 124.

One element of these "affairs," and repressions in Eastern Europe more generally, was their relationship to the Soviet discourse of dangerous Jewish nationalism and anti-Semitism in the Soviet Union. Just as the MGB in 1946 and then Suslov in 1947 sent memos warning of Jewish danger to a Soviet leadership not yet responsive to construing Jewish nationalism as a threat, Soviet advisers and Eastern European leaders complained of Jews in Eastern European leadership positions, at first without any resonance from Moscow.

But then, Polish Jewish communist leaders, who had been so instrumental in removing the bourgeois nationalist deviant Gomulka in the summer of 1948, soon found themselves caught up in the projection of the anti-cosmopolitan campaign from Moscow. Having just reported to Moscow in March 1948 that Minc, Berman, and Zambrowski were Moscow's most reliable allies, in July 1949, Ambassador Lebedev wrote to Vyshinsky and Stalin that "Bierut is the most serious and reliable party and state leader in Poland." He went on to charge that "Berman, Minc, and Zambrowski haven't freed themselves from strong nationalistic prejudices." Evidence against Berman was that his older brother was a leader of "Jewish nationalistic organizations" in Poland. The Joint Committee still hadn't been liquidated in Poland, despite Moscow's advice, because of Berman's resistance. Minc had no "Polish" deputies in the Ministry of Industry. The MGB, beginning with deputy ministers and including all department heads "hasn't a single Pole. All are Jews. Only Jews work in the intelligence department." His conclusions were that "Bierut is isolated from other Polish communists by a group of people who clearly suffer from Jewish nationalism" and a "Pole must be made MGB head who will be Bierut's right hand and gradually purge the apparat."[96]

On February 10, 1950, a Soviet MGB adviser in Budapest, Kartashov, sent a report to the Soviet leadership, in which he wrote how he was "struck by how many Jews there are in leading state and party positions." Jozsef Revai, a Jew, was a big nationalist who was close to Rajk and objected against his arrest, saying the accusations were contrived by Hungarian state security. Politburo members Mikhail Farkas and Zoltan Vas, both Jews, were compromised by their close ties to the American spy, a Jew, Dr. Benedek. Too many Jews had penetrated the security police. A significant number of Hungarian Jews, he went on, have "vast family, commercial, and political ties with America...." Even the "fascist Horthy government protected them (Hungarian Jews) from the Germans. Kartashov then closes the circle, linking Hungarian Jews to American intelligence and the presumed danger to the Soviet Union.[97] At this particular time however, when

---

[96] Lebedev's advice ironically resonates with his March 1948 advice to surround Gomulka with the three Jewish Communists he now typifies as exerting a baneful influence on Bierut. Volokitina et al., *Vostochnaia Evropa v Dokumentakh Rossiiskikh Arkhivov, 1944–1953 gg. Tom II*, 172–77.

[97] Volokitina et al., *Sovetskii Faktor v Vostochnoi Evrope*, 260–67.

the anti-Semitic campaign had waned in Moscow, affairs against Jews did not resonate with the Soviet leadership.[98]

In May 1951, a Soviet MGB adviser in Prague sent Minister of State Security Viktor Abakumov a memorandum informing him that the subversive activities of Jewish nationalists had penetrated top party and state ranks in Czechoslovakia. Slansky came from an old Jewish family, the MGB adviser continued, and has great influence in the party and "all bourgeois Jewish nationalists are oriented toward Slansky."

As was argued in chapter 2, the Russian nation was identified both officially and popularly, both explicitly and incidentally, as the predominant ethnonational core of the Soviet Union. In so doing, the Orthodox religion was treated much more leniently than religions that were understood as fostering non-Russian national identities, such as Catholicism, Islam, Judaism, or Lutheranism. This set of identity-spawned concerns was reflected in the treatment of religious beliefs in Eastern Europe. Fears of nationalist deviation were often connected to fears that the local non-Orthodox churches were breeding grounds for such threats. For example, just six months before his death, Stalin chided Poland's Bierut for not adopting a harsher policy toward the Catholic clergy, underestimating their connection to bourgeois nationalism in Poland.[99] There were also the many slips of the tongue that demonstrated the taken for granted quality that Russia as the Soviet Union's implicit nation enjoyed. For example, in negotiations with Mao in January 1950, Stalin referred to "Russian troops" in Port Arthur.[100]

While I argue that Soviet efforts to replicate itself in Eastern Europe were the product of its domestic discourse of danger, where any differences from the model could entail the overthrow of socialism in the Soviet Union, it would be a mistake to underestimate the interaction effects between this domestic identity and events in the world. And the one external event that had the biggest influence on reinforcing Soviet feelings of insecurity before the United States only reaffirms the importance of paying attention to domestic Soviet identity in the first place. It turns out that the European Recovery Program, or Marshall Plan, as it is most commonly known, was the single event that most convinced the Soviet leadership of the danger the United States posed to allied regimes in Eastern Europe.

By shifting, if only unintentionally, the currency of the competition from military power to economic wherewithal, from Soviet strength to its very weakest suit, the United States amplified all Soviet insecurities about the possible

---

[98] Murashko and Noskova, "Repressii Kak Element Vnutripartiinoi," 552.

[99] Volokitina et al., *Sovetskii Faktor v Vostochnoi Evrope*, 696.

[100] Dieter Heinzig, *The Soviet Union and Communist China, 1945–1950: The Arduous Road to the Alliance* (Armonk, NY: M.E. Sharpe, 2004), 331.

erosion of the Soviet position in Eastern Europe, and accelerated the process of Stalinization, of creating in Eastern Europe domestic orders as closely imitative of Soviet identity as possible. The most threatening weapons the United States had in the early years of the Cold War were economic and cultural, not military.

For most observers, and IR theorists of the Realist persuasion, it would have made sense had Moscow reacted with greater alarm to the declaration of the Truman Doctrine by the US president before a joint session of Congress in March 1947 than to the proposal of the European Recovery Plan by US Secretary of State George Marshall at the June 1947 Harvard University commencement. But they would be wrong. Instead, the growing need to have no deviation from Stalinism in even the smallest matters at home translated into Soviet alarm at the prospect of its European socialist allies forming economic relationships with the imperialist West. And the alacrity with which so many of them opted for attending the Paris planning meetings for the Marshall Plan was still more evidence of how dangerously alluring US economic power could be. The Truman Doctrine, or the US assumption of British security obligations in Turkey and Greece, was nothing new—just the substitution of one imperialist for another.

This is not to say that the Marshall Plan should not be interpreted as part of US containment policy. It no doubt was, but it was not intended to unravel Soviet control over Eastern Europe, as Stalin inferred. It was instead a way to pump money into Europe to help finance their purchase of US exports, and then, when their own industries recovered, to help them earn dollars through exports to the US market. All this, of course, was aimed at helping Europe re-establish itself as an independent bulwark against Soviet expansionism, reducing the burden on the United States. In fact, one of the main arguments offered by the Truman Administration to Congress was that the Marshall Plan aid would obviate the need for increased defense budgets in the United States.[101]

On June 5, 1947, US Secretary of State George Marshall delivered the commencement address at Harvard University in which he made the offer of substantial U.S. economic assistance to Europe, or what later came to be known as the Marshall Plan. Two weeks later, England and France invited the Soviet Union to participate in a June 27 foreign ministers meeting in Paris to discuss the plan. The Politburo met to discuss the invitation on June 21, and on June 24 approved Molotov's trip to Paris. Throughout the meeting, Molotov's major objection concerned control over the disbursement of resources, arguing for each state's right to ask for aid without US "interference" in how the aid was to be spent. Ultimately unsatisfied on this point, as well as the fact that aid was available for Germany (from which reparations would end), Molotov announced

---

[101] Fred L. Block, *The Origins of International Economic Disorder* (Berkeley: University of California Press, 1977), 87–88, 104–05.

Soviet opposition to the plan on July 2. On July 5 Molotov sent a telegram to all Eastern European allies advising them to go to the forthcoming Paris meeting on the ERP, but in order to undermine it by each leaving it, declaring it a mask for US domination of Europe. Just two days later, however, Molotov rescinded the previous telegram, this time advising each country not to attend, leaving "motives for rejections at their own discretion."

This last telegram put the Czechoslovakian government in the most difficult position, having already accepted the British/French invitation and appointed its delegation. On July 9, Stalin demanded Gottwald come to Moscow, and harangued him into joining other Eastern European states in declining the invitation, arguing that one could not be both "friendly to the Soviet Union" and attend the Paris meeting. On July 11, Prague annulled its decision to attend, and foreign minister Tomas Masaryk commented famously: "I went to Moscow as a free minister, but returned as Stalin's lackey!"[102]

Rejection of the Marshall Plan only deepened the unpopularity of communists in Eastern Europe, not least of all in Czechoslovakia. In the May 1946 parliamentary elections, Czechoslovakian communists had won 38 percent of the vote. Four months after Masaryk's humiliating return from Moscow, they garnered only 20 percent in university student elections, boding none too well for the upcoming May 1948 parliamentary contest. According to available intelligence, the Prague government's ultimate rejection of the invitation to the Paris meeting on the Marshall Plan resulted in western governments consigning Czechoslovakia to the Soviet sphere of influence, thus reassuring Czechoslovak communists during their assumption of power in February 1948. What has most often been termed a "coup" was in fact a series of blunders by noncommunist democrats accompanied by swift and ruthless opportunism by the communists. Democrats resigned from the coalition government on February 20, 1948, protesting against communist penetration of the police forces. Instead of Masaryk and social democrats resigning too, thus forcing new elections, the Czechoslovakian president Edvard Benes accepted the new majority communist government, who immediately used the instruments of the state they had so carefully penetrated, as well as mobilized aktiv on the streets, to purge and persecute the remaining opposition. Benes resigned in June and died in September.[103] As Gottwald later remarked, "I couldn't believe it was so easy."[104]

The formation of the Cominform should also be seen in light of both the discourse of danger emanating from Moscow and Eastern European receptiveness

---

[102] Danilov and Pyzhikov, *Rozhdenie Svekhderzhavy*, 45–49.
[103] Lukes, "The Czech Road to Communism," 44, 252–58.
[104] Mastny, *The Cold War*, 42.

to the Marshall Plan. Egorova argues that the Cominform was created in response to Stalin's surprise and irritation at the independent actions of the French and Italian communist parties in May 1947, their decisions to leave their respective coalition governments. Stalin was not informed in advance of their decisions.[105] Zhdanov wrote to the French communist leader Maurice Thorez on June 2, 1947, to criticize the party for the no-confidence vote and for not consulting with Moscow first.[106] This kind of "freelancing" was not consistent with a Soviet understanding of itself atop a hierarchy of subordinate parties.

Of critical importance, and reflected in Zhdanov's notes for his plenary speech that were vetted by Stalin, however, was the Eastern European responsiveness to the Marshall Plan. From Moscow's perspective, it revealed the Achilles Heel of Soviet strategy in Eastern Europe: its economic weakness relative to the United States. Intentionally or not, most probably not, the United States had shifted the competition over Europe to an arena of Moscow's greatest weakness, its weakest suit. Not only was the United States materially superior, but Moscow's Eastern European allies had enthusiastically responded to the lure of sacrificing their one-sided dependence on Moscow for the corrosive integration into Western capitalist markets.[107]

Zhdanov ascribed four errors to western communist parties in the draft of his speech at the September 22, 1947, formation of the Cominform. These were: the "self-liquidationism" of Browder in the United States; "parliamentary illusions," rather than ratcheting up of the class struggle; belief in the electoral path to socialism; and the idea of "national roads" to socialism, all ascribed to the French and Italians.[108] At the Cominform meeting itself, Zhdanov criticized the Italian Communist Party (PCI) for not opposing the Marshall Plan effectively, although he didn't advocate unleashing a civil war in Italy like Tito did. In March, Molotov was prompted to telegram Palmiro Togliatti, the PCI general secretary, advising him to stop listening to the Yugoslavs and not initiate any kind of armed conflict.[109]

---

[105] Nataliia I. Egorova, "Stalin's Foreign Policy and the Cominform, 1947–53," in *The Soviet Union and Europe in the Cold War, 1943–53*, ed. Francesca Gori and Silvio Pons (New York: St. Martin's Press, 1996), 197.

[106] Gibianskii, "Kak Voznik Kominform," 141.

[107] This interpretation is consistent with Scott Parrish, "The Marshall Plan, Soviet-American Relations, and the Division of Europe," in *The Establishment of Communist Regimes in Eastern Europe, 1944–1949*, ed. Norman Naimark and Leonid Gibianskii (Boulder: Westview Press, 1997), 285–86, with the exception that I place greater emphasis on Soviet preferences for reparations over economic welfare in Eastern Europe.

[108] Silvio Pons, "A Challenge Let Drop: Soviet Foreign Policy, the Cominform and the Italian Communist Party, 1947–8," in *The Soviet Union and Europe in the Cold War, 1943–53*, ed. Francesca Gori and Silvio Pons (New York: St. Martin's Press, 1996), 247.

[109] Silvio Pons, "Stalin, Togliatti, and the Origins of the Cold War in Europe," *Journal of Cold War Studies* 3, no. 2 (Spring 2001): 17–22.

While not advocating armed overthrow of the French and Italian governments, Stalin did not foreclose the possibility of armed conflict between communists and their governments, and was prepared to arm them for that eventuality. Symbolically, just a week before what would be the last meeting of the CFM, Stalin met with Thorez in Moscow and asked him how matters stood with weapons. Thorez said the party had hidden quite a few. Stalin said French communists need weapons if attacked, and the Soviet Union "can give them to you if necessary."[110]

A word needs to be said about the peculiar institutional arrangements that accompanied Soviet foreign relations, especially with Eastern Europe. Not surprisingly, Stalin mostly handled foreign policy almost single-handedly, helped only by Zhdanov and Molotov on Eastern European affairs, and Anastas Mikoyan, who undertook a variety of foreign assignments.[111] Molotov was also the foreign minister as well as CC Secretary for foreign affairs, so enjoyed the closest of relations with Stalin on matters of foreign policy.[112] The Politburo as a whole met only three times from October 1946 until Stalin's death in March 1953.[113] Instead, policy was decided by Stalin and a small number of the party leadership, at meetings at the Kremlin beginning late at night, and often continuing into the morning at one of his dachas. The results were then often written up and sent around for signatures to the Politburo members. To our knowledge, no one ever refused to sign such a document.[114] All these arrangements maximized the institution of Stalin's arbitrary power.

Special relations were enjoyed by those Eastern European communists who had spent time in Moscow. In August 1945, for example, Georgii Dimitrov, a Bulgarian communist who had emigrated to the Soviet Union in 1923, becoming an official in the Central Committee's Department of Relations with the International Communist Movement, asked Stalin's advice about how to run as a candidate in Bulgarian parliamentary elections while simultaneously already being a Supreme Soviet deputy in the Soviet Union! Stalin recommended he resign from the Soviet parliament, and Dimitrov returned home to Bulgaria for the first time in 22 years. Even so, he kept an apartment in Moscow, and visited the grave of his son, Mitia, there.[115]

---

[110] Mikhail M. Narinskii, "I. V. Stalin i Moriz Torez. Zapis Besedy v Kremle, 1947 g.," *Istoricheskii Arkhiv* 1 (1996): 13.

[111] William Taubman, *Khrushchev: The Man and His Era* (New York: W. W. Norton, 2003), 329–30.

[112] And even during his replacement by Vyshinsky as foreign minister from 1949 to 1953, Molotov was still at the center of all foreign policy decision-making.

[113] Iu. N. Zhukov, "Borba za Vlast v Rukovodstve SSSR v 1945–1952 godakh," *Voprosy Istorii* 1 (1995): 28.

[114] Zubovka, "The Rivalry with Malenkov," 71–72.

[115] Dimitrov, *The Diary of Georgi Dimitrov*, 378, 387, 411.

Other scholars have noted that spending the war in Moscow was a great advantage to any Eastern European communist upon returning home, while those who had either fought against the Nazis at home, been imprisoned by them, or had emigrated to other countries, were disadvantaged in Moscow.[116] Years spent in Moscow allowed one to cultivate relationships with the Soviet party elite, while not being in Moscow made Stalin suspicious that contacts with foreigners, especially Europeans, and even German Nazi jailers, would somehow have made someone less politically reliable. Being a resistance fighter might have made you into a nationalist, that is, someone more loyal to her home country than to Moscow.[117] This, of course, was precisely the phenomenon that developed at home with regard to returning Soviet POWs, or to authors who cited too much Western literature in their own work.

In the case of postwar Poland, for example, the Moscow communists included Bierut, Berman, Minc, and Roman Zambrowski; the nationalists were Gomulka, Marian Spychalski, Zenon Kliszko, and Ignacy Loga-Sowinski.[118] Among other foreign communist leaders, Palmiro Togliatti of the PCI, and Maurice Thorez of the French communist party (PCF), both spent the war in Moscow. As late as 1949 in East Germany, there were 165 highly-ranked communist party members with Soviet citizenship. Many who spoke about "our" party had in mind the CPSU in Moscow.[119] After the Soviet liberation of Rumania in August 1944, both Anna Pauker and Laszlo Luka returned from Moscow to the leadership of the Rumanian party.[120] The Hungarian communist party general secretary, Matias Rakosi, had spent the war years in Moscow, while Rajk, who would be arrested, tried and executed in 1949, had the misfortune of having fought in the Spanish Civil War against fascism, and having spent World War II in French, Hungarian and German prisons and concentration camps. These experiences made Rajk simultaneously a serious political rival of Rakosi and a serious political risk for Moscow, as he hadn't "arrived on the Moscow wagon train" after the war, unlike Rakosi.[121]

---

[116] Murashko and Noskova, "Repressii Kak Element Vnutripartiinoi," 516.

[117] For instance, General Petrushevskii, main military adviser in the Bulgarian army, identified local Bulgarian communists as nationalists in his reports to the "Center." Murashko and Noskova, "Repressii Kak Element Vnutripartiinoi," 516.

[118] Taras, "Gomulka's 'Rightist-Nationalist Deviation.'"

[119] Norman M. Naimark, *The Russians in Germany: A History of the Soviet Zone of Occupation, 1945–1949* (Cambridge: Belknap Press of Harvard University Press, 1995), 292; and Giles MacDonogh, *After the Reich: The Brutal History of the Allied Occupation* (New York: Basic Books, 2007), 104.

[120] Eastern European militaries were also liberally populated by officers who had spent the war in exile in the Soviet Union. Murashko and Noskova, "Repressii," 463–94; and Volokotina et al., *Moskva i Vostochnaia Evropa*, 138.

[121] Murashko and Noskova, "Institut Sovetskikh Sovetnikov," 520–21; and Bela I. Zhelitski, "Tragicheskaia Sudba Laslo Raika. Vengriia 1949g," *Novaia i Noveishaia Istoriia* 2 (2001): 125–34.

Beyond the hundreds of Eastern European communists who spent years in Moscow and returned home, there were many who stayed in Moscow to work in the CC FPD, writing memoranda, training cadres, working as couriers, or making radio broadcasts.[122] These communists provided yet another transmission belt between Moscow and its Eastern European allies. Some Moscow communists returned home as intelligence agents for the Soviet Union. For example, Professor Arnost Kolman at Charles University in Prague had spent 30 years in the Soviet Union, had taught at the Higher Party School in Moscow, and, upon his return to Czechoslovakia in 1945, became an informant for the Soviet embassy.[123]

In Tatiana Volokitina's edited volume on Soviet policy toward Eastern Europe, the authors argue that a peculiar dynamic developed among the leaders of individual Eastern European allies, as well as among the leaders of the countries themselves. They were constantly vying among themselves to gain "the right to be the source of information for Moscow" and to become Stalin's "only trusted person" in their country and in the bloc, if possible.[124] Anxiety on this score was expressed by Rakosi, who complained to a Soviet MGB adviser in Budapest that he was "offended by how far away from Stalin he had to sit during Stalin's birthday celebrations in Moscow."[125]

One of the more striking and tragicomical examples of this competition for Stalin's favor were the extraordinary efforts taken by Soviet allies in Eastern Europe to demonstrate their ecstasy on the occasion of his 70th birthday, celebrated on December 21, 1949. Czechoslovaks, for example, assured the Soviet ambassador Mikhail A. Silin that they had gathered 8 million birthday greetings, or over 90 percent of the population over 6 years of age, that they would erect a monument to Stalin in the center of Prague, and that they had prepared 15 to 20 railroad wagonloads of gifts for transport to Moscow. According to Volokitina, celebration plans for all Eastern European allies were vetted with Soviet advisers before implementation.[126]

Another institution familiar from the Soviet domestic scene was mortal fear of telling Moscow anything it didn't want to, or expect to, hear. This entailed withholding information that might contradict the assumptions underlying current Soviet policy, or sending doctored information so as to justify that policy.[127] This was of course always counterproductive for Soviet policy aims, perhaps nowhere

---

[122] Gibianskii, "Poslednii Vizit Tito," 137.
[123] Murashko and Noskova, "Institut Sovetskikh Sovetnikov," 512.
[124] Volokotina et al., *Moskva i Vostochnaia Evropa*, 11.
[125] Volokitina et al., *Sovetskii Faktor v Vostochnoi Evrope*, 260.
[126] Ibid., 214–16.
[127] See, for example, Andrei M. Ledovskii, a Soviet consular officer in China in the 1940s, "12 Sovetov I. V. Stalina Rukovodstvu Kompartii Kitaia," *Novaia i Noveishaia Istoriia* 2 (2004): 126–27.

greater than in eastern Germany. When German communists finally summoned up the courage to tell Stalin that the number of rapes committed by Red Army soldiers was hugely costly to them politically, Stalin's reply was, "I will not allow anyone to drag the reputation of the Red Army through the mud."[128] Needless to say, the matter wasn't pursued. Meanwhile, in occupied Germany, when rapes were reported, albeit rarely, in the local press, the perpetrator was invariably referred to as "a man in a Red Army uniform," never as a Red Army soldier.[129]

One can see how delicately one had to talk when meeting the "Great Friend." Stalin asked the Hungarian prime minister Ferenc Nagy, during an April 1946 meeting in Moscow, whether Hungarians resented the Soviet armed forces, and intimated that he should speak frankly. The latter replied that the occupation army had no disagreements with the Hungarian people, and there were few incidents. "Often dishonorable Hungarians themselves abuse the occupation army," he said. He did add, however, that it cost Hungary a lot to pay for the occupation. Stalin replied that the Hungarian people cannot be morally offended by the Red Army . . . and that these forces will be gradually withdrawn, unburdening the Hungarian economy.[130]

Another peculiarity of the Soviet-East European relationship was the level of control Moscow exercised over not only broad strategic decision-making in Eastern Europe, but also the most minute of details, just as if the Central Committee in Moscow were ordering obkom and raikom secretaries in the Soviet Union what to do. For example, Soviet advisers wrote East Germany's land reform legislation.[131] Kynin concluded that "there is no evidence in any archives, German or otherwise, that the German communist party participated in developing the land reform," which was decided upon in August 1945.[132] Soviets in East Germany insisted on the presence of flowers at party meetings,

---

[128] Naimark, *The Russians in Germany*, 71.

[129] Reports from Major General Sergei Tiulpanov, propaganda director of the Soviet Military Administration—Germany (SVAG) to Moscow also included the "disguised as Red Army" phraseology when reporting on crimes against the German people. Georgii P. Kynin and Johan P. Laufer, "Vvedenie: Politika SSSR po Germanskomu Voprosu (9 maia 1945 g.—3 oktiabria 1946 g.," in *SSSR i Germanskii Vopros*, vol. II (Moscow: Mezhdunarodnye Otnosheniia, 2000), 344. Complaining about the excesses of the local Soviet security forces could get you arrested, as it did Lt. General K.F. Telegin, who was imprisoned for "animosity toward the NKVD." Naimark, *The Russians in Germany*, 104, 561 n. 169.

[130] Volokitina et al., *Vostochnaia Evropa v Dokumentakh Rossiskikh Arkhivov, 1944–1953 gg., Tom I*, 1–10.

[131] Georgii P. Kynin and Johan P. Laufer, "Vvedenie: Politika SSSR po Germanskomu Voprosu (9 maia 1945 g.—3 oktiabria 1946 g.)," in *SSSR I Germanskii Vopros*, vol. II (Moscow: Mezhdunarodnye Otnosheniia, 2000), 36–37.

[132] Kynin and Laufer, "Vvedenie: Politika SSSR po Germanskomu (9Maia 1945g.—3 Oktiabria 1946g.)," 738.

re-choreographed the ceremonies accompanying party membership card distribution, and demanded that banners, red scarves, and musical instruments all be present at Pioneer meetings, all according to common Soviet practice.[133]

In September 1949 Ambassador Silin complained to the head of Czechoslovakia's CC ID, Bedrich Geminder, about the obviously reduced number of portraits of Stalin and Soviet flags on display during official holidays. It "both surprises and troubles us," he said. In his report of the conversation to the foreign ministry, Silin concluded that "Geminder and Slansky will draw the necessary conclusions."[134]

It would be most misleading to consider either the Soviet Union or any of its Eastern European allies as unitary actors. Instead, there were many institutionalized channels through which Moscow both gathered information about its allies and exerted influence and pressure on them. Among these channels were Soviet embassies, journalists, the MVD, MGB, and Cominform, as well as the many Soviet delegations that visited these countries. Almost all the latter routinely wrote reports to the Central Committee analyzing the state of political play in the country they had visited, often pointing out various risks of dangerous deviance they had noted during their visits. At the same time, Eastern Europeans tried to use these many channels to not only exert influence on Moscow, but to gain political advantage against competitors at home, and in other Eastern European countries.

One such common technique was providing Moscow with compromising materials or "kompromat," on one's political rivals. Eastern European communists were acutely attuned to the fine-grained twists and turns of official Soviet discourse in Moscow, which better enabled contriving the most resonant collection of charges against a rival. Rumania's leader Gheorge Gheorgiu-Dej, for example, fed Soviet representatives information on his rival Luka, accusing him of a loss of "vigilance" and connections with Zionists and "right-opportunist deviationism," all calculated to resonate with the predominant discourse of danger prevailing in Moscow in April 1951.[135]

Rakosi was perhaps the most diligent in spreading kompromat about his purported communist allies in Eastern Europe, especially Czechoslovakia's Gottwald and Poland's Gomulka. During his June 4–21, 1949, visit to Prague, Rakosi gave Gottwald a list of 675 purported Anglo-American spies in Czechoslovakia, including two Politburo members, Minister of the Interior

---

[133] Naimark, *The Russians in Germany*, 285, 315.

[134] Volokitina et al., *Sovetskii Faktor v Vostochnoi Evrope*, 171–72.

[135] On the more general phenomenon of passing kompromat to Moscow, see Murashko and Noskova, "Institut Sovetskikh Sovetnikov," 645–49; and Pokivailova, "Moskva i Ustanovlenie Monopolii," 339.

Vaclav Nosek, and Minister of Foreign Affairs Clementis.[136] In July 1949, as Rajk's interrogation dragged on, Rakosi told one of the visiting MGB advisers on the affair that despite informing Gottwald of a "chain of espionage" throughout Eastern European communist parties connected to the Rajk affair, "Czech communist leaders still haven't taken any kind of measures."[137] Planting these charges with both MGB advisers and Cominform representatives had its effect. In September 1949 Bierut, not wishing to appear less vigilant than his Hungarian counterpart, appealed to Stalin to arrange a meeting in Moscow so he could discuss with Stalin the Gomulka and Spychalski affairs "in connection with the Budapest process. . . ."[138] Also in response to Rakosi's efforts to impugn the credentials of his Eastern European competitors, both MGB representatives from Poland and Czechoslovakia arrived in Budapest to familiarize themselves with the materials of the affair and search for criminal ties between Rajk and his "accomplices," and their own party elites. But even after reviewing the materials, Gottwald asked Rakosi, through Rakosi's visiting brother and CC member, Zoltan Biro, whether, during Rajk's trial, the names of implicated Czechoslovakians could go unmentioned. Rakosi refused. Gottwald and Romania's Gheorgiu-Dej subsequently appealed to Moscow to send MGB specialists to help them prepare their "affairs." Stalin personally replied to Gottwald's request on September 23, 1949, promising to send the necessary advisers to Prague.[139]

Rakosi continued his campaign against Gottwald during Stalin's birthday celebrations in Moscow in December. He told Boris Ponomarev at the CC FPD that Interior Minister Nosek, Defense Minister Svoboda, and Foreign Minister Clementis were all connected with English intelligence.[140] In an April 8 letter to Gottwald, Stalin demanded Svoboda's removal. He was dismissed on April 25.[141] Even after Rajk's execution and the prosecution of affairs in Poland, Rumania, and Czechoslovakia, Rakosi complained to a Soviet MGB adviser in Budapest, whose report of the conversation was distributed to the Soviet leadership in Moscow, that "Gottwald and Slansky are [still] indecisive and liberal toward hostile elements in the party." [142]

---

[136] Volokitina et al., *Vostochnaia Evropa v Dokumentakh Rossiiskikh Arkhivov, 1944–1953 gg. Tom II*, 171.

[137] Ibid., 181–82.

[138] Murashko and Noskova, "Repressii Kak Element Vnutripartiinoi," 530.

[139] Volokitina et al., *Vostochnaia Evropa v Dokumentakh Rossiiskikh Arkhivov, 1944–1953 gg. Tom II*, 171, 219–23; and Murashko and Noskova, "Institut Sovetskikh Sovetnikov," 621–22.

[140] Volokitina et al., *Sovetskii Faktor v Vostochnoi Evrope*, 244.

[141] Murashko and Noskova, "Repressii kak Element," 482.

[142] Ibid., 258–59.

Peculiar institutions yielded peculiar conversations. In May 1949, behind Rakosi's back, Hungary's political police, under Moscow's direct control, reported to Pavel Iudin and L. S. Baranov in the CC FPD in Moscow that the Hungarian party was not paying sufficient attention to the struggle with Trotskyites in the party. Rakosi was furious and demanded from the Soviet ambassador Georgii M. Pushkin to be told who had given the "Russians" this information. Rakosi accused them, his own police, of trying to sour relations between Moscow and himself.[143] Pushkin had reported the same day to Moscow that while "the Hungarian police are still inexperienced and young, the main thing is they are devoted to the Soviet Union."[144]

But it wasn't only at the highest level that compromising information was passed on to Soviet officials. A Rumanian consular official in Poland sent Suslov a report "on the political and social life of Poland" in October 1948 in which he reported seeing only "one portrait of Comrade Stalin on May Day, and even that was very small. The parade itself was boring, and the marchers looked coerced." On June 22, liberation day for Poland, "criminally little was said or written about the Soviet heroes who saved the Polish people." And "nothing at all happens" on Soviet Aviation or Navy Day. He also reported what Soviet advisers noticed, the deep penetration of American and Western culture in Polish daily life: the availability of newspapers, books, and magazines from England and the United States, and posters for their films.[145]

In addition, it was taken for granted that Soviet officials would participate in their allies' Central Committee and Politburo meetings. For example, Soviet ambassador M. F. Bodrov was invited to a closed (to Bulgarian party members) Central Committee meeting in May 1950 to examine personnel changes on the CC.

Perhaps most well-known, a Soviet citizen, Marshal Konstantin Rokossovsky, was appointed Polish defense minister in November 1949. Soon the overwhelming majority of the Polish command staff was Soviet. Of 45 generals in March 1950, 27 were Soviet; by December, 40 of 52. Rokossovsky communicated directly to the Chief of the General Staff in Moscow, bypassing Bierut and the Polish defense ministry.[146] In May 1950 Rokossovsky was made a Polish Politburo member. Jakub Berman recalled that in both his offices at the Council of Ministers and at the Central Committee, he had two phones. One was a local line, the other was connected directly to Moscow, and Stalin's hours of business had the same effects in Warsaw as they had in Moscow, compelling

---

[143] Pokivailova, "Moskva i Ustanovlenie Monopolii," 340–41; Volokitina et al., *Vostochnaia Evropa v Dokumentakh Rossiiskikh Arkhivov, 1944–1953 gg. Tom II*, 95–97.

[144] Murashko and Noskova, "Repressii Kak Element Vnutripartiinoi," 521.

[145] Bordiugov, *SSSR-Polsha*, 263–66.

[146] Murashko and Noskova, "Repressii," 485–88.

thousands to remain awake into the wee hours of the morning, lest the Great Friend from Moscow call.[147]

These complicated loyalties of Eastern European communists manifested themselves after the Soviet-Yugoslav split. More than 500 Yugoslavians in the Soviet Union at the time of Tito's excommunication from the bloc refused to return to Yugoslavia.[148] Within the Yugoslavian party itself, more than 55,000 members, or 12 percent of the total, and 52,000 candidate members, identified with the position of the Cominform (of course drafted by Moscow) against Tito and their own party. Tito's response was harsh. More than 16,000 were sent to labor camps, and 5,000 emigrated. Over 172,000 were arrested from 1948 to 1952, about 100,000 in 1948–49 alone.[149]

B. The Excommunication of Tito's Yugoslavia in 1948

Up until months before being excommunicated from the Soviet bloc, Yugoslavia had been regarded by Soviets as its most similar and reliable ally in Eastern Europe, at least as far as its domestic transformation was concerned. Indeed, the original draft of the Yugoslav constitution in 1946 was almost a literal translation of the Soviet constitution of 1936.[150] In the run-up to the founding of the Cominform in September 1947, the CC FPD produced analytical reports on each Eastern European ally. Yugoslavia's domestic policies were extolled, far more so than any other Eastern European ally, although its foreign policy was criticized for insubordination and recklessness: on Trieste, on its role in the Balkans and Albania, and on the Bulgarian constitution.[151] Gibianskii concluded, "In leading Soviet circles they were very sensitive to . . . the danger of a violation of hierarchy in relations between the Soviet Union and peoples' democracies."[152] In a report prepared for Zhdanov's speech at the opening of the Cominform in September

---

[147] Toranska, *Them*, 335.

[148] Pokivailova, "Moskva i Ustanovlenie Monopolii," 359.

[149] Volokitina, "Istochniki Formirovaniia Partiino-Gosudarstvennoi Nomenklatury," 214–18.

[150] Tatiana V. Volokitina, "Oformlenie i Funktsionirovanie novogo Mekhanizma Gosudarstvennoi Vlasti," in *Moskva i Vostochnaia Evropa. Stanovlenie politicheskikh rezhimov sovetskogo tipa (1949–1953). Ocherki istorii*, ed. Tatiana V. Volokitina et al. (Moscow: ROSSPEN, 2002), 235.

[151] Leonid Ia. Gibianskii, "Kominform v Deistvii. 1947–1948 gg. Po Arkhivnym Dokumentam," *Novaia i Noveishaia Istoriia* 2 (1996): 164–68.

[152] Ibid., 168; Gibianskii's work, relying as it does on the most exhaustive use of archival sources in multiple countries, is the single best source on Soviet-Yugoslavian relations from 1945 to 1953. For far greater detail than I can offer here, see Gibianskii, "Sekretnaia Sovetsko-Iugoslavskaia Perepiska 1948 Goda," *Voprosy Istorii* 4, 6, and 10 (1992); Gibianskii, "Kak Voznik Kominform."; Gibianskii, "Kominform v Deistvii, 1947–1948 gg. Po Arkhivnym Dokumentam," *Novaia i Noveishaia Istoriia* 2; and Gibianskii, "Na Poroge Pervogo Raskola."

1947, Yugoslavia was singled out for eliminating "the roots of capitalism more thoroughly than in other Eastern European states."[153] The January 1948 round of CC FPD reports also gave Yugoslavia a clean bill of health.[154]

The excommunication of Yugoslavia from the Soviet bloc is probably best understood in relationship to a series of independent actions by Soviet communist allies in Europe that demonstrated that any continuing tolerance of difference, as expressed in "national roads" to socialism, was too risky, threatening a reversal of socialist construction domestically, as well as closer economic, political, and diplomatic relations with the imperialist West. Yugoslavia's own actions, decisions by the French and Italian communist parties to force the collapse of their coalition governments, and the alacrity with which Eastern European allies met the idea of the Marshall Plan, made Tito's Yugoslavia a possible exemplary case of deviationism that Stalin could use to re-establish the hierarchy within the bloc.

Soviet targeting of Tito and Yugoslvia, the country most advanced on the socialist road, very closely parallels the treatment of deviants at home. Tito was chosen as an exemplar, a model who had been consistently praised for his adherence to the Soviet model.[155] For example, the philosopher Georgii Aleksandrov, the film director Sergei Eisenstein, and the author Vsevolod Kochetov, all of whom had just received Stalin Prizes, were singled out during anti-cosmopolitan and anti-kowtowing campaigns, demonstrating that even the most revered and seemingly unblemished of Soviet models could still err and could still require rectification by the party. So, how could a lesser light possibly be innocent of some dangerous deviation, even if unintentional?

Soviet displeasure with Tito's foreign policy built up over the six months prior to his March 1948 excommunication. Stalin sent a telegram to Tito in August 1947 criticizing him for unilaterally announcing a treaty with Bulgaria without consulting Moscow. Just a few months later, Tito, again without consulting Moscow, proposed sending a Yugoslav army division to Albania. Tito backed down in both cases, and in a February 1948 meeting in Moscow among the Soviet leadership, Bulgaria's Dimitrov and Kostov, and Yugoslavia's foreign minister Edvard Kardelj and Politburo member Milovan Djilas, the Soviet allies confessed their errors and signed an agreement to consult with Moscow in advance on any foreign policy move thereafter. But almost simultaneously, Tito

---

[153] RGASPI f575 op1 d3, 103.

[154] Leonid Ia. Gibianskii, "Kominform v Deistvii. 1947–1948 gg. Po Arkhivnym Dokumentam," *Novaia i Noveishaia Istoriia* 1 (1996): 170.

[155] It couldn't have helped Tito that in Moscow they were well aware of his and Yugoslavia's popularity in other Eastern European countries. G. P. Murashko and A. F. Noskova, "Sovetskoe Rukovodstvo i Politicheskie Protsessy T. Kostova i L. Raika," in *Stalinskoe Desiatiletie Kholodnoi Voiny: Fakty i Gipotezy*, ed. I. V. Gaiduk, N. I. Yegorova, and A. O. Chubarian (Moscow: Nauka, 1999), 24.

was defying Soviet orders by continuing to arm Greek partisans. And just three weeks after the agreement in Moscow, on March 1, 1948, Tito argued in the Yugoslavian Politburo for authority to press Moscow to reverse itself, and allow Yugoslav troops in Albania, and a Yugoslvian-Albanian union.[156]

It is worth noting that Belgrade's relationship with Albania was not dissimilar from Moscow's relationships with its Eastern European allies. Just as the Soviet Union expected to participate in the inner workings of central decision-making in Poland or Czechoslovakia, for instance, Yugoslavia had a representative from the Yugoslavian communist party in the Albanian communist party's central committee, too.[157]

Much of the danger from Tito's independence arose from the identity relations that characterized Moscow and its Eastern European allies. Sitting atop the hierarchy of the socialist community meant that any actions by its subordinates were attributed to Moscow's orders. Danger came from imperialist enemies inferring that whatever Moscow's allies did was at the direction of Moscow and from socialist allies inferring that if Yugoslavia could act independently, whether in foreign or domestic policy, so could they. In the February 10, 1948, meeting with their Bulgarian and Yugoslavian counterparts, the Soviet leadership warned that the reckless Yugoslavian-Bulgarian treaty, for example, would only give "English and Americans a pretext to intervene in Greece," and Dimitrov's ill-advised remarks about a Balkan confederation only made it easier to create a Western bloc. Molotov pointed out that Polish comrades had thought Moscow had authorized Yugoslav and Bulgarian actions, and the Albanians told Moscow they thought the Soviet leadership had agreed to the introduction of Yugoslavian troops into Albania. Otherwise, why would Tito suggest it?[158]

Stalin went on to explain the connection between allied actions and American domestic and foreign policy:

> You are giving reactionary elements in America food to convince public opinion that America won't be doing anything special if it creates a Western bloc, because a bloc already exists in the Balkans.... Heading

[156] Gibianskii, "Sekretnaia Sovetsko-Iugoslavskaia Perepiska 1948 Goda," *Voprosy Istorii* 4, 120–23; Gibianskii, "Na Poroge Pervogo Raskola," 96; Adibekov, *Kominform I Poslevoennaia Evropa*, 100–01; and Jeronim Perovic, "The Tito-Stalin Split," *Journal of Cold War Studies* 9, no. 2 (Spring 2007): 32–63. The Soviets found out on March 23 that Tito had recommended not only an Italian communist seizure of northern Italy in the event of a US military intervention in the country, but also a communist uprising in Austria to create a divided country with a communist east. Gibianskii, "Kominform v Deistvii, 1947–1948 gg. Po Arkhivnym Dokumentam," *Novaia i Noveishaia Istoriia* 2, 164.

[157] Perovic, "The Tito-Stalin Split," 44.

[158] Gibianskii, "Na Poroge Pervogo Raskola," 96–97.

America are real moneybags, not intelligents [*sic*], who hate us passionately and only look for a pretext.... They can fail at the elections if we give progressive elements arguments by our conduct.... But if these money magnates end up in office again, then we will be significantly guilty through our behavior.[159]

Tito's actions were communicated immediately to Moscow, through its ambassador, Anatolii Lavrentiev, and by one of its allies on the Yugoslavian Politburo, the finance minister, Sreten Zhuiovich.[160] Gibianskii argues that "everything changed when Moscow received Lavrentiev's report about the Yugoslav Politburo meeting."[161] Most importantly, the Soviet leadership learned that their Yugoslav comrades denied Soviet advisers and diplomats access to data about the Yugoslavian economy, had rejected Stalin's order that Bulgaria and Yugoslavia pursue an immediate confederation, and, despite Stalin's admonitions to end the Greek civil war, had instead met with the Greek CP General Secretary, Nikos Zakhariades, and informed him that Yugoslavian military aid would continue, despite Stalin's objections.[162] On March 18, 1948, the Soviet Union withdrew all its military and civilian advisers from Yugoslavia over Yugoslav objections, the first material manifestation of the breach that would last until 1955.[163]

What ultimately served as the foundation for the bill of particulars levied on Yugoslavia was received by Suslov on March 27 from his CC FPD analysts. The subsequent report was distributed simultaneously to Tito and the entire eastern bloc. The report was titled, "On the Anti-Marxist Positions of the Leaders of the Communist Party of Yugoslavia on Questions of Foreign and Domestic Policy."[164] The new binary of the discourse of danger was evident. On page one, under the section entitled "Scorn for Marxist Theory," the authors quoted Lenin in "What's to Be Done?" Lenin had written that "only two ideologies exist: socialist and

---

[159] Gibianskii, "Na Poroge Pervogo Raskola," 98. This is a rare moment: Stalin recognizing the possible effects foreign policy might have on US domestic politics. Note, however, it is Dimitrov's and Tito's conduct that risks tipping the election, not Stalin's. So, the coup in Czechoslovakia, progressive Stalinization of Eastern Europe in general, formation of the Cominform, and the soon-to-be declared blockade of Berlin are not understood, at least not in the archival records, as actions that could "give food" to American reactionaries.

[160] Gibianskii, "Kominform v Deistvii, 1947–1948 gg. Po Arkhivnym Dokumentam," *Novaia i Noveishaia Istoriia* 2, 160; and Pokivailova, "Moskva i Ustanovlenie Monopolii," 349.

[161] Gibianskii, "Kominform v Deistvii, 1947–1948 gg. Po Arkhivnym Dokumentam," *Novaia i Noveishaia Istoriia* 2, 161.

[162] Perovic, "The Tito-Stalin Split," 55–56.

[163] Murashko and Noskova, "Institut Sovetskikh Sovetnikov," 610.

[164] RTsKhIDNI f17 op128 d1163, 9–24. This is in the same series as the rest of the drafted reports about Eastern European allies.

bourgeois. There is no middle. Therefore, any reduction in socialist ideology, any dismissal of it, means the strengthening of bourgeois ideology."[165] No gray areas of innocuous difference existed here. Yugoslavia had ignored its place in the hierarchy by "ignoring the Soviet Union as the decisive force" and minimizing the role of the Red Army in Yugoslavia's liberation. The smallest details of deviation on the "Yugoslav national path to socialism" were now excoriated as dangerous bourgeois degeneration, matters such as not wearing the red scarves of Soviet Young Pioneers, not publishing the full text of the Soviet CC Resolution on Muradeli's opera, *The Great Friendship*, and not accepting a visit of the Red Army song and dance ensemble in December 1946. In addition to the foreign policy unilateralism, enumerated above, socialist construction in Yugoslavia was now criticized, unlike in the reports of just months before. Most ironic, however, were the charges made against Tito himself: his "vozhdizm, vanity, and presumptuousness," and his concentration of power, which meant "he practically alone leads the entire sociopolitical life of the country and its foreign policy."[166]

Eastern European allied responses to the March 27 letter against Tito could only have confirmed Stalin in his suspicion that hierarchy needed to be imposed strictly on the bloc. The most immediate, and only unprompted, support Moscow received was from Rakosi's Hungary, on April 8. The Rumanian and Czechoslovakian parties didn't even hold Politburo meetings to discuss the letter. The Polish party didn't respond for almost a month, and then did so only after Gomulka told the Soviet ambassador that he didn't believe the charges.[167] Some Bulgarian and Czechoslovakian party members approved "the courage and independence of Tito" at local meetings.[168]

In their April 13 response to Stalin and Molotov, Tito and Kardelj denied the charges, suggested that this must just be a big misunderstanding, attributed Soviet charges to bad intelligence from disgruntled informants, and asked that the Soviets send a delegation to discuss matters.[169] But the May 4, 1948, reply from Stalin and Molotov, also sent simultaneously to Eastern European allies, allowed for no compromise. Two weeks later, Suslov generously invited Tito to attend a June Cominform meeting where he could listen to his own denunciation. Tito declined the opportunity.[170]

---

[165] Ibid., 11.
[166] Ibid., 16–21.
[167] Murashko and Noskova, "Repressii Kak Element Vnutripartiinoi," 498–500.
[168] Volokitina, "Nakanune," 54–55.
[169] Gibianskii, "Sekretnaia Sovetsko-Iugoslavskaia Perepiska 1948 Goda," *Voprosy Istorii 6*, 160–66.
[170] Ironically, Tito had been one of the most vociferous supporters of the Cominform, as it was aimed against what he considered "rightist deviationism" in French, Italian, and Czechoslovakian parties. Zubok and Pleshakov, *Inside the Kremlin's Cold War*, 135.

Just as the identification of Zoshchenko and Akhmatova as deviants, and Eisenstein, Aleksandrov, and Kochetov as New Soviet Men who could nevertheless make dangerous errors, had warned average Soviets that the boundaries of acceptable Soviet identity had become much more narrow, identifying the hero Tito as a dangerous deviant sent a chilling message throughout Eastern Europe. National roads to socialism, with their toleration of religious believers, private agriculture, Western cultural influence, and other contextual differences, let alone independent foreign policy action, were now punishable offenses. Of course such a punishment, being driven out of the bloc and possible dependence on the West, would probably have been voted for by most Eastern European publics. But it was a terrifying prospect for thousands of Moscow's allies in power in these countries.

Just how dangerous Tito's deviance must have been thought to be to Soviet security—understood as the need to have regimes in Eastern Europe as similar to the Soviet model as was possible to achieve—is evident in the fact that Moscow abandoned an ally, and even turned an ally into a potential enemy, just after the creation of the West European Union and days before announcing the blockade of Berlin. Mastny argues that the problem was "the incompatibility of Stalinist affinities."[171] There is truth in the argument that the very closeness of Soviet and Yugoslav identities made differences between them that much more dangerous to the Soviet project. The more socialist Yugoslavia was understood to be, the closer it was to the Soviet model, the more dangerous any of its "national" deviations or foreign policy ventures were, as they resonated in the bloc as authoritative alternatives to the model on offer from Moscow.

Stalin expressed the paternalistic and hierarchical logic of these identity relations in a February 1950 reception at the Hotel Metropol in Moscow: "Yugoslavia has placed itself outside the family; it wanted to take an impossible separate path; it will return to the family sooner or later."[172]

C. The East German Exception

Tatiana Volokitina opens her book on Soviet foreign policy toward eastern Europe after the war by explaining that East Germany had been excluded from the book because "in Soviet policy the GDR (German Democratic Republic) occupied a special place, apart from Eastern European countries...."[173] This special place reflected Soviet aspirations that Germany would be reunited, maximally as

---

[171] Mastny, *The Cold War*, 37.
[172] Heinzig, *The Soviet Union*, 366.
[173] Volokotina et al., *Moskva i Vostochnaia Evropa*.

a Soviet ally, minimally as a demilitarized, neutralized country friendly to the Soviet Union. So long as there was any hope that unification on acceptable terms could be effected, East German adoption of the Soviet model, in all its Stalinist details, had to be deferred. As Norman Naimark, perhaps the foremost historian of Soviet-GDR relations, concluded: "The Soviet Union had different intentions than it did in [the rest of Eastern Europe]. In Germany, the Soviets were interested in maintaining maximum flexibility to accommodate to a four-power agreement on unification, demilitarization, and neutralization of the country."[174]

As was the case with Soviet allies in Eastern Europe more generally in the year or two after the war, Stalin counseled caution and moderation to his East German friends. In a June 1945 meeting with Wilhelm Piech and Walter Ulbricht, Stalin proposed that the German party publicly declare that the Soviet model was inappropriate for Germany and a parliamentary democracy must be established, and guarantee that farmers with large landholdings shouldn't fear confiscation.[175] In addition, German communists "should stop speaking so glowingly about the Soviet Union."[176] In a subsequent memorandum on land reform in eastern Germany from Molotov and Vyshinsky to Stalin, they explicitly differentiated the more moderate terms of the expropriations, as compared to those being undertaken in the rest of Eastern Europe.[177]

However, even before Stalinization in eastern Germany, which came several years after it had already begun in the rest of Eastern Europe, the Soviet appetite for reparations made eastern Germany an incredibly unattractive model for those Germans living in the West. From 1945 to 1947, around 17,000 boxcars of dismantled German factories arrived in the Soviet Union.[178] A reasonable estimate is that one-third of East Germany's industry was removed, and then reparations continued from ongoing East German production. Having promised to end reparations in May 1946, partly in order to affect the autumn elections in eastern Germany, the dismantling of German factories continued until January 1947.[179] As late as October 1947, when Stalin agreed to reduce Soviet troops in

---

[174] Naimark, *The Russians in Germany*, 351.

[175] Wilhelm Piech would become the first president of the German Democratic Republic (GDR) in 1949, and Walter Ulbricht would become first secretary of the communist party in 1953.

[176] Dimitrov, *The Diary of Georgi Dimitrov*, 372. Soviet representatives in eastern Germany had to go around painting over the red stars that their German communist allies had put on buildings. Stalin also had to reverse the German communists' announced ban on all other political parties in June 1945. Filitov, "The Soviet Administrators," 111.

[177] Kynin and Laufer, "Vvedenie: Politika SSSR po Germanskomu (9Maia 1945g.—3 Oktiabria 1946g.)," 37, 218–19.

[178] Danilov and Pyzhikov, *Rozhdenie Svekhderzhavy*, 113.

[179] Kynin and Laufer, "Vvedenie: Politika SSSR," 40–48, 178; and *SSSR I Germanskii Vopros*, vol. III (Moscow: Mezhdunarodnye Otnosheniia, 2003), 705.

East Germany by 40 percent, he agreed with First Deputy Minister of Internal Affairs Ivan Serov over the objections of General Sokolovskii, commander of Soviet forces in Germany, that the freed up food supplies should not be left for local Germans, but transferred to the Soviet Union.[180] More amusing, but still telling, was widespread resentment among Germans of Soviet requisitioning of potatoes to make vodka for themselves. Graffiti appeared, replacing SED (Socialist United Party) with Soviet Property of Germany.[181]

The Soviet Union was obsessively interested in reparations, repeatedly demanding $10 billion of transfers, not only from eastern zones, but western zones, too, this figure having been discussed at the Yalta Conference in February 1945, though never formally agreed to. In November 1946, Molotov offered the French deputy foreign minister, Maurice Jacques Couve de Murville a deal: If France supported the Soviets on the $10 billion, they could rely on Soviet support for French claims on the Saar.[182] In his January 1947 meeting with East German leaders, Stalin acknowledged that the continued "dismantling had influenced the mood before the Berlin elections."[183]

Not only Soviet reparations made the close identification of German communists with Moscow politically costly in eastern Germany, but so too did the issue of German prisoners of war in the Soviet Union, of whom there were 4 to 5 million by the end of the conflict.[184] Colonel Sergei Tiulpanov, head of the Soviet occupation's Propaganda Department, succeeded in getting 120,000 freed in time for the September 1946 parliamentary elections at the request of East German communists who were fearful of the popular resentment engendered by not only the POW issue itself, but the fact that Soviets didn't allow letters to be exchanged between the POWs and their families in East Germany.[185] As of March 1947, there were still one million German POWs in the Soviet

---

[180] Naimark, *The Russians in Germany*, 197. Similarly, Molotov, in February 1947, rejected Rumanian requests that Moscow pick up expenses for maintaining Red Army forces in Rumania, saying this would happen only after peace treaties were ratified by the three Powers. Volokitina et al., *Vostochnaia Evropa v Dokumentakh Rossiskikh Arkhivov, 1944–1953 gg., Tom I*, 567.

[181] Naimark, *The Russians in Germany*, 160–69, 384.

[182] Kynin and Laufer, "Vvedenie: Politika SSSR," 181.

[183] *SSSR I Germanskii Vopros*, vol. III, 256. Not until May 1950 did the Soviet Union write off what it claimed to be the remaining half of its reparation bill: $3.7 billion, though the estimate is very rough. Kynin and Laufer, "Vvedenie: Politika SSSR," 42. In his April 1947 meeting with Secretary of State Marshall in Moscow, Stalin complained that the Soviets had received only $2 billion in reparations from Germany, when "the Russians at Yalta had said $10 billion, and the Americans had said this is not so much." Kynin and Laufer, "Vvedenie: Politika SSSR," 358. Note as well Stalin's conversational substitution of Russians for Soviets.

[184] For similar concerns in Rumania, see *Tri Vizita*, 223–25.

[185] Kynin and Laufer, "Vvedenie: Politika SSSR," 85–86.

Union. Although the Soviets agreed to free them all at the December 1948 CFM meeting in Moscow, the promise went unfulfilled until 1956, although the numbers had dwindled to 30,000 by 1951.[186]

Added to the political burden of local communists were the up to two million rapes committed by Soviet soldiers in East Germany in 1945 and 1946. These didn't end until the Soviet army isolated itself in its own camps by 1948. Not until January 1949 did the USSR Supreme Soviet pass a law with strict punishments for rapes by Soviet citizens in Germany. Many Soviet representatives reported back to Moscow that the rapes were costing the communists political support.[187] In addition, there was the brutal reality of up to 80,000 workers forced to work in the uranium mines near the Czechoslovak border in order to fuel the Soviet atomic bomb program. Exposed to radiation poisoning and only the most rudimentary of living quarters, thousands fled westward.[188]

The 2+ million POWs, rapes, reparations, and overall repression resulted in dismal local election results in September 1946, and still worse in Berlin elections the next month. In the local elections, both the Liberal Democratic Party (LDP) and Christian Democratic Union (CDU) outpolled the communists, and in Berlin the Social Democratic Party (SDP) got 49 percent of the vote, the CDU 22 percent, and the German communists only 20 percent. Not surprisingly, German women voted in far greater numbers against the communists than did men.[189]

Soviet analysts recognized that the SDP had won so many votes because it had demanded a re-examination of Germany's eastern borders, the return of Silesia and other eastern provinces, the end to reparations, the return of POWs, and the end to harsh Soviet rule. Of course, the German communist party was wrong-footed on all these issues by Soviet policies.[190] As late as May 1947, Tiulpanov reported to the foreign ministry that even some members of the German Communist Party were suggesting negotiations with Poland on adjusting the border.[191]

---

[186] Ibid., 68; and MacDonogh, *After the Reich*, 420–21.

[187] Naimark, *The Russians in Germany*, 79–132.

[188] Ibid., 244–49.

[189] Ibid., 121, 329.

[190] Kynin and Laufer, "Vvedenie: Politika SSSR," 196–204. Piech asked Stalin during his January 1947 Moscow meeting whether "even small changes could be made in the eastern border." Stalin said it was impossible. *SSSR I Germanskii Vopros*, vol. III, 261.

[191] *SSSR I Germanskii Vopros*, vol. III, 339. It should be noted that the movement of Polish borders westward was originally raised not by Stalin, but by Polish exiles in London, in 1942, and was agreed to by Stalin, Roosevelt, and Churchill only at Yalta in February 1945. Giles MacDonogh, *After the Reich: The Brutal History of the Allied Occupation* (New York: Basic Books, 2007), 13.

In a long meeting with Stalin in March 1948, Piech had to take a most circuitous route to get to the point of asking Stalin to rein in Soviet police in eastern Germany, who were arbitrarily arresting young men, many of whom would disappear without a trace. Piech started by talking about anti-Soviet propaganda taking its toll on the German people, and then raised the issue of the arrests. Stalin asked, "Who is arresting these Germans?" Then Stalin suggested they were "foreign agents and spies." Finally, Stalin asked, "Why haven't you written me about this before?" Piech responded that he didn't want to bother him with trivialities. Stalin exclaimed, "What bother?!"[192] Ulbricht continued to complain the following month to Tiulpanov about the food situation, the continuing dismantling of factories, and the disappearances of party members who had been arrested by Soviet authorities without charge, all of which reduced public support for the party and its program.[193]

Soviet occupiers proved equally obtuse on seemingly more minor, but politically sensitive issues, such as refusing to heed German communist requests to stop displaying portraits of Soviet military leaders in public, or showing movies glorifying Imperial Russian Generals Kutuzov and Suvorov, or, still worse, showing the Red Army's triumphal march into Berlin, including scenes of German POWs marching east, the same POWs whose fate went unknown for years to the Soviet Union's putative allies in Germany.[194] While A. A. Smirnov, head of the 4th European Department of the MFA, recommended to Molotov in June 1947 that Buchenwald and Sachsenhausen, both former Nazi concentration camps, be shut down, Deputy Minister of Internal Affairs and Deputy Chief of SWAG, Ivan Serov, refused.[195]

It is worthwhile to compare Soviet to Western occupation policy, since Moscow and Washington were both ultimately competing for the hearts and minds of Germans. Soviet policy had two major disadvantages. First, the United States was completely uninterested in reparations for itself, having reaped huge economic dividends from the war, while avoiding almost all of its devastation. Meanwhile, the Soviets, as shown, were vitally interested in extracting resources from conquered Germany, both for reasons of need and retribution. Second, Soviet understanding of what kind of domestic political order was necessary in Germany in order for the Soviet Union to be secure became increasingly Stalinist, and therefore unattractive, to Germans with a choice. Meanwhile, the system on offer from the United States, liberal democratic capitalism, was not

---

[192] "Za Sovetami v Kreml," 10.
[193] Kynin and Laufer, "Vvedenie: Politika SSSR," 663.
[194] Naimark, *The Russians in Germany*, 308, 420.
[195] *SSSR I Germanskii Vopros*, vol. III, 412.

so horrible, in comparison. It might seem, given the electoral returns and refugee flows, that the West must have followed a far more benign policy toward the defeated Germans than Moscow. But the picture is more mixed, and the differences point out the huge advantages the United States and the West had in prosecuting the ensuing Cold War with the Soviet Union.

For example, if the Soviets re-used Auschwitz, Sachsenhausen, and Buchenwald as camps for German prisoners, the Americans so used Dachau and the British, Bergen-Belsen. While Germans under Soviet occupation frequently complained about disappearing friends and family, arbitrarily arrested by Soviet police forces, it was in the American occupation zone that almost 170,000 denazification cases were tried, compared to only 18,000 in the Soviet zone. Significantly, while the United States began to release them en masse in 1949 to support Chancellor Adenauer's government, the growing Stalinization of eastern Germany was underway. Germans in the Soviet zone, at least for the first two years, were fed better than Germans in western occupation zones, a starvation diet being one of the ways western occupiers thought Germans should be punished for the war.[196]

In a December 1948 meeting with the German leadership, Stalin chided them with being too openly militant, reminding them, "Old Teutons went naked into battle with the Romans, but suffered losses. . . . One must mask oneself." Stalin went on to recommend against the planned expropriations of property. He criticized Piech, Grotewohl and Ulbricht for their "premature" efforts to build socialism. "One must wait. . . . Socialism must be approached by zigzags, not directly. . . . Conditions in Germany dictate a more cautious policy." He again differentiated Soviet from East German experience, and joked he had become an opportunist in his old age.[197] Unlike other Eastern European constitutions that were religiously copied from the Stalinist Soviet constitution of 1936, the GDR's constitution of October 1949 was explicitly modeled on the Weimar Republic constitution.[198]

Granted greater leeway from adhering to the Stalinist model of course didn't mean anything was permitted. It only looked like toleration of difference in comparison to what was happening in the Soviet Union itself, and in other Eastern European countries. Even in the exceptional case of eastern Germany, "by force of habit as well as conviction, Soviet political officers encouraged . . . [German communists] to follow similar patterns of organization and behavior. They were

---

[196] MacDonogh, *After the Reich*, 355–66.

[197] Volokitina, "Nakanune," 39; Naimark, *The Russians in Germany*, 312–13; "'Nuzhno Idti k Sotsializmu ne Priamo, a Zigzagami:' Zapis Besedy I. V. Stalina s Rukovoditeliami SEPG. Dekabr 1948 g.," *Istoricheskii Arkhiv* 5 (2002): 5–12.

[198] Danilov and Pyzhikov, *Rozhdenie Svekhderzhavy*, 41.

the schoolmasters of the [German communist party] and the headmaster [was] Colonel Tiulpanov.[199] For example, the German Academy of Sciences was taken to task by Soviet advisers for not pursuing Lysenkoism in biology, as it was being done in the Soviet Union.[200] The campaign against foreign influence on Soviet culture was followed by the banning of foreign plays in Germany in August 1946. While verbatim translations of the Soviet CC resolutions on *Zvezda*, with their crude invective against Akhmatova and Zoshchenko, remained unpublished in the East German press until 1952, apparently in order not to scare away support for local communists, Alexander Dymshits, head of the Culture Department under Tiulpanov, wrote a series of articles about socialist realism and its application to East German culture.[201] Just as foreign trophy films were shown in the Soviet Union with rewritten subtitles, and a political interpretation appended to the opening of the film, Tiulpanov insisted that every film shown in Germany be accompanied by an opening monologue by a party official to "explain" the film to its German audience.[202]

Only after Western rejection of the Soviet note of March 1952 suggesting a unified, democratic, neutral, and demilitarized Germany did Stalin authorize, on July 8, 1952, the construction of socialism in the GDR, openly and according to the Soviet model. The German exception was over.[203] In communications with the German leadership after the note, Stalin advised, finally, collectivization of German agriculture. Ulbricht, in particular, jumped at the chance, having been restrained by Moscow for the last seven years. Collectivization was accompanied by a round of show trials of "terrorists and saboteurs," just like in the Soviet Union in the 1930s.[204]

D. Relations with China

Soviet relations with China, or more precisely the Chinese Communist Party (CCP) and the nationalist Kuomintang government, followed the same pattern of moderation in the first year or two after the end of World War II and was generally characteristic of Soviet relations with the rest of the world, and of identity relations

---

[199] Naimark, *The Russians in Germany*, 284.

[200] Ibid., 235.

[201] David Pike, "Censorship in Soviet-Occupied Germany," in *The Establishment of Communist Regimes in Eastern Europe, 1944–1949*, ed. Norman Naimark and Leonid Gibianskii (Boulder: Westview Press, 1997), 224–32.

[202] Naimark, *The Russians in Germany*, 284.

[203] Wilfried Loth, "Stalin's Plans for Post-War Germany," in *The Soviet Union and Europe in the Cold War, 1943–53*, ed. Francesaca Gori and Silvio Pons (New York: St. Martin's Press, 1996), 31.

[204] Mastny, *The Cold War*, 138–39.

at home. Much scholarship has appeared in recent years on Sino-Soviet relations, based on archival openings in both China and Russia.[205] A general picture emerges of a Soviet balancing act. At first openly restraining Mao, and behaving correctly toward Chiang Kai-shek's Kuomintang, and then increasingly providing material support to the Chinese communists, while still maintaining the pretense of even-handedness. Once the People's Republic of China (PRC) was established in September 1949, Stalin still moved cautiously in establishing an alliance with China, again fearing a provocation of the United States. But any such fear was put aside in Stalin's April 1950 agreement to back Kim Jong Il's invasion of South Korea, with the proviso that Chinese armed forces would provide whatever military support North Korea might need. From 1950 until Stalin's death, significant quantities of Soviet economic and military aid flowed into China, but China used much of this aid in Korea and was continually restrained from pursuing its primary strategic objective, the reconquest of Taiwan by Soviet refusal to support it.

Soviet Temporization and Moderation

On August 14, 1945, the Soviet Union and the Kuomintang signed a "Treaty of Friendship and Alliance," resulting in Soviet military bases in Port Arthur, Dairen, control of Manchurian railroads, and independence for Outer Mongolia, or the People's Republic of Mongolia. (PRM) On the very same day, Japanese

---

[205] The best examples include Lorenz Luthi, *The Sino-Soviet Split: Cold War in the Communist World* (Princeton: Princeton University Press, 2008); Heinzig, *The Soviet Union*; Boris T. Kulik, *Sovetsko-Kitaiskii Raskol: Prichiny i Posledstviia* (Moscow: Institut Dal'nego Vostoka RAN, 2000); Elizabeth Wishnick, *Mending Fences: The Evolution of Moscow's China Policy from Brezhnev to Yeltsin* (London: University of Washington Press, 2001); Kathryn Weathersby, "Sovetskie Tseli v Koree, 1945–1950," in *Kholodnaia Voina: Novye Podkhody, Novye Dokumenty*, ed. M. M. Narinskii (Moscow: Institute of General History, 1995), 315–33; Kathryn Weathersby, "New Russian Documents on the Korean War," *Cold War International History Project Bulletin* Issues 6–7 (Winter 1995/1996): 30–84; Kathryn Weathersby, "Stalin, Mao, and the End of the Korean War," in *Brothers in Arms: The Rise and Fall of the Sino-Soviet Alliance, 1945–1963*, ed. Odd Arne Westad (Stanford: Stanford University Press, 1998), 90–116; Niu Jun, "The Origins of the Sino-Soviet Alliance," in *Brothers in Arms*, 47–89; Andrei M. Ledovskii, "Na Diplomaticheskom Rabote v Kitae v 1942–1952 gg.," *Novaia I Noveishaia Istoriia* 6 (1993): 102–32; Andrei M. Ledovskii, "Peregovory I. V. Stalina s Mao Tszedunom v Dekabre 1949-Fevrale 1950 g. Novye Arkhivnye Dokumenty," *Novaia I Noveishaia Istoriia* 1 (1997): 23–47; Andrei M. Ledovskii, "Stenogrammy Peregovorov I. V. Stalina s Czhou Enlaem v Avguste-Sentiabre 1952 g.," *Novaia I Noveishaia Istoriia* 2 (1997): 69–86; Andrei M. Ledovskii, "Stalin, Mao Tszedun i Koreiskaia Voina 1950–1953 Godov," *Novaia i Noveishaia Istoriia* 5 (2005): 79–113; Shen Zhihua, "Sino-Soviet Relations and the Origins of the Korean War: Stalin's Strategic Goals in the Far East," *Journal of Cold War Studies* 2, no. 2 (Spring 2000): 44–68; and Sergei N. Goncharov, John W. Lewis, and Xue Litai, *Uncertain Partners: Stalin, Mao, and the Korean War* (Stanford: Stanford University Press, 1993).

Emperor Hirohito broadcast his message of surrender, and within hours, Stalin cabled Mao suggesting that the CCP negotiate with the Kuomintang and resolve their differences peacefully.[206] A two-pronged Soviet policy ensued. In October 1945, the Soviet army left enough captured Japanese equipment to outfit 300,000 People's Liberation Army (PLA) soldiers. But on November 19, 1945, Moscow informed the CCP of its decision to transfer all cities along the Changchun railroad to the Kuomintang government, and advised all CCP cadres to evacuate. In early December 1945, Soviet forces allowed the Nationalist army to land at Mukden. But in March 1946, Stalin supported CCP plans to occupy all of Changchun, Harbin, and Quiqihaer, dropping his insistence that the CCP participate in a coalition government with the Kuomintang.[207] As late as April 1947, Molotov assured US Secretary of State George Marshall that Moscow wanted a common policy in the Far East that would adhere to the Four Power agreements reached during the wartime conferences.[208]

Reflecting Moscow's abiding fear of provoking the United States, Soviet weapons supplies to the PLA were kept secret. Even into 1949, Soviet weapons were replaced by American ones, so it could be argued they had been captured from the Nationalists.[209] Persistent Soviet reluctance to allow Mao to travel to Moscow to meet Stalin is probably accounted for by this Soviet fear that an official and public reception of Mao would only risk increasing US interest in providing support to the Kuomintang. In early 1947, Mao expressed his interest in traveling to the Soviet Union. On June 15, the Soviets assented, but only a secret visit. But just two weeks later, Stalin changed his mind and advised the visit's postponement.[210] In July 1948 Stalin recommended delaying Mao's visit until November, this time deploying the flimsiest of excuses: Soviet leaders had to see to the harvest![211] On November 21, 1948, Mao asked again, and again Stalin suggested a later date.[212] On January 11, 1949, Stalin again advised Mao against visiting because "it would be used by enemies to discredit the CCP as a force allegedly dependent on Moscow...."[213]

---

[206] Jun, "Origins," 52.

[207] Ibid., 55–60; and Heinzig, *The Soviet Union*, 92–98, 114.

[208] Jun, "The Origins," 61.

[209] Heinzig, *The Soviet Union*, 101. The June 26–August 14, 1949, Liu Shaoqi visit to Moscow was kept so secret that Western scholars only heard about it in the late 1980s. Heinzig, *The Soviet Union*, 176.

[210] Ledovskii, "Stenogrammy Peregovorov," 23.

[211] Heinzig, *The Soviet Union*, 124. Perhaps Stalin used this transparent evasion because of his embarrassment over allowing his fear of possible US reactions to influence his relationship with Mao.

[212] Ledovskii, "Stenogrammy Peregovorov," 24.

[213] S. L. Tikhvinskii, "Perepiska I. V. Stalina s Mao Tszedunom v Ianvare 1949 g.," *Novaia I Noveishaia Istoriia* 4–5 (1994): 135.

Consistent with an application of a discourse of difference, and Moscow's understanding of itself as atop the hierarchy of socialist modernity, was the frequent advice from Stalin and other Soviet leaders to Mao and the CCP to moderate their ambitions for a rapid socialist transformation of China. It should be said that, despite Mao not visiting Moscow, there was constant communication between the two parties, most often in the form of Chinese communists sending Moscow long memos and reports on what they were doing and asking advice on what they should be doing. For example, replying to Mao's telegram of November 30, 1947, on April 20, 1948, Stalin advised against "following the examples of the Soviet Union and Yugoslavia," in eliminating all other political parties from the political stage. Instead, China should have a coalition government, because it will be a "national revolutionary-democratic government, not a communist one. . . ." Nationalizing the land and property of the bourgeoisie would be a mistake.[214]

The Alliance with China

By early 1949 it was clear to Stalin that Mao's forces were going to win in China. This victory was understood by Stalin to be a huge boon to Soviet security, and that of socialism in general. He told Ivan Kovalev, his personal envoy to Mao, in May 1948, that "if socialism is victorious in China, and our countries go along the same path, then the victory of socialism in the world can be considered guaranteed. We will not be threatened by any contingencies."[215] Herein is concealed the ultimate rupture in identity relations. So long as the Soviet Union and China, as two socialist countries, were on "the same path," security and victory were assured. But, in just ten years, identity differences would result in disastrous results for Sino-Soviet relations.

In a January 1949 telegram to Mao, Stalin, while for at least the fourth time refusing to entertain Mao in the Soviet Union, sent Anastas Mikoian as his personal representative to meet with Mao, and recognized Mao's "victorious liberation war." Soviet understanding of China changed as it became clear that victory was close at hand. While Mikoian repeated Stalin's recommendation of a coalition government, he also urged Mao to collectivize the peasantry, not just expropriate landlords. China was to become more like the Soviet Union every day. At the March 1949 CCP CC Plenum, Mao made Chinese imitation of the Soviet Union official, thus making any future differences between Moscow and Beijing that much more consequential.[216]

---

[214] APRF f39 op1 d31, 298–99.
[215] Holloway, *Stalin and the Bomb*, 274.
[216] Heinzig, *The Soviet Union*, 140; Goncharov, Lewis, and Litai, *Uncertain Partners*, 39–45.

Another very significant identity that emerged for China during Mikoian's visit was China's role as vanguard for revolutionary movements in the decolonizing world; a division of labor was emerging, with the Soviet Union atop the hierarchy, responsible for revolutionary movements in the modern, developed West, and China, subordinate, but still responsible for national liberation movements in the East. It came about after Mao kept calling himself a "pupil of Stalin," inexperienced, a bad Marxist, etc. Finally, Mikoian told him that the Chinese experience was of "theoretical value for revolutionary movements in Asian countries," thus opening the door to a particular kind of alliance relationship.[217]

What would later become the topics of negotiation between Mao and Stalin during their first and only meeting in Moscow from December 1949 to February 1950 were also discussed by Mao and Mikoian. Mikoian telegrammed Moscow on February 6, 1949, reporting that Mao and the Chinese were surprised that the Soviets considered their treaties with China to be unequal, and expressed no interest in their revision.[218] But Mao did ask whether Inner and Outer Mongolia could be merged into one Chinese province, something neither Stalin nor any subsequent Soviet leader found imaginable, given the existence of the People's Republic of Mongolia. Mao also asked about Soviet military support for the PLA's efforts to crush the rebels in Sinkiang. Mikoian refused the request, but Liu Shaoqi raised it again with Stalin in July–August 1949 in Moscow, and Stalin assented.[219] Indeed, there was a significant increase in Soviet military aid to China, including military advisers and pilots, in the first half of 1949, antedating Mao's "lean to one side" speech on June 30, 1949, conventionally marked as the beginning of the Sino-Soviet alliance.[220]

Sandwiched between Mikoian's week with Mao in China and Mao's ten weeks with Stalin in Moscow was Liu Shaoqi's ten-week stay in Moscow in June–August 1949.[221] Liu, at the time the second-ranking member of the CCP behind Mao, raised the issue of the August 1945 Soviet treaty with the Kuomintang, but Stalin replied he didn't want to discuss its revision or renunciation yet, as it would allow Britain and the United States to selectively renege on all the agreements reached at Yalta.[222] However, he did agree to discuss it with Mao

---

[217] Heinzig, *The Soviet Union*, 148; Goncharov, Lewis, and Litai, *Uncertain Partners*, 46.

[218] Ledovskii, "Peregovory I. V. Stalina," 28.

[219] Zhihua, "Sino-Soviet Relations," 55–57. At this meeting with Liu, Stalin offered 40 Soviet fighter planes, as well advising that China "Sinicize" Sinkiang, and its borders more generally. Danilov and Pyzhikov, *Rozhdenie Svekhderzhavy*, 61–62.

[220] Goncharov, Lewis, and Litai, *Uncertain Partners*, 74.

[221] Ibid., 64 (arguing that Stalin met with the delegation six times); cf. Heinzig, *The Soviet Union*, 177 (arguing only two).

[222] Stalin's abiding fear of provoking the West resulted in his telegramming Mao in June 1949, warning against deploying the PLA too close to China's borders with Western colonies. Holloway, *Stalin and the Bomb*, 274.

during his upcoming visit, and offered to evacuate Port Arthur immediately, if the Chinese wished. Liu demurred.[223]

During Liu's visit, on July 25, Mao telegrammed Stalin declaring that "we need to seize Formosa" and asked to have 1,000 Chinese pilots trained in Moscow over the next six months or a year, and be supplied with 100 to 200 fighter planes and 40 to 80 bombers. Mao also requested that Stalin send volunteer pilots and covert military units to aid in the capture of Taiwan. Stalin refused the requests to aid in the liberation of Taiwan, saying it would entail conflict with both the US Navy and Air Force and would "provide a pretext for unleashing a new world war." He said instructors are available anytime, but the other aid requests should be thought about and discussed later. Stalin suggested to Mao, instead of invading the island, why not send special forces to foment rebellion? The latter might have been Stalin calling Mao's bluff, since Mao had assured Stalin of the ease with which the PLA could take Taiwan, since the masses would rally to the CCP's side.[224] Fear of provoking the United States also spurred Stalin's desire to hide the $300 million loan Moscow offered China, either as a loan to Manchuria or as a secret party to party agreement, to be formalized only when a new Chinese government was established. He also advised China not to join the Cominform.[225]

Other Soviet behavior manifested anxiety about unnecessarily provoking the United States in China. Stalin personally, for example, kept the official recognition of the PRC on October 2, 1949, a low-key matter. He even kept it off the front page of *Pravda*, overruling Gromyko. Moreover, to maintain legal niceties, Stalin had kept a Soviet ambassador, Nikolai Roshchin, in Nanking until September 30, 1949, despite repeated requests from Mao to remove this Soviet representative to the Kuomintang.[226]

Chinese subordination to Moscow was fully evident by this time. Prior to visiting Moscow, Liu had sent to Stalin a report, "On the Question of Relations between the CPSU and CCP," which asserted that "Mao and the CCP CC think that the CPSU is the headquarters of the international communist and workers' movement, and CCP is only the staff of one of the fronts. The interests of the

---

[223] Zhihua, "Sino-Soviet Relations," 57.

[224] Goncharov, Lewis, and Litai, *Uncertain Partners*, 69; Heinzig, *The Soviet Union*, 131; and Ledovskii, "Peregovory I. V. Stalina," 32–33. Yet again another case of an ally promising a short and easy war to entice its great power partner to participate.

[225] Heinzig, *The Soviet Union*, 179, 206.

[226] Ibid., 256. What is worse, Stalin appointed Roshchin, as the Soviet Union's first ambassador to the PRC, despite having been ambassador to the Nationalist government. In a January 1950 meeting with the head of the Soviet MFA's Far East section, I. F. Kurdiukov, Mao asked that Roshchin be replaced. The request was never passed on to Stalin. Ledovskii, "Na Diplomaticheskom Rabote v Kitae," 127. Only in July 1950, with the appointment of Pavel Iudin, did Mao get a Soviet ambassador to his liking.

parts must be subordinate to international interests, and therefore the CCP subordinates itself to the decisions of the CPSU. If differences emerge between the two parties, then the CCP, having expressed its viewpoint, will subordinate itself and will fulfill the decisions of the CPSU."[227] What could be better than that, from the viewpoint of Moscow? China had declared itself to be a peripheral oblast to the Moscow center.

But Stalin didn't endorse this kowtowing before Moscow. He reportedly said it seems strange to us, "the party of one state subordinating itself to the party of another.... It is impermissible.... You shouldn't take the thoughts we express as orders. They are a kind of fraternal advice.... We can advise you, but not order you, since we are insufficiently informed about the situation in China...."[228] Stalin instead repeatedly emphasized China's unique contribution to the world revolutionary movement—in the decolonizing world. It was during this meeting that Stalin and Liu explicitly agreed that China, not the Soviet Union, would be responsible for relations with, and aid to, Ho Chi Minh in Vietnam.[229] Stalin said that "Asians are looking to you with hope," and the CCP has many "pupils."[230] But Liu would have nothing to do with Stalin's elevation of China's role. At the farewell banquet for Gao Gang, Stalin proposed a toast in which he said, "While today you call us older brother, a younger brother can catch up and surpass him." But Liu protested and refused to raise his glass to this, exclaiming, "We will always learn from our older brother!"[231] What is more, in direct contravention of the cult of infallibility in place at home, Stalin admitted to Liu that "we know we have made ourselves a hindrance to you.... We may give you erroneous advice because we don't understand the real situation in your country. Whenever we err, you should let us know."[232]

---

[227] Goncharov, Lewis, and Litai, *Uncertain Partners*, 47.

[228] Rakhmanin, "Vzaimootnosheniia I. V. Stalina," 83.

[229] Ilya V. Gaiduk, *Confronting Vietnam: Soviet Policy toward the Indochina Conflict, 1954–1963* (Stanford: Stanford University Press, 2003), 2. Chen Jian, *Mao's China and the Cold War* (Chapel Hill: University of North Carolina Press, 2001), 120; and Zubok and Pleshakov, *Inside the Kremlin's Cold War*, 57.

[230] Heinzig, *The Soviet Union*, 207. Later, in a September 1952 meeting with Zhou Enlai, Stalin told him that "China must become the flagship of Asia. It [not the Soviet Union] should be supplying other Asian countries with specialists." Shu Guang Zhang, *Economic Cold War: America's Embargo against China and the Sino-Soviet Alliance, 1949–1963* (Washington: Woodrow Wilson Center Press, 2001), 109.

[231] Heinzig, *The Soviet Union*, 218.

[232] Ibid., 208. A very similar exchange occurred between Stalin and Zhou Enlai on September 19, 1952, with Zhou asking for orders and Stalin insisting on giving only advice. Ledovskii, "Stenogrammy Peregovorov," 85. In his February 10, 1948, conversation with Dimitrov, Kostov, Kardelj, and Djilas in Moscow, Stalin famously admitted to being wrong about China: "[T]hey turned out to be right; we turned out to be wrong...."

Stalin also tried to restrain Chinese enthusiasm for immediate socialist construction, as he had in Eastern Europe until 1947, and would in East Germany until 1952. He advised Liu to include the national bourgeoisie in the Chinese government and to not confiscate imperialist investment hastily.[233] Stalin endorsed moderation because of his understanding China as lower on the hierarchy of socialist development than Eastern European people's democracies, let alone the Soviet Union itself. In a February 1950 meeting on the new edition of Stalin's textbook on political economy, it was agreed that China still lagged behind on the road to socialism. It had only a dictatorship of "the proletariat and peasants" and had "feudal relations" in the countryside, not unlike the early stages of Soviet rule in Central Asia. They concluded that China was "still in the first phase of development."[234]

Finally, Mao arrived for his first, and only, visit with Stalin, on December 16, 1949, remaining in Moscow until February 17, 1950. Mao wasn't "abandoned" or given the cold shoulder by Stalin during his trip, contrary to earlier historiography on the subject. He stayed at "Blizhnaia," the dacha used by Stalin when he didn't stay at the Kremlin. Stalin met Mao the day he arrived, and then Mikoian and Vyshinsky on the 18th, Molotov and Mikoian on the 20th. Nikolai Fedorenko, MFA Far Eastern Department head, met him every day, and Kovalev met him mostly every day. At Stalin's birthday celebration at the Bolshoi Theater on December 21, Mao was given the seat of honor beside Stalin on his right, with Khrushchev on Stalin's left. He was next to Stalin at the banquet the following day and was the first foreign guest invited to speak.[235]

At the first meeting, on the afternoon of December 16, Stalin said revision of the 1945 treaty was not advisable, as it was part of the Yalta agreements, and any changes would afford a pretext to the United States and Britain to reopen other questions, such as the Kurile islands or Sakhalin. Stalin instead suggested keeping the treaty but withdrawing Soviet troops from Port Arthur. To Mao's request for Soviet pilots to help in the reconquest of Formosa, Stalin temporized, saying aid hasn't been ruled out, but we should consider its form. And then, invoking the well-known danger, he said, "What is most important here is to not give Americans a pretext to intervene...."[236] In late December, Mao complained to Kovalev

---

[233] Heinzig, *The Soviet Union* 201–02. Stalin's copy of Liu Shaoqi's report has numerous "Yes[ses]!" in Stalin's blue pencil beside passages that acknowledge China's long road to socialism ahead, and current demand for moderation. APRF f45 op1 d328.

[234] Ethan Pollock, *Stalin and the Soviet Science Wars* (Princeton: Princeton University Press, 2006), 180.

[235] Heinzig, *The Soviet Union* 268, 281–84.

[236] "Record of Conversation, Stalin and Mao Zedong, December 16, 1949," in *Brothers in Arms*, 315–16.

that they had come to Moscow for nothing: "Why had he come, just to eat, shit, and sleep every day?"[237] On January 2, 1950, Molotov and Mikoian told Mao that a new treaty could be negotiated.[238] Discussions between Mao and Stalin began on January 22, at which time Stalin said the Port Arthur agreement wasn't equitable, and that China and the Soviet Union should share equally in the control of the Changchun railroad.[239]

The Treaty of Friendship, Cooperation, and Mutual Assistance, signed on February 14, 1950, replacing the August 1945 treaty with the Nationalist government, resulted in the return of Port Arthur to China no later than December 31, 1951, instead of by 1975, as provided for in the 1945 treaty.[240] It also obligated both sides to offer military assistance if either was involved in military hostilities with Japan or its allies. China also got concessions on the Changchun railroad, as well as elimination of Soviet extraterritorial rights on Chinese soil.[241] The joint stock companies for the exploration and exploitation of Chinese mineral resources, suggested by China in January 1950, were agreed to by the Soviet side. But the "secret protocols" were the humiliating "bitter pills," as Mao referred to them some years later, that reeked of the "unequal treaties" of the nineteenth century. For example, China agreed to keep all foreigners and foreign investment, other than Soviet, out of Manchuria and Sinkiang, and the Soviets had the right to move troops on the Manchurian railroad without informing China, while China, despite repeated demands during the talks, didn't enjoy reciprocal rights. Stalin himself introduced the idea of prohibiting "citizens of third states" in Manchuria and Sinkiang, and "[t]he Chinese delegation met the idea with bewildered silence."[242]

On January 8, Soviets advised Mao to demand the Kuomintang seat on the UN Security Council (UNSC). The Soviet Union began boycotting UNSC meetings on January 16.[243] At the January 22 meeting, Stalin agreed with Mao's proposal to occupy Tibet.[244]

---

[237] Heinzig, *The Soviet Union*, 288.

[238] Zhihua, "Sino-Soviet Relations," 57–58.

[239] "Record of Conversation, Stalin and Mao Zedong, January 22, 1950," in *Brothers in Arms*, 325–326.

[240] Later in 1950, the Soviets agreed to evacuate Dairen by the beginning of 1951. In September 1952, China asked Moscow to prolong its troop presence in Port Arthur, and Moscow did so until May 1955. Heinzig, *The Soviet Union*, 356–57.

[241] On September 15, 1952, Stalin agreed with Zhou Enlai to transfer railroad to China by the end of that year. Ledovskii, "Stenogrammy Peregovorov," 81.

[242] Ledovskii, "Na Diplomaticheskom Rabote v Kitae," 121–26; and Heinzig, *The Soviet Union*, 349–58, 373–76.

[243] Heinzig, *The Soviet Union*, 299.

[244] Ledovskii, "Peregovory I. V. Stalina," 41.

The Korean War

> The North Koreans have lost nothing in this war except the victims.[245]
> —Stalin, August 25, 1952

When Stalin was asked at Yalta in February 1945 what the Soviet Union wanted for participation in the war against Japan, he asked for nothing in Korea. At Potsdam, six months later, he agreed to the division of Korea at the 38th parallel, and ordered a stop to the Soviet advance weeks before US soldiers had even arrived in the South. In September 1947, Moscow suggested a mutual withdrawal of foreign forces and withdrew all Soviet forces by December 1948, seven months before the United States completed its exit.[246] In late 1949, Stalin even accepted his ambassador's proposal to dismantle Soviet naval and air bases in North Korea.[247]

Consistent with the caution shown toward the Chinese civil war unfolding next door, the Soviets refused to sign a treaty of alliance with North Korea, holding out hope for an ultimately united Korea. Pursuant to Kim's persistent pleas for Soviet help in a war of reunification against the South, including Kim's presentation of a plan of attack to Stalin in March 1949,[248] Stalin asked the Soviet embassy in Pyongyang to evaluate a possible attack by the North. Its September 14, 1949, report was pessimistic about North Korean prospects. The Politburo two weeks later agreed with the conclusions made by its foreign ministry officials in North Korea.

Its conclusions were included in a subsequent telegram to Kim. It argued that the North didn't enjoy military superiority, the guerilla movement and popular uprising had not been prepared in the South, and "the possibility of a prolonged war would give the Americans an excuse to interfere in Korean affairs."[249] Stalin's consultations with Mao in early October resulted in a telegram on October 27 from Gromyko to the Soviet ambassador in Pyongyang, Terentii

---

[245] Stalin, arguing against accepting armistice conditions, August 25, 1952.

[246] Weathersby, "Sovetskie Tseli v Koree," 315–322.

[247] Zhihua, "Sino-Soviet Relations," 48.

[248] Stalin replied at the time that "it is not necessary to attack the South, although in the case of a southern attack on the North, it would be possible to go over on the counteroffensive." Mastny, *The Cold War*, 90.

[249] Zhihua, "Sino-Soviet Relations," 50.

Shtykov, warning the North Korean leadership, once again, to cease provocations on the border.[250]

Despite repeatedly verbally restraining Kim, Soviet military aid to North Korea accelerated throughout 1949.[251] On January 5, 1950, Truman announced the end of military assistance to the Nationalist Chinese on Taiwan. A week later, Secretary of State Dean Acheson gave a speech in which he removed both Taiwan and South Korea from the US defense perimeter in Asia. On January 30, Stalin telegrammed Kim, agreeing, finally, to his request to discuss his invasion plans in April in Moscow. While the sequence certainly looks like a compelling causal story, it should be said that nobody has yet turned up any Soviet documentation linking these two American speeches to Stalin's change of heart.[252]

During his secret March 30–April 25, 1950, visit to Moscow, Kim Jong Il promised Stalin a fait accompli, a war so short that the United States would not have time to intervene effectively. In particular, he reassured Stalin that it would be a surprise attack and last three days; 200,000 South Korean communists would rise up in support of the invasion; and southern guerillas would support the North Korean army. Not only Soviet, but even Chinese help would not be necessary, Kim argued.[253] Stalin approved the attack, but told Kim the Soviets would not fight, even if the United States intervened, and any military assistance would have to come from China, reflecting the new division of labor forged between Moscow and Beijing a year earlier.[254] North Korea was so convinced of its short war theory that it didn't even plan beyond 30 days.[255]

Kim went from Moscow to China, visiting Mao on May 13. The Chinese appealed to Moscow for clarification, and Vyshinsky cabled Mao that Stalin had indeed approved Kim's plans, "but it is up to you, China, to decide." Not only did Mao approve, releasing some 70,000 Koreans from the PLA to help North Korea,

---

[250] Evgueni Bajanov, "Assessing the Politics of the Korean War, 1949–1951," *Cold War International History Project Bulletin* 6–7 (Winter 1995/1996): 54, 87; and Andrei M. Ledovskii, "Stalin, Mao Tszedun i Koreiskaia Voina 1950–1953 Godov," *Novaia i Noveishaia Istoriia* 5 (2005): 92. It should be kept in mind that both the North's Kim and the South's Syngman Rhee had continually claimed sovereignty over all of Korea, and sporadic military clashes between the two across the 38th parallel were a common occurrence right up to the onset of the war in June 1950. As Gaddis concluded, both Rhee and Kim tried to push their Great Power patrons into a war, and Stalin ultimately took the bait. John Lewis Gaddis, *We Now Know: Rethinking Cold War History* (Oxford: Oxford University Press, 1997), 70–75.
[251] Zhihua, "Sino-Soviet Relations," 48.
[252] Ibid., 52.
[253] Ibid., 53, 66.
[254] Goncharov, Lewis, and Litai, *Uncertain Partners*, 137.
[255] Ibid., 155.

but prepared to invade Taiwan, too. Mao further assured Kim that the United States wouldn't intervene as "the US won't risk World War III for such a small territory."[256]

Manifesting his continued concern about the United States, Stalin refused to provide even military advisers to North Korea before the attack.[257] The war began on June 25. By June 28, Seoul had fallen. Meanwhile, Stalin was pushing Kim to advance faster, fearing a US intervention otherwise. By July 5, Stalin pressed China to deploy nine divisions on its border with Korea, just in case, promising air cover.[258] Buoyed by North Korea's initial success, Stalin termed the July 13 British proposal of a return to the 38th parallel "impudent and unacceptable." Stalin again requested those nine Chinese divisions, promising Soviet air cover.[259] Meanwhile, China had already felt out India about exchanging a return to the 38th parallel for the permanent seat on the UNSC. In his reply to Stalin, Mao ignored the request for the nine divisions but thanked him for the offer of Soviet air support.[260]

At this time, Stalin was very satisfied with the turn of events in Korea. In his August 27 rejection of Gottwald's[261] suggestion that boycotting the UNSC meetings on Korea was a mistake, Stalin outlined the following strategic logic:

> America has now involved itself in a military intervention in Korea, an opportunity to commit new stupidities so that public opinion can see the true face of the American government. Now hardly any honest person can doubt that America is an oppressor and aggressor, and that they are not as militarily strong as they advertise. Besides, it is clear that the USA is now distracted from Europe. Isn't this a plus for us in the balance of world forces? Unconditionally.
>
> Let's assume that the American government will tie itself up in the Far East and involve China in the struggle for freedom in Korea. What can happen then?
>
> First, America can't deal with China's huge armed forces. . . . [I]f only America should overextend itself in this struggle. Second, America will be unable to launch World War III in the near future. . . . There will be time to strengthen socialism in Europe. . . . [262]

---

[256] Zhihua, "Sino-Soviet Relations," 67; Mastny, *The Cold War*, 94; Ledovskii, "Stalin, Mao Tszedun," 94; Weathersby, "New Russian Documents," 39; At the time of the Korean War, Andrei M. Ledovskii was Soviet consul-general in Mukden, China.

[257] Zhihua, "Sino-Soviet Relations," 62.

[258] Weathersby, "New Russian Documents," 43; and Mastny, *The Cold War*, 99.

[259] Ledovskii, "Stalin, Mao Tszedun," 100.

[260] Ibid., 101.

[261] I must say I have not come across another instance of an Eastern European ally having the courage/audacity/risk-acceptance to directly criticize any of Stalin's foreign policy decisions.

[262] Ledovskii, "Stalin, Mao Tszedun," 96–97.

Given the many rewards Stalin expected the war in Korea to bring the Soviet Union and the socialist camp, he would plausibly have been dismayed over the success of the Inchon landing in South Korea behind North Korean lines on September 15.

Just three days after the landing, Stalin urged North Korea to redeploy its forces from the southeast to the defense of Seoul and to build air defenses for Pyongyang, warning that the Korean Peoples' Army (KPA) was in danger of being destroyed by unchallenged US air power and a double envelopment by US forces. But North Korea ignored the advice for over a week. Seoul fell to US forces less than two weeks after the landing. The same day, the Soviet Politburo decided the KPA should retreat back across the 38th parallel and concentrate on defending North Korea. Kim appealed to the Soviet Union and China on October 1 for direct military intervention to save North Korea.[263] Stalin asked Mao the same day to send five to six Chinese divisions, with Soviet air cover.[264] The initial Chinese response was negative, arguing that it was too dangerous, Chinese forces were too weak, they should wait, North Korea can be lost, and Kim can lead a guerilla war.[265] On October 5, the Soviet Politburo resigned itself to the loss of North Korea, not wishing a direct military conflict with the United States. But Stalin still urged Mao to intervene, arguing that China would never get Taiwan back if the United States occupied all of Korea, and that war with the United States (if China fights it) was better now, than later, when Japan recovers.[266] On October 9, Mao tentatively agreed to ultimately send nine divisions, with Soviet air cover, the same day US forces crossed the 38th parallel.[267] Not until October 13 did Mao agree to intervene, and Chinese forces crossed the border on October 24.[268]

On November 24, MacArthur began his offensive toward the Yalu River border between North Korea and China. The Chinese counterattack resulted in Chinese forces retaking Pyongyang on December 4. The Chinese having the US forces on the run, Stalin agreed with Mao's conditions for a cease-fire on December 7: withdrawal of all foreign troops from Korea, withdrawal of US forces from Taiwan and the straits, the UNSC seat for the PRC, and a conference on a peace treaty with Japan.[269] Through December, both Stalin and Mao pushed the Chinese

---

[263] Ledovskii, "Stalin, Mao Tszedun," 103.

[264] Aleksandr V. Vorontsov, "'Okazat Voennuiu Pomoshch Koreiskim Tovarishcham,'" *Istochnik* 1 (1996): 124–30.

[265] Ledovskii, "Stalin, Mao Tszedun," 104.

[266] Ibid., 105; and Vorontsov, "Okazat Voennuiu Pomoshch," 132–33.

[267] Vorontsov, "Okazat Voennuiu Pomoshch," 134.

[268] Alexandre Y. Mansourov, "Stalin, Mao, Kim, and China's Decision to Enter the Korean War, September 16–October 15, 1950: New Evidence from the Russian Archives," *Cold War International History Project Bulletin* Issues 6–7 (Winter 1995/1996): 95–104; and Ledovskii, "Stalin, Mao Tszedun," 110.

[269] Weathersby, "New Russian Documents," 52.

commander, Peng Dehuai to capture Seoul and push US forces farther south. On December 31, Chinese forces retook Seoul.[270]

The front having roughly stabilized at the 38th parallel over the last six months, on June 5, 1951, the Soviet ambassador to the UN, Iakob Malik, informed George Kennan that the Soviet government would like a peaceful resolution of the Korean War as soon as possible.[271] The same day, Stalin telegrammed Mao to not "accelerate the war, since a drawn out war gives the possibility for Chinese troops to study contemporary warfare, shakes up the Truman regime in America, and harms the military prestige of Anglo-American soldiers." If we were to summarize positions on a possible armistice from May 1951 to June 1953, we could say the Soviets wished to prolong the war; the Chinese wavered, but ultimately supported a prolonged war unless the United States made significant concessions, and the North Koreans increasingly wished to end the war as soon as possible.[272]

By July 1951, Stalin agreed to Mao's negotiating position, dropping the issues of Taiwan and the UNSC seat, but demanding a cease-fire, POW exchange, withdrawal of all foreign forces, and a return of refugees.[273] In August 1952, Zhou Enlai and Stalin met in Moscow, mostly to coordinate strategy in Korea. Zhou said that the Americans wanted to return 76,000 POWs, while keeping 13,000 Chinese. The Koreans wanted this deal, arguing that their daily losses were greater than the number of POWs whose return the North Koreans, Chinese, and Soviets were arguing for. Zhou reported that Mao was for continuation of the war as it "hinders US preparation for World War III." Stalin agreed.[274]

After endorsing Kim's decision to launch the war, Stalin did all he could to reduce the probability of a direct military clash between Soviet and US forces. Most obviously, he induced Chinese forces to do all of the ground combat, while Soviet military engagement remained in the air.[275] Stalin refused to allow Soviet Koreans to fight on the side of the KPA. US bombing of a Soviet airbase 100 kilometers inside the Soviet border resulted in a quiet Soviet protest, not in a pretext to deepen Soviet involvement. The redeployment of Soviet air defense forces to Manchuria was done in secret, and the planes Soviets flew had North Korean markings, their pilots wore North Korean uniforms, and on the radio, they spoke only Korean.[276]

---

[270] Holloway, *Stalin and the Bomb*, 284.
[271] Ibid., 288.
[272] Weathersby, "New Russian Documents," 52–59, 71–78; Mastny, *The Cold War*, 124–48.
[273] Weathersby, "New Russian Documents," 67.
[274] Ledovskii, "Stenogrammy Peregovorov," 74–75.
[275] During the war, the Soviet Union supplied China with materiel for 64 army and 22 air force divisions, leaving China with $650 million to repay, which they did so by 1965. Jian, *Mao's China*, 61.
[276] Weathersby, "Sovetskie Tseli v Koree," 327–29.

E. The Irrelevant Third World

We might reasonably expect that the decolonizing world would have been seen by the Soviet leadership as the richest possible source of allies against the United States, a huge opportunity for an expansionist Soviet Union to challenge the prevailing status quo in the imperialist camp. On the contrary, under Stalin, given his fear of difference, and distrust for any but the most loyal communists who were committed to the Soviet model in detail, these nationalist leaders of anti-colonial movements were not regarded as potential allies, but rather as potential lackeys of the imperialists.

An August 1945 conversation between Molotov and the French ambassador to the Soviet Union, Georges Catroux, is illustrative. The latter asked Molotov about the Soviet attitude toward the re-establishment of French sovereignty in Indochina. Molotov asked incredulously why anyone would oppose this? Catroux answered that Roosevelt opposed it.[277]

Stalin resisted even recognizing Ho Chi Minh's Democratic Republic of Vietnam (DRV) in January 1950, in contrast to the PRC's enthusiastic and public acclamation. When Ho visited Moscow in February 1950, while Mao was still there, he had to do so in secret, and he was told to make any aid requests to China, not the Soviet Union.[278] Stalin even later said he regretted recognizing the DRV, saying he had done so too hastily.[279]

Now, of course, one can plausibly argue that Molotov and Stalin still thought of France as a major player in Europe, an important potential ally on managing the occupation of their common German enemy. But this could not explain similar attitudes toward rebellious colonies held by other imperial powers, or the continued indifference toward these revolutions after the lines in Europe were already drawn. Scholars who have made the connection between Soviet hopes for French help on Germany and Soviet restraint on Indochina or Algeria have not cited any primary evidence in making the claim.[280] My claim that Soviet indifference toward Vietnam was just part of a more general indifference to the decolonizing world, because of fear of its likely betrayal of socialism and the Soviet Union, seems more plausible, as it accounts for a wide range of outcomes, not only Soviet attitudes toward national liberation movements (NLMs) in French colonies.

---

[277] Kynin and Laufer, "Vvedenie,", 225.

[278] Goncharov, Lewis, and Litai, *Uncertain Partners*, 107–08; Jian, *Mao's China*, 121.

[279] Heinzig, *The Soviet Union*, 306.

[280] I have in mind Goncharov, Lewis, and Litai, *Uncertain Partners*, 107, and Gaiduk, *Confronting Vietnam*, 3. For example, the latter argues the Soviets didn't want to undermine the French Communist Party's chances of joining a French government. But the PCF had already been ousted from a coalition government in May 1947, three years before Ho Chi Minh was given the cold shoulder in Moscow.

It is interesting to see how Stalin regarded UN trusteeships. The issue arose at the November 1946 New York CFM meeting, and Molotov cabled Stalin to say he saw no reason for the Soviet Union to participate in them. On the contrary, Stalin cabled back, we should express our interest, so we can use them as bargaining chips to be traded on issues of more importance. To ensure Molotov got the point about Soviet lack of interest in decolonization per se, he explained that "we shouldn't be more leftist than the leaders of these territories. They... mostly are corrupt and care not so much about the independence of their territories, as the preservation of their privileges.... The time is not yet ripe for us to clash over the fate of these territories...."[281] In one of his very few available commentaries on revolutionary prospects in the "East," Stalin wrote a letter to the Indonesian Communist Party, cautioning it to "reject revolutionary Leftism," and, instead, concentrate on political work among the people.[282] He went on to remind its members that they were not China; they did not share a border with the Soviet Union, who could provide them refuge from encirclement.[283]

Ironically, given future alignment patterns in the Middle East, and the anti-cosmopolitan campaign that began in 1948 in the Soviet Union, the one anti-colonial movement Stalin did support was that of Israel. Soviet Ambassador to the UN Andrei Gromyko's General Assembly speech in June 1947 calling for an Israeli state in Palestine was a moving appeal for justice for the world's Jews: "An enormous number of surviving European Jews have ended up without homeland, shelter, or means of existence. Hundreds of thousands wander around different countries in search of refuge. The greater part of them are in refugee camps.... It is time, not in words, but in deeds, to help these people.... The fact that not a single west European state was able to defend the elementary rights of the Jewish people, and defend it from the violence of fascist butchers explains the aspiration of Jews to create their own state. It is impossible to justify the denial of such a right for Jews."[284]

Not only did the Soviet Union immediately recognize the state of Israel on May 15, 1948, but had covertly supplied the Jewish resistance with weapons through Czechoslovakia and Yugoslavia for years after the war. The recruitment of Jewish fighters and purchase of arms was so obvious in Prague that US Secretary of State George Marshall protested to the Czechoslovakian foreign minister, Clementis, accusing Prague of violating the UN arms embargo on Palestine. In the autumn of 1948, the Czechoslovakian consulate in Israel gave transit visas to members of the

---

[281] Vladimir O. Pechatnov and Vladislav M. Zubok, "The Allies are pressing on you to break your will, " Cold War International History Project Working Paper (Washington, D.C.: Wilson Center, 1999), 22.
[282] Gaiduk, *Confronting Vietnam*, 8.
[283] Westad, *The Global Cold War*, 67.
[284] Zhukov, *Stalin: Tainy Vlasti*, 475.

terrorist Stern gang so they could flee to Prague after assassinating the UN envoy to Palestine, Count Folke Bernadotte.[285] The Soviet Union also supported Israel diplomatically at the UN during the war that ensued after Israel's declaration of independence. Soviet UN Ambassador Yakov Malik, for example, called for a cease-fire in the war in November 1948, leaving Israel in possession of previously Arab territory.

The case of Soviet support for Israel clearly runs contrary to my hypotheses about the link between societal understandings of Soviet identity and relations with the external world. If we recall from chapter 2, Solomon Mikhoels was arrested in January 1948, popular anti-Semitism was tolerated throughout the media and in official institutions, and in November 1948, the Jewish Anti-Fascist Committee was shut down. All this occurred during staunch Soviet support for Israel, and months before the Soviet Union ended the covert supply of weaponry to Israel in February 1949.[286]

Consistent, however, with the more general Soviet indifference to the decolonizing world, ending support for Israel didn't result in support for its Arab neighbors or the Palestinians. When asked about the Soviet position on aid for Palestinian refugees, Gromyko replied that the Soviet Union wouldn't participate "since this problem was created by other countries."[287] The overthrow of Egypt's King Farouk in July 1952 went almost unremarked in Moscow.[288]

F. Relations with the United States

> The main weapons of America are stuffed animals, cigarettes, and other goods for sale.
> —Stalin to Zhou Enlai, August 1952, Moscow

Stalin made this statement to Zhou Enlai with ridicule, but in fact he had put his finger on one of the prime sources of the US advantage in the Cold War: its economic prowess. The United States was the Soviet Union's most Significant Other in world politics from 1945 until 1991. Indeed, both often referred to themselves as "the only two great powers" in the world.[289] Indeed, any other categorization of

---

[285] Ibid., 462–465. The assassination of Bernadotte had been approved by none other than Yitzhak Shamir, future Likud prime minister of Israel. Bowyer Bell, "Assassination in International Politics," *International Studies Quarterly* 16, no. 1 (March 1972): 59–82.

[286] Zhukov, *Stalin: Tainy Vlasti*, 469.

[287] Volokitina et al., *Sovetskii Faktor v Vostochnoi Evrope*, 134.

[288] Gaddis, *We Now Know*, 166.

[289] For example, General Lucius Clay in conversation with Marshal Sokolovsky in Berlin in October 1945. Kynin and Laufer, "Vvedenie: Politika SSSR po Germanskomu (9 Maia 1945g.—3 Oktiabria 1946g.)," 248. US Ambassador Walter Bedell Smith in conversation with Sokolovsky and Semenov in Moscow in March 1946. Kynin and Laufer, "Vvedenie: Politika SSSR po Germanskomu (9 Maia 1945g.—3 Oktiabria 1946g.)," 435.

the Soviet Union was a violation of the hierarchical and patriarchal order of things. As Molotov told the Soviet ambassador to the United States a few days after Truman's announcement of aid to Greece and Turkey, such declarations will not "convert us into obedient good little boys."[290] Soviet relations with every other country were in some way understood in relationship to Soviet relations with the United States, or imperialism. All the foregoing discussions could have been presented with the United States as a player, but most central in this relationship were the fate of Germany and Soviet security in Eastern Europe. Conditioning these relations were Soviet expectations of a new world war with the United States, and concern that Moscow, or its allies, not unnecessarily provoke the United States into a more forceful posture against the Soviet Union or its allies.

1. Fear of a New War with the United States

It seems safe to say that Soviet leaders never feared that the United States would attack the Soviet Union, either conventionally or atomically. One material indicator of how confident the Soviet Union was of US intentions was the reduction of Soviet armed forces from 11 to 3 million between 1945 and 1948, and a decline in the military budget from 138 to 55 billion rubles in the same period. Even during the four years of American atomic monopoly, Stalin appears to have been unconcerned about the possibility of an unprovoked US attack on the Soviet Union. He thought, for example, that the United States had only a few atomic bombs in any case, maybe five or six. In fact the United States had nine by mid 1946.[291]

Moreover, Stalin was unimpressed by the destruction wrought on Hiroshima and Nagasaki. The reports he received from Japan attributed the level of destruction to the flammability of wood and paper houses, Japan's lack of air defenses, the lack of strategic warning, and the failure to evacuate civilians. Soviet military planning in the early postwar years took all these Japanese vulnerabilities into account. Civilian defense, strategic warning, and bombing of US bombers in theater before they could take off to deliver their atomic munitions were the nucleus of early Soviet postwar planning.[292]

Nevertheless Stalin both devoted precious resources to the acceleration of the Soviet atomic program, as well as expressed relief at its successful test on August 29, 1949, telling one of its main "fathers," Igor Kurchatov, that "if we had been a year or 18 months later, we would surely have felt it on ourselves," perhaps

---

[290] Nikolai V. Novikov, *Vospominaniia Diplomata* (Moscow: Politizdat, 1989), 379.
[291] Holloway, *Stalin and the Bomb*, 152–53.
[292] Ibid., 227–32.

reflecting fear of the chatter in the United States about the expedience of a preventive war against the Soviet Union.[293]

Stalin's other source of "hope" against a US attack was that, theoretically speaking, inter-imperialist wars were inevitable, but not imperialist wars against the Soviet Union. The latter could only occur indirectly, as a result of the former. Underlying this hope, besides Lenin's theory of imperialism, was Stalin's conviction that the US economy was in another state of capitalist crisis, and so would be forced to compete with Britain, and other imperialist powers, for markets to exploit. This would explain his view that the United States was trying to repress German economic development, that denial of the Marshall Plan to Eastern European allies would deal a blow to the US economy, and that the US was desperate to trade with Eastern Europe and China. Talking with Sergei Eisenstein about his sequel to *Ivan the Terrible*, Stalin offered his theory of US warmaking: "Americans bombed Czechoslovakian industry. They adhered to this line all across Europe. For them it was important to destroy industry that competed with them. They bombed with gusto!"[294]

What Stalin and the Soviet leadership apparently never felt was fear that the United States would attack the Soviet Union, or that there was any high probability of war between the two countries. Of more than a few direct quotes from Stalin, with many different interlocutors, only once did he express fear of a war with the United States. In August 1948, for example, despite tensions over the unification of the Western zones in Germany in March 1948, the Soviet surface blockade of West Berlin initiated on April 1 and the June 4 US Senate passage of the Vandenberg Resolution committing the United States to the stationing of troops in Europe, Malenkov told Pietro Nenni, general secretary of the Italian Socialist Party, in August 1948 that the Soviets were convinced of a low probability of war.[295]

In a May 1949 conversation with his envoy to Mao, Ivan Kovalev, Stalin said that "war isn't advantageous for the imperialists.... They aren't ready to fight.... America is less ready to attack the USSR than the USSR is to repulse an attack...."[296] While Stalin warned Togliatti in January 1951 that a new world war could break out at any moment,[297] in February Stalin told a journalist that "the peace movement can prevent a new world war."[298]

---

[293] Ibid., 271.

[294] Andrei Artizov and Oleg Naumov, eds., *Vlast i Khudozhestvennaia Intelligentsiia: Dokumenty TsK RKP(b)-VKP(b), VChK-OGPU-NKVD, o Kulturnoi Politike, 1917–1953 gg.* (Moscow: Demokratiia, 1999), 615.

[295] Pons, "Cold War in Europe," 22.

[296] Holloway, *Stalin and the Bomb*, 263–64.

[297] Pons, "Cold War in Europe," 25.

[298] Holloway, *Stalin and the Bomb*, 288.

In discussing the Korean War with Zhou Enlai in Moscow in August 1952, Stalin asserted:

> The Korean War has shown the weakness of the Americans.... Americans aren't at all capable of conducting a big war, especially after Korea. All their power is in planes and the atomic bomb.... America can't beat tiny Korea.... Every American soldier is a speculator.... The Germans conquered France in 20 days. The United States, already for two years, can't deal with tiny Korea. What kind of power is that? They want to subjugate the world, but can't deal with tiny Korea. No, Americans don't know how to fight.... They place their hopes on the atomic bomb and bombing, but you can't win a war like that. You need ground forces, but their ground forces are few and weak. They fight with little Korea, but in the United States they are already crying. What will happen if they start a big war? Then, perhaps, they all will cry."[299]

2. Fear of Provoking the United States

As was seen from Stalin's discussions with Eastern European and Chinese leaders, his fear of the United States continued after expectations of some kind of co-hegemony with Washington had been dashed. Stalin criticized the Bulgarian leadership in August 1947 for signing a treaty with Yugoslavia before peace treaties had been signed between the Allies and Yugoslavia, Czechoslovakia, and Poland, since this just gave a pretext for the "US to increase support for Greece and Turkey." Replying to his "Great Friend" Stalin, Dimitrov agreed to table the treaty.[300] At the same meeting in March 1948 Stalin told Yugoslavian representatives Kardelj and Djilas to not deploy an army division in Albania; otherwise, both the English and Americans would have a pretext to intervene.[301] Stalin advised the East German leadership in December 1948 not to join the Cominform as "one shouldn't give new arguments to one's enemies."[302]

---

[299] Ledovskii, "Stenogrammy Peregovorov," 75.

[300] Dimitrov, *The Diary of Georgi Dimitrov*, 423. "Velikii Drug" or "Great Friend" was the code name for Stalin in Dimitrov's telegrams to Moscow.

[301] Gibianskii, "Na Poroge Pervogo Raskola," 99.

[302] "Nuzhno Idti k Soltsializmu," 22.

3. Germany and Eastern Europe

What becomes a central problem in relations between the United States and the Soviet Union—the Stalinization of Eastern Europe—was born during the wartime conferences, when it was collectively agreed that these regimes would be simultaneously "free and friendly toward the Soviet Union." This was oxymoronic. Somehow, Roosevelt and Churchill either believed, or disingenuously repeated the expectation, that Eastern Europeans would freely choose to be friendly to Moscow, and Stalin repeated that such friendly regimes would be freely chosen. Perhaps a useful myth to keep the coalition together, it was a delayed action mine in the relationship, as Western publics were increasingly horrified by the Stalinization of Eastern Europe, and Stalin felt increasingly betrayed by Western insistence that these governments be populated by parties and individuals he felt were hostile to the Soviet Union.

Given the level of destruction suffered by the Soviet economy, the US suspension of Lend-Lease in May 1945 was a serious blow. According to Gosplan, Lend-Lease and imports accounted for 55 percent of trucks and cars, 21 percent of tractors, 42 percent of locomotives, 41 percent of aluminum, 99 percent of tin, and all the natural rubber used in the Soviet Union from 1941 to 1945. Lend-Lease was worth about $11 billion and in 1944 was fully 19 percent of Soviet GNP.[303] So, although, the Truman Administration cut all Lend-Lease recipients off at the same time, the shock done to the already reeling Soviet economy was massive, and doubtless underappreciated in Washington. This came along with oddly protracted negotiations over a $5 billion US loan to the Soviet Union that had been promised by Roosevelt at both Teheran and Yalta.[304] Instead, the Soviet Union was granted a credit of $244 million in October 1945.

In September 1945 at the London CFM meeting, US Secretary of State James Byrnes raised the possibility of a US-Soviet treaty that would "keep Germany disarmed for 20–25 years." Informed by Molotov of the US proposal, Stalin replied that, while it was "hard to reject," Molotov should ask for a pact against Japan, as well.[305] In June 1946 Molotov sent a memo to Stalin on Byrnes's proposed treaty, after gathering comments from many MFA officials. Molotov found nothing good in the proposal he claimed was pursuing the following goals: reduce the time Germany is occupied; reduce Soviet reparations; weaken

---

[303] Danilov and Pyzhikov, *Rozhdenie Svekhderzhavy*, 122–23.

[304] Stalin expressed his confusion over both Lend-Lease and the elusive credits when Secretary of State George Marshall visited Moscow in April 1947. Kynin and Laufer, "Vvedenie: Politika SSSR," 356.

[305] Volokotina et al., *Moskva i Vostochnaia Evropa*, 33; Pechatnov and Zubok, "The Allies are pressing," 5.

control over Germany; weaken Soviet influence in Germany; preserve German economic and military power; accelerate Germany's potential so as to use it against the Soviet Union; and re-examine all Allied decisions on Germany.[306]

In the discussions leading up to Molotov's memo Marshal Zhukov weighed in, arguing a demilitarized Germany would be followed by US demands that Soviet troops leave Poland and the Balkans. Molotov's deputy, Solomon Lozovsky (later executed in the Leningrad Affair), expressed fear of economic competition with the West, as the troop withdrawal would "lead to US economic domination of Germany."[307] Perhaps the unlucky Lozovsky was most prescient, as it would be the US economic threat to Soviet gains in Eastern Europe, or rather the alacrity with which Eastern Europeans welcomed such a threat, that would prove most alarming to Moscow.

In September 1946, perhaps in response to the speech given by Secretary of State Byrnes on September 6 in Stuttgart announcing a turn in US policy in Germany from occupation to reconstruction, Molotov instructed Nikolai Novikov, then ambassador to the United States, to join him in Paris for the CFM meeting. He then asked Novikov to write a memorandum on the state of US-Soviet relations, in effect dictating what should be in it. In it Novikov warned Moscow that US intentions in Germany were to rapidly withdraw from western Germany, leaving an ally of the United States in its place.[308]

Just a month after Britain and the United States announced the unification of their zones of occupation in western Germany on January 1, 1947, Stalin met with Piech, Ulbricht and Grotewohl. Stalin elaborated on what he took to be US and British plans for Germany. He argued that they feared Germany's rise as a global competitor on world markets, and so were for its underdevelopment, division, and weakness. The USSR opposed this because A) German and Japanese recovery would lead to better and cheaper goods on world markets; B) an economically repressed Germany will only be a revanchist Germany; and C) the USSR sympathizes with German workers who deserve to live better. Stalin suggested in the worst case, the eastern zone would have to be unified, and promised to delay reparations, end dismantling German industry, and reduce the number of Soviet armed forces on East German territory.[309] This line of argumentation contradicted Molotov's memorandum rejecting the Byrnes proposal

---

[306] Kynin and Laufer, "Vvedenie: Politika SSSR po Germanskomu (9 Maia 1945g.—3 Oktiabria 1946g.)," 575.

[307] Pechatnov and Zubok, "The Allies are pressing," 18.

[308] Loth, "Stalin's Plans," 28; and Noikov, *Vospominaniia Diplomata*.

[309] "'Nasha Liniia Takaia . . . ' Dokumenty o vstreche IV Stalina s rukovoditeliami SEPG. Ian-fev 1947g." *Istoricheskii Arkhiv* 4 (1994): 40; Loth, "Stalin's Plans," 26–27; and Kynin and Laufer, "Vvedenie," 247–60.

just six months before, in which it was argued the United States was trying to make a German counterweight to the Soviet Union in Europe.[310]

While Molotov interpreted Truman's enunciation of his eponymous doctrine on March 12, 1947, as evidence that the United States would support reactionary regimes and try to subvert Soviet allies in Eastern Europe, the real threat to Soviet positions in Eastern Europe was to come from a less expected source: an offer of economic aid.[311] The US offer of economic aid to all European countries reinforced Soviet fears of losing Eastern Europe. By shifting, if unintentionally, the currency of the competition from military to economic power, the United States amplified Soviet insecurities about the possible erosion of the Soviet position in Eastern Europe and accelerated the process of Stalinization—of creating in Eastern Europe domestic orders as closely imitative of Soviet identity as possible.

Moreover, Marshall Plan aid recipients would have to open themselves up to hundreds, if not thousands, of American and Western European officials who would assist in the distribution of that aid, this at a time when Stalin at home was doing everything possible to reduce his population's exposure to the noxious influence of Western culture. This fear of exposure to the West was a major incentive to prohibit Eastern European allies from accepting ERP aid. After all, at the end of his life, Stalin even accused Molotov and Mikoian of having "fallen under the influence of Western imperialist countries." Both having been in America, "they returned from there under the great impression of the economic might of America.... They were apparently frightened by the overwhelming power they saw in America...."[312] Not only was the ERP understood as possibly corrosive of the necessary socialist orders in Eastern Europe, but given Stalin's theory of imperialism, the United States needed the ERP to sustain its tottering capitalist economy.[313]

On July 7, 1947, Secretary of State George Marshall replaced Directive JCS (Joint Chiefs of Staff) 1067 of July 17, 1945, which officially governed US occupation policy in Germany, with Directive JCS 1779, the latter advocating a

---

[310] Consistent with this view is SVAG's report to Molotov on US intentions, delivered on February 8, 1947. Kynin and Laufer, "Vvedenie: Politika SSSR," 266–67.

[311] I discussed the effects of the Marshall Plan on Soviet-Eastern European relations above, in Section A.

[312] Mikoyan, *Tak Bylo*, 574.

[313] Mikhail M. Narinskii, "The Soviet Union and the Berlin Crisis, 1948–9," in *The Soviet Union and Europe in the Cold War, 1943–53*, ed. Francesca Gori and Silvio Pons (New York: St. Martin's Press, 1996), 58. This theory extended to Stalin's expectations for US investment in China, with Stalin telling Liu Shaoqi in July 1949 that "the crisis in the US will force it to value highly trade with China." Heinzig, *The Soviet Union*, 466.

"stable and productive Germany."[314] On August 30 Marshal Sokolovsky protested US and British moves to create Bizonia, pointing out that the Allied Control Commission (ACC) was supposed to reach unanimous decisions for all of Germany on matters such as industrial production.[315]

On October 14, 1947, the Soviet Union decided to sign treaties of alliance with its Eastern European allies, this time aimed at "all aggression," not just German.[316] In justifying these treaties to the Hungarians in February 1948, Molotov spoke only of the German threat and cited Ernest Bevin's January 1948 speech about including Germany in the West European Union (WEU), to be launched in March.[317] The Brussels Pact, which created the WEU, was regarded by the Soviet leadership as the "first official military-political alliance of the Western bloc under US direction" because its preamble didn't limit itself to the German threat, but spoke of "armed aggression in Europe" in general.[318]

At the November-December 1947 CFM meeting in London, the Western powers suggested setting up a separate state in the Western zones of occupation. While Western powers saw this as the only way to ensure the economic viability of western Germany in the face of Soviet obstructionism, the Soviets understood the proposal, on the heels of the Marshall Plan, as an open violation of wartime agreements on a unified approach to postwar Germany, and a sign of Western plans to include what would become West Germany in a Western military alliance.[319] In early 1948, the Western powers announced a Feburary 19 meeting in London to discuss a separate agreement on West Germany.

At the London meeting, Molotov continued to pursue a united Germany, but Soviet demands for reparations made it unacceptable to the other three occupying powers. France joined Bizonia and in December 1947, all reparations to the Soviet Union from Trizonia were ended.[320] At a March 1948 meeting of US, British, French, and Benelux foreign ministers that had been going on since February 23 in London, it was decided to go ahead with a separate German state.[321] A week later, foreshadowing the Berlin Blockade, A. A. Smirnov wrote Molotov a memo on "Our Measures with respect to Germany in the Near Future," in which he said that "we can no longer limit ourselves to protests . . . [s]ince the

---

[314] MacDonogh, *After the Reich*, 238.

[315] Kynin and Laufer, "Vvedenie: Politika SSSR," 57.

[316] Dimitrov, *The Diary of Georgi Dimitrov*, 430.

[317] Volokitina, "Nakanune," 45–48.

[318] Yegerova, "NATO i Evropeiskaia Bezopasnost," 62.

[319] Volokitina, "Nakanune," 43.

[320] Narinskii, "The Soviet Union and the Berlin Crisis," 60.

[321] These meetings were importantly separate from both the CFM and ACC meetings, both of which included the Soviet Union.

Western powers have destroyed the ACC and CFM and renounced previously adopted decisions, agreements on ... zones of occupation have lost their force. The Soviet government will therefore be compelled to close its zone...."[322]

On March 20, 1948, Sokolovsky abandoned the Allied Control Commission (ACC) in Germany. A week later, Stalin met with the German communist leadership in Moscow, reassuring them that if Germany remained divided it would be West Germany that would suffer, as East Germany would have assured markets in the East. Meanwhile, unification might still take years.[323] On April 1, the Soviets began to blockade all land routes for travel to Berlin. On April 17, SVAG reported to Moscow that "Germans think that the Anglo-Americans have retreated before the Russians...." Dratvin and Semenov went on to claim that "Clay's attempts to create an airbridge have failed. The Americans have realized it is too costly...." On 24 June, the blockade was extended to all ground transportation.[324]

On July 3, Sokolovsky announced what it would take to end the blockade: Western abandonment of plans to create a separate West German government. At his August 2 meeting with the French, British, and US ambassadors, Stalin retreated a bit, linking the end of the blockade to acceptance of the Soviet Deutschmark in all Berlin and Western suspension of its efforts to create a separate government until a Four Power meeting could be held. Meanwhile, Soviet officials in Germany continued to report to Moscow all sorts of problems with the Western airlift, especially emphasizing the coming difficulties in autumn and winter. After the airlift demonstrated its capacity through the winter, Stalin dropped his currency demands, and settled for a Four Power meeting, with no commitment from the West not to create the Federal Republic of Germany (FRG). The blockade was lifted on May 12, 1949, just two weeks after the not unrelated creation of the North Atlantic Treaty Organization (NATO), uniting the United States, Canada, and WEU members Iceland, Portugal, Iceland, Italy, and Norway in alliance against the Soviet Union.[325]

---

[322] Kynin and Laufer, "Vvedenie: Politika SSSR," 57; Paul Steege, "Holding on in Berlin: March 1948 and SED Efforts to Control the Soviet Zone," *Central European History* 38, no. 3 (September 2005): 438–42.

[323] "Za Sovetami v Kreml," 23–24.

[324] For the untold story of of just how porous the blockade was, and how Soviets even encouraged West Berliners to get their food and coal from the Soviet zone, see William Stivers, "The Incomplete Blockade: Soviet Zone Supply of West Berlin, 1948–49," *Diplomatic History* 21, no. 4 (Fall 1997): 569–602.

[325] Narinskii, "The Soviet Union and the Berlin Crisis," 64–72.

In September 1950, not least because of the increased fear of the Soviet threat generated by the launching of the Korean War in June, the United States officially proposed the rearmament of the FRG within NATO. In September 1951, Western allies announced West Germany's integration into the European Defense Community, as an alternative to NATO membership. On March 10, 1952, the Soviet government sent a note to all Western occupying powers in Germany proposing, for the last time, a reunified, neutral, demilitarized, and democratic Germany. Western rejection of the proposal on March 25, 1952, spurred "Stalin to abandon hope for a united Germany, telling Piech" he must organize his own state.[326] What the note showed was that Stalin preferred a neutral united non-communist Germany to an armed West Germany in NATO.[327] On May 28, 1952, the European Defense Treaty creating the EDC was signed.

At Stalin's death in March 1953 it is hard to disagree with Vojtech Mastny's conclusion that Stalin had left the world around the Soviet Union in a pretty fair mess. To a significant degree, the mess that Stalin's successors inherited was the product of a discourse of danger prevailing at home in the Soviet Union. This was a discourse that could tolerate not the slightest deviation from the Soviet model of socialism. Consequently, Eastern European socialist regimes must become Stalinist regimes. The process of Stalinization in Eastern Europe did more than anything, before the Korean War, to ensure a Cold War between the Soviet Union and the West. At the same time, however, the discourse of danger fenced off one enormous arena of possible conflict and competition between the United States and the USSR: the decolonizing world. After Stalin's death, we will see that the discourse of difference, while certainly most welcome to Soviet citizens, was no unequivocal dampener of the Cold War, but in fact expanded its reach.

---

[326] Loth, "Stalin's Plans," 30–31.

[327] Iurii V. Rodovich, "O 'Note Stalina' ot 10 Marta 1952 g. Po Germanskomu Voprosu," *Novaia i Noveishaia Istoriia* 5 (2002): 63–79; and Gaddis, *We Now Know*, 126–28.

4

The Thaw at Home, 1953–58

The death of Stalin killed the institution of Stalinism, and so released the forces of change in Soviet society. The previously repressed discourse of difference was almost instantly empowered against the literally dead Stalinist discourse of danger. This reversal occurred in virtually every domain of Soviet domestic life, from high politics to daily life on the kolkhoz.

On virtually every single defining element of Soviet identity, the official post-Stalin discourse adopted, or accommodated itself, in greater or lesser degree, to previously repressed societal visions of Soviet identity. This is not to say that the societal view won; it did not. Throughout the four years after Stalin's death and up to the removal of the "anti-party" group led by Molotov at the June 1957 CC Plenum, a multifarious array of societal understandings continued to push for more tolerance of difference, even as the official view had given some way. The picture is a very complicated and contradictory one. The societal discourse was seemingly officially blessed by Khrushchev's denunciation of Stalin at the Twentieth Party Congress in February 1956, but then put on severe notice after the Soviet military intervention crushed the Hungarian rebellion in November 1956, only to be given yet another endorsement by the removal of the most Stalinist of figures, Molotov, from the Presidium in June 1957.

It would be easy to associate all these changes with the person of Khrushchev himself. But I think this would be a serious misreading of the situation, and an underestimation of the influence of society more generally. With Stalin's death, the institution of Stalinism disappeared, but what would replace it was not so obvious, had one based predictions on the prior behavior or positions of any of the Presidium members, whether Nikita Khrushchev, Viacheslav Molotov, Georgii Malenkov, or Anastas Mikoian. Instead, within weeks and even days of Stalin's death, elements of the societal vision of the Soviet Union made themselves known in official policy. What is more, a vast number of changes occurred at the behest of the very least likely carrier of any kind of reformist ideas: secret police chief, serial rapist, and executioner, Lavrentii Beria.

As Zubkova recounted the first three months after Stalin's death, Beria proposed the transfer of camps and labor colonies from the MVD to the Justice Ministry; the reduction of forced labor; the end to grand construction projects; the re-examination of postwar purges; the abolition of torture; and de-Russification campaigns in Belarus, western Ukraine, and the Baltic republics.[1]

The fact that Khrushchev eventually adopted many of the positions of Beria raises questions about the justifiability of relying on personalities to account for what happened to Stalinism after Stalin's demise. It would seem that a more structural, in this case, societally structural, account is necessary. Perhaps Beria was just a more astute politician than his rivals. He sensed the change broader society wanted for the Soviet Union and started announcing policies to reflect these desires. In doing so, he caught his rivals on the Presidium by surprise, and forced them to either consent to his ideas, or, what eventually happened in June 1953, realize just how dangerously adept he was at garnering public support and remove and execute him, as was done in December 1953.

But where did these ideas about an alternative Soviet identity come from? Given that almost all of them were already evident in the societal discourse that was suppressed under Stalin, it would seem misplaced to attribute them to Beria himself, or to Malenkov and Khrushchev, who continued and deepened the Thaw that was already initiated by Beria. And even if the three men were just using the emerging discourse of difference instrumentally and had no genuine personal commitments to any of its elements, this would further strengthen the argument in favor of a societal structuralist account. Perhaps still more, as it would demonstrate that even when political elites don't believe what they are doing, they do it in any case, either because it is politically rewarding, narrowly speaking, or simply reflects available societal understandings of what alternatives to a discredited past there might be.

Let's assume that Beria, Malenkov, and Khrushchev each wanted to succeed Stalin. We are still left with the critical question of what kind of Soviet identity would they offer to garner political support. Indeed, perhaps the most expected outcome was a competition to be the true Stalinist, not the repudiator of Stalin. The fact that the outcome played itself out within the societal discourse of difference, and not within the discourse of danger, points to the importance of these societal understandings of Soviet identity as the prime source of the substance of whatever political struggle would emerge.

In what follows, I describe the immediate de-Stalinization that occurred upon Stalin's death, and then devote separate sections to each of the primary elements of the new discourse of difference, and how they were articulated in different domains of Soviet society at the time.

---

[1] Zubkova, *Russia After the War*, 154.

Immediate De-Stalinization

Just one day after Stalin's death, Komsomol First Secretary, and later Politburo member, Aleksandr N. Shelepin phoned Khrushchev to announce that the Komsomol secretariat had voted unanimously to change the name of the All-Leninist organization to the All Leninist-Stalinist organization. Khrushchev called him back later that night, recommending against it.[2] On March 10, 1953, the day after Stalin's burial, Malenkov invited CC Ideology Secretary Mikhail Suslov, his deputy Boris Ponomarev, and *Pravda* editor Dmitrii Shepilov to the Presidium meeting. He showed them the latest issue of *Pravda* and pointed out that his funeral speech was in bold and covered most of the front page, while speeches of Molotov and Beria were in small type. Moreover, a doctored photo of him appeared to show him sitting between Stalin and Mao. Malenkov criticized these manifestations of the "cult of personality," and ordered that the "tendency be corrected."[3]

Other media outlets got the message. By March 19, it was impossible to find any articles in newspapers or magazines about Stalin. The change was so abrupt that the CC got a stream of letters from readers demanding an explanation for the disappearance. The CC didn't offer any explanation at the time.[4] Konstantin Simonov later concluded that Khrushchev had removed him as editor of *Literaturnaia Gazeta* on March 21 because of his lead editorial after Stalin's death recommending that the main task of Soviet writers should be to "glorify the genius Stalin."[5]

On April 22, it was decided to omit Stalin's name from all May Day slogans.[6] On May 9, all portraits were banned from parades and demonstrations, including Stalin's.[7] In July 1953, all of the gifts to Stalin were removed from display at the Pushkin Museum.[8] No detail was too small to be noticed as a possible Stalinist vestige. On December 23, 1953, Alexei Rumiantsev reported to the CC Presidium

---

[2] Mariia R. Zezina, *Sovetskaia Khudozhestvennaia Intelligentsiia I Vlast v 1950-e—60-e Gody* (Moscow: Dialog-MGU, 1999), 120–21. Shelepin apparently didn't get the message, since he suggested to the Presidium on March 26 that the Komsomol's newspaper, *Komsomolskaia Pravda*, change its name to *Stalin's Generation*. Zhukov, *Stalin: Tainy Vlasti*, 638. Similarly, the request of the director of the Lenin Museum to add Stalin to its name was rejected by CC Secretary Petr N. Pospelov in May 1953. Pikhoia, *Sovetskii Soiuz*, 106.

[3] Iurii V. Aksiutin, "Khrushchevskaia "Ottepel" i Obshchestvennye Nastroeniia," in *SSSR v 1953–1964* (Moscow: ROSSPEN, 2004), 34.

[4] Zhukov, *Stalin: Tainy Vlasti*, 638.

[5] Simonov, *Glazami Cheloveka*, 250–51. Konstantin Simonov was a renowned wartime poet and secretary of the Union of Soviet Writers from 1946 to 1959.

[6] Zhukov, *Stalin: Tainy Vlasti*, 644.

[7] This was Beria's idea, and was reversed two months later. Pikhoia *Sovetskii Soiuz*, 98.

[8] Zhukov, *Stalin: Tainy Vlasti*, 673.

about the removal of an Azerbaijani carpet from display at the Museum of the Revolution. They had sent it out to have the image of Beria woven out of the carpet, but then had discovered the entire carpet was suffused with "the spirit of the cult of personality," and so had it removed to basement storage.[9]

From 1954 until Khrushchev's secret speech on February 25, 1956, at the Twentieth Party Congress denouncing Stalin, there was an evident pause in the removal of Stalin from official discourse, though de-Stalinization continued in many other ways. The first anniversary of Stalin's death was marked in *Pravda* with a largely laudatory front page editorial.[10] At a meeting in Leningrad in April 1954 explaining the rehabilitation of those implicated in the Leningrad Affair of 1948, Khrushchev said that Viktor Abakumov, the Minister of State Security at the time, was behind the affair, not Stalin.[11]

This "pause" ended during the months preceding the Twentieth Party Congress. At the November 5, 1955, Presidium meeting, Soviet leaders discussed how to observe Stalin's upcoming birthday on December 21. From the notes taken at the time, we have the following elliptical discussion. Voroshilov said, "[P]eople will take it badly if we don't hold meetings at factories.... Bulganin: Don't hold meetings on the 21st. We must emphasize the difference. Mikoian: Don't hold any meetings; don't oblige ourselves.... We must reconsider Stalin Prizes when we don't have Lenin Prizes.... Khrushchev's final word: He slaughtered party cadres and military officers...."[12]

The Discourse of Danger Meets the Discourse of Difference

The two elements of the discourse of danger whose change during the Thaw had the most ramifications for how Soviets understood themselves were insecurity and infallibility. The discourse of danger was predicated on the Soviet Union and socialism being under threat at home and from abroad. The discourse of difference

---

[9] RGANI f5 op17 d451, 282. Kornei Chukovskii's diary shows rumors in his community outstripped reality, but not by much. It was said the Kremlin would be opened (done in December 1953), the Stalin Prize would be abolished (done in August 1956), and kolkhoz conditions would improve (agricultural turnaround begun in 1954). But the Writers' Union (WU) was not disbanded, the militia was not reduced in size by 80 percent, and Aleksandr Fadeev wasn't fired but committed penitential suicide in 1956. Kornei Chukovsky, *Diary, 1901–1969* (New Haven: Yale University Press, 2005), 374.

[10] And Stalin's birthday was officially commemorated in December 1954, as was his death in March 1955.

[11] Vladimir P. Naumov, "Byl li Zagovor Berii? Novye Dokumenty of Sobytiiakh 1953 g.," *Novaia I Noveishaia Istoriia* 5 (1998): 37.

[12] Aleksandr A. Fursenko, ed., *Arkhivy Kremlia. Prezidium TsK KPSS 1954–1964*, vol. 1 (Moscow: ROSSPEN 2003), 56. Lenin Prizes replaced Stalin Prizes in August 1956.

was based on precisely the opposite assumption: Socialism at home was secure. Soviet identity under Stalin also propagated the notion that the party and its leaders knew best and did not make errors of consequence. The Thaw, however, revealed fundamental errors made not only by the party, but by Stalin himself, thus opening the field to an idealized Soviet citizen capable of making mistakes, and still remaining a good Soviet patriot.

A more secure and fallible Soviet Union implied broader freedom for a more tolerant discourse of difference, one that would foresee the daily contestation of many elements of Soviet identity.

Table 4.1 lays out the new identity topography. Each of the elements under Contested Terrain were pieces of Soviet identity from the societal discourse under Stalin that were both incorporated into the official discourse of difference after Stalin's death, although to greatly varying degrees, and remained the grounds for continuing conflict among society and the party and state. On the other hand, understanding the Soviet Union as atop a hierarchy of modernity continued to be an element of shared identity. Finally, a new challenge to the official discourse emerged under the Thaw, the idea that true Soviet socialism was being corrupted by a "new class" of embourgeoised bureaucrats.

In sum, the new Soviet identity was one that understood the Soviet Union as more secure, did not treat deviations as dangerously anti-Soviet, valued realistic portrayals of Soviet reality, admitted to fallibility, accepted ambiguous representations of reality, allowed that contradictions in society need not entail fatal conflicts, accepted gray areas rather than zero-sum dichotomies, granted individuals some private space where they need not worry about the public meaning of their actions, and accepted that the average Soviet was not a child any longer.

Table 4.1 **The Discourse of Difference after Stalin**

Contested Terrain	Continuity	New Challenge
External Others	Hierarchy	The New Class
Russian Nation/Orthodoxy	Modernity	
Center-Periphery		
Public-Private		
Paternalism-Maturity		
Optimistic-Realistic		
Clarity-Ambiguity		

The More Secure Soviet Union

A material demonstration of the new official understanding of a more secure Soviet Union was the Presidium's members' abandonment of their armored ZIS-110 limousines. The only, and meaningful, exception was Molotov, who kept his.[13] Another material manifestation of reduced danger was the reallocation of budgetary resources away from the military and heavy industry to agriculture and consumer goods production. As early as March 27, 1953, just three weeks after Stalin's burial, Beria proposed redirecting investments from some defense plants to agriculture.[14] Prime Minister Malenkov's budget foresaw a 9 percent reduction in defense spending for 1954. The budget that finance minister Arsenii Zverev presented to the Supreme Soviet in April 1953 reflected these new priorities, although it had to be edited to remove all references to Stalin's *Economic Problems of Socialism in the USSR*.[15]

Soviet armed forces were significantly reduced during the Thaw, as well. From March 1953 to July 1955, Soviet troop strength diminished from 5.4 to 4.8 million. In August 1955, Khrushchev announced an additional reduction of 640,000 by December. In fact, only 340,000 were demobilized, leaving 4.4 million in January 1956. In May 1956, however, a further cut of 1.2 million was announced.[16] All these reductions were material manifestations of a heightened sense of Soviet security, spawned as well by Soviet advances in both nuclear and missile technologies in the period.

A July 1953 CC resolution reduced taxes on peasants by more than one-half. Agricultural production grew by 35 percent over the previous five-year plan. The period from 1954 to 1958 is considered the most successful in the entire history of the Soviet countryside.[17] The gains were primarily due to private plots. From 1953 to 1957, more than half the growth in meat production, 36 percent of the

---

[13] Sergei N. Khrushchev, *Nikita Khrushchev and the Creation of a Superpower* (University Park: Pennsylvania State University Press, 2000), 31. Khrushchev took an armored limousine to the July 1953 Presidium meeting that charged and arrested Beria. Taubman, *Khrushchev*, 252.

[14] Naumov, "Byl li Zagovor Berii," 24.

[15] Zhukov, *Stalin: Tainy Vlasti*, 639, 674–77. The January 1955 Presidium decision to reverse this favoring of consumer goods appears to have been a tactical move by Khrushchev to discredit Malenkov, who was replaced at the next CC Plenum as prime minister, and not as an indication of any heightened sense of official Soviet insecurity. For an original analysis of post-Stalinist politics, see George W. Breslauer, *Khrushchev and Brezhnev as Leaders* (London: Allen and Unwin, 1982).

[16] Matthew Evangelista, *Unarmed Forces: The Transnational Movement to End the Cold War* (Ithaca: Cornell University Press, 1999), 93.

[17] Elena Iu. Zubkova, "Malenkov i Khrushchev: Lichnyi Faktor v Politike Poslestalinskogo Rukovodstva," *Otechestvennaia Istoriia* 4 (1995): 111.

growth in vegetables, milk, and wool, and 87 percent of the growth in eggs and tobacco production came from the private plots.[18]

In an unusually high-level and public repudiation of Soviet insecurity, Molotov was forced by the Presidium to publish an article in a September 1955 issue of the party's main theoretical journal, *Kommunist*, in which he admitted he had been wrong in a previous article (in February) in writing that the Soviet Union had only built the "foundations of socialism," and not socialism itself.[19] In other words, Molotov had argued the Soviet project was still immature and vulnerable, a clear manifestation of the discourse of danger. He was compelled to recant, acknowledging the Soviet Union, and socialism in the Soviet Union, was more secure and developed than he had previously argued.

What constituted dangerous "anti-Soviet activity" also changed. Under Stalin, possession of any works by any "enemies of the people" could earn one a long prison sentence. During the Thaw, the absence of evidence of distributing this literature implied the absence of "counter-revolutionary intent," and so possession was treated more leniently.[20] An example that would be amusing if it had not resulted in two years of imprisonment was the case of a resident of Northern Osetia, who was condemned in March 1952 for ripping Stalin's portrait from his apartment wall, throwing it on the floor, and tearing it with the broken shards of glass he had already created by smashing dishes while fighting with his wife. The RSFSR Supreme Court reversed the sentence in 1954, reasoning that there was "nothing anti-Soviet in these actions," as he had made no anti-Soviet statements during the fight with his spouse and only inadvertently slandered Stalin.[21]

On March 27, 1953, the Supreme Soviet amnestied almost half the 2.5 million prisoners in Soviet labor camps and penal colonies, although rejecting Beria's more far-reaching proposal of freeing all those who had been condemned by the extra-judicial special commissions and "troikas."[22] Insofar as many of the falsely condemned had been tortured into confessing to crimes of anti-Sovietism, espionage or terrorism, official abrogation of these sentences and recognition of their groundlessness simultaneously acknowledged that the Soviet project had not

---

[18] Aleksandr V. Pyzhikov, "Problema Kulta Lichnosti v Gody Khrushchevskoi Ottepeli," *Voprosy Istorii* 4 (2003): 47–57, 263.

[19] For a discussion of this event, see James Richter, *Khrushchev's Double Bind: International Pressures and Domestic Coalition Politics* (Baltimore: Johns Hopkins University Press, 1994), 73; and Pyzhikov, "Problema Kulta Lichnosti," 53.

[20] Vladimir A. Kozlov and Sergei V. Mironenko, eds., *Kramola: Inakomyslie v SSSR pri Khrushcheve i Brezhneve, 1953–1982 gg.* (Moscow: Materik, 2005), 26.

[21] Ibid., 174.

[22] These were banned in September 1953. Dmitrii T. Shepilov, "Politicheskii Arkhiv XX Veka. Vospominaniia," *Voprosy Istorii* (August 1998), 14; Aksiutin, "Khrushchevskaia 'Ottepel,'" 35; Pikhoia, *Sovetskii Soiuz*, 93; and Zubkova, *Russia After the War*, 164.

been a target of the vast foreign conspiracy previously proclaimed. In Beria's April 2, 1953, report to the Presidium about Solomon Mikhoels' 1948 murder, for example, it was revealed that those arrested for the crime had been coerced into their confessions.[23] On April 4, 1953, Beria signed an order prohibiting the arrest of innocent people, beatings, round the clock handcuffing of prisoners behind their backs, sleep deprivation, and keeping naked prisoners in cold rooms.[24]

The July 1953 CC Plenum devoted to justifying the arrest of Beria became a forum for elaborating just how much more secure the Soviet Union was than had been appreciated since the war. Khrushchev said, "Let's take a look at the last 10 years. Let's figure out what kinds of plots inside our country were revealed by the MVD [Ministry of Internal Affairs] and MGB [Ministry of State Security]. With the exception of false and exaggerated ones, none. Voroshilov: Right, none. . . . Khrushchev: The doctors' plot is an odious affair for all of us; it is a lie. If you take the Mingrelian affair, the Georgian affair, they are lies. . . . I ask you, do we really have such a stream of counter-revolutionary uprisings? . . . The sword of our socialist state must be sharp and pointed. We still have many enemies. We have the strongest capitalist countries and their agents in our country. . . . But this sword must be aimed against enemies, and not against our own people." This was precisely the issue during the Thaw: Who was a real enemy? Khrushchev concluded, to laughter, "If we were now to look through the archives of the MVD, I am convinced that 80 percent of the Soviet people has an MVD dossier, and for each of them, they are working on an affair."[25] In other words, Soviet insecurity was greatly exaggerated. Indeed, for all of 1956 and 1957, not a single Soviet was tried for espionage.[26]

In September 1955, the Supreme Soviet amnestied all those imprisoned for collaboration during the war, meaning all those who had been imprisoned for having the misfortune of being captured as POWs by advancing German armies, or being transported as slave labor to German concentration camps and liberated by the Red Army in 1944–45.

At the July 1954 Central Committee meeting at which it was decided to remove Aleksandr Tvardovsky as editor of *Novyi Mir*, Khrushchev cited how strong the Soviet Union had become to justify going easy on Tvardovsky.[27]

---

[23] Naumov, "Byl li Zagovor Berii," 22.

[24] Pikhoia, *Sovetskii Soiuz*, 94. Any resemblance of these interrogation techniques to those approved by US Defense Secretary Rumsfeld in 2002 is coincidental.

[25] RGANI f2 op1 d29, 8–22.

[26] Kozlov and Mironenko, *Kramola: Inakomysliev*, 35.

[27] Tvardovsky was a poet and three-time winner of the Stalin Prize in literature. He is most closely associated with defending *Novyi Mir*'s role as a publishing outlet for less orthodox work, including Ehrenburg's *The Thaw* in 1954. He was its editor from 1950 to 1954 and 1958 to 1970.

While prefacing his remarks with a nod to Stalin, Khrushchev concluded that even deviance such as Tvardovsky's poem, "Terkin in the Other World," was no grave threat. He said that while "enemies hoped that after the death of Stalin the party line would be revised, they were wrong. . . . We are Leninists, Stalinists." But "we should try to save him, [Tvardovsky] if he is so inclined. We shouldn't adopt a devastating CC resolution on the journal. We must treat it more quietly. We are so strong that no dead Terkins can shake the foundations of the state."[28] Khrushchev, in an explicit admission of fallibility, blamed the party leadership itself: "We ourselves are guilty in that we didn't explain a lot about the cult of personality. That's why the intelligentsia is tossing about."[29] Tvardovsky was replaced as editor by Konstantin Simonov.

Part of the Thaw concerned a softening of consequences for expressions of difference. Instead of being treated as criminally dangerous, writers, directors, and artists demanded that, at a minimum, their transgressions be understood as honest mistakes that any good Soviet could make, so long, of course, as they owned up to them, if only eventually. One should not be officially reprimanded by the party, barred from publication, demoted, or expelled from the party or professional institutions, let alone internally exiled, arrested, or imprisoned for words the party later deemed deviations from the acceptable.

For example, in defending Vasilii Grossman, if not Grossman's novel *For a Just Cause*, to the CC Presidium on October 16, 1953, just before opening the 14th Plenum of the Writers' Union, Fadeev argued that "one must not confuse criticism of our Soviet writers who wish to correct mistakes with hostile elements in literature, conscious bearers of ideology hostile and alien to Soviet society." He went on to defend writers, such as Mukhtar Auezov, who had been justly criticized for bourgeois nationalism, but who simultaneously were not "fundamentally or mainly characterized by these errors. . . ." He called this unjustifiable practice of condemning writers forever based on isolated errors "an infantile sickness," of course evoking Lenin's characterization of "left-wing communism" in his 1920 essay.[30]

Security, however, remained a relative concept. In asking Khrushchev's permission to allow weather reports for agricultural purposes to be extended from a three-day to a five- or seven-day forecast, Glavlit reassured him that this would only include temperature, rainfall, and strong winds, but of course "without indicating their direction."[31]

---

[28] Aksiutin, "Khrushchevskaia 'Ottepel,'" 86–87.
[29] Vladimir Lakshin, *Novy Mir vo Vremena Khrushcheva* (Moscow: Knizhnaia Palata, 1991), 17.
[30] RGANI f5 op 17 d437, 138–40.
[31] A. V. Blium, ed., *Tsenzura v Sovetskom Soiuze: 1917–1991* (Moscow: ROSSPEN, 2004), 375.

The Fallible Soviet Union

Clearly one of the most visible and dramatic changes after Stalin's death was the admission by the party and state of errors in the arrest and execution of literally hundreds of thousands of innocent Soviet citizens. This process had many aspects, from posthumously rehabilitating party elites executed by Stalin in the 1930s to restoring membership in the Writers' Union of those expelled by Stalin in the 1950s. Already in the weeks after Stalin's death, Beria ordered the creation of five special commissions to investigate the Doctors' Plot, Mingrelian Affair, and the affairs of artillery factory workers, MGB workers, and the aviation industry. In each case, it was admitted the affairs had been fabricated.[32]

The Thaw was marked as well by public criticism of various aspects of Soviet reality, heretofore either ignored or relegated to rare elite discussions or obfuscated with muddled language. In the last week of July 1953, however, no less an important mass outlet than *Pravda* published Valentin Ovechkin's "On the Brink," a critical expose of the failings of Soviet agriculture. This article was closely accompanied by equally critical works in *Novyi Mir* by Gavriil Troepolskii ("From the Notes of an Agronomist"), and Fedor Abramov ("People of the Kolkhoz Countryside"). These were followed by the official publication of a summary of the September 1953 CC Plenum on agriculture at which Soviet performance was publicly acknowledged to be inadequate.

Of course, the most important confession of fallibility was to come at the Twentieth Party Congress in Khrushchev's secret speech denouncing Stalin. On December 30, 1955, the "Special Commission for Studying Materials on the Mass Repressions from 1935–40" was created under the chairmanship of Pyotr Pospelov. On February 1, 1956, the Presidium met to consider its report. The notes of the meeting show a most reluctant Molotov, Voroshilov, and Kaganovich. Molotov: "But we must recognize Stalin as a great leader." Mikoian objected to Molotov. Kaganovich agreed with Molotov, "We can re-examine a lot, but Stalin was the leader for 30 years." Molotov: "We should say that Stalin was a great continuer of the cause of Lenin." Bulganin disagreed. Voroshilov added that "the party should know the truth, but present it as life dictated it. The period was dictated by circumstances.... We can't pass by the many abominations of Stalin, but we must not throw the baby out with the bath water." Molotov agreed with Voroshilov, saying, "[Y]es, re-establish the truth, the truth that under Stalin's leadership socialism was victorious. And we must compare that with the odious matters...." Khrushchev concluded: "Stalin was dedicated to the cause of socialism, but by all barbaric means. He destroyed the party. He was not a

---

[32] Naumov, "Byl li Zagovor Berii," 20.

Marxist-Leninist. He obliterated everything sacred in man. Everything was subordinated to his whims.... At the congress we must put Stalin in his place. Get rid of his posters and pictures in the literature before the congress."[33]

A week later, the Presidium met again to discuss the speech, this time pointing out that Soviet society would take matters into its own hands if the party did not come clean about Stalin's crimes, reflecting the power of societal understandings to constrain the party elite. Molotov again resisted the wholesale declamation of Stalin, arguing that "for thirty years we lived under Stalin's leadership and we industrialized. After Stalin, a great party emerged." Kaganovich added, "We are responsible. But the situation was such that we couldn't object." He then spoke of his own brother who committed suicide when threatened with arrest. "But I agree with Comrade Molotov that we proceed cool-headedly.... We must not unleash any spontaneous events...." Bulganin suggested dividing Stalin into two periods: "In the second stage, Stalin stopped being a Marxist-Leninist...." Mikoian agreed with Bulganin, saying he usurped power and destroyed Soviet agricultural production but was right to struggle with Trotskyites.

Nikolai Shvernik warned that "the CC cannot be silent now—otherwise it will be the street that speaks...." Shepilov agreed, "We must tell the truth; otherwise they will not forgive us. Tell the truth that the party didn't need to imprison millions and the state didn't have to send 100s of thousands to the executioner's block."[34] The day before the congress opened, on February 13, the Presidium approved reading the speech. On February 22, a draft was circulated in the Presidium and approved with minor emendations.[35]

The Soviet Union's External Others

During Stalin's reign, external others, but especially the capitalist West and the United States as its apotheosis, were mortal dangers, posing deadly threats to the very existence of the Soviet Union. The Thaw went some small way to alleviate this danger, but there remained a chasm between societal identification with the West, and official fear of over-exposure of Soviet citizens to its noxious influence.

What was dangerous about any particular article, novel, or play? Criticism of Soviet reality was barely tolerable, so long as it didn't argue that reality was inherent to, or generally characteristic of, the Soviet system. But the red line was

[33] Fursenko, *Arkhivy Kremlia Prezidium*, 95–97.
[34] Ibid., 99–103; and Aleksandr N. Iakovlev, ed., *Reabilitatsiia: Kak eto Bylo. Dokumenty Prezidiuma TsK KPSS i Drugie Materialy*, vol. 1 (Moscow: Mezhdunarodnyi Fond "Demokratiia," 2000), 349–51.
[35] Aksiutin, "O Podgotovke Zkrytogo Doklada," 111–14.

often outside of any Soviet writer's control because it lay in the Western reaction to Soviet writings. Using Vladimir Dudintsev's *Not by Bread Alone* as an example, Boris Polevoi, a Writers' Union executive officer, wrote a letter to Pospelov complaining that "some writers have strange and perverse opinions that our policy has changed to NEP.... This has given food to imperialist propaganda about the 'crisis of impotence' of Soviet literature...."[36] It began with Pomerantsev's article which "repeats everything foreign enemies have said about Soviet literature in the postwar period."[37] Soviet intellectuals had to fear that what they wrote might be picked up in the West, or cited there as a criticism of Soviet reality. A student at Moscow State University (MGU) had the misfortune to allow her enthusiasm for a visiting French actor to manifest itself as an impromptu dance with him that was photographed. Unfortunately, it later appeared abroad with the caption: "She was waiting for her prince." She was expelled from the Komsomol, and then the university.[38]

It was also out of bounds to criticize the Soviet Union, even implicitly, before a Western audience. Mikhail Zoshchenko, who had just been restored to the Writers' Union (WU) a year before, found that out after his comments before a group of visiting British writers in Leningrad in May 1954. After a few questions about his treatment after Zhdanov's denunciation of him and Akhmatova in 1946, he rejected Zhdanov's criticism and said, "[F]rom now on I'll write what my conscience dictates," of course implying that socialist realism demanded the opposite. Three weeks later, he was condemned at a party meeting of the Leningrad section of the WU for being "antipatriotic," that is, critical of the Soviet Union before a foreign audience.[39]

Zoshchenko tried to defend himself at this meeting, declaring that "I wrote [in his "confession" to get readmitted to the UW] that I was wrong about a lot, and had lapses, but I don't agree that I am a *non-Soviet* writer, and I never was."[40] Here Zoshchenko desperately tries to avoid the label of danger attached to him by his accusers. Simonov's response played on this external threat: "A delegation comes from abroad, fundamentally bourgeois, and a Soviet writer, readmitted to the UW.... appeals to these bourgeois puppies and wrests applause from them."[41] This will become an abiding theme for the years going forward, that non- or anti-Soviet

---

[36] The reference here is to the New Economic Policy adopted by the Bolsheviks after the civil war. It was marked by free-ish markets in agriculture, retail trade, and services. In this context, it implies a surrender to capitalism.

[37] RGANI f5 op30 d84, 113.

[38] "'Volnodumstvo' v MGU: Dokumentalnoe Povestvovanie po Protokola. 1951–1959 gg.," *Istochnik* 3 (2002): 91.

[39] RGANI f5 op17 d486, 76–78.

[40] RGANI f5 op30 d83, 56.

[41] Ibid., 79.

intellectuals pander to the West for cheap applause, while betraying the Soviet Union. Simonov went on at the meeting to accuse Pomerantsev of disloyalty, of having "the psychology of a Tashkenter," portraying him as a coward who fled to Uzbekistan during the Great Patriotic War, rather than fighting at the front.[42]

Some Soviet intellectuals survived repeated offenses of the type for which Zoshchenko was punished. In particular, Ilya Ehrenburg led a charmed existence, repeatedly provoking party minders abroad and at home to write memos to Moscow authorities declaiming his unpatriotic conduct in front of foreigners. The Ehrenburg exception remains a mystery.[43] In January 1956, the CC Culture Department sent the Presidium a catalogue of Ehrenburg's most recent transgressions. While at an October 1955 meeting with Hungarian writers in Budapest, he had said that "what he hated more than anything in the world were the red and blue pencils of editors and that he didn't agree with Soviet criticism of his novel, *The Thaw*, and was working on its second part." He spoke "scornfully" of the Soviet "production novel." He had shown unseemly admiration for "contemporary bourgeois decadent and formalist art, Hemingway's impotent and naturalistic *Old Man and the Sea*, and the extremely formalistic and gloomy Faulkner." In a meeting with a Mexican writer in Moscow, he said he and some of his friends were tired of propagandistic art. He has resigned from the editorial board of *Inostrannaia Literatura/Foreign Literature* to escape its conservatism."[44]

Meanwhile, exposure to the West was growing. In March 1954, the first Italian film festival was held in Moscow. The deputy head of the Science and Culture Department, P. Tarasov, reported with alarm what visitors had written in the guest books at the Indian and Finnish art exhibitions in late 1953: "[G]ive us art without politics, fresh air, Gaugin, Monet and Marc. Save us from the Gerasimovs, Sokolov-Skalias, etc. Give us art!" There were also many requests to reopen the Museum of New Western Art, which had been closed in 1947.[45] From May to September, the Pushkin Museum exhibited European artworks "saved" from the Dresden gallery. In October 1955, there was the first week of French film in Moscow. In preparation for Khrushchev's official visit to Great Britain in April 1956, there was a week of English films shown in Moscow. In just one week, more than one million Muscovites, or over 20 percent of Moscow's total population, attended these films.[46]

---

[42] Ibid., 84.
[43] For views of the charmed life of Ehrenburg, see Rubenstein, *Tangled Loyalties*.
[44] RGANI f5 op36 d3, 67–70. Ehrenburg was summoned to a meeting in the CC Culture Department in September 1956 at which he apologized and smoothed things over.
[45] RGANI f5 op17 d454, 34.
[46] Zezina, *Sovetskaia Khudozhestvennaia Intelligentsiia*, 238.

The steady revival of the Soviet film industry at least began to displace the predominance of Western films on Soviet screens. In 1953, 31 of the 67 new films shown were still foreign.[47] But in 1954, 38 local films were released, increasing to nearly 70 in 1956.[48] But as Soviet films re-emerged, Western music was beginning to penetrate Soviet air space. The Science and Culture Department reported to the CC in August 1954 that this music "is heard every day for many hours in pioneer camps, sanatoria, rest homes, parks, railroad stations, stadiums," wherever masses of people congregate. Why? Market incentives. "For the sake of commercial interests, our record factories have increased production of Western dance music" from almost nothing in the first quarter of 1953 to over half the 1.2 million records produced in the first quarter of 1954. But "even 25-fold growth in a single year cannot meet the demand."[49]

Under Stalin, admiration for Western ideas, products, and culture was termed "servility" and "kowtowing" and meant one was unpatriotic and indeed dangerous. None of these extreme positions were evident in official Soviet discourse after Stalin's death, although admiration for the West was certainly not officially appreciated either.[50] Chukovsky's diary entry for November 11, 1954, reflects the reversal in climate in literature. He reflects on the editorial comments on his page proofs for *Nekrasov's Craft*: "I had strict orders from the censor not to praise Russian literature at the expense of foreign literature. They deleted the passage containing Chernyshevsky's statement that 'Fielding is good, but he is not Gogol.' War has been declared on chauvinism in general."[51]

But official comparisons with the West generally resulted in a conclusion of Soviet superiority. So, at the September 1953 CC Plenum on agriculture, Khrushchev asserted that Soviet agriculture was "the most mechanized agriculture in the world." And what modern technology existed in the West "is concentrated in the hands of a small group of capitalist farmers; the overwhelming majority of farmers use manual labor and primitive technology."[52]

By May 1957, Khrushchev, buoyed by the results of agricultural reforms and the virgin lands campaign, declared that the Soviet Union would "catch up and overtake" the United States in the production of many foodstuffs. In making the case, Khrushchev acknowledged that in per capita terms, the average American consumed three times more meat and 50 percent more milk. But, he said, "we will catch

---

[47] RGANI f5 op17 d501, 7.
[48] RGANI f5 op30 d131, 50.
[49] RGANI f5 op17 d496, 111–12.
[50] Stalin's 1947 ban on Soviet citizens marrying foreigners was repealed in 1956.
[51] Chukovsky, *Diary*, 388.
[52] RGANI f2 op1 d48, 4.

up by 1960." He ridiculed the economists he consulted who had said 1975, at the earliest.[53]

The defeat of Lysenkoism in Soviet science demonstrated a new tolerance for interaction and comparison with the Western world. In a clever rhetorical strategy, biology professor Nikolai Dubinin argued in a March 1954 letter to Malenkov and Khrushchev that because of Stalin's protection of Lysenko, great Soviet ideas had been suppressed that were later found to have been developed in the West with great success. He cited, in particular, Iosif Rapoport's work on chromosomes and heredity and Nikolai Vavilov's work on hybrid seeds.[54] He gave numerous examples of promising research discontinued in 1948, research that had produced hybrids in the United States that "have increased grain yields by 66%, allowing them to harvest 20–25 million tons more corn" than otherwise would be possible. A letter from biology professor Anton Zhebrak pointed out that British and American scholars who are friendly to the USSR consider the views of Lysenko to be "an anachronism, reminiscent of the denial of evolution in many parts of America."[55] Lysenko was finally removed in April 1956 as head of the Academy of Agricultural Sciences, which he had headed since 1938.

In his speech on industry at the July 1955 CC Plenum, Nikolai Bulganin reported that the Soviet textile industry was half as efficient as its counterpart in the West and its quality was lower. He said the US paper industry was 150 percent more productive because Soviet "machine production is technologically backward . . . with only 30% automation" compared to total automation in the US, such that "our labor productivity is 250% less than leading US enterprises." His conclusion, unthinkable before Stalin's death: "We must constantly study everything new that is being created in world science and technology."[56] Of course, the outcome would be ultimate Soviet superiority, as the best technology, when married to the best social(ist) system, would guarantee the surpassing of capitalism.

At the Twentieth Party Congress in February 1956, Mikoian was the first Soviet leader to utter Stalin's name in a critical light at the congress. In this case, Mikoian went to the very heart of Stalin's cult of infallibility and Soviet superiority, his

---

[53] Lev A. Kirshner and Svetlana A. Prokhvailova, eds., *Svet i Teni "Velikogo Desiatiletiia:" N. S. Khrushchev I ego Vremia* (Leningrad: Lenizdat, 1989), 116.

[54] Nikolai Vavilov was arrested for his scientific views in 1940 and died in a Saratov prison in 1943. He was posthumously rehabilitated in 1955. Rapoport's Jewish ethnicity didn't help his research under Stalin, either.

[55] RGANI f5 op17 d463, 17–58. In the highest-level public rebuke possible, Khrushchev criticized Lysenko in the March 21, 1954, issue of *Pravda*. A January 1955 CC Resolution further purged Soviet biology and agronomy of Lysenkoism. RGANI f5 op17 d464 27.

[56] RGANI f2 op1 d148, 29–58.

very theory of socialism as expressed in *Economic Problems of Socialism in the USSR*. He refuted the core argument of economic calamity in capitalist countries after the war, calling it "hardly accurate" and saying that "an analysis of the economies of modern capitalism hardly can be helped."[57]

The achievements of the West also became a way of justifying the re-direction of resources to one's own area of interest. So, Culture Minister Nikolai Mikhailov, reporting in June 1955 to the Presidium on the state of Soviet cinematography, pointed out that while Moscow had 49 theaters, Paris had 351, London 327, New York 624, and Rome 231, and New York had 80 seats per every 1000 viewers, while Moscow had all of five. He concluded by proposing "we build 400 more theaters by 1958."[58]

Stalin's successors also discovered that it was very hard to counter bourgeois propaganda without having read it. There had to be exposure to the West in order to formulate credible arguments against it. Apparently, Stalinist fear was so great that any exposure would be dangerous that the directors of the Academy of Sciences Institute of Philosophy after Stalin's death requested the Central Committee grant their scholars in the Section on the Criticism of Contemporary Foreign Bourgeois Philosophy access to the works they were supposed to criticize. They reported to Pospelov that "this very significant sector really has no possibility to familiarize itself with the philosophical and sociological books of contemporary bourgeois authors. They not only know nothing about new philosophy books published abroad, but have no access even to the translations we have already done...."[59]

The Soviet Russian Nation

Under Stalin, as we have seen in chapter 2, the Russian nation was explicitly and officially celebrated as the senior brother to all others. And its centrality was closely associated with both official anti-Semitism and the privileging of Russian Orthodoxy over other religious beliefs. Much of the explicit official sanctification of Russian national identity disappears after Stalin's death, but the unintentional reproduction of Russian national centrality continues, as does the broad and deep societal resonance of such a discourse.[60] But, unlike in Stalin's time, Russocentrism did not go unchallenged. As Brandenberger concludes, "Soviet

---

[57] Iurii V. Aksiutin, "Novoe o XX Sezde KPSS," *Otechestvennaia Istoriia* 2 (1998): 110.

[58] RGANI f5 op30 d131, 53.

[59] RGANI f5 op17 d 424, 163–64. Pospelov gave his permission on August 5, 1953.

[60] One example of the official unintentional reproduction of Russian exceptionalism are the pavilions that opened in 1954 for each of the republics at the All-Union Economic Exhibition. While all the non-Russian buildings had some folkloric elements, Russia's alone was a neoclassical temple.

ideologists promoted a non-ethnic, all-Union sense of popular identity more aggressively during the 1950s and 1960s than they had under Stalin, with images of modernization, progress, urbanization, and optimism."[61]

Even so, the Russian nation remained the taken for granted background nation for the Soviet Union. The mere fact that other, non-Russian cultures, languages, and literatures, were referred to as "national," while the Russian language or Russian novels were not, suffices to show the difference between being the invisible essence of Soviet national identity and the visible pre-modern vestige that must be transcended.[62] For just one taken for granted example, Supreme Soviet meetings were arranged with Russia, Ukraine, and Belarus, front and center in that order, with the back rows and sides occupied by Georgia, Tajikistan, Udmurtiia, and other non-Russian representatives.[63]

The Russian Nation and Anti-Semitism

One of the earliest moves acknowledging fallibility after Stalin's death was the official rehabilitation of those 37, mostly Jewish, doctors accused in the Doctors' Plot just two months before Stalin's demise. Just a week after Stalin's burial, Beria ordered the MVD to investigate the Doctors' Plot's fabrication. On April 3, the Presidium accepted the MVD report commissioned by Beria outlining the torture used to extract confessions from those arrested. Just the day before, Beria had reported that Solomon Mikhoels, of the Jewish Anti-Fascist Committee, had been murdered by KGB operatives.[64] Among the most prominent victims of Stalin's anti-Semitic campaign, Molotov's wife, Polina Zhemchuzhinaia, was rehabilitated in May 1953.[65]

As developed in chapter 2, it appears that official Soviet anti-Semitism found broad and wide societal support, to the extent that party and state officials had to differentiate cosmopolitanism from Judaism and protect Jews from attack, verbal and otherwise. The pattern continued during the Thaw. The Ukrainian party

---

[61] Brandenberger, *National Bolshevism*, 244.

[62] For more on the the centrality of Russian national identity, see Ted Hopf, *Social Construction of International Politics: Identities and Foreign Policies, Moscow, 1955 and 1999* (Ithaca: Cornell University Press, 2002), 55–69.

[63] For the seating map, RGANI f5 op30 d97, 58–59.

[64] Kostyrchenko, *Gosudarstvenni Antisemitizm v SSSR*, 481–483; and Naumov, "Byl li Zagovor Berii," 20–21. All members of the Jewish Anti-Fascist Committee were rehabilitated in November 1955. On April 2, 1953, the Presidium took the medals away from those who had been awarded them for their work in Mikhoels's murder. Mikhoels, on the contrary, had his Order of Lenin posthumously restored. Kostyrchenko, *Gosudarstvenni Antisemitizm v SSSR*, 119, 201–10; and Iakovlev, *Reabilitatsia: Politicheskie Protsessy*, 264–67.

[65] Kostyrchenko, *Gosudarstvenni Antisemitizm v SSSR*, 164–66.

first secretary, L. G. Melnikov, for example, fired the editors of the republic daily *Pravda Ukraina*, for "allowing an anti-Jewish letter" in its pages, and reported to Khrushchev that "individual cases of incorrect attitudes toward Jewish people" have been dealt with by the relevant party organs.[66]

Pravda carried the news of the fabricated Doctors' Plot on April 5 and ran a lead editorial condemning "national hostility" the next day. But the public response to the absolution of these Jews was hardly reassuring to the victims. A report to Khrushchev on workers' comments at Moscow enterprises the day after the news was made public shows broad skepticism of the victims' innocence.[67] A few days later, Shepilov sent Khrushchev a summary of letters to *Pravda*, of which he was the editor. Of the 28 letters excerpted, 5 were openly anti-Semitic. One anonymous (perhaps mindful of the official position against anti-Semitism) letter writer asked, "Why begin with the exaltation of Jews and humiliation of Russians? How many innocent victims of repressions are still in the camps, but they aren't the first to be rehabilitated, instead a group of Jews!" He went on to repeat the canard of Jews not fighting for the Motherland during the war, but "now they squeeze us." Another anonymous writer threatened: "You think that you'll change our views of Jews. No, you won't. Jews were parasites in our eyes and will remain so. They squeeze us Russians out of all cultural institutions; they do no heavy labor. You should smash them and not absolve them."[68]

The chairman of the Council on Affairs of Religious Cults (CARC), Polianskii, reported on April 22, 1953, "hooligan attacks on synagogues in some cities," apparently not unrelated to the official denunciation of the Doctors' Plot.[69] Nevertheless, he also reported dramatic increases in synagogue attendance on Rosh Hashanah in October 1953: in Moscow from 7,000 in 1952 to 10,000; in Tashkent, from 2,500 to 7,000, and in Kiev, from 10,000 to 25,000, with another 15,000 out on the street, also apparently in reaction to the official repudiation of anti-Semitism.[70]

It seems that MVD employees were also not enthusiastic about the rehabilitation of Jews after the Doctors' Plot and Jewish Anti-Fascist Committee affairs were renounced. In recordings of meetings of more than 1,600 MVD functionaries with its minister, Sergei Kruglov and CC Secretary N. N. Shatalin after Beria's arrest in July 1953, the police largely disagreed with terminating the Doctors' Plot, with ending Jewish "affairs" more generally, and blamed Beria for prematurely stopping them.[71]

---

[66] RGANI f5 op30 d6, 9–10.
[67] RGANI f5 op30 d19, 10–17.
[68] RGANI f5 op30 d5 9, 14.
[69] RGANI f5 op30 d10, 23.
[70] RGANI f5 op17 d452, 202–03.
[71] Pikhoia, *Sovetskii Soiuz*, 113–14.

More than a few Soviet Russian writers resented the rehabilitation of Jewish writers.[72] Tikhon Semushkin, for example, opposed the appointment of Simonov to the Writers' Union secretariat because of "his bias for a group of one nationality." In September 1955, *Novyi Mir*, under Simonov's editorship, became the first journal to publish Yiddish poetry since 1948.[73] Semushkin also opposed the removal of Anatolii Sofronov, who represented "the purely Russian foundation of our literature."[74] Sofronov himself reported to the CC Science and Culture Department that Fadeev's defense of a group of writers of "one nationality provokes the decisive protest of another group, including Panferov, Pervents, Bubennov, Romanov, Gonchar, Brovka, and others."[75]

Fadeev, asking for guidance about his upcoming introductory address to the 14th Plenum of the Union of Writers in October 1953, raised the issue of "Sofronov and those who support him." He was especially outraged at their suggestion to introduce a new "personal membership card" for WU members which would include one's nationality, that of one's spouse, whether your or your relatives ever belonged to anti-party groupings (which of course nullified the whole point of subsequent rehabilitation), and whether any relatives had been investigated, prosecuted, tried, and/or punished. Fadeev objected to this "intimidation."[76]

Nikolai Mitrokhin has concluded that "the main grouping of Russian nationalists outside the party-state apparatus was formed inside the Union of Writers of the USSR. [Its] division into two contending camps became obvious immediately after Stalin's death...."[77] At the 2nd Writers' Congress in December 1954, L. S. Sobolev, "one of the founders of the fraction of Russian nationalists" raised the issue of "gruppovshchina" as an important problem, that is, the group of Jews in the writers' community, and their mutual aid society therein.[78]

By December, Alexei Surkov, Secretary of the WU, appealed to the Presidium for advice on what to do with the many requests he was getting from the relatives of rehabilitated Jewish writers to publish the banned works of their repressed relatives. He was especially uncertain about whether to publish any works in

---

[72] Zezina, *Sovetskaia Khudozhestvennaia Intelligentsiia*, 149.

[73] Frankel, *Novy Mir*, 81. In his December 1956 "Literary notes" that appeared in *NM*, Simonov publicly apologized for his participation in the anti-cosmopolitan campaign of 1949.

[74] This letter was in October 1953.

[75] RGANI f5 op17 d437, 121–24. In a December 28, 1954, letter to Rumiantsev, Fyodor Gladkov complained that Mikhail Bubennov had telephoned him to accuse him of "leading the struggle of cosmopolitans against Russian writers." RGANI f5 op17 d486, 263–64.

[76] RGANI f5 op17 d437, 149–55. The identity card was subsequently abandoned.

[77] Nikolai Mitrokhin, *Russkaia Partiia: Dvizhenie Russkikh Natsionalistov v SSSR 1953–1985 gody* (Moscow: Novoe Literaturnoe Obozrenie, 2003), 141.

[78] Ibid., 148.

Yiddish, as this has "general state significance."[79] Five months later, Dmitrii Polikarpov, who replaced Rumiantsev as chair of the CC Culture Department in 1955, replied to Surkov, suggesting "for starters" the WU publish a Yiddish literary almanac and a number of books. Why? Because the absence of Jewish theaters and literary outlets has "strengthened the activities of synagogues" in Jewish life. The lesser of two evils, apparently.[80]

Mitrokhin divides the Russian nationalist writers into two groups: "those who distinguished themselves in the struggle against cosmopolitans, red patriot-anti-Semites," including Mikhail Sholokhov, Mikhail Bubennov, Anatolii Sofronov, and Alexei A. Surkov, and those "cynical and well-masked Orthodox monarchists," including Sergei V. Mikhalkov, Leonid Leonov, Natalia P. Konchalovskaia, N. P. Smirnov, and others.[81] Some Russians felt sufficiently aggrieved to form organizations such as "The Rossian National-Socialist Party," whose three dozen members pledged to "beat cops and communists" and "revive the Russian nation."[82]

The Russian Nation and Non-Russian Nations

In mid April 1953 Beria commissioned reports that attacked the official Russocentrism of the party in its Russification campaigns of local party and governmental organs in western Ukraine, Belarus, Lithuania, Latvia, and Estonia. Beria supervised all these investigations, except for Latvia, which Khrushchev led. The reports were considered in the Presidium in May and June.[83] The reports did not pull punches with regard to the excesses committed in the name of Soviet "security." In the report on western Ukraine, for example, the catalogue of victims included almost 500,000 repressed, including 134,000 arrested, 153,000 executed, and the rest exiled.[84]

Had the discourse of danger been controlling, we should expect to see the imperialist threat invoked to explain these policing measures. Instead, while noting the danger of local nationalism and its imperialist patrons, the reports and the Presidium's decisions also pointed the finger at Russian nationalist excesses in whipping up "bourgeois nationalism" unnecessarily. With respect to Lithuania,

---

[79] RGANI f5 op36 d2, 126–34.

[80] Ibid., 152–53. In 1955, "Science" was dropped from the Science and Culture Department.

[81] Mitrokhin, *Russkaia Partiia*, 150–52.

[82] Quotes from Mitrokhin, *Russkaia Partiia*, 191–92. For details, see 191–95. I am introducing the neologism "rossian" to differentiate it from the ethnic "russian," which correspond to the Russian words "rossisskii" and "russkii," the former being those living in Russia, the latter being those who are ethnically Russian. These correspond to what is now know as civic national, and ethnonational, identities.

[83] Naumov, "Byl li Zagovor Berii," 22–24; and Zhukov, *Stalin: Tainy Vlasti*, 665.

[84] RGANI f5 op8 d27, 84.

for example, "the main cause of the bad situation is errors and distortions made by party and soviet organs in their political work and collective farm creation."

These admissions of error were accompanied by critiques of "administrative methods ... little knowledge of the Lithuanian language ... groundless application of punitive measures and repressions that sometimes needlessly affect broad strata of the population, enrage them, and create the soil for the activities of the anti-Soviet nationalistic underground." Additional errors included "inadequate inclusion of Lithuanian cadres, over-reliance on non-Lithuanian immigrants [Russians] ... and the baseless distrust of people who found themselves on territory temporarily occupied by Germans." The report concluded that it is "intolerable that official business is conducted in Russian, which provokes the just indignation of the locals." Consequently the CC recommended the correction of all the above errors, including banning, as a rule, the practice of non-indigenous secretaries at all party and state levels, the use of Russian in official business, and stipulated the mandatory study of Lithuanian by all communists.[85] Ukraine's first secretary, Melnikov, was replaced by Alexei Kirichenko, and Belarus' Nikolai Patolichev by Mikhail Zimianin.

As in the case of Jews, the official Soviet discourse of supranational equality was not matched with the same level of liberalism in society as a whole. In the collection of letters Shepilov passed on to the Presidium from *Pravda* readers in August 1953 concerning violations of nationality policy in Ukraine, Belarus, and the Baltic, about half defended locals from Russians, and half complained about new discrimination against Russians.[86]

Stalin's death opened up space for non-Russians to demand more faithful adherence to Leninist nationality policy. One illustrative example was the fate of the Kazakh writer, Mukhtar Auezov. In June 1953, A. Petrosian, a party official at the Institute of World Literatures, wrote a letter to Pospelov, informing him of "attempts to discredit the honorable name of this outstanding Soviet writer" with charges of bourgeois nationalism. Petrosian cited a recent article slandering Auezov, and asked about Auezov: "Is he our man, or is he not our man?" In other words, are we going to continue to dichotomize the world into us and them along previous Stalinist lines? "Can certain facts in Auezov's biography never, and in no way, be erased?" Are we to ignore his Stalin Prize for his novel *Abai*? How could a work of socialist realism awarded such a prize be the product of a nationalist? Auezov never gets credit for eliminating errors from subsequent works.

Petrosian apparently got no response, so in May 1954 he sent another letter to Pospelov, this time generalizing Auezov's fate to "the punishment/shelmovanie

---

[85] RGANI f5 op30 d6, 11–13. Similar reports and recommendations were made for Ukraine on the same day, ibid., 16–18; and for Latvia on June 6. Ibid., 20–29.
[86] RGANI f5 op30 d6, 107–10.

[a czarist device of the early eighteenth century] of eminent national writers in other Central Asian republics, especially in Turkmenistan and Kyrgystan." Finally, in August 1954, one of Pospelov's deputies, P. Tarasov, agreed that "these are vulgar attacks on an honored writer," and said that Auezov should be restored to the department chair from which he had been "incorrectly" removed.[87]

Meanwhile, reports filtered into the Presidium about violations of nationality policy at other levels, too. On June 17, 1953, V. S. Kruzhkov, head of the Agitprop Department and Alexei Rumiantsev, head of the CC Science and Culture Department reported to the Presidium "On the Gross Distortion of Nationality Policy by the Mordovskii Obkom." They criticized the party for not developing the local language, literature, or theater. What is worse, in an Orientalist twist, the local Mordvin "intelligentsia disdain the Mordvin language," instead relying on Russian.[88]

Another avenue for non-Russians to challenge the centrality of Russia to the Soviet project was to question prevailing Soviet historiography that claimed they had benefited from Russian imperial rule rather than been repressed by it. Their champion in Moscow was Anna Pankratova, a leading historian on Central Asia and CC member, who supported the view that Central Asia had been developing before Russian rule. She was appointed editor of *Voprosy Istorii/Questions of History* in June 1953, and used it to further her point of view. She was supported in this effort by many local historians from the periphery.[89]

In July 1954, those ethnic groups who were exiled during and after the war, Germans, Crimean Tatars, Kalmyks, and Balkyrs, had their "offenses" decriminalized, were given the right to leave their settlements and to find work, and their children had the official stigmata removed from their dossiers. In March 1955, the Presidium lifted all restrictions on these "special settlers" who were party members, and restored the passports of Chechens, Ingush, and Karachaevtsy,

---

[87] RGANI f5 op17 d492, 64–78.

[88] RGANI f5 op16 d582, 66–73. For complaints about the arrested development of Turkmen culture and literature, see RGANI f5 op17 d403, 7–10. On Tajikistan, RGANI f5 op17 d403, 11–17. Much longer and in-depth reports and discussions resulted from the March 5–9, 1956, riots in Georgia after Khrushchev's de-Stalinization speech. It was ultimately concluded by the CC that ethnic Georgians had mistakenly repressed the national aspirations of Osetians, Abkhazians, and Armenians, but Russian-Georgian relations were fine. Vladmir A. Kozlov, *Mass Uprisings in the USSR: Protest and Rebellion in the Post-Stalin Years* (Armonk: M. E. Sharpe, 2002), 112–35; Aleksandr Fursenko and Timothy Naftali, *Khrushchev's Cold War* (New York: W.W. Norton 2006), 283–95; and Aleksandr N. Iakovlev, ed., *Reabilitatsiia: Kak eto Bylo. Fevral 1956—Nachalo 80-x Godov*, vol. II (Moscow: Mezhdunarodnyi Fond "Demokratiia," 2003), 150–56.

[89] Eli Weinerman, "The Polemics between Moscow and Central Asians on the Decline of Central Asia and Tsarist Russia's Role in the History of the Region," *Slavic and East European Review* 71, no. 3 (July 1993): 448–49.

but did not restore the right to return to the homes from which they were expelled. In February 1957, the Autonomous Soviet Socialist Republics of Balkaria, Chechnia-Ingushetia, Kalmykia, and Karachaev were re-established.

In sum, the official Soviet national identity is contested, both from within and from below. While officially supranational, the party and state continues its implicit privileging of Russia as its nation, but simultaneously publicly criticizes and punishes manifestations of Russocentrism. Meanwhile, non-Russians, including Jews, are pushing back against all varieties of Russocentrism. Finally, Russians themselves, feeling increasingly aggrieved, reassert the centrality of Russia to the Soviet project.

The Implicit Soviet Nation and its Russian Orthodox Church

While religious belief in general continued to be officially treated as a pre-modern vestige concentrated among the backward and among old women, Orthodoxy continued to be privileged relative to non-Orthodox faiths. As under Stalin, the Council on the Affairs of the Russian Orthodox Church, (CAROC) through its chairman, Georgii Karpov, continued to defend believers from "administrative measures—filling in wells, sanitary quarantines, banning pilgrimages, and other inappropriate actions, that only raise religious activeness."[90] The number of Orthodox churches grew from 11,000 in January 1953 to almost 13,500 four years later, and its income from 180 million rubles in 1948 to 667 million in 1957.[91]

Typical of the Council's achievements was the Belarussian party's return to parishioners of a church it had illegally turned into a granary three years before, in violation of the December 1944 law "On Orthodox Churches and Prayer Houses."[92] In October 1954, V. S. Kruzhkov reported to the CC that the party had taken disciplinary action against party officials in Mogilev, Cherkassk, Zhitomir, and Lipetsk for "gross administrative interference in the activities of the church and insulting the religious feelings of believers" in response to complaints from the Council.[93]

But Karpov's bid to carve out more institutional autonomy and authority for his Council was rejected. In June 1953 he asked that the Council be

---

[90] This is excerpted from the report of April 29, 1953, but is representative of dozens more over the next four years.

[91] RGANI f5 op17 d452, 1; and Mikhail V. Shkarovskii, *Russkaia Pravoslavnaia Tserkov i Sovetskoe Gosudarstvo v 1943–1964 Godakh. Ot "Peremiriia" k Novoi Voine* (Saint Petersburg: DEAN+ADIA-M, 1995), 56.

[92] RGANI f5 op17 d452, 52.

[93] RGANI f5 op16 d669, 141.

allowed, without referral to the CC, to approve the opening of up to 25 churches a year, decide on publications, and deal with party obkoms directly when the latter committed "administrativnost" against believers.[94] But Karpov was not deterred, making similar requests in April 1954. This time he justified opening new churches, pointing out that petitioners cite Article 127 of the Soviet Constitution, and that opening a limited number each year will help in "preventing unhealthy political feelings among believers . . . and in the struggle against underground meetings of worship." He further asked, in light of the unauthorized seizure of churches by local party and state institutions for granaries, or just for harassment, that all such seizures be required to have the approval of the CAROC. The response from CAROC's institutional "Other," the CC Agitprop Department, was both negative and accusatory, asserting that Karpov's requests were "essentially aimed at strengthening the position of the church in the country."[95]

In June 1953, Rumiantsev and Khrushchev approved Chairman of the Council on Affairs of Religious Cults (CARC) Ivan Polianskii's request for the publication of a Baptist bimonthly.[96] It is interesting to note the external dimension to Soviet deliberations about religious freedom, as well. Those pushing for more tolerance often invoked the foreign audience to justify their requests. For example, it was argued that the May 1954 decision to publish 2,000 copies of the Koran in Arabic "would significantly dispel the slanderous propaganda in the countries of the Moslem East about the alleged persecution of Islam and the prohibition on any kinds of religious Muslim literature."[97]

Polianskii recognized the privileged position of the Russian Orthodox Church, (ROC) and Karpov's CAROC, in his arguments against Karpov's proposed merging of the two Councils. In his May 1956 letter to the CC, Polianskii argued that "abroad they well understand that the ROC, as the most powerful church organization, is closer than other churches to the Soviet government and that the Soviet government devotes special attention to this church. . . ." He goes on to say that non-Orthodox believers will feel unrepresented if CAROC takes over both councils, as they see in the Council on Cults "a state organ free from the overwhelming power of the ROC. . . ."[98] Karpov's proposed merger was rejected.

---

[94] RGANI f5 op16 d542, 120–26.

[95] RGANI f5 op16 d669 10–16, 27–28.

[96] RGANI f5 op17 d452, 39–44. The requested circulation was reduced from 5,000 to 3,000 on Rumiantsev's recommendation. This seems like a common "over-insurance"/cover your ass/perestrakhovanie approach to requests for violations of the ideals of the New Soviet Man.

[97] RGANI f5 op16 d670, 74.

[98] RGANI f5 op16 d642, 127–34.

In the memorandum setting the stage for the July 1954 CC Resolution "On Big Inadequacies in Scientific-Atheistic Propaganda and Measures for its Improvement," Kruzhkov and Rumiantsev in March 1954 began by remarking on the recent religious revival, especially among "the backward part of the population." Orthodox churches had grown from 3,000 in 1940 to 13,500 in 1953, and 18,600 houses of worship overall, including synagogues, mosques, and other Christian churches. What's worse, the unregistered Muslim clergy in Central Asia includes "former mullahs, sheikhs, merchants, basmachis, kulaks, and criminals. . . ." They then enumerated the many pilgrimages and holidays, the main danger again being all the young people who participated. They said the party is lax in its agitprop work and erroneously believes that "during the construction of communism, religion becomes obsolete spontaneously."[99]

For the next four months, local party committees reported back to the CC Agitprop Department on the serious religious revivals occurring in their communities and what they were doing to implement the July 7, 1954, CC Resolution to combat them.[100] By September Karpov was complaining in the name of the CAROC about people taking matters into their own hands, hooligans breaking windows, swearing at the clergy, defiling icons, etc.[101] In September in Kiev, an iconostasis was smashed and icons stolen; in Sverdlovsk, the 12-year-old daughter of a local priest was beaten by classmates to the chants of "beat the holy daughter."[102]

Finally, on November 5, 1954, the Central Committee, acknowledging its fallibility, passed a new resolution, "Errors in Conducting Scientific-Atheistic Propaganda among the People," aimed at correcting the excesses committed in the name of the July resolution. The new resolution situated the church within socialist society rather than identifying it as a "bourgeois capitalist remnant," again expanding the boundaries of what it meant to be Soviet. Second, and related, it paid tribute to honorable believers who were building socialism. And third, it recognized religion as a private matter, although reserving to the party the right to conduct propaganda against it, but without "administrativnost." The Orthodox Church responded with gratitude, as did the Orthodox churches of Finland and Romania.[103]

Just as after the July 1954 CC Resolution, local party officials began sending reports to the CC Agitprop Department confessing their sins of excessive zeal in

---

[99] RGANI f5 op16 d650, 18–21.
[100] From Grodno obkom in Belarus, e.g., RGANI f5 op16 d693, 44–48.
[101] Chumachenko, *Church and State*, 131.
[102] RGANI f5 op16 d694, 57–58.
[103] Chumachenko, *Church and State*, 134.

implementing the party's apparent desires, and elaborating steps they were taking to correct those errors in light of the November resolution.[104]

As Mikhail Shkarovskii concludes his study of the Russian Orthodox Church and Soviet rule, "[T]he period from 1955–7 became the most favorable for the church since 1947." He cites the fact that in February 1955 CAROC was given the right to register unregistered communities of worship, so in 1955, 41 new churches opened.[105] In addition, in March 1955, Kruzhkov, approved Karpov's request for the publication of 50,000 hymnals, 35,000 bibles, and 250,000 prayer books. In August, Metropolitan Nikolai was awarded the Order of the Red Banner of Labor. The November 1954 Resolution became an institutional tool Karpov could use to justify additional requests, such as the construction of a church in Rostov oblast, which had been delayed for four years. It was approved in February 1956.[106]

The Muscovite Center of Soviet Russia

As in the Stalinist period, Soviets understood themselves in a hierarchical manner radiating from Moscow, then Russia, and then the periphery or "glubina," literally, depths. This spatialization was mapped onto the modern/premodern binary and the unstated centrality of the Russian nation to the officially supranational Soviet identity. An especially evocative example comes from Chukovsky's diaries. It is striking for its unwitting bluntness. He describes a meeting of Moscow writers before the 2nd Writers' Congress where Alexei Surkov, then 1st secretary of the WU, warned the 1,000+ Muscovite writers in attendance against "leaving the room whenever an Azerbaijani or Tatar got up to speak."[107]

Both official and societal discourses continued to distinguish between the paradigmatically modern Soviet project and those parts of Soviet reality marked by backwardness, always understood as the periphery. Central Asia, in particular, was singled out for its place on the lower rungs of the ladder of development. Reporting to the Presidium in June 1953, Rumiantsev and Kruzhkov wrote about the conditions prevailing in Turkmenistan: feudal attitudes toward women, more than a few cases of women immolating themselves, incidents of polygamy, the payment of bride prices, and under-aged marriages.[108]

---

[104] See, for example, memo from Grozny obkom chair. RGANI f5 op16 d689, 20–22.

[105] Mikhail V. Shkarovskii, *Russkaia Pravoslavnaia Tserkov pri Staline I Khrushcheve* (Moscow: Graal, 1999), 52–54.

[106] RGANI f5 op16 d754, 23–26.

[107] Chukovsky, *Diary*, 389. Apparently, the Russian writers didn't listen, as Marina Francicevich, a Yugoslavian guest, reported that whenever writers from the periphery got up to speak, "the buffets and corridors filled up." AVPRF f144 op16 d740, 14.

[108] RGANI f5 op17 d403, 4.

The periphery had its moments to strike back, one being the 2nd congress of the WU. The meetings were punctuated with sarcastic and ironic jabs from "peripheral" writers inviting Muscovites and Leningraders to come visit when they have a chance, saying they might find out "we no longer fell trees by hand." More seriously, Ukrainian writers complained at the congress about a three-volume work on Soviet literature that included only Russian authors and a Moldovan author wondered aloud in his speech about whether all the Moldovan books he had sent for display at the congress had been lost, since they were not being exhibited.[109]

The Soviet center was modern, its periphery pre-modern. But the Muscovite Russian center could be a vanguard for the pre-modern periphery, helping its more under-developed little brother into socialism. A survey of the Academy of Sciences Institute of Ethnography's journal, *Sovetskaia Etnografiia*, reveals dozens of articles in which non-Russian areas of the Soviet Union were depicted as modernizing parts of the Soviet Union being helped by Moscow Center.[110]

More Private Space to be Soviet

A new valorization of the private over the public was evident in several popular movies in the period. In Vsevolod Pudovkin's *Return of Vasilii Bortnikov*, Marlen Khutsiev's *Spring on Zarechnaia Street*, and Iosif Heifits' *Big Family* and *The Rumiantsev Affair*, the main heroes were simple people with banal problems making their way through everyday life, not great collective farm workers, or machine tool makers, overfulfilling the plan. New protagonists appeared: the hero-loser and the good-for-nothing small fry.[111] All this, and more, implied the Soviet system had become so secure it need not penetrate every nook and cranny of every citizen's life to ensure fidelity to the cause.

The official critique of works that privileged the private used the term "bezideinost" to characterize these works, that is, an absence of an ideological cast or lesson for the readers. All literary works should be publicly meaningful; mere description of private lives, at work, at home, and in love were deemed not necessarily dangerous, but at least unnecessary, and certainly unworthy of the broad and deep public enthusiasm they continually, and annoyingly, provoked.

The Central Committee's Science and Culture Department stood as the guardian against the danger of expanding the private too far. By early 1954, its deputy head, P. Tarasov, was sounding the alarm, pointing out examples of "apolitical" writings

---

[109] For more from the congress, see Hopf, *Social Construction of International Politics*, 53–55, 62–64.
[110] Ibid., 45–46, 49–51.
[111] Nancy Condee, "Cultural Codes of the Thaw," in *Nikita Khrushchev*, ed. William Taubman, Sergei Khruschev, and Abbott Gleason (New Haven: Yale University Press, 2000), 165.

and "nonideological art," that is, work that focused on newly private spaces, outside of public meanings of partiinost and ideinost. He identified cases of "exaltation of decadent Western art" and the danger of rehabilitated writers looking for revenge. Overall, he concluded that there had emerged a dangerous "faith in some kind of ideological NEP," that is, a backsliding in socialist development. These writers justified themselves by citing the party's own directives against varnishing Soviet reality. But being labeled with "NEP" was a very serious charge, implying one's willingness to go back in time, before the construction of socialism in the Soviet Union, to compromise with private landowners and the petit bourgeoisie, more generally.[112]

Pomerantsev's "On Sincerity in Literature" ended up as the poster child for this danger. Published in the December 1953 issue of *Novyi Mir*, it was a sensation among Soviet readers. Its simple call for writers to be honest in describing Soviet reality resulted in letters from readers pouring in to the editors at *Novyi Mir, Literaturnia Gazeta, Znamia* and other journals and newspapers.[113] Alexeyeva recalls the atmosphere in the Lenin Library's smoking room after Pomerantsev's article appeared: "Old-line Stalinist views had a right to exist. Nothing more.... They had been downgraded to views that could be tolerated."[114]

Besides much else he allowed to be published in *Novyi Mir* in the first 18 months of the Thaw, Aleksandr Tvardovsky, its editor, was held responsible for Pomerantsev's work. The entire editorial board of *NM* was called into CC Secretary Petr Pospelov's office in June 1954 and criticized for its publication policies. Pospelov recommended Tvardovsky's immediate dismissal as editor, a wish that would be fulfilled by August. Meanwhile, *NM* was excoriated in the press for its liberal bent.[115]

The day after his "processing" by Pospelov, Tvardovsky wrote a bold letter to the entire Presidium, rejecting the criticism of *NM*'s choices, including Pomerantsev, while admitting to isolated errors.[116] Tvardovsky insisted there was no "line" at the journal, trying to avoid the far more serious charge of establishing some kind of coherent and organized group opposed to the official Soviet position.[117]

---

[112] RGANI f5 op17 d454, 33–35.

[113] Zezina, *Sovetskaia Khudozhestvennaia Intelligentsiia*, 134–35.

[114] Alexeyeva, *The Thaw Generation*, 73.

[115] Zezina, *Sovetskaia Khudozhestvennaia Intelligentsiia*, 139–40. For an enlightening history of *Novyi Mir*, see Frankel, *Novy Mir*, 81.

[116] "Processing" referred to security police treatment of those they are interrogating. Tvardovsky's deliberate use of it was aimed at reminding Presidium members that Pospelov had operated contrary to the new "socialist legality" that had been promulgated by the party since Stalin's death.

[117] RGANI f5 op30 d84, 29.

The new editor of *NM*, Konstantin Simonov, made the case for the private world in his speech at no less official a meeting as the 2nd Congress of the Union of Writers in December 1954. He said "to depict people only at work . . . would be to show them in a one-sided way. . . . How many raikom secretaries in our novels . . . are deprived of the right to dreams, meals, medical attention—not to mention love and personal happiness—and all in the name of the senselessly harsh, and the main thing, unlikely affirmation, of the primacy of public interests over personal interests."[118]

In one of his last acts as first secretary of the Writers' Union, Aleksandr Fadeev wrote a memo to Khrushchev and Malenkov in October 1953, in which he defended writers' individuality from efforts to impose a false template of socialist realism. He wrote that "the party has its artistic program. . . . But the position of Lenin in his article on party literature is rarely cited, where he speaks of the attention to creative individuality, about the room for thought and fantasy in artistic creativity. . . . If Lenin had used his power against Mayakovsky [whose poetic style he didn't like], he would never have become the outstanding poet Mayakovsky."[119]

Soviet People are Adults

The paternalistic view of the Soviet project was reflected in other dichotomies: modern and pre-modern, core and periphery, Russian and non-Russian, insecure and secure. A typical title, "The Young Art of the Turkmen People," reflected the essence of this relationship perfectly. Non-Russian Turkmen are necessarily in need of the guidance of their "older brother" Russians in achieving modernity, as if Turkmen art didn't really exist before the Russian vanguard came along to develop it.[120] Ilya Ehrenburg demanded that a stop be put to this infantilization of the Soviet people, who had already proved themselves in the war to be capable of defending socialism from the most powerful and dangerous of aggressors: Nazi Germany. In defending his novel, *The Thaw*, at the 2nd Congress of Writers in December 1954, he asked, "Isn't it time to open a section in the Writers' Union for adult literature?"[121]

---

[118] *Vtoroi Vsesouznyi Syezd Sovetskikh Pisatelei: 15–26 Dekabria 1954 goda, Stenograficheskii Otchet* (Moscow, 1956), 102.

[119] RGANI f5 op17 d437, 61–79. In his accompanying letter to Khrushchev on December 24, Rumiantsev more or less rejects each of Fadeev's criticisms, reflecting the intstitutional clash between the Writers' Union and the CC Culture Department.

[120] *Pravda*, October 21, 1955.

[121] *Vtoroi Vsesouznyii Syezd*, 143.

A More Realistic Soviet Union

Pomerantsev's novel was the occasion for Alexei Surkov to sketch out the two extremes that must be avoided in depicting Soviet reality: "the complacency of boastful and conceited, leftist, bombastic assaults of the neo-RAPPist vulgarizers and the nihilist whine of petty bourgeois panic-mongerers ready to slander the wealth of experience we have accumulated."[122] Of course there was a vast terrain between these two extremes, and the debate over the boundaries would never be definitively resolved. Those in favor of more difference accused their foes of being Stalinist vulgarizers; their foes accused them of being dangerous proponents of bourgeois restoration. In the Statutes of the WU, adopted at its 2nd congress in December 1954, the chasm remained: "Socialist realism demands the truthful representation of reality (stop here for the discourse of difference) in its revolutionary development" (stress the latter to return to 1946).[123]

One of the most popular movies of 1957, *Delo bylo v Penkove/It Happened in Penkov*, exemplifies the new attention to the everyday life of average people in Soviet mass culture during the Thaw. Village life is shown with all its poverty and squalor, slushy rutted roads, ramshackle homes, but without any kind of commentary. The conditions are not in the process of being overcome; the villagers are not thirsting for modernity; nor is it being delivered by any avid party workers. The conditions just are. Matvei, the philandering hero, is a complicated figure from a hard-working, though not ideologically inspired, peasant family, who poisons his neighbor's chicken with vodka. His extra-marital romance with Tonia is simply presented, not moralized upon in any way.

In the July 1954 issue of *Oktiabr*, Surkov joined the orthodox crusade against *New Times* and its presentation of gritty Soviet reality, criticizing those works where "everything that is evil and rotten occurs among the leading groups of our society; our government and party workers, scientists, and intellectuals appear as the principle negative characters."

Soviet Gray between Black and White

In Vera Panova's novel, *Span of Time*, the main characters were marked by their ambiguity: Heroes were flawed; antagonists were not wholly unsympathetic. In Leonid Zorin's play *Guests*, published in the February 1954 issue of *Teatr*, he depicts three generations of the Kirpichev family. The father, Alexei, is an old Bolshevik revolutionary hero; his son, a Justice Ministry official, is a careerist,

---

[122] "Pod Znamenem Sotsialisticheskogo Realizma," *Pravda*, May 25, 1954.
[123] Swayze, *Political Control of Literature*, 114. Or see the lead editorial in the last issue of *Kommunist* for 1955, "K Voprosu o Tipicheskom v Literature I Iskusstve," 14.

corrupted by desire for power and prestige, living in a bourgeois style; and Alexei's grandson Tema, is a bon vivant, dining in the best restaurants, riding in his chauffeured car. A clearly complex and critical view of Soviet reality, perhaps the play's most dangerous implication is that this bourgeois deviation is not the product of Western influence, but rather, implicitly, is the natural outgrowth of the Soviet system itself.[124]

Ilya Ehrenburg's novel, *The Thaw*, first appeared in the May 1954 issue of *Znamia*. It proved immensely popular. While an average Soviet novel had a production run of 30,000, *The Thaw*'s initial edition run was 45,000. It was still sold on the black market for exorbitant sums and was circulated in typescript copies, as well.[125] It was "bought up, read, and heatedly discussed in editorials, at different plena, in kitchens and living rooms, in student corridors, and at village youth meetings [posidelki], in both drunken and sober company, and in the metro and on trams," Anatolii Cherniaev recalled in his memoirs.[126]

The broad popular response was evoked by the many ambiguous shades of gray used to describe average Soviet citizens. The novel opens with a public meeting decrying a recently published romantic novel for its lack of "ideinost," and its overly explicit depictions of love and lust. Upon returning home, Koroteyev, an engineer, is criticized by Savchenko, an artist who is unsuccessful because he refuses to paint socialist realist depictions of Soviet reality. Savchenko claims Koroteyev, the party man, just parroted the party line. Volodya, the cynical and successful producer of socialist realist kitsch, defends Koroteyev, saying it is always better to hide what one thinks; one should always behave strategically. Pukhov, the honorable Old Bolshevik, assails his son, Volodya, for such attitudes. Pukhov's daughter, Sonya, a true believer, defends her father because the party is right: A novel must educate, not confuse the reader. Of all these characters, only Sonya would have been acceptable prior to Stalin's death.

In the dichotomous, hierarchical, binarized world of the discourse of danger, the working class was in utter opposition to the dangerous bourgeoisie. *The Thaw* complicated this crystal clear marking of boundaries but did not erase them. The Stalin Prize-winning novels of Vera Panova (*Span of the Year*) and Leonid Leonov (*The Russian Forest*), as well as many other cultural productions, presented good Soviets with "bad" class backgrounds who were able to transcend their origins, as well as social miscreants with "good," solid proletarian

---

[124] Swayze, *Political Control of Literature*, 98–99.

[125] Maurice Friedberg, *A Decade of Euphoria: Western Literature in Post-Stalin Russia* (Bloomington: Indiana University Press, 1977), 155; and Edward Crankshaw, *Russia without Stalin* (New York: Viking Press, 1956), 136.

[126] Anatolii S. Cherniaev, *Moia Zhizn i Moe Vremia* (Moscow: Mezhdunarodnye Otnosheniia, 1995), 219.

backgrounds.[127] While criticized in predictable quarters for such representations, subsequent novels, films, and plays in the period did not shy away from such blurring of the boundaries.

Ehrenburg defended *The Thaw* and the Thaw at the December 1954 Writers' Congress by condemning those who lived in a world of "black and white," those authors who embellish communal apartments with gold, make workshops look like laboratories, collective farm clubs like noble mansions, "with creatures who have nothing in common with Soviet people, with their complicated, deep internal lives."[128]

In 1957, Grigorii Chukhrai's first film, *The Forty-First* won a special prize at Cannes. This film, set during the Soviet Civil War, involved a romance between a Red Army sharpshooter and her White Guard lover. A far cry from the usual dichotomization of the evil rapacious Whites and freedom-loving Reds, the film's ending sees a tearful sniper squeezing the trigger to gain her 41st kill, her politically incorrect lover.

But that is not to say a proletarian identity was not preferred. The tale of Tvardovsky trying to get his party identification card "corrected" is most telling. In April 1954, Tvardovsky wrote directly to Khrushchev to get his parents reclassified from kulaks to "middle peasants." The matter was turned over to CC Secretary Ekaterina Furtseva, who commissioned a report from the Smolensk obkom party secretary. The latter wrote that Tvardovsky's father had "two cows, a horse, and hired temporary labor for harvesting, but did not have permanent employees.... There was no constant wage labor." Nevertheless, the Krasnopresnenskii raikom in Moscow rejected Tvardovsky's application in November 1954. But the Moscow gorkom, which Furtseva chaired, overruled the lower party committee, approving the change just two days later.[129]

The New Soviet Class

A new challenge to the official discourse of Soviet identity were the increasing charges from society that an emerging new class of embourgeoised party and state bureaucrats lived privileged lives at the expense of the Soviet people whom they were purportedly serving. This challenge was spawned from critiques of corruption and thievery, which in themselves, and as isolated deviations, were tolerated by the party in articles, novels, and plays. It also was related to the periphery's resentment of the privileges and arrogance of the Moscow Center. This, too, was tolerated as a justified response to flagrant violations of the party's

---

[127] For more details, see Hopf, *Social Construction of International Politics*, 41–45.
[128] *Vtoroi Vsesouznyii Syezd*, 142–44.
[129] RGANI f5 op30 d84, 2–10.

dominant discourse of equality and leveling between urban and rural, Russian and non-Russian, Moscow and the sticks. But increasingly there were public condemnations of the emergence of a "new class" that was enriching itself at the expense of the Soviet people. Soviet officials were hyper-sensitive to this new challenge to their aura of self-sacrificing idealists.

In the August–October 1953 issues of *NM*, Vladimir Dudintsev's novel, *Not by Bread Alone*, appeared. It was about a lone inventor, Lopatkin, who had to struggle against party and state bureaucrats to get his idea accepted. In the meantime, he was unjustifiably imprisoned by his opponents who are not punished, but are promoted. That the invention is ultimately adopted is credited to a lone party official, Galitsky. The main villain, Drozdov, gave his name as a popular synonym for bureaucratic evil. This, like *The Thaw*, was an enormously popular best-selling book.[130]

Dudintsev's novel pushed the boundaries of difference in several different ways. Drozdov was depicted as typical, not an exception. Galitsky was not a devotee of Marxism-Leninism, but just a good man, indicating that adherence to socialism was neither a necessary nor sufficient condition for being a good Soviet. Morevoer, Dudintsev has Lopatkin and Galitsky, the heroes, continually being accused of apolitical idealism, the typical orthodox charge. Moreover, the novel showed a party bourgeoisie living very well.[131]

Ensuing discussions of the novel only reinforced the fears of Culture Department officials. At an October meeting of the Moscow UW devoted to *Not by Bread Alone*, the author Konstantin Paustovskii declared that "there were 1,000s of Drozdovs" and that there is "a new petit bourgeois caste, rapacious people, with nothing in common with the revolution, our regime, or socialism."[132] It would be hard to go beyond calling what is officially socialist, non-socialist, or the socialists themselves, or at least the party and state officials who claim to be socialists, a new class of plunderers.

One episode, recalled by Raisa Orlova, captures the two discursive treatments of Dudintsev nicely. She was meeting at a friend's house in November 1956. "Two of my girlfriends, almost crying, 'What will this lead to? Our kids, reading the likes of Dudintsev, will stop respecting us and their teachers and Soviet power.' I replied that such books can only help re-establish the Soviet power destroyed by Stalin...."[133] One sees danger in critique; the other sees critique as restoring a deeper security. Indeed, not only does greater security make critique possible, criticism increases that very same security.

---

[130] Dunham, *In Stalin's Time*, 242.

[131] Frankel, *Novy Mir* 84; and Swayze, *Political Control of Literature*, 165–66.

[132] Zezina, *Sovetskaia Khudozhestvennaia Intelligentsiia*, 182.

[133] Raisa Orlova and Lev Kopelev, *Myi Zhili v Moskve* (Moscow: Kniga, 1990), 39.

Ovechkin, for example, at the 2nd Writers' Congress in December 1954, criticized those living in expensive Moscow apartments and the Peredelkino writers' community of dachas, and those who wrote only for awards and prizes and who served on committees only to receive stipends. He accused them of leading bourgeois lifestyles.[134] Zorin's 1954 play *Guests* was condemned by the CC Culture Department for giving a "false and slanderous characterization of social relations.... Our state essentially was depicted as degenerate and bureaucratic and ... it said there is a bourgeoisie of state workers." This was said in the context of trying to ban Zorin's new play, *Alpatov*.[135]

The idea of a "new class" in Soviet life was not limited to novels and plays. Leaflets distributed in Kemerovo Oblast after the September 1955 strike of conscripted construction workers declared that "they had struck against the illegal actions and tyranny of the Soviet bourgeoisie, and not against Soviet power.... The reality is that the riches in life are enjoyed by a small clique of people—the Soviet bourgeoisie and their toadies...."[136] Shortly after the Twentieth Party Congress, the "Socialist Union of Struggle for Freedom" was created by three students in Kiev. During their interrogations, they argued the need for such a party since in the USSR, "Soviet power doesn't exist; instead an anti-popular power exists of a narrow group of irresponsible people who rely on the bureaucracy." The current bureaucratized system has "no democratic liberties: no freedom of speech, press, or assembly; this encourages anti-Semitism, and excessive taxation of the peasantry."[137] In April 1957, a teacher at a technical school in Minsk, V.N. Tiurin, was sentenced for creating the "All-Russian Workers-Peasant Party" after events in Hungary, the explicit aim of which was to "overthrow the dictatorship of the party bureaucracy." Its party program was titled "On the Need for a Socialist Revolution."[138]

In sum, we can imagine an idealized pair of speeches from Molotov, representing the seriously discredited discourse of danger, and Ehrenburg, representing the newly empowered discourse of difference.

Molotov: The Soviet Union and the socialist project remain gravely insecure, both from the threat of bourgeois degeneration from within and from imperialist

---

[134] *Vtoroi Vsesouznyii Syezd*, 248–52.

[135] RGANI f5 op17 d542, 173–176. Andrei Sakharov recalled that his very first letter of protest to the Soviet leadership was to defend Zorin's play for its accurate depiction of a new Soviet bourgeoisie. Sakharov, "Pismo Prezidentu," *Znamia* 3, no. 2 (1990): 59.

[136] Kozlov, *Mass Uprisings in the USSR*, 71. For more on events in Kemerovo, see esp. 65–71.

[137] The three young men were sentenced to six, four, and one year in a corrective labor camp. Kozlov and Mironenko, *Kramola: Inakomysliev*, 346–50. Other small groups who declared their struggle against the new bureaucratic class included the "Union of Revolutionary Leninists" in Leningrad and the "Workers-Peasants Underground Party" in Rostov Oblast. See ibid., 350–55 for details.

[138] Ibid., 332. Tiurin was amnestied in 1963.

penetration from without. While Stalin made individual mistakes, the party collective as a whole makes correct decisions for our socialist nation. We must protect our developing Soviet people from the pernicious influence of Western ideas, especially when it comes to the less advanced parts of the Soviet Union, and especially in Central Asia. We must constantly publicize all the achievements of socialism, and ensure that there is no room for treating isolated mistakes and shortcomings as if they were common tendencies or general conditions. We must hold each and every Soviet citizen up to an ideal standard of conduct, both in the public sphere, and at home. Deviations from this ideal only encourage immature people to imagine that being Soviet is a flexible concept. This is a slippery slope to anti-Soviet, counter-revolutionary, bourgeois ideas of overthrowing Soviet power.

Ehrenburg: The Soviet project of socialism is fundamentally secure. It has proven itself in the war against fascism and the economic progress made since 1945. In fact, the main threat to Soviet security is the exaggeration of its insecurity, and its unavoidable entailment of repression of innocent people who in fact are good Soviet men and women, as interested in building socialism as the most committed party member. The party must realize that the Soviet people have grown up; they are adults now, and their individual initiative must not only be trusted but welcomed, if we are to catch up and overtake the West economically. The party should be comfortable with stretching the ideal Soviet model to encompass all who are not openly anti-Soviet, rather than the Stalinist default of threatening anyone with repression whom the party could construe as not demonstrably adhering to the flawless ideal. The more secure the Soviet project, the more difference should be tolerated; in exchange, such toleration will result in a stronger, more prosperous, and hence, more secure Soviet Union.

From the Twentieth Party Congress to the Invasion of Hungary

"On the Cult of Personality and its Consequences" was delivered by Khrushchev to a closed session of the Central Committee on February 25, 1956. A short summation would be that Stalin's bloody excesses were unnecessary for the construction of socialism in the Soviet Union and must not be repeated. According to Khrushchev, Stalin's perception of danger was pathologically exaggerated. "Stalin introduced the concept of 'enemy of the people' and use of the term eliminated the need for any evidence or proof. . . ." Khrushchev compared Lenin's relative tolerance for dissent with Stalin's ruthlessness. According to Khrushchev, Lenin welcomed Zinoviev and Kamenev back into the party even after they opposed the revolution. Stalin, on the other hand, used more extreme measures even after "socialism was secure," than Lenin did when the revolution was still imperiled.

Khrushchev went on to explicitly condemn the "theory" underlying this discourse of danger, the idea that as socialism gets stronger, the class struggle becomes more intense, and so the threat to socialism grows. "When socialism in our country was fundamentally constituted, when the exploiting classes were mostly liquidated . . . when the social basis for political movements and groups hostile to the party had contracted . . . then repression directed against them began."[139]

Khrushchev's denunciation of Stalin dramatically shifted the balance of discursive power in favor of those who favored increased tolerance for difference in Soviet society and against those who still adhered to Stalin's model of dangerous deviance.[140] This was still more the case as Khrushchev had legitimized the understanding of the Soviet Union and the socialist project as fundamentally secure at home, a position the societal discourse of difference had propounded since the end of World War II.

If the Soviet project was secure, then what possible rationale could there be for not allowing full-blown criticism of flaws in that system? After all, had not the very lack of such criticism allowed 30 years of tyranny to endure? Wasn't unquestioning sycophancy and faith in the infallible paternalism of the party responsible for all the crimes laid out in Khrushchev's speech? Wasn't the commitment to dividing society up into black and white enemies and allies responsible for the unnecessary repression of millions? Wasn't the discourse of difference, its understanding of what the Soviet Union was and should be, the best defense against any return of a "cult of personality and its consequences?"

The weeks and months after the speech witnessed a literal flood of interpretations of Stalinism that the official discourse had a hard time controlling, at least until the revolution in Hungary reverberated back into the Soviet Union, and so alarmed the party elite that it simply demanded a halt to any additional thawing of Soviet political and social life. One might think of the post-congress period as an enormous window of opportunity thrown open for advocates of difference, an opportunity to press the thaw as far as possible, to push the boundaries of permissible difference as far away from the New Soviet Man, in as short a time as possible. There were many such efforts, both by intellectuals and by Soviet officials in this period.

---

[139] Kirshner and Prokhvailova, *Svet i Teni*, 52–57.

[140] Only in Georgia did public demonstrations break out in support of Stalin Fursenko. Fursenko, *Arkhivy Kremlia Prezidium*, 111–12; and Fursenko and Naftali, *Khrushchev's Cold War*, 283–90. This is not to say that many Soviets at public meetings to discuss the speech did not express confusion, skepticism, and simple refusal to believe what was said about Stalin.

Just after the congress, a meeting of the Moscow section of the WU turned into a broad attack on anti-Semites like Anatolii Safronov and against the luxurious living standards of a new class of bureaucrats. Even the sexual debauchery of Georgii Aleksandrov, minister of culture until his removal for arranging sexual liaisons with theater students of his choosing, was an object of discussion.[141] Composers demanded the repeal of the 1948 CC resolutions condemning Shostakovich and other "abstract" composers. Even Zoshchenko's cause was taken up by a group of writers appealing to the CC.[142] Simonov gave a talk condemning Zhdanov's 1946 CC Resolutions before Russian language teachers at MGU in late October 1956 that was greeted by "deafening applause."[143]

From June to October, *Novyi Mir*, under Simonov's editorship, published poems by Nikolai Zabolotsky, who had just been released from the camps, and by Boris Pasternak. In the June issue of the journal, Simonov declared, following Fadeev's suicide, that Fadeev's first version of *Young Guard* was superior to the later version Stalin demanded he write, even after awarding the first one a Stalin Prize. In July 1956, Meyerhold's work was officially re-evaluated, and allowed to be performed.[144]

A month after the speech, the Soviet government decided to dramatically accelerate the release of prisoners from the camps. It created 97 three-person commissions to travel around the country in place of the glacially slow judiciary. The March 26 decree was titled "On Measures for the Most Rapid Liquidation of the Consequences of the Criminal Activities of Beria and his Accomplices." In just seven months, 176,000 cases were reviewed, resulting in over 120,000 releases and 28,000 sentence reductions.[145] Isaac Babel and Iurii Olesha were officially rehabilitated and their previously banned works published.[146]

In April 1956, the Presidium created a commission chaired by Molotov to investigate the trials of Bukharin, Rykov, Zinoviev, Kamenev, and others, as well as the murder of Kirov.[147] Reflecting official recognition of Soviet strength, the

[141] John Gordon and Carol Garrard, *Inside the Soviet Writers' Union* (London: Tauris, 1990), 72–73; and Chukovsky, *Diary*, 393–94.

[142] Zezina, *Sovetskaia Khudozhestvennaia Intelligentsiia*, 177.

[143] Veniamin A. Kaverin, *Epilog* (Moscow: Moskovskii Rabochii, 1989), 332; Zezina, *Sovetskaia Khudozhestvennaia Intelligentsiia*, 177–78.

[144] Meyerhold himself had been posthumously rehabilitated in November 1955.

[145] Aleksandr A. Fursenko, ed., *Arkhivy Kremlia. Prezidium TsK KPSS 1954–1964*, vol. 2 (Moscow: ROSSPEN 2006), 221–22; and Kathleen E. Smith, "Gulag Survivors and Thaw Policies," unpublished manuscript, 2006, 9–10.

[146] Swayze, *Political Control of Literature*, 151. In May 1956, at Ehrenburg's urging, Lev Gumilev, Anna Akhmatova's son, was released from prison. Rubenstein, *Tangled Loyalties*, 286–87.

[147] The chairmanship of Molotov and the revolution in Hungary doubtless contributed to the December 1956 decision to not rehabilitate these victims or charge Stalin with Kirov's murder. Nikolai A. Barsukov, "XX Sezd v Retrospektive Khrushcheva," *Otechestvennaia Istoriia* 6 (1996):175; and Iakovlev, *Reabilitatsiia*, vol II, 73–74, 204–07. Tukhachevskii and Yakir were, however, rehabilitated by the commission.

government repealed the criminalization of tardiness and absenteeism at work in late April. Three days later, on April 28, the Supreme Soviet decreed that "special settlers" exiled by Stalin during the war be restored their legal rights.[148] After hearing the Marshal Zhukov commission report on June 29, the Presidium accepted its recommendation to amnesty, release, and compensate those Soviet POWs from the war who were still in prison camps.[149]

A representative example of the kinds of reactions from the broader public provoked by Khrushchev's speech can be found in Anna Pankratova's report to the CC on her nine meetings she held in Leningrad from March 20 to 23, to discuss the speech.[150] These meetings attracted over 6,000 people who asked 825 questions. It is the questions that reveal the trends in thinking that were most troubling to official Moscow.

According to Pankratova, her audience asked how they should now assess Stalin? Many wrote notes asking why we were not also condemning those who supported the cult.[151] Questions were raised about the responsibility of former Presidium members for the cult. Others asked what objective conditions of socialism gave rise to the cult. "What is the material foundation for the cult of personality? Perhaps it is the absence of competition in industry and agriculture? Perhaps it is the creation of a big stratum of Soviet bureaucracy which raises doubts about the socialist essence of our social and state system?" She termed "unhealthy" critiques raised against collectivization and dekulakization. Others raised the issue of "real" democracy. One suggested a new cult was emerging around Khrushchev. Many notes raised the issue of anti-Semitism and why we are not struggling more against it. Many teachers suggested cancelling exams until new history textbooks were available. She wrote, "Knowing the situation in schools (she is a Professor of History at Moscow State University and editor of *Questions of History*), I fully support the teachers' request."[152]

Based on the materials reported from all levels of discussions of the speech—oblast, raion, city, and primary party organizations—the overwhelming concern of the CC in Moscow, beyond the many remarks that went far beyond critiques of Stalin himself, was the failure or unwillingness of local party officials to "give

---

[148] Liudmila M. Alekseeva, *Istoriia Inakomysliia v SSSR* (Vilnius: Vest, 1992), 94–111. Although Tatars and Meshketians were barred from returning home to Crimea and Georgia, respectively.

[149] Iakovlev, *Reabilitatsiia*, vol. II, 129–32.

[150] After the congress, the speech was distributed to all party committees for a public reading and discussion, from obkom to primary party organizations in factories or university departments.

[151] Perhaps they would have been heartened by the example of Alexander Fadeev, who committed suicide in May 1956. At his funeral, Boris Pasternak said, "He has rehabilitated himself." Rubenstein, *Tangled Loyalties*, 294.

[152] RGANI f5 op16 d747, 74–90.

an appropriate rebuff" to those making these allegedly anti-Soviet remarks. This was especially true at the local levels beneath the obkom.[153]

One example of someone going too far was Iurii Orlov, at the time a graduate student researcher at the Institute of Theoretical and Experimental Physics in Moscow, who made the following impermissible remarks: "Our country is socialist, but not democratic. It is wrong to compare socialism with capitalism, better to compare it with a slave system.... Property belongs to the people, but power belongs to some small group of scoundrels.... Our party is penetrated by the spirit of slavery." He was expelled from the party and the institute. The meeting at the institute resulted in a special CC resolution on 5 April devoted specially to his words.[154]

Most alarming was the move from criticizing Stalin to criticizing the Soviet system, socialism, its absence of democracy, its failure to be what it claimed to be. Having digested all these reports from thousands of party meetings, Leonid Brezhnev was instructed to draft a letter, "On the results of the discussions of the decisions of the 20th party congress," for all party aktiv. Sent out on 30 June, it was measured in identifying "isolated" episodes of "anti-party speeches" and efforts to "run down and discredit the state and party apparatus." A key issue was the separation of Stalin from socialism, since "there are still communists [nb: still we/us] who don't understand or don't want to understand that the cult should not be seen as *inherent to the nature of Soviet society*..." (emphasis added).

The letter concluded by invoking the danger of the External Other. "Hostile imperialist propaganda influences individual Soviets.... Growing economic and cultural ties with capitalist countries, more tourists and delegations create conditions for the penetration into our country of specially selected people, disguised as tourists, whose aim is the subversion of the Soviet system and anti-Soviet propaganda."[155]

A most complicated picture emerged after the first round of discussions of the speech. As Polly Jones described it, "never again would the party unleash such a

---

[153] Polly Jones, "From the Secret Speech to the Burial of Stalin: Real and Ideal Responses to de-Stalinization," in *The Dilemmas of De-Stalinization*, ed. Polly Jones (London: Routledge 2006), 42–47.

[154] Iakovlev, *Reabilitatsiia*, vol. II, 52–57, 64–65; Aksiutin, "Novoe o XX Sezde KPSS," 118; Alexeyeva, *The Thaw Generation*, 86; Vladimir Naumov, "Repression and Rehabilitation," In *Nikita Khrushchev*, ed. William Taubman, Sergei Khrushchev, and Abbott Gleason (New Haven: Yale University Press, 2000), 107; and Iurii Orlov, *Opasnye Mysli* (Moscow: Argumenty i Fakty, 1992), 126–29. Meetings at the Leningrad Writers' Union, Institute of Oriental Studies and the Gorky Institute of World Literature also became nationally renowned for their "incorrect" interpretations of the speech. Aksiutin, "Novoe o XX Sezde KPSS," 118–19.

[155] Iakovlev, *Reabilitatsiia*, vol. II, 157–62.

torrent of conflicting and controversial views from the Soviet public."[156] The discourse of difference, borne of a sense of greater Soviet security, continued in both the official and cultural domains.

The Chill: From Hungary to the Anti-Party Group Plenum

Events in Hungary showed Soviet leaders what might happen in the Soviet Union if the societal discourse of difference ever came to power at home. The number of Soviets tried and convicted for "anti-Soviet agitation and for spreading false stories slandering the Soviet state and social system" peaked in 1957; almost 2,000 Soviet citizens were so condemned, compared to less than 500 the year before. Moreover, almost half of those imprisoned were workers.[157] Although Soviet leaders were alarmed, there was no re-Stalinization, no going back to the discourse of danger. There was a pause, and then a resumption of the same contradictory struggle that had characterized Soviet reality since Stalin's death. It culminated in the ouster of the potential carriers of any return to Stalinism: Molotov, Lazar Kaganovich, Kliment Voroshilov, "and Shepilov who joined them."[158]

Events in both Poland and Hungary had effects in the Soviet Union that were troubling for the Soviet leadership. The challenges to orthodoxy abroad encouraged non-Russians recently colonized by Moscow to express their solidarity with their Hungarian comrades. In Kaunas, Lithuania, for example, crowds sang the hymn "Lithuania Our Homeland," and shouts of "Long live Hungary," "Down with Moscow," and "Hooray for the independence of Lithuania," rang out from the crowd.[159]

Public opposition to the Soviet invasion itself was concentrated primarily "among the educated or relatively educated Marxist or 'protoliberal' romantics."[160] A group of Leningrad students united as the "Union of Communist-Leninists" and distributed leaflets at Leningrad University in November 1956, declaring that "[i]n the communist citadel cracks are appearing. In Hungary and Poland ... popular freedom was crushed by the treads of Soviet

---

[156] Jones, "From the Secret Speech," 41.

[157] Kozlov and Mironenko, *Kramola: Inakomysliev*, 36–39.

[158] This was the official description of Shepilov at the Plenum, as he joined in opposing Khrushchev, but was not accused of the other opponents' Stalinist predilections.

[159] Kozlov, *Mass Uprisings in the USSR*, 164. For other nationalist, anti-Soviet effects from Hungary, see "SSSR: Narody i Sudby," *Voennye Arkhivy Rossii* 1 (1993): 246–70.

[160] Kozlov and Mironenko, *Kramola: Inakomysliev*, 37.

tanks. . . . In Hungary it was precisely students who first defended the suppressed democracy." They went on to ask, "Where is the freedom won by Lenin?" and pledged that "under the banner of Leninism we will destroy political bureaucratism." The four party members were sentenced from one to ten years each.[161]

Even those who had pushed most to expand the boundaries of the permissible fell into line immediately after the Soviet military intervention. Tvardovsky, Ehrenburg, Paustovsky, Margarita Aliger, and 62 other writers signed a lead editorial supporting the suppression of Hungary in the November 24, 1956, *Literaturnaia Gazeta*, titled "See the Whole Truth."

The ruling Soviet elite shortly concluded that events in Hungary had spun out of control partly because of the Hungarian party's permissive attitude toward its own intelligentsia, who also had been pushing the boundaries of difference there. Of course, the Culture Department minders merely saw the fallout from Hungary as a happy circumstance to revive their campaign for the discourse of danger they had been prosecuting as an institutional mission for years.

The first salvo here was a memo from CC Culture Department Head Dmitrii Polikarpov and his deputy, Boris Riurikov, "On Some Questions on Contemporary Literature and on Facts of Incorrect Sentiments among Some Writers," sent to the Presidium on December 1, 1956. This memo was used to once again condemn Dudintsev and Zorin, and to raise the issue of Boris Pasternak's new novel, *Doctor Zhivago*. They claimed the authors' works had spawned "unhealthy" interpretations of Soviet reality, critiques of not "bad and unfit leaders, but of leaders and leadership in general." They warned that writers were increasingly frequently demanding a re-evaluation of Zorin's *Guests*, despite the fact that "leading workers are represented as a class of bourgeoisie" in it. They also remembered Simonov's denunciation of the 1946 CC Resolutions against *Zvezda, Leningrad*, and the film *Big Life*.

However, it shows just how far the discourse of difference had penetrated even Soviet officialdom that Polikarpov and Riurikov didn't condemn the content of Simonov's remarks, but rather the unsuitable non-party audience: "[I]t introduces confusion and undermines party authority in their eyes."[162]

They concluded by pointing out that *Doctor Zhivago* "is penetrated with hatred for the Soviet Union. And although the novel wasn't accepted for publication [rejected by *NM*], manuscripts are circulating among authors and Pasternak enjoys, especially among student and youth, the glory of an unrecognized

---

[161] Ibid., 350–54.

[162] Although Riurikov did defend these resolutions "in essence" in an article in #17/1956 *Kommunist*, "Lenin and Socialist Culture."

genius."[163] As is frequently the case with the discourse of danger, it is the intelligentsia, students, and young people who are considered the weakest links in the socialist system, most susceptible to bourgeois penetration.

A week later, the CC held an official meeting on literature, presided over by Dmitrii Shepilov, at which the connection between the Hungarian "counter-revolution" and the discourse of difference in the Soviet Union was officially proclaimed. Boris Polevoi, a UW board member, opened with an expression of danger: "It was precisely with a critique of partiinost and socialist realism that began all those loathsome events we have seen in Poland and Hungary." Polevoi's assertion that "we are still firing back [at those who write anti-Soviet articles] with small calibre weapons" prompted Brezhnev to interrupt, "[Y]our volleys cannot be heard."

Previously criticized works of Tvardovsky, Zorin, and Pomerantsev were now elevated to a higher level of danger after the events in Hungary. So, Rumiantsev accused Zorin of spreading "Trotskyite ideas about the appearance of a new bourgeoisie, about the appearance of a new class, which exploits the working class of our country...."[164]

On the second day of the meeting, Simonov boldly defended his public position against the 1946 Resolutions, asserting that they contradicted the Twentieth Party Congress [165] However, he went on to defend their timeliness in 1946, when the country was more insecure, again implying that greater security should foster greater tolerance for difference. When Pospelov interjected that the conditions of 1946 "remain in full force even now," Simonov didn't back down, but said that "Zhdanov's position was one-sided and didn't call for the revelation of obstacles in our path, and was silent about them instead...."[166]

Simonov then turned to Dudintsev, defending his work as part of the struggle against the cult of personality. Again, Pospelov objected that one must not struggle "with the system." Simonov continued his defense, arguing that "we think that this novel was written from a Soviet position." He then invoked the External Other to differentiate Dudintsev from Pasternak, arguing that by sending *Doctor Zhivago* abroad to be published, Pasternak "showed hostility to the Soviet

---

[163] RGANI f5 op36 d14, 99–107. Apparently, they didn't know that Pasternak's manuscript had been smuggled by an Italian communist visiting Moscow to Feltrinelli, a publisher in Rome, in October 1956.

[164] One might imagine being compared to Trotsky, who ended up with an axe in his back, would send chills through the spines of not only Zorin, but all those sitting in the audience who defended him.

[165] These resolutions were not officialy rescinded until 1989.

[166] One's position on the 1946 Resolutions said much about one's position on the discourses of danger and difference. Simonov very cleverly fashioned a position that supported the resolutions in their time, under the conditions that prevailed when the Soviet Union was weak and vulnerable. In doing so, he simultaneously rejected the idea that these resolutions were wrong after the war and that they were relevant in the 1950s.

people."[167] Simonov continued by attacking critics for their "stupid and harmful provocations," calling N. Smirnov a "bomb-thrower" for his attack on Yevtushenko. Using official concern for youth to his rhetorical advantage, Simonov claimed this was hardly a case of "nurturing" a young poet.

Polikarpov ended the day's proceedings by attacking Simonov for publishing Nazym Khikmet's popular play *Was that Ivan Ivanovich?*, comparing it to Zorin's *Guests*, and brought up again Simonov's disparaging remarks about the 1946 Resolutions, this time concentrating on his irresponsibility in saying such things before a non-party audience.[168] His recommendation was to return Surkov and Polevoi to the WU secretariat.

The next and last day of the CC meeting, December 10, was opened by the Ukrainian writer and Khrushchev favorite, Aleksandr Korneichuk, who accused Simonov of being dangerously unpatriotic. He asked rhetorically, "Comrade Simonov, why have you opened the doors to demagogues, to black slanderers? Why, at this moment, when the kasha is boiling in Poland and Hungary, and when some of our youth have begun to waver...? Don't you understand there is a battle going on?"

Shepilov, the highest ranking party official at the meeting, spoke from the position of Soviet strength advanced in the discourse of difference. While imperialists are trying to exploit the Twentieth Party Congress he said, "they forget the elementary truth that the very severity of self-criticism is a sign of our great power, and not our weakness." Consequently, "the worst thing would be an administrative ban, to not influence or discuss. This would mean drawing the sickness in, and dressing authors in wreathes of martyrs with all the ensuing consequences...." Shepilov concluded in a compromise: "[W]hat remains in force from the 1946–48 CC decisions are a high ideological content for literature against apolitical, pessimistic kowtowing [presumably, before the West]."

Pospelov followed Shepilov, saying, "Simonov had spoken correctly about how the 1946 CC decisions were evoked by a particular international situation." He pointed out, citing secret TASS documents, that "in 1952, in light of our steel production, Eisenhower decided against a preventive war." He then attributed the current Soviet strength to the 1946 Resolutions. But he came back to the Hungarian danger lurking within Simonov's positions, and their connection to the external danger. "Is it really accidental that the entire bourgeois press has

---

[167] After all, it was Simonov, as editor of *NM*, who had rejected Pasternak's submission there. It is as if Simonov was willing to sacrifice Pasternak in exchange for maintaining freedom for the Thaw for the rest.

[168] In a private meeting in the Culture Department chaired by Polikarpov, Simonov confessed his error in criticizing the 1946 Resolutions before a non-party audience, but continued to defend Dudintsev. RGANI f5 op36 d35, 16–17.

raised a joyful battle around the Dudintsev novel, saying that precisely this novel gives a full picture of Soviet society? One must think, comrade Simonov, why our enemy praises it."[169]

Yet another letter from the CC was sent out on December 19, in light of events in Hungary and continuing unacceptable reactions to the Twentieth Party Congress. Again drafted by Brezhnev, it linked the inadmissible interpretations of the cult with the counter-revolution in Hungary, and identified as most vulnerable and in need of party tutelage students, young people, and the intelligentsia.[170] At the following CC Plenum, a week after the party circular was distributed, Khrushchev even expressed a kind of regret for emptying the camps, saying that "many 1,000s have been freed... But they were not all pure. And some were very impure—Trotskyites, Zinovievites, Rightists, all kinds of riffraff.... Some have rejoined the party as enemies of the party.... We must expel them and if they are corrupting the party, arrest them."[171]

These warnings from on high were rapidly reflected in a number of notable rejections in the cultural world. Sergei Mikhalkov's screenplay for *First-Class Chauffeur/Shofer Ponevole* was shelved at the behest of Riurikov in January 1957.[172] As Riurikov described it, the main hero is a Soviet minister who uses his official car and driver to go on vacation. His driver takes ill, so the minister has to drive himself: "This way he rubs up against the reality of life and finds out about the defects in the ministry he heads." The movie "pits elites against masses. The minister is depicted as representative of the 'embourgeoised' stratum of Soviet society."

The driver, mistaken for the minister, gets special menus in restaurants and hotel rooms are cleared out for his convenience. He ends up in a hospital where he is "surrounded with exaggerated concern and attention. A young woman even shows him special personal sympathy and hopes to marry him." Mistaken as the driver, the minister experiences the life of "an average Soviet person. He encounters bureaucratism and indifference." The main reason for rejecting this "contrived and essentially odious theme" is that the situation is depicted "not critically, but as the normal and daily conditions of contemporary Soviet reality."[173]

---

[169] RGANI f5 op36 d12, 22–214. Ironically enough, just a month after this demonization of Dudintsev and his novel at the CC meeting, no one other than Polikarpov and Riurikov recommended its publication by Young Guard publishers in a print run of 30,000 to 50,000, down from the 500,000 originally planned by Roman-Gazeta, but remarkable all the same. The explanation they gave the Presidium was that its publication would "deprive demagogues from having an occasion to argue that the novel was banned." RGANI f5 op36 d37 6b.

[170] Pikhoia, *Sovetskii Soiuz*, 144–46.

[171] Aksiutin, "Khrushchevskaia 'Ottepel.'"

[172] It came out in 1958, directed by Nadezhda Kosheverova.

[173] RGANI f5 op36 d50, 1–2.

The same fate met screenwriter Vladimir Tendriakov and director Mikhail Shveitser's *Tugoi Uzel/Tight Knot*, which didn't see the light of day until 1989, although an unrecognizably diluted version came out as *Sasha Vstupaet v Zhizn/Sasha Embarks on Life* in 1957. According to the January 4, 1957, Mosfilm studio's party committee, the original film "insistently and consistently shows all representatives of the party . . . as cowardly, careerist, hypocritical, and criminally indifferent to the needs of the people."[174] At an April 1957 meeting at Mosfilm with Tendriakov and Shveitser, Mikhail Romm, Ivan Pyrev, Tvardovskii, Emmanuil Kazakevich, and Aliger supported reworking the film, while the party committee secretary, V. Ageev, and the deputy culture minister, Surin, opposed even this possibility.[175]

A real blast from the Stalinist past appeared in Polikarpov's review of the previous year's theater repertoire, wherein he used the August 1946 CC Resolution as a measure, this time singling out plays that glorify the Western bourgeois Other: "As a rule what is performed . . . idealizes the bourgeois way of life. . . . There are often ideas of class peace, 'good or humane' capitalists. . . . Bourgeois life is depicted like some kind of idyll. . . . Scenes occur in rich fashionable apartments of businessmen . . . luxurious toilets, jazz music. . . . an advertisement for the bourgeois way of life." Of course, youth were singled out for their vulnerability in being exposed to these kinds of plays.[176]

He further found fault with all the plays about "rehabilitated communists returning from prison, as if they are the conscience of the people." He singled out Zakhar Agranenko's *We are Together* being staged at Moscow's Pushkin Theater, where heroes are sailors who spent time in both Hitler's camps, "where they behaved honorably and our Soviet camps in which one of them dies of beatings and the other barely survives." The third objectionable genre Polikarpov identified were spectacle-memoirs, that is, "plays of the '20s and '30s which were banned because of their authors' arrests.[177]

The saga of *Doctor Zhivago* deserves attention here not only because of its notoriety, but because of what it says about Soviet identity at the time, and the acute reaction the foreign publication of a work rejected by Soviet censors produced. The actual content of the novel was largely irrelevant. It was neither more

---

[174] RGANI f5 op66 d50, 30. Meanwhile, mirroring Dudintsev's contradictory case above, Tendriakov's novel *Tugoi Uzel* was nominated for a Lenin Prize, and the book was published in an edition of 500,000. RGANI f5 op36 d50, 26–27.

[175] RGANI f5 op36 d50, 26–45.

[176] On similar comments about adoration of the bourgeois decadent formalistic abstract West in the visual art world, see Culture Minister Nikita Mikhailov's January 21, 1957, memo on the artistic intelligentsia of Moscow and Leningrad to the CC, in RGANI f5 op36 d48, 17–22.

[177] RGANI f5 op36 d44, 1–5.

nor less ambiguous, anti-Soviet, non-ideological, etc., than other works. But the fact that Pasternak had sent it to the West elevated the novel into an unpatriotic, hostile, even treasonous act. It was if he had forsaken his Soviet identity to ally with the imperialists.

The manuscript for *Doctor Zhivago* was completed by February 1955. For the next year, Pasternak shopped it around the most liberal Soviet journals. He started at *Literaturnaia Moskva/Literary Moscow*, but Emmanuil Kazakevich read it and said, "Judging by the novel, the October Revolution was a misunderstanding and never should have occurred." Simonov then rejected it at *Novyi Mir*. Pasternak's son, Yevgeny, has written that a visiting Italian communist, Sergio D'Angelo, asked for and received the manuscript from his father in the summer of 1956. He never returned it and passed it on to the leftist Italian publisher Giorgio Feltrinelli, who notified his father he intended to publish it in Italian. In June 1956, Boris Pasternak wrote a letter to Feltrinelli warning of grave consequences if the novel came out in Italian before it was published in the Soviet Union.[178]

In January 1957, Boris Ponomarev, head of the CC Department on Ties with Foreign Communist Parties, wrote to Riurikov that Pasternak had agreed to send a telegram to the publisher Fetrinelli saying he needed the manuscript back in order to rework it for publication. The Italian communist party deputy secretary Luigi Longo agreed to intercede with the publisher on Pasternak's behalf.[179] Feltrinelli went ahead with the publication nonetheless.

Dudintsev also fell afoul of Western appreciation for his work. It didn't help that *Not by Bread Alone* was being produced on Broadway at the time, and that Hollywood had invited him to come make a movie of his novel.[180] In a local party meeting on Dudintsev, the chair of the Moscow section party committee, Sytin, concluded that "we should arm ourselves with the 1946–48 CC Resolutions. They are only untimely in part, but fundamentally correct in directing our literature and art."[181]

On May 13, 1957, Khrushchev himself appeared at a UW Plenum meeting. Before he spoke, both Ehrenburg and Simonov defended Dudintsev. Ehrenburg again expressed his confidence in the security of Soviet socialism: "They say this

---

[178] Chukovsky, *Diary*, 407–08.

[179] RGANI f5 op36 d37, 2.

[180] Furtseva announced this to the June CC Plenum, evoking "noise in the hall." RGANI f2 op1 d230, 50.

[181] Zezina, *Sovetskaia Khudozhestvennaia Intelligentsiia*, 201. Again, ironically, just a week after Dudintsev's "processing" at the Moscow writers' meeting, Riurikov recommended to the Presidium that they not prevent the publication of Dudintsev's novel abroad "because of the big noise it would raise in the press." RGANI f5 op36 d37 6b.

list of books [the usual suspects] is very harmful, harmful due to the political situation. I have a more optimistic view of our society and our people...." Consequently, one need not take extreme measures against those with whom one might disagree. "Dudintsev's novel is artistically weak. I repeat, artistically.... It was an incorrect approach, but from that, against which one can object, right up to an absolute ban—is a big step. Can't we really have a discussion about books?... We need to somehow avoid the administration of literature.... We need to permit maximum initiative...." Simonov defended Dudintsev by criticizing himself and other editors for not doing a better job of helping Dudintsev revise his manuscript, but said "it was a novel with honorable intentions"[182]

Khrushchev then gave a two-hour address. He made the connection between the dangerous turn of events in Hungary and Dudintsev: "The rebellion in Hungary wouldn't have happened had they imprisoned two or three bawlers. Some of our writers are trying to knock the legs from under Soviet literature by imitating the Petofi circle [of Hungarian intellectuals who demanded reform] ... and it is absolutely right that the state hit them on the hands...." The problem is, Khrushchev went on, that some have incorrectly understood the essence of the party critique of the cult of personality, "ignoring the world-historical successes of the Soviet country in the construction of socialism...." He then made the connection with the external Other: "In Dudintsev's little book, which reactionary forces abroad now try to use against us, negative facts are tendentiously selected...." The author "intentionally rejoices at the inadequacies in our life."

To make himself more clear, Khrushchev invited some 300 to 400 writers and artists with their spouses to his suburban dacha at Semenovka, where he was apparently not exactly sober. He shouted, "If anyone is getting ready to go on the same path as Hungary or Poland, against the line of the party, we will crush them into dust...." He especially attacked Margarita Aliger, one of the editors of *Literaturnaia Moskva* and the recent widow of Aleksandr Fadeev, saying: "You are a throwback to the capitalist West!" She replied, "Nikita Sergeevich, what are you saying? I am a communist, a party member...." "You lie! I don't believe communists such as you," he replied.[183]

Literaturnaia Moskva was dreamed up and edited by Kazakevich who intended it to come out twice a year, its first issue appearing in Feburary 1956,

---

[182] RGANI f5 op36 d33, 94–106.

[183] Aksiutin, "Khrushchevskaia 'Ottepel,'" 217–20. Khrushchev repeated his arguments connecting Dudintsev, Aliger, and Kazkevich to the events in Hungary at the CC Plenum in June. Plenum, 11th session, June 28, 33–34. It is significant, however, that unlike CC Culture Department functionaries, Khrushchev did not argue that the 1946–48 CC Resolutions were still defensible. *Literaturnaia Moskva* was shut down in March 1957, before its third issue could appear, accused of propagating "nihilism and despondency." Zezina, *Sovetskaia Khudozhestvennaia Intelligentsiia*, 200.

and available in Kremlin book stalls during the Twentieth Party Congress. It included poems by Zabolotskii for the very first time, Tvardovsky's *Za daliu dal*, Pasternak's notes on translating Shakespeare, and Ehrenburg's article on Tsvetaevaia, as well as many less challenging pieces.[184] One of the most challenging, however, was Alexander Iashin's *Levers*, a short story about some kolkhoz managers and party officials sitting around complaining about the plight of their farm, the party's ignorant interference in its operation, etc., followed by a meeting of the party aktiv, where each one of the former malcontents just mouths all the hackneyed party slogans and brooks no dissent. It was the first public revelation of a common phenomenon in Soviet life: thinking one thing in private, but publicly doing what was required, under pain of punishment.

Veniamin Kaverin, one of the editors of the almanac, recalled his meeting with Iashin about his submission. "At the meeting, I asked him to make some insignificant changes, and he asked is that all? Yes, I said. He was silent and shrugged his shoulders. "But last year when I brought the story to *NM*, Krivitskii (the secretary of the editorial board there) told me, 'Take this story as far away from me as possible and burn it or bury it so that no one ever sees it. It would be good if you only got 10 years...'"[185]

But the discourse of difference didn't disappear. The recently posthumously rehabilitated Vsevolod Meyerhold's production of *Mandat* premiered in a Moscow theater less than three weeks after the Soviet military intervention in Hungary. A day after the conclusion of the CC meeting with writers, Boris Pilniak was posthumously re-admitted to the WU. One of the most popular plays in the 1956–57 season was Turkish émigré communist Nazym Khikmet's *But Was that Ivan Ivanovich?*, a satire already published in the March 1956 issue of *NM*. It allegorically depicted how the Soviet system created the possibility for every leading worker to have his or her own cult of personality. It was adopted by 30 theaters, translated into several languages, and premiered in May 1957 at the Moscow Theater of Satire, to positive reviews in the press.[186]

One extraordinary fact in this period that might go unnoticed, but is critical in revealing the huge change after Stalin's death, is the resistance officially criticized authors felt they could offer in response to the party. Their own personal feelings of security were unthinkable just a few years before. The responses of

---

[184] Zezina, *Sovetskaia Khudozhestvennaia Intelligentsiia*, 191. The issue also included Tvardovsky's poem, "Meeting with a Friend," about an innocent exile who spent 17 years in a hard labor camp and Kazakevich's *A House on the Square*, a novel about the Red Army that included not only heroic soldiers, but thieving parasites, too.

[185] Veniamin A. Kaverin, *Literator: Dnevniki i Pisma* (Moscow: Sovetskii Pisatel, 1988), 106–08.

[186] Zezina, *Sovetskaia Khudozhestvennaia Intelligentsiia*, 187.

Simonov, Aliger, Ehrenburg, Dudintsev, and others cited above are examples of the fundamental change in the boundaries of permissible difference.

Just a month after Khrushchev's drunken threats to Soviet writers, the main carriers of the discourse of danger—Molotov, Kaganovich, and Voroshilov—were removed from power. On the morning of June 22, 1957, Central Committee members were greeted with charges against this "anti-party group," accused of plotting against Khrushchev, the Presidium, party policy, and much else. Ironically, from June 18 to 21, there was an anti-Khrushchev majority on the Presidium. Molotov, Kaganovich, Malenkov, Bulganin, Voroshilov, Pervukhin, and Saburov all argued for Khrushchev's removal as first secretary, largely due to his rude and crude treatment of his colleagues, and tendency to publicly announce new policies without consulting the rest of the Presidium. Only Mikoian, Brezhnev, Suslov, Furtseva, and Pospelov defended Khrushchev, a 7–6 majority for demotion.[187]

But over these three days, Khrushchev arranged the meeting of the full Central Committee where he had a majority of supporters.[188] While there were many charges against Molotov and Co., the outcome was a big victory for the discourse of difference over the discourse of danger at the very pinnacle of Soviet political power. As Mikoian summarized in his memoirs: "Why did I support Khrushchev? It was clear to me that Molotov, Kaganovich, and partially, Voroshilov, were dissatisfied with the revelations of Stalin's crimes...."[189]

On the first day of the plenum, Marshal Zhukov listed thousands of Stalin's victims shot under the signatures of Molotov and Kaganovich.[190] Given a chance to defend himself, Molotov criticized Khrushchev for his tardy and unnecessarily crude treatment of writers like Dudintsev, who should have been dealt with long before.[191] Mikoian accused Molotov of remaining a Stalinist, saying that Molotov was trying to tar Khrushchev with the same "Rightist label" Stalin had tried to smear Molotov with at the October 1952 CC Plenum.[192] The next day, Brezhnev accused the anti-party group of wanting to restore mass repressions. Furtseva accused them of "covering up the economic inadequacies" of the country. Consequently, "agriculture was brought to the brink of collapse."[193]

---

[187] Lazar Kaganovich, *Pamiatnye Zapiski* (Moscow: Vagrius, 1996), 515–17; and Aksiutin, "Khrushchevskaia 'Ottepel,'" 225.

[188] Between March 1953 and March 1956, Khrushchev had replaced 45 of 84 first party secretaries in republics and oblasts.

[189] Mikoyan, *Tak Bylo*, 597.

[190] Plenum, 1st session, June 22, 15. I will deal in more detail in the next chapter with Molotov's foreign policy errors as enumerated at this Plenum. They are reflections of his Stalinist line at home.

[191] Plenum, 2nd session, June 24, 73.

[192] Plenum, 4th session, June 25, 40.

[193] RGANI f2 op1 d230 26, 37–42.

On the morning of June 27, Kuusinen noted that after the Twentieth Party Congress, "we thought that Stalin and Beria were guilty of arbitrary violence.... But now we have found out that Malenkov, Kaganovich, and Molotov, even without pressure from Stalin, acted violently against many dedicated communists, directly encouraged torture . . . and false confessions."[194] This "processing" of Molotov and Co. went on until June 29.

Institutions and Identities

During the Thaw, the institutional landscape of Moscow shifted dramatically in favor of societal understandings of identity. The death of Stalin had the most important institutional effect of destroying the single most powerful obstacle to the dissemination of counter-hegemonic understandings of what it meant to be Soviet. Fear of sanctions and its consequence of over-insurance and anticipation of Stalin's wishes gave way to experimentation with the boundaries of the possible. There were some notable institutional continuities, however. The Central Committee Culture and Agitprop Departments continued to be guardians of the discourse of danger. Boundaries of permissibility continued to be established by official campaigns against exemplary deviations: Tvardovsky, Pomerantsev, Dudintsev, Zorin, Iashin, and Pasternak, in this period.

One important institutional hold-over from Stalin, and indeed pre-dating him, was the primacy of the general secretary on the Presidium, such that once Khrushchev had stated a position at a meeting of the Presidium, most of the other members were loathe to object, for fear of disrupting the unity of the party elite before the eyes of the public. The repeated violation of this norm by Molotov figured prominently in his removal in June 1957. The consequence of this was to give extraordinary power to the general secretary for the execution of his own personal preferences in party and state policy.

Shepilov, no fan of Khrushchev after his removal from the Presidium in June 1957, wrote in his memoirs about why he didn't oppose either the virgin lands or the fetishization of corn cultivation advanced by Khrushchev, despite the fact that, "as an economist-agronomist I of course understood the deep flaws in these plans. But I, as my entire generation of communists, was brought up in the spirit of party possession/oderzhimost and strictest discipline, and I would consider as sacrilege any kinds of doubts about party directives."[195]

---

[194] RGANI f2 op1 d232, 30–31.
[195] Dmitrii T. Shepilov, "Politicheskii Arkhiv XX Veka. Vospominaniia," *Voprosy Istorii* (September 1998), 7.

An additional Stalinist institutional hold-over, though in less extreme form, was the norm of telling higher authorities what they wanted to hear about reality, a kind of institutionalized varnishing/lakirovka of reality. Consequently, Khrushchev's efforts to get to the bottom of the agricultural crisis in the latter half of 1953 were impeded by the Central Statistical Administration's failure to offer accurate figures.[196]

But the same institutions that nurtured difference under Stalin—the creative unions, editorial boards, the intelligentsia, the culture market, and the councils on religious affairs—not only continued as carriers of difference, but asserted themselves more strongly, in the absence of the threats promised by Stalin.

Examples abound in the period of the preferences of the Culture and Agitprop Departments being ignored, challenged, over-ridden, and ridiculed. The Science and Culture Department suffered a serious defeat in the efforts of P. V. Volobuev and Anatolii Cherniaev to concoct a *"Questions of History* affair" against Anna Pankratova and her editorial board.[197] Aleksandr Saveliev calls this event "a battle between the apparat and the nomenklatura," since Pankratova, beyond being an academician, doctor, and professor, was a CC member, too.

In late 1954, Volobuev and Cherniaev solicited letters about the journal. The April 1955 meeting staged to criticize *Voprosy Istorii* was postponed because of Pankratova's health. The Department itself was split on pursuing the affair, Rumiantsev once exclaiming to Volobuev, "Don't you know you are dealing with Pankratova—a CC and Supreme Soviet Presidium member?!" Pankratova, meanwhile, kept up her own direct correspondence with CC Department leaders and Presidium members Shepilov and Pospelov, in fact complaining in May 1955 about her critics and their baseless claims against the journal. Finally, in March 1956, Shepilov rejected any further "processing" of Pankratova or her journal. At the time of her death in May 1957, Pankratova had stopped publishing additional works of historians who had been repressed, satisfying her more orthodox critics.[198]

The Writers' Union was not itself an advocate of difference, since it represented virtually all points of view, but it was a venue for an airing of these debates as the 2nd congress clearly showed in December 1954. Prior to the 2nd congress of writers, the Moscow section met, and in a secret ballot, voted against Nikolai

---

[196] Taubman, *Khrushchev*, 261.

[197] Cherniaev would go on to become one of Gorbachev's most trusted "new thinkers." Journals such as *Voprosy Istorii* and other more academic publications had additional institutional power in that they were not subjected to the same level of pre-publication censorship from Glavlit as the mass literary journals, like *Novyi Mir*. Aleksandr V. Saveliev, "Nomenklaturnaia Borba Vokrug Zhurnala 'Voprosy Istorii' v 1954–1957 Godakh," *Otechestvennaia Istoriia* 10 (2003): 151.

[198] Ibid., 149–58.

Gribachev attending the congress as one of their delegates. The Leningrad section did the same to Vsevolod Kochetov.[199]

It was also an institutional home for subcultures within the literary community, most prominently, as shown above, between conservative Russian nationalists and liberal Soviet writers. The former scored a huge institutional victory after Khrushchev's attendance at the UW's Third Plenum in May 1957: A UW for the RSFSR was founded, in clear opposition to the UW of the USSR. Apparently, Russian national identity was getting too diluted while serving as the implicit national identity for all Soviets.[200]

The Moscow and Leningrad sections of the Writers' Union were powerful institutional carriers of the Thaw. The Moscow section had its own publication, *The Moscow Literator*, in which, for example, Paustovsky's speech against the "new class" of Soviet rulers was published. In contrast, *Literaturnaia Gazeta*, the official organ of the Writers' Union itself, refused to publish a transcript of the UW meeting following the Twentieth Party Congress its editor, Vsevolod Kochetov, calling it "revanchist."[201] Of course, it was *Literaturnaia Gazeta*, under Boris Riurikov's editorship in 1954, that had "processed" the more liberal Tvardovsky's *Novyi Mir*.[202] Efforts to create a new institution could go too far, as well, as we have seen in the case of the almanac *Literaturnaia Moskva*, which was shut down after just two issues in 1957.

The newly-created Ministry of Culture somewhat diluted the CC Departments' direct supervision of cultural production, and even represented to a degree the more expansive understanding of Soviet identity advocated by many writers and artists. It had a rather rocky start. Its first minister, Panteleimon K. Ponomarenko, the former first party secretary of Belarus, lasted only until March 1954, when he became first party secretary of Kazakhstan.[203] His successor, Georgii Aleksandrov, was removed within months, for sexual indiscretions. Nikolai Mikhailov became the new minister in 1954, not retiring until 1960.[204]

Market incentives were also in conflict with ideological orthodoxy. As under Stalin, the Culture Ministry pushed for the purchase of foreign films, as ticket receipts were revenue for them. The CC Culture Department realized

---

[199] RGANI f5 op17 d486, 246–247. In the domain of visual arts, as Nikita Mikhailov himself testified, "it is characteristic that socialist realists were not chosen as delegates to the Moscow meeting of artists in December 1956." RGANI f5 op36 d48, 18.

[200] Frankel, *Novy Mir*, 138.

[201] Zezina, *Sovetskaia Khudozhestvennaia Intelligentsiia*, 191–92.

[202] Allied with *Novyi Mir* in advancing a discourse of difference was the journal *Iunost*. Mitrokhin, *Russkaia Partiia*, 150.

[203] Ponomarenko went on to become Soviet ambassador to Poland from 1955 to 1957, and then to India and Nepal, from 1957 to 1959.

[204] Zezina, *Sovetskaia Khudozhestvennaia Intelligentsiia*, 105–06.

this and accused the ministry of "not attaching due significance to these acquisitions. . . . The Ministry proceeds mainly from considerations of how much income can be received . . . and less than anything to the ideological side of the question." The Culture Department rejected ten of the ministry's requests.[205] The Culture Department lamented the "incorrect mercenary attitude of local publishers" who publish "huge editions of second-rate foreign writers" to make money.[206]

Individual Soviet artists were also understood as dangerous and profitable commodities. In June 1956, the Presidium agreed with the Culture Ministry's request to allow the pianist Stanislav Richter to attend a Robert Schumann celebration in the GDR, noting that "almost all the biggest countries in the world are asking to organize tours for Richter on extremely profitable terms."[207] But just five months later, the Presidium denied permission for Richter to go to England for a concert, citing the fact that his mother had decided to stay in Germany after the war and his father had been executed by Soviet authorities.[208]

One of the informal, but widespread, institutional forms to emerge after Stalin's death was the "kompaniia" or "kruzhok." These were small groups of friends looking for opportunities to drink, chat, listen to music, and dance, mostly in each other's apartments. They were also places for discussions of the novels, plays, articles, and movies that constituted the Thaw.[209] There was an upsurge in the creation of literary circles in institutes and universities among students and staff, and informal journals of criticism appeared.[210] Some of these discussion groups became well-known because their members were arrested. The "Krasnopevtsev group" of nine Moscow State University students was arrested in August 1957 and the "Pimenov group" of 11 students, mostly from the Leningrad Library Institute, was arrested in March 1957. They were all charged with forming an illegal group and distributing illegal literature and leaflets.

The phenomenon of mass public poetry readings had just begun in 1957, as well. Boris Riurikov, deputy head of the CC Culture Department, reported in May 1957 of "troubling meetings of poets at the Gorky Literature Institute with young people preferring Pasternak and Mayakovsky, considering realism old-fashioned."[211] The

---

[205] RGANI f5 op36 d30, 115–19.
[206] RGANI f5 op36 d14, 97.
[207] RGANI f5 op36 d24, 72.
[208] Zezina, *Sovetskaia Khudozhestvennaia Intelligentsiia*, 242.
[209] Alexeyeva, *The Thaw Generation*, 83.
[210] Swayze, *Political Control of Literature*, 154.
[211] RGANI f5 op36 d32, 64.

party itself, especially its lowest links, on the factory floor, at institutes, but also right up to oblast committee meetings, became, as we saw, sites of full-blown debates about Soviet identity after the Twentieth Party Congress Unable to define precisely what the Soviet Union was after declaring it was not Stalin, the party gave only broad and vague instructions to party officials. It took three different directives from the Center to restore some sense of acceptable order to these discussions within the party itself.

Aware of the power a creative union like the WU could have, and taking advantage of the window of opportunity opened by the Thaw, Romm and Pyrev lobbied the Presidium for the creation of a Union of Cinematographers, against the wishes of the Ministry of Culture, fearful of the creation of a "second center of power" and succeeded in 1957.[212]

Implications for Foreign Policy

The discourse of difference transformed domestic life in the Soviet Union. Societal constructivists would expect, given these new elements of Soviet identity, that Soviet relations with the external world would change, too. First, we should expect that the Soviet Union would understand itself as more secure and powerful in the world. This has indeterminate effects, as more power might produce more propensity for risky adventures, or, on the contrary, being more secure might allow the Soviet Union to be more relaxed about the imperialist threat.

Second, we should expect the Soviet Union to be more tolerant of difference within the socialist camp, since dangerous deviance is not so common as was once thought. This would imply a de-Stalinization of the Soviet bloc, as well as a greater tolerance for deviations in places such as China, which are lower on the rungs of modernity and socialist development. In addition, we would expect the bourgeois nationalist leaders of the developing world to be more welcome as potential Soviet allies, because the dichotomous division of the world into us and them has been eroded at home.

Third, the Soviet Union should admit to mistakes in its treatment of other states in the past. Fourth, the ethnonational Russian nation should creep into elite Soviet discussions of foreign relations, even while officially forswearing such a pre-modern vestige. As for timing, there should be immediate changes in

---

[212] Ian Christie, "Canons and Careers: The Director in Soviet Cinema," in *Stalinism and Soviet Cinema*, ed. Richard Taylor and Derek Spring (London: Routledge, 1993), 167; Vladimir Baskakov, "'Serebrianyi Vek' Sovetskogo Kino," in *Kinematograf Ottepeli: Dokumenty i Svidetelstva* (Moscow: Materik, 1998), 180–81; and Swayze, *Political Control of Literature*, 146.

Soviet foreign policy, since de-Stalinization occurred within days after Stalin's death at home. One continuity should be the maintenance of the Soviet Union atop a hierarchy of socialist modernity when compared to others in the socialist camp. This would also be the case with regard to the decolonizing world, which would frequently be regarded as pre-modern.

5

The Thaw Abroad, 1953–58

Just as Stalin's death had immediate and revolutionary effects on Soviet identity in Moscow, it had similar consequences for Soviet foreign policy. The discourse of danger, with its fundamentally vulnerable Soviet Union, its socialist project under constant threat, its understanding of deviations from the Soviet model as always potentially catastrophic for the construction of socialism, and its division of the world into a rigidly binarized "us" and "them," was immediately countered by the societal discourse of difference that had been surviving, often underground and in private, the previous years.

The emergence of a Soviet Union that understood itself as more secure, its socialist project more assured, deviations from its model as tolerable, even if not welcomed, and the world as an arena of grays, not blacks and whites, a world not of "us" and "them," but rather "us," "them," and "not them," profoundly affected Soviet relations with its Eastern European allies, its Chinese ally, and its newly possible allies in the developing world.

In Eastern Europe, the rise of the discourse of difference in Moscow meant the discrediting of the model of socialist development Eastern European communists had been pursuing for the last half dozen years. The "new course" recommended by Moscow discredited tens of thousands of party functionaries, and rehabilitated hundreds of thousands of executed, imprisoned, and repressed. Most important, it meant that those leaders who had been installed on a wave of Stalinist "affairs" were now themselves vulnerable. In welcoming Yugoslavia back into the socialist fold, the Soviet Union blessed versions of socialism, belief in which could have gotten oneself killed just years before. The Soviet invasion of Hungary in November 1956 re-established some sort of boundary of allowable difference beyond which Soviet socialist allies were loath to go, but still far beyond what was permissible in 1953.

The discourse of difference initially improved relations with China, as the Soviet Union realized that its economic and military agreements with China had been unequal. However, the continued understanding of socialism in the Soviet Union as a de-Stalinizing project ran head on into the growing Chinese understanding of socialism as precisely Stalinist. The Thaw met the Great Leap Forward. The seeds of the Sino-Soviet split were sown by the discourse of difference in the Soviet Union.

In the developing world the discourse of difference meant the Soviet Union had interests in places and people that were completely absent under Stalin's more orthodox rejection of difference as dangerous deviance. Bourgeois nationalists such as Nasser or Nehru, previously scorned as imperialist lackeys, became potential allies. The principle of "who is not against us is potentially with us" replaced the Stalinist principle of "who is not with us is against us." This change in Soviet identity would open up Asia, Africa, and Latin America to 30 years of intense, and deadly, competition between Moscow and Washington.

Relations with the United States were the least affected area of Soviet foreign policy, at least as compared to Eastern Europe, China, and the developing world, perhaps because so much of the identity relationship between the Soviet Union and the United States was generated in the interactions between the two states internationally, such that the Soviet great power identity was reinforced daily in relations with the United States and the West.

Acknowledgement of fallibility affected all of Soviet foreign policy. Admission that it was a mistake to Stalinize Eastern Europe brought rapid changes to almost all those regimes. Recognition that the Soviet Union had erroneously excommunicated Yugoslavia from the socialist community resulted in a high-level Soviet delegation visiting Belgrade to apologize and lay out a course for rapprochement between the two socialist countries. Realizing that economic, political, and military relations with China were unfortunately redolent of the unequal treaties of the nineteenth century resulted in much more equitable relations between the two socialist allies. Determining that nationalist bourgeois leaders like Nehru, Nasser, and Nu need not be communist to be reliable allies against imperialism opened up the entire decolonizing world to Soviet foreign policy. Finally, recognizing that its hard line on Berlin, Austria, Korea, etc., as well as its large conventional army, had unnecessarily provoked the West to arm itself in response led to the first postwar détente in Soviet-Western relations.

Hungary: The Boundary between Danger and Difference

Soviet policy toward Hungary from the time of Stalin's death until the aftermath of the military suppression of the Hungarian revolution in November 1956 reflected the ongoing struggle between the discourses of danger and difference in Soviet identity politics in the period. Just as inside the Soviet Union, where there was an immediate de-Stalinization after Stalin's death, Soviet leaders demanded that Hungary follow suit. When toleration for difference got out of control in Hungary, the Soviets responded with armed force to restore a more orthodox leadership in Budapest. But even after the intervention, Soviet leaders continued to recommend a relatively reformist course for Hungarian politics. This tracks neatly with the Hungarian effects at home in the Soviet Union, where the Thaw was slowed, but not reversed.

Just three months after Stalin's death, at a meeting in Moscow in June 1953, the Soviet leadership insisted on Matyas Rakosi's resignation as Hungarian prime minister. This reflected the post-Stalin realization in the Soviet Union of the dangers of the concentration of power in a single autocrat's hands, and the need for collective leadership. At Soviet behest, Imre Nagy replaced him. He then embarked on a series of reforms. Even before the Hungarian delegation arrived in Moscow, it had been instructed by Soviet leaders to replicate in Hungary what was already being implemented in the Soviet Union: reallocate investment away from industry to consumer goods and services, reduce taxes on the peasantry, and separate the positions of general secretary and prime minister.[1]

Having already admitted their own fallibility at home, Soviet leaders insisted at their June 13–16 meeting that their Hungarian counterparts do the same. Malenkov told them that "our impression is that our Hungarian comrades underestimate their shortcomings." Soviet admission that their many "affairs" and repression in general were concocted and unnecessary was replicated in the attacks of Beria and Malenkov on Rakosi for the excessive use of police power. Malenkov assured them that "we are correcting the mistakes we have made in this respect in our country."[2] Beria, of all people, inquired, "How could it be acceptable that in Hungary, a country with 9.5 million people, one and one half million are persecuted. . . .?"[3] Beria also told Rakosi, "Enough glorifying of leaders, of Stalin!"[4] The unexpected level of anti-Stalinism displayed by Beria at home in the early months after Stalin's death manifested itself as well in foreign affairs.

At the end of the meeting, Rakosi agreed to reduce investments in heavy industry, allow peasants who had been forced to join collective farms to leave them, to declare an amnesty for political prisoners, and to resign as prime minister. At its June 27–28 plenum, the Hungarian party officially adopted this New

---

[1] Bela Zhelitski, "Nazrevanie Obshchestvennogo nedovolstva I Politicheskogo Krizisa v Vengrii v Pervoi Polovine 50-x godov," in *Vengriia 1956 goda: Ocherki Istorii Krizisa*, ed. Bela Zhelitski, T. M. Islamov, and Iu. S. Novopashin (Moscow: Nauka, 1993), 23.

[2] Charles Gati, *Failed Illusions: Moscow, Washington, Budapest, and the 1956 Hungarian* Revolt (Palo Alto: Stanford University Press, 2006), 27–29.

[3] Taubman, *Khrushchev*, 247.

[4] Aksiutin, "Khrushchevskaia 'Ottepel,'" 41.

Course. The number of collective farmers dropped by 39 percent; investment in heavy industry declined by 40 percent, and private services even received government loans.[5] On July 25, the Hungarian government declared an amnesty that would free and/or rehabilitate almost 750,000 Hungarians by November.[6]

But Rakosi and his allies never abandoned their efforts to undermine Nagy and the New Course. Nagy confided to the Soviet ambassador, Evgenii Kiselev in July 1953 that he was surprised that Rakosi and others "mistakenly equate the demands of working people with the hand of the enemy."[7] Rakosi, like Molotov in the Soviet Union, was a carrier of Stalin's discourse of danger. In late 1954, while resting in the Soviet Union, Rakosi took advantage of his access to Soviet leaders to tell them that Nagy was an anti-Soviet nationalist, a Right deviationist, an opportunist, and—the coup de grace—a favorite of the West. The result was a January 8, 1955, meeting in Moscow with the Hungarian leadership where, unsurprisingly, Molotov declared that "in Hungary there is no better leadership than the leadership of Rakosi."[8] Molotov's Stalinist ally on the Presidium, Lazar Kaganovich, made the dangerous charge of comparing Nagy to Bukharin. Khrushchev pointed out the limit of "national" paths to socialism, the boundary beyond which difference becomes danger, warning that "the Voice of America is hoping there will be Soviet, Yugoslavian, and Hungarian socialisms. . . ." With Soviet backing, the March 1955 Hungarian party plenum condemned Nagy's "right deviationism." On March 28, Nagy was asked to resign as prime minster and was replaced by Andras Hegedus, a Rakosi protege. In April, Nagy was removed from the Politburo; and in December, from the party.[9]

But the period from Nagy's restoration to the eve of the Twentieth Party Congress in February 1956 was marked by the growing power of the discourse of difference in the Soviet Union. Its foreign policy consequences were manifest in the May 1955 treaty neutralizing Austria, the June 1955 visit of atonement to Yugoslavia, the July 1955 Geneva summit with the leaders of the United States,

---

[5] Gati, *Failed Illusions*, 56.

[6] Bela I. Zhelitski, "Imre Nad," *Voprosy Istorii* (August 2006): 33, 56. The future Hungarian leader, and former party general secretary and interior minister, Janos Kadar, was freed from life imprisonment in May 1954.

[7] Tatiana V. Volokitina et al., *Moskva i Vostochnaia Evropa. Stanovlenie politicheskikh rezhimov sovetskogo tipa (1949–1953). Ocherki istorii* (Moscow: ROSSPEN, 2002), 787; and Mark Kramer, "The Early Post-Stalin Succession Struggle and Upheavals in East-Central Europe," *Journal of Cold War Studies* 1, no. 1 (Winter 1999): 30.

[8] Zhelitski, "Nazrevanie Obshchestvennogo Nedovolstva," 43–47; Gati, *Failed Illusions*, 115–23. One of the many charges leveled at Molotov at the Anti-Party Plenum in June 1957 that dismissed him from power was a dangerously close and enduring relationship with Rakosi.

[9] What amounted to "national roads to socialism" would be proclaimed permissible at the Twentieth Party Congress in February 1956, just a year later.

France, and Britain, and the September 1955 establishment of diplomatic relations with West Germany. All these events only served to embolden Hungarian reformers and discredit Rakosi's disavowal of the New Course.

A November 1955 memorandum from the second secretary of the Soviet embassy in Budapest, Boris Gorbachev, expressed growing unease about how far difference was advancing in Hungary, despite Rakosi's leadership. He wrote that the influence of "right opportunist views," those of Nagy, continued to be substantial among the intelligentsia. Writers who were critical of Rakosi were "met with stormy approval" from the audience at the Writers' Union. As in the Soviet Union, Hungarian youth were identified as the weakest link. Gorbachev pointed out the dangers of admitting one's mistakes. Writers here "cite the errors of the party in industrialization and collectivization, and unjustified repressions.... the Rajk affair and Yugoslavia" to justify opposition to the party's line today.[10]

The Twentieth Party Congress in Moscow in Feburary 1956 further discredited Rakosi's efforts to thwart the course of reform in Hungary. At the March 12–13 plenum at which the Hungarian party leadership discussed the consequences of Khrushchev's revelations, Rakosi persisted in defending his actions against Nagy, while Kadar demanded that Mihaly Farkash be prosecuted for his role in the Rajk Affair.[11] Rakosi was forced to announce the rehabilitation of Rajk in late March.[12] More generally, confusion reigned in Hungary, as Moscow did not give its ambassador in Budapest, Iurii Andropov, any clear instructions for how Rakosi was to respond to the new authorization of still deeper de-Stalinization.[13]

On April 29, 1956, Andropov sent an alarming telegram to Moscow about the political situation in Hungary.[14] Most critically, he opposed Rakosi's consent to restore Kadar to the Hungarian Politburo. "We think that our Hungarian comrades are making a serious concession to the Right and demagogic elements, hoping to weaken their criticism.... It would be expedient to speak to them about this, frankly stating our fears about Kadar."[15] From June 8 to 14, 1956, Mikhail Suslov was sent to Hungary by the Politburo and sent back far more reassuring messages about the scene in Hungary than Andropov. In his June 13

---

[10] RGANI f5 op36 d3, 13–31.

[11] Matiash Rakosi, "Liudiam Svoistvenno Oshibatsia," *Istoricheskii Arkhiv* (January 1999): 14.

[12] Roi Medvedev, *Neizvestnyi Andropov: Politcheskaia Biografiia Iuriia Andropova* (Moscow: Prava Cheloveka, 1999), 28.

[13] Vladimir Kriuchkov, *Lichnoe Dela. Chast Pervaia* (Moscow: Olimp, 1996), 46.

[14] Andropov, who had been serving as a counselor in the Budapest embassy, replaced Kiselev in December 1955.

[15] "Vengriia, Oktiabr-Noiabr 1956 goda," *Istoricheskii Arkhiv* (May 1993): 106.

memo to the Politburo, Suslov concluded from his meeting with Kadar that "I doubt he will be negatively inclined toward the Soviet Union. His inclusion in the Politburo will significantly appease some of the dissatisfied, and Kadar himself will feel morally bound."[16] While advising that Rakosi not be replaced, Suslov reassured that "there is no talk about a 'crisis' in the party leadership or distrust for the party, and the mood of the workers and peasants, especially peasants on cooperatives, is healthy." He went on to argue "it would be wrong to consider as Right opportunists all those who are dissatisfied. Among them are many honorable communists who are dissatisfied with Rakosi because of his serious violations of legality in 1949–52. . . ." He recommended that Farkash be tried and supported Kadar's inclusion on the Politburo.[17] Suslov's views reflected well the new discourse of difference prevailing in Moscow: whoever is not against us is potentially one of us.

The Poznan riots in Poland on June 28–29 only inspired Hungarians to demand that the New Course be deepened, especially in light of Khrushchev's speech at the Twentieth Party Congress.[18] Mikoian was sent to Budapest to participate in the Hungarian party plenum on July 13. Mikoian told the Hungarian leadership that "anything unexpected and unpleasant like Poznan cannot be permitted here." He said that Hungarian "CC members distrust Rakosi because of the pre-1953 repressions" and recommended he retire from the Politburo. In his report to Moscow on his conversations with Rakosi, Hegedus, and Erno Gero, Mikoian concluded that "so long as Rakosi heads the party, the CC will not be able to defend itself from accusations of unjustified repressions. . . . I suggested he voluntarily step down and rest for his health in our country. Comrade Rakosi said he would, if we considered it useful."[19]

It is important to note that the Soviet leadership could have followed Andropov and Molotov, and supported Rakosi's continued resistance to any meaningful reform. But given the discourse of difference's rise in the Soviet Union at the time, and especially after the authority of the Twentieth Party Congress was behind it, Soviet understanding of what it meant to be a socialist state did not permit re-Stalinization. Instead, as expressed by Mikoian and Suslov, good communists had good reason to reject Rakosi and his Stalinist program. As

---

[16] Rakosi, "Liudiam Soistvenno Oshibatsia," 68 n. 102. The explanatory notes in Rakosi's memoirs are written by the editors of *Istoricheskii Arkhiv*, the journal in which they are serialized.

[17] Medvedev, *Neizvestnyi Andropov*, 30; V. L. Musatov, "SSSR I Vengerskie Sobytiia 1956 g.," *Novaia i Noveishaia Istoriia* (January 1993): 7; and "Vengriia, Oktiabr-Noibr," 109.

[18] Bela Zhelitski, "Budapesht—Moskva: god 1956-I" in *Sovetskaia Vneshniaia Politika v Gody "Kholodnoi Voiny (1945–1985),"* ed. L. N. Nezhinskii (Moscow: Mezhdunar otnosheniia, 1995), 252.

[19] "Vengriia, Oktiabr-Noibr," 110–14.

Kadar told Mikoian on July 14, "We fear that comrade Rakosi will again return to the old practice of tyranny, and put us in prison."[20] On July 19, Kadar returned to the Politburo.

By mid-September, there was growing unrest in Hungary, culminating in tens of thousands attending the reinterment of the remains of Laszlo Rajk on October 6, not coincidentally the date of an 1849 Austrian execution of 13 Hungarian rebels. During the week of street demonstrations that followed there were demands for a renewal of socialism and a deepening of the New Course that had been abandoned by Rakosi.[21] On October 12, Andropov reported to the MFA a conversation with Gero. Gero said dissatisfaction has now gone far beyond the intelligentsia to include workers and peasants. Demonstrators at the reburial of Rajk demanded Nagy's restoration to the Politburo and the open trials of Rakosi and Farkash.[22] Andropov concluded, "One must foresee that eventually Nagy will have to be accepted into the leadership of the party, maybe even on the Politburo, because the pressure is very strong." Nagy refuses to admit any errors as the price for readmission to leadership, citing the fact that in October 1954 he had demanded the rehabilitation of Rajk, and now that's what has been done. Gero thinks that Nagy is a pawn for anti-Soviet forces and that if "Nagy takes power, Hungary will be even less socialist than Yugoslavia. . . ." Anti-Soviet feelings have markedly increased, even among workers and in the party. Gero requests that the Soviets make Rakosi stay in the Soviet Union and announce that he will remain there for a long time on account of his health. Despite Gero's anxiety, Andropov concluded that "we think that Gero's assertion of dissatisfaction and anti-Soviet feelings in the working class is incorrect." The Hungarian party leadership just doesn't explain and defend its policies well.[23]

The next day, Nagy's party membership was restored and the December 1955 resolution justifying his expulsion was annulled. The following week, student demonstrators demanded the return of Nagy to power and the withdrawal of Soviet armed forces from Hungary. Nagy returned to the Politburo on October 23. But it was too late, as violence broke out in Budapest the same day, with 100,000 demonstrators on the streets, the razing of Stalin's statue and the torching of the main radio station. For the next 10 days, the Soviet Presidium would meet daily about what to do in Hungary. On the 23rd, everyone on the Presidium, except Mikoian, agreed to deploy Soviet armed forces to Budapest to

---

[20] Pikhoia, *Sovetskii Soiuz*, 137. Ironically, Mikoian would express similar fears about Molotov, Kaganovich, and Voroshilov to justify his vote for their removal at the "anti-party" plenum in June 1957.

[21] Medvedev, *Neizvestnyi Andropov*, 33.

[22] Farkash and his son were arrested the same day.

[23] "Vengriia, Oktiabr-Noibr," 131–34.

re-establish order. Even Nagy did not oppose this offer. Mikoian and Suslov were sent to Budapest.[24] By the 24th, 6,000 of an eventual 31,000 Soviet troops had entered Budapest. By noon, 25 demonstrators had been killed, and 200 wounded.[25]

To further demonstrate that the Rakosi era was over, Nagy became prime minister on the 24th, and Mikoian and Suslov recommended Gero resign as first secretary; Kadar replaced him on the 25th. Continuing to allow difference to reign, Mikoian and Suslov agreed to Nagy's proposal to expand the government to include non-communist parties, small farmers, social democrats, and peasants, a true "popular front."[26] Not unpredictably, Molotov, Kaganovich, and Voroshilov criticized Mikoian's moderation during a meeting of the Presidium that day.[27] Khrushchev defended Mikoian both that day, and on the 26th, when the criticism was renewed. Meanwhile, Mikoian and Suslov reported on the 26th from Budapest that they had objected to Nagy's announcement that he would enter into negotiations with Moscow on the withdrawal of all Soviet forces from Hungary, but still said, "[W]e think the main thing now is not military measures, but is the possession of the masses."[28]

On the 27th, Mikoian and Suslov were still more reassuring, reporting that "in general, the government is reliable in the sense of being more authoritative among the public."[29] On the other hand, they also told Kadar that he could have as many Soviet troops as "are needed."[30] On the 28th, Nagy declared that those who had participated in the unrest until this point were patriotic workers expressing just demands for reform. On the same day, the Soviet Presidium was split between those who thought events were heading in the right direction, and those who thought it was already past time for a military suppression of what they deemed to be a counter-revolution.

Khrushchev noted that the situation was getting more complicated in Hungary, and that "Kadar's mood is to negotiate with the hotbeds of resistance." He remarked that workers support the uprising. Voroshilov adopted a more

---

[24] Fursenko, *Arkhivy Kremlia Prezidium*, 176–77.

[25] Mark Kramer, "New Evidence on Soviet Decision-Making and the 1956 Polish and Hungarian Crises," *Cold War International History Project Bulletin* 8–9 (1996/1997): 365–67. This would grow, according to Suslov, to 350 dead, 3,000 wounded, and 600 Soviet casualties, by the 28th. Fursenko, *Arkhivy Kremlia Prezidium*, 184.

[26] Zhelitski, "Budapesht—Moskva," 264–70.

[27] Kramer, "New Evidence on Soviet-Decision Making," 367.

[28] Fursenko, *Arkhivy Kremlia Prezidium*, 180; and "Vengriia, Oktiabr-Noibr," 137–39.

[29] Perhaps reflecting the strength of the discourse of difference in Moscow, Suslov, Mikoian, and Andropov never suffered professionally or personally from their serious misreadings of Hungarian realities.

[30] "Vengriia, Oktiabr-Noibr," 139.

aggressive stance, arguing that "we must decisively suppress them. Nagy is a liquidator." Molotov agreed, calling the current situation the road to capitulation. He criticized Mikoian for "appeasing them," and asked to open a discussion on the "help of our armed forces." Kaganovich supported Molotov, but Malenkov, defending the merits of allowing reform to work its way, said, "Don't blame our comrades. They are pursuing the line of suppression firmly." Voroshilov returned to his criticism of Mikoian, and now Suslov, arguing that "American agents are operating more actively than" the Soviet envoys. Bulganin disagreed, warning that "in Budapest there are forces that want to overthrow the government of Nagy and Kadar." This was the heart of the difference. Molotov, Kaganovich, and Voroshilov wanted to militarily suppress those "forces," with or without the consent of Nagy and Kadar, while Khrushchev, Malenkov, Bulganin, Mikoian, and Suslov all saw Nagy and Kadar as allies against those "forces." The only question was whether Nagy and Kadar had the capacity and the will, without Soviet military intervention, to effect an outcome that would leave Hungary a socialist ally, or not. Bulganin laid out the choice: "We should support the present government. Otherwise we must support occupation. This will involve us in an adventure." Kaganovich, apparently swayed, agreed with Bulganin.[31] The upshot was to wait and continue to rely on Nagy and Kadar, at least for another day.

On the 29th, the Hungarian government recharacterized the rebels as a "movement of working people for the satisfaction of just demands." Suslov and Mikoian reported back to Moscow that this move, along with an amnesty for demonstrators, had led to "armed groups beginning to lay down their arms." The subsequent Presidium meeting is marked by all, save Khrushchev, expressing alarm at Mikoian's "capitulationism."[32]

The next day, October 30, marks the apogee of Soviet toleration of difference, not just in Hungary, but in the socialist world more generally. On that day, the Presidium adopted and published the "Declaration on the Principles of Development and Strengthening of Friendship and Cooperation between the Soviet Union and Other Socialist Countries." In it the Soviet Union confesses to errors in the past, violations of sovereign equality, and promises to withdraw military advisors, and military forces, in accordance with the requests of its socialist allies. It is a stunning repudiation of hierarchy, infallibility, and center-periphery relations. As Gati argued, "the declaration was an extension of de-Stalinization to the realm of Moscow's relations with countries in the Soviet bloc."[33] It lasted less than 24 hours.

---

[31] Fursenko, *Arkhivy Kremlia Prezidium*, 181–85.
[32] "Vengriia, Oktiabr-Noibr," 143.
[33] Gati, *Failed Illusions*, 179.

Khrushchev, early in the October 30 Presidium meeting, suggested adopting the Declaration. The only debate was just how far to go in admitting previous errors. Even Molotov, arguing that "an anti-revolutionary government has been created" in Hungary, recommended entering into negotiations about the withdrawal of Soviet forces. Shepilov supported a withdrawal from Hungary. Zhukov agreed, but raised doubts about leaving the GDR and Poland. Voroshilov cautioned, "[C]riticize ourselves, but justly."[34] Kaganovich alone objected to any self-criticism at all. Bulganin argued against "softening the self-criticism—mistakes were made." Khrushchev expressed readiness to withdraw military and security advisers and said we support the government of Nagy and Kadar. Khrushchev concluded with the choice facing Moscow: "There are two paths: military—the path of occupation, and peaceful—the withdrawal of forces and negotiations."[35] While the Declaration was published in *Pravda* the very next day, already in the early morning hours, the sentiment among Soviet leaders had shifted.

By the October 31 Presidium meeting, Nagy had endorsed leaving the Warsaw Pact, declared neutrality, and had opened talks with Mikoian and Suslov on Soviet troop withdrawals.[36] Khrushchev opened the meeting, declaring, "We should re-examine our assessment and should not withdraw our troops from Hungary and Budapest." For the first time, he invoked the loss of credibility the loss of Hungary would entail for Moscow: "If we depart from Hungary, it will encourage the Americans, British and French—the imperialists. They will perceive it as weakness on our part and go on the offensive.... To Egypt, they will then add Hungary. We have no other choice."[37] Molotov, referring to the Declaration he had agreed to only the day before, said, "[Y]esterday was a half-assed decision."[38] Upon receiving his orders, Marshal Ivan Konev promised the Presidium on October 31 that it would take only three to four days to "crush the counter-revolution in Hungary."[39] He was right.

Prior to the launching of "Operation Whirlwind" on November 4, the Soviet Presidium continued to meet. Mikoian, back in Moscow on November 1, continued,

---

[34] See chapter 4 for similar discussions on the draft of Khrushchev's secret speech at the Twentieth Party Congress. Criticize, but carefully.

[35] Fursenko, *Arkhivy Kremlia Prezidium*, 187–91; and "Kak Reshalis 'Voprosy Vengrii'," *Istoricheskii Arkhiv* (February 1996): 97–104.

[36] Kramer, "New Evidence on Soviet-Decision Making," 369.

[37] "'Malin' Notes on the Crises in Hungary and Poland, 1956," *Cold War International History Project Bulletin* 8–9 (1996/1997), 393. Britain and France had joined Israel's invasion of Egypt on October 31. The change of Soviet mind is consistent with the argument that the Suez Crisis tipped the balance in favor of an invasion of Hungary, since now Soviet credibility was on the line as a great power, but there is not yet explicit archival evidence to support that conclusion.

[38] Fursenko, *Arkhivy Kremlia Prezidium*, 192.

[39] Kramer, "New Evidence on Soviet-Decision Making," 375.

alone, to oppose the use of military force. Others, however, enumerated the dangers of inaction. In particular, they had received alarming reports of the spread of unrest in support of the Hungarian revolution in Czechoslovakia, Romania, and the USSR itself.[40] As Shepilov put it, "If we don't embark on a decisive path, things in Czechoslovakia will collapse."[41]

But Mikoian argued that "the demand for the withdrawal of (our) forces has become universal. Anti-Soviet feelings have risen.... Force now will help nothing. Enter negotiations. Wait 10 to 15 days." But at the same time, he repeatedly said that "we shouldn't allow Hungary to leave our camp." The others were already convinced that only military suppression would guarantee that commonly desired outcome. Suslov, for example, replied that "the danger of a bourgeois restoration has come.... Only by occupation can we have a government that supports us." Zhukov chimed in, "We must remove all the trash and disarm the counter-revolution." But Mikoian clung to his position, arguing at the second Presidium meeting on November 1 that "if Hungary is becoming a base of imperialism, then there is no conversation. [But] we are talking about the situation today. We shouldn't permit a schoolboyish [*shkoliarskii*] approach. We have three days yet to think, to get the advice of our comrades. We should maintain contact with them." Nobody agreed.[42]

Meanwhile, Kadar had disappeared to the Soviet Embassy in Budapest, and would arrive in Moscow the next day. Nagy, aware of the arrival of Soviet forces, declared Hungary's withdrawal from the Warsaw Pact and appealed to the UN to recognize Hungary's neutrality. Over the next two days, Kadar and Ferenc Munnich joined in the Presidium discussions in Moscow. Kadar, it seems, only reluctantly went along with the decision to use Soviet forces.

At the November 2 meeting, Kadar, sounding a lot like Nagy, argued that "most rebels are not counter-revolutionaries; they just want people's democracy and a Soviet troop withdrawal." He confessed that "at first, we didn't see this, and qualified them as counterrevolutionaries, and thereby turned the masses against us." He supported the coalition government, arguing they "don't want a counter-revolution." They are "against the return of landlords and capitalists." He praised the already moot Moscow Declaration of October 31, saying it had "made a good impression," but its effects were undermined by Soviet troop movements. He complained about Andropov lying to the government about Soviet troop movements. He suggested that Soviet forces withdraw for two to three months, during which time "our party and other parties could fight against the counter-revolution." He argued the "use of

---

[40] Mark Kramer, "The Soviet Union and the 1956 Crises in Hungary and Poland," *Journal of Contemporary History* 33, no. 2 (1998): 196–98; and Zubkova, *Russia After the War*, 196–97.

[41] "'Malin' Notes," 395.

[42] Fursenko, *Arkhivy Kremlia Prezidium*, 193–95.

military force will reduce the moral situation of communists to zero.... The authority of socialist countries will suffer."[43]

But Soviet leaders were far beyond any compromise, instead occupying themselves with how to present their decision to use force to the world. They drafted a "plan for measures on Hungary" that included "speaking about the threat of fascism" from the Horthyites, the "threat to our Motherland," using "how they want Hungary as a base against us," and so on.[44] It is interesting to note here that the imperialist threat rarely, if ever, came up in the months leading up to the intervention. Of course, the United States would take advantage of any overthrow of socialism in Hungary, but only rarely in internal deliberations was the United States identified as the source of the rebellion, only its main beneficiary.

The next day, the Presidium met with Kadar and Munnich again. This time, Khrushchev lamented Soviet errors of previous months: They had not pursued a policy of accepting difference in Hungary soon enough. "We asked for Rakosi's removal far too late. Mikoian and I are to blame for suggesting Gero and not Kadar.... They are honorable dedicated communists, but they did many stupid things. Expelling Nagy from the party was a mistake."[45] Kadar agreed, asking, "Why did we choose Gero in the summer? Soviet comrades always helped, but it was a mistake. Our Soviet comrades only trusted three to four Hungarian comrades: Rakosi, Gero, and Farkash.... Rakosi told us that our Soviet comrades shared the opinion about expelling Nagy from the party."[46] It is notable that Khrushchev confessed to not being liberal enough early enough, not to being too weak and tolerant.

Khrushchev left that night to meet secretly with Tito on the island of Brioni off the Yugoslav coast to ask for Belgrade's support for Operation Whirlwind. According to the memoirs of the Yugoslavian ambassador to Moscow, Veljko Micunovic, who was in attendance, Khrushchev wondered whether Nagy was just an instrument of reaction or a conscious agent of imperialism. Regardless, events were leading to the restoration of capitalism. "What is left for us to do, he asked. If we reconcile ourselves, the West will consider us idiots and cowards. We cannot agree to such a turn of events, neither as communist internationalists, nor as the Soviet Union, a great power." At the end of the meeting, Khrushchev and Malenkov again blamed the previous Stalinist order in Hungary for the crisis at hand: "Rakosi and Stalin cooked up a porridge in Hungary that now we have to eat."[47]

---

[43] "Kak Reshalis 'Voprosy Vengrii'," *Istoricheskii Arkhiv* (March 1996): 97–101; and Fursenko, *Arkhivy Kremlia Prezidium*, 197–99.
[44] Fursenko, *Arkhivy Kremlia Prezidium*, 196.
[45] "Kak Reshalis," (March 1996), 109–10.
[46] Fursenko, *Arkhivy Kremlia Prezidium*, 199–200.
[47] Veljko Micunovic, *Moscow Diary* (New York: Doubelday, 1980), 138–40.

As Operation Whirlwind began on November 4, the Presidium met in Moscow.[48] Once again, Khrushchev and Molotov faced off over where to draw the line between difference and danger. One might think that the Hungarian revolution would have forged a consensus behind the re-Stalinization of the bloc, but as we have seen in the Soviet Union itself, events in Hungary caused a pause in the Thaw, not a rollback. The same was to be true in Hungary, despite Molotov's resistance. At the meeting, Molotov took issue with Kadar's plans to "condemn the Rakosi-Gero clique. This can be dangerous. We must convince them to refrain from this." Khrushchev replied, "I don't understand Molotov; he comes up with the most pernicious ideas." Bulganin agreed with Khrushchev. But Shepilov supported his predecessor as foreign minister, saying, "We will be giving them the opportunity to besmirch the entire 12 years of the work of the party...." Putting his finger on the danger of dominoes falling in a reformist direction in eastern Europe, he warned that "tomorrow there will be an 'Ulbricht clique.'" Kadar went ahead with his radio address.[49]

Just two days later, Molotov returned to the issue at the November 6 Presidium meeting, with the same result. Molotov and Kaganovich demanded that the expression "Rakosi clique" be dropped. Molotov warned that "what is going on is the creation of a new Yugoslavia," thereby succeeding in restating his opposition to the rapprochement with Yugoslavia, as well. But Malenkov noted that without condemning Rakosi, "[W]e will not strengthen the leadership" of the new Kadar government. Zhukov agreed, and Averky Aristov made the stakes plain, accusing Molotov and Kaganovich of "clinging to the cult of Stalin." Khrushchev concluded, "Molotov doesn't say it, but he is thinking of returning Hegedus and Rakosi. Rakosi did colossal harm and for this he must be held responsible and expelled from the party. Comrade Kaganovich, when will you correct yourself and stop bootlicking? What a backward position you take!" Only Shepilov agreed with Molotov that "we will be putting a blot on the socialist past."[50]

The revolution in Hungary forced the Soviet leadership to decide how far difference could go before it became dangerous, how far a country could de-Stalinize, and reform its socialist model, before it was no longer a socialist ally, but a potential ally of the imperialist enemy. The dialogue between Molotov and his supporters, and Khrushchev and his, illustrates that debate. And

---

[48] The operation would last a week and entail 2,700 Hungarian and 700 Soviet deaths. Medvedev, *Neizvestnyi Andropov*, 45.

[49] Fursenko, *Arkhivy Kremlia Prezidium*, 201–02.

[50] Ibid., 204–06; "'Malin' Notes," 398–99; and "Kak Reshalis," (March 1996), 116. At the June 1957 anti-party plenum, Khrushchev accused Molotov of wanting to restore Rakosi as late as March 1957, but I can find no corroborating archival evidence of such a stance by Molotov. CC Plenum, June 24, 1957, 26.

Khrushchev and the discourse of difference won, at least in averting a return to Stalinist orthodoxy. Molotov's continued opposition to the new de-Stalinized Soviet identity resulted in his ouster from power in the June 1957 "Anti-Party Plenum."

Poland: Dodging a Bullet

Just as Stalin's death had called a halt to the Doctors' Plot and other contrived "affairs," Moscow advised Poland on May 15, 1953, to end its "germ warfare" affair, an open show trial on which Soviet and Polish officials had been working since 1952. Just a month later, the Soviet government recommended that the planned show trial of bishop Kachmarek be reconsidered because "the available evidence is insufficiently convincing to confirm the accusations" against him. The Polish government went ahead nonetheless, sentencing Kachmarek to 12 years in September 1953.[51]

Just as Ulbricht and Rakosi were invited to Moscow soon after Stalin's death to discuss the need for immediate de-Stalinization, Boleslaw Bierut's delegation received the same advice in July 1953. And, like Rakosi and Ulbricht, he resisted, only announcing a "new course" on October 29, and only implementing it superficially.[52]

In late December 1953, the Soviet ambassador to Poland, Georgii Popov and Mikhail Zimianin, the MFA official in charge of relations with Poland, co-authored a critical memo to Molotov on Poland's domestic circumstances. The analysis reflected a combination of the discourses of difference and danger. First, unlike Soviet communists, who had at last begun to recognize their own fallibility, Polish comrades "overestimate their successes and are uncritical toward their errors in economic policy." Mirroring recent policy changes in the Soviet Union, they note that the rates of growth in consumer goods and food production are too low and there is no collective party leadership.

On the other hand, the Polish leadership was criticized for not being sufficiently orthodox, as well. They allow too many individual farmers; their "attitudes toward kulaks are still vague"; and bourgeois nationalism, Catholicism, and social democracy are still strong ideological threats to Polish socialism. Popov and Zimianin complain the trials against Gomulka and former defense minister Marian Spychalski have been "extremely protracted."[53] They should be

---

[51] Volokitina et al., *Vostochnaia Evropa v Dokumentakh Rossiiskikh Arkhivov, 1944–1953 gg. Tom II*, 803, 903–05.
[52] Kramer, "The Early Post-Stalin," 32.
[53] Gomulka was freed from prison in December 1954.

organized as "they would promote the unmasking of bourgeois nationalism in Poland and raise the political vigilance and militance of the party."[54]

Just as Soviet keepers of orthodoxy at home were constantly worried that the discourse of difference might go too far in the cultural world, Soviet keepers of orthodoxy abroad followed closely cultural developments of their socialist allies. So, the June 1954 Polish Writers' Union congress was marked as a site of "reactionary sentiments" in favor of replacing socialist realism. In particular, Pomerantsev's "On Sincerity in Literature" had become widely known and discussed in Poland. These unhealthy phenomena were reported to Pospelov.[55] It was typical for Soviet critics in eastern Europe to single out for attack the exact same works that were then under fire in Moscow; another example of the transfer, in detail, of Soviet identity politics to Soviet socialist allies.

It was not until the Twentieth Party Congress that the discourse of difference really took off in Poland. In a scenario too strange to be untrue, Bierut was in a Kremlin hospital with pneumonia when a copy of Khrushchev's secret speech was delivered to him. He had a heart attack after reading it, and died on March 12, 1956.[56] De-Stalinization was received with great enthusiasm in Poland. Rakosi recalls that he found out about Khrushchev's speech only after reading the Polish party newspaper, *Tribuna Liudu*. Its first page was covered with pictures of the Polish communists in the 1930s who had just been rehabilitated by Khrushchev at the Twentieth Party Congress.[57]

On March 15, Khrushchev led a Soviet delegation to Warsaw for Bierut's funeral, and supported the choice of Edvard Ochab as Bierut's successor, deliberately rejecting more Stalinist alternatives.[58] The Polish party distributed copies of Khrushchev's speech to all party cells in late March. At the meetings where

---

[54] Volokitina et al., *Sovetskii Faktor v Vostochnoi Evrope*, 854–61. This combination of concerns was reflected in conversations of the Soviet leadership with Berut in Moscow on December 28, 1953. Ibid., 874–76. Apparently Ambassador Popov was too zealous in his insistence that his Polish comrades reduce the influence of Jews (Mints, Berman, and Zambrovskii) on the Polish Politburo. At the March 29, 1954, Soviet Presidium meeting at which his removal was discussed, Khrushchev declared that Popov had "showed himself to be an anti-Semite." Fursenko, *Arkhivy Kremlia Prezidium*, 881–83. He was replaced by Pantemelion Ponomarenko. The end to official anti-Semitism in Moscow was transferred to Soviet relations with its socialist allies.

[55] Fursenko, *Arkhivy Kremlia Prezidium*, 449; RGANI f5 op17 d454, 103–04. This transfer of vigilance abroad was continued across the period. Ambassador Ponomarenko reported to Foreign Minister Shepilov in February 1957 about the dangerous "revisionists" to be found in the Polish Academy of Sciences, Warsaw University, Ministry of Education, and academic and cultural institutions more generally. A 90-page summary of dozens of articles in the Polish press that exhibited these dangerous deviations was appended to the memo. RGANI f5 op30 d229, 19–20.

[56] Taubman, *Khrushchev*, 290.

[57] Matiash Rakosi, "'Videl, kak voznikaet kult lichnosti'," *Istoricheskii Arkhiv* (January 1997): 135.

[58] Pikhoia, *Sovetskii Soiuz*, 137.

the speech was read, anti-Soviet and anti-Russian protests erupted.[59] In April, Ochab exonerated Gomulka of all charges of "hostile and diversionary activity."[60]

Reminiscent of East Berlin three years before, Poznan erupted in workers' riots June 9–28, 1956. Demonstrators demanded bread, religious freedom, and an end to communism and Soviet occupation. Seventy demonstrators were shot by Polish security forces.[61] The immediate Soviet response was also not unlike its response to unrest in East Germany: publicly blame the imperialists, and, as if acknowledging the true cause of the discontent, rush to provide more economic aid so as to avert any future revolts. On July 9, the Soviet government approved a new economic aid package for Poland. On July 14, Khrushchev told the Yugoslavian ambassador, Micunovic, that "they wanted to go to the West, to break up the camp. Behind it all stood the US. This time the West dared to provoke a revolt in Poland, tomorrow it would be somewhere else; they thought the time had come to change the results of World War II."[62] Ochab later recalled that the Soviets had advised him to blame the imperialists for Poznan, but he told them there wasn't enough evidence to sustain the claim.[63]

Poznan, like the Twentieth Party Congress three months before, accelerated the de-Stalinization of Poland. Gomulka's party membership was restored in August. On October 4, the Soviet Presidium approved Ochab's request to remove all Soviet KGB advisers from Poland.[64] A week later, Gomulka rejoined the Polish Politburo; on October 17 he became the party's first secretary. As was the case in Hungary, no Stalinist option was discursively available in the face of political unrest. The discourse of difference had taken its place.

Meanwhile, the Soviet leadership, alarmed at the accelerating pace of change in Poland (not to mention Hungary), took the desperate measure of flying uninvited to Poland on October 19, to participate in the Polish party's CC plenum. Before leaving for Warsaw, the Soviet leadership had mobilized Soviet armed forces in Poland under the guise of "exercises." Only as a Soviet tank brigade was approaching Warsaw shortly before his arrival did Khrushchev order Marshal Konev to halt his forces. Poland had mobilized its own internal security troops

---

[59] A. M. Orekhov, "Sobytiia 1956 goda v Polshe i Krizis Polsko-Sovetskikh Otosheii," in *Sovetskaia Vneshniaia Politika v Gody "Kholodnoi Voiny," (1945–1985)*, ed. L. N. Nezhinskii (Moscow: Mezhdunarodnii Otnosheniia, 1995), 223; and Taubman, *Khrushchev*, 284. Ochab later recalled that he was reproached for allowing Khrushchev's speech to be published in the Polish press while at the June 1956 CMEA meeting. It wasn't published in the Soviet Union in full until 1962. Toranska, *Them*, 56.

[60] Rakosi, "Liudiam Soistvenno Oshibatsia," 64.

[61] Pikhoia, *Sovetskii Soiuz*, 2000, 137; Toranska, *Them*, 224.

[62] Micunovic, *Moscow Diary*, 86–87.

[63] Toranska, *Them*, 63.

[64] Fursenko and Naftali, *Khrushchev's Cold War*, 2006, 433; and Luthi, *The Sino-Soviet Split*, 56.

in light of Soviet actions.[65] Khrushchev arrived in Poland with the commander of the Warsaw Pact, Konev, as well as 11 other Soviet generals in dress uniform. In light of Soviet troop movements, Gomulka told Khrushchev that "if you talk with a revolver on the table you don't have an even-handed discussion. We cannot continue discussions under these conditions."[66]

The uninvited Soviet guests did not get off on the right foot. Upon his alighting the plane, Khrushchev greeted the Soviet generals who awaited him, while shaking his fist at the Polish party leadership. He yelled, "We spilled blood for the liberation of this country and you want to give it to the Americans, but you will not succeed!" He refused to shake hands with his Polish comrades and called them traitors. Gomulka introduced himself to Khrushchev saying, "I am Gomulka, the one you kept in prison for three years."[67]

While the discussions resolved little, they at least arrested the brewing crisis in Polish-Soviet relations. Upon returning to the Kremlin the next day, Khrushchev was still considering to "do away with what is in Poland." He fulminated against Ponomarenko who he accused of misjudging both Ochab and Gomulka.[68] By the next day, however, Khrushchev outlined two choices: "[I]nfluence and follow events, or go onto the path of interference." He concluded, "[W]e must refrain from armed interference and show patience." He agreed to withdraw all Soviet advisers from the Polish secret police and defense ministry as well as Soviet officers from the Polish armed forces. He swallowed the Polish Presidium's decision to not re-elect the Soviet Pole and Polish defense minister Konstantin Rokossovsky to the Polish Presidium. He also admitted that the Soviet Union should stop demanding Polish coal at below world market prices as reparations. "The sooner we get along without Polish coal, the better," he said. At the time, the Soviet Union was paying $1/ton while the world price was $10/ton. The Soviets also annulled $538 million in Polish debt.[69]

Mass popular support for Gomulka was duly noted at Soviet Presidium meetings discussing Poland. From October 22 to 24, hundreds of thousands of Poles took to the streets in support of Gomulka's "new course." Also of great importance

---

[65] Nikolai Bukharin, "Otnosheniia mezhdu Sovetskim Soiuzom I Polskoi Narodnoi Respublikoi (1944–1989 gg.)," *Voprosy Istorii* (October 2007): 102; and Taubman, *Khrushchev*, 293.

[66] Gati, *Failed Illusions*, 142.

[67] Orekhov, "Sobytiia 1996 goda," 229.

[68] In any event, Ponomarenko lasted until October 1957, when he was replaced by Petr Abrasimov.

[69] "SSSR i Polsha: Oktiabr 1956-go," *Istoricheskii Arkhiv* (May–June 1996): 182–86; Fursenko, *Arkhivy Kremlia Prezidium*, 174–75; and Bukharin, "Otnosheniia," 103. Rokossovsky retired on November 13, returned to the Soviet Union, and became a deputy defense minister. His replacement was none other than Spychalskii, whom Zimianin and Orlov had recommended be publicly tried with Gomulka three years before.

in ultimate Soviet restraint was Gomulka's reassurance on October 24 that Poland had no intention of leaving the Pact.[70]

The events in Poznan and Gomulka's restoration resonated throughout the Soviet Union, provoking more energetic support for the discourse of difference at home, and thereby alarming the Soviet leadership that they were approaching the boundaries of danger. At the October 23 Presidium meeting, it was decided to not publish Gomulka's CC Plenum speech in the Soviet press, fearing its positions on the Catholic church, private agriculture, multi-party governance, in short, a Polish path toward socialism.[71]

In a November 4 report from the Lithuanian party to the CC in Moscow, it was noted that the Polish CC Plenum's decision to dissolve unprofitable collective farms had found support among "groups here who express hope for the dissolution of Lithuanian kolkhozy."[72] Moreover, over two thousand ethnic Poles have applied to emigrate to Poland from Lithuania in the last two weeks, compared to just 260 all last year. The report continued to describe student demonstrations in Kaunas of up to 35,000 people, with anti-Soviet slogans reflecting both nationalist and religious sentiments.[73]

It must have been unusually alarming for Soviet leaders in Moscow to learn from their Lithuanian CC Secretary Antanas Snechkus that the October 31 Declaration on Relations with Socialist Countries was being interpreted in Lithuania as if such relations should prevail between the Russian and Lithuanian Socialist Republics![74] Some students at the State Historical Archive Institute in Moscow toasted events in Poland and Hungary as signaling "the impending fourth Russian revolution."[75]

The GDR: Still a Special Case

Despite the GDR's exceptional position, it too was affected by immediate de-Stalinization in the Soviet Union. Just two weeks after Stalin's death, Molotov reversed Stalin's recent agreement to close the Berlin border. In his orders to

---

[70] Kramer, "New Evidence on Soviet-Decision Making," 361; "'Malin' Notes," 389; and Orekhov, "Sobytiia 1996 goda," 231–34.

[71] "SSSR i Polsha," 186.

[72] According to an April 1957 MFA Information Committee report, Poland was in last place among socialist countries in terms of percentage of collectivized agriculture: 6 percent. RGANI f5 op30 d130, 133.

[73] "USSR/Russia—Egypt: 50 Years of Cooperation," *International Affairs* (October 1993): 247–52.

[74] Aksiutin, "Novoe o XX Sezde KPSS," 257–59.

[75] Taubman, *Khrushchev*, 301.

Marshal Vasilii Chuikov, chairman of the Soviet Control Commission and Vladimir Semenov, Moscow's main political adviser to the SCC, he justified the reversal by citing the "bitterness and dissatisfaction from Berliners" that would be directed against the GDR and Soviet Union if such a move were made.[76] But it was not until May 1953 that a full re-evaluation of Ulbricht's Stalinist regime was performed, and the Soviet leadership recommended a "New Course" for East Germany. Although too late to prevent the workers' demonstrations and riots on June 16–17, the changed model for constructing socialism, consistent with Soviet advice to all its socialist allies, including China, was a substantial deceleration of the process of socialist construction.

Soviet relations with the GDR remained exceptional in the sense that Germany was a defeated, divided, and occupied recent former enemy in the middle of Europe. It was also the strategic prize of the great patriotic war and the most immediate strategic threat of the early Cold War. In the early post-Stalin period, the new Soviet discourse of difference and its public commitment to ultimate German reunification both militated toward a new course for the GDR. Molotov's complaints about Ulbricht to the Presidium in May 1953 captured the strategic aspect of the relationship perfectly. He said that Ulbricht's speech on Marx's birthday on May 5, with its talk about the "dictatorship of the proletariat" and the construction of socialism, was killing any chances of influencing West German domestic politics in the direction of reunification. Molotov further recommended, foreshadowing the new course that would be officially adopted in a month, that Ulbricht be advised to stop the creation of new agricultural cooperatives and the campaign against private farmers.[77]

On that very day, May 14, Ulbricht's government was further turning the screw, announcing a 10 percent increase in labor output norms, the Soviet Presidium agreed with Molotov's view of developments in the GDR, including advising Ulbricht to abandon his Stalinesque plans for his 60th birthday celebration.[78] A few days after this Presidium discussion, Marshal Chuikov, his political adviser Pavel Iudin, and Iudin's deputy, Ivan Ilyichev, sent the Presidium a detailed report on the situation in the GDR, especially highlighting the accelerating flight of refugees across the border to the West, which the Soviet authors blamed on the "squeezing of capitalist elements out of industry, commerce, and agriculture. . . ."[79] They also

---

[76] Hope M. Harrison, *Driving the Soviets Up the Wall* (Princeton: Princeton University Press, 2003), 19.

[77] Kramer, "The Early Post-Stalin," 32; and Alexei Filitov, "SSSR I GDR: God 1953-i," *Voprosy Istorii* (July 2000): 124.

[78] Harrison, *Driving the Soviets*, 24.

[79] 120,000 East Germans had fled West in the first four months of 1953 alone, including 3,000 party members. Naumov, "Byl li Zagovor Berii," 25; and Aksiutin, "Khrushchevskaia Ottepel," 38.

criticized excessive religious persecution and the groundless linkage of disgruntled youth to West German fascists.[80]

The memoranda from Berlin, Beria, and Molotov leading up to the June Presidium meeting that formulated the new course for the visiting GDR leadership all agreed that it was Ulbricht's excessively Stalinist model of socialism that urgently needed to be changed if the regime were to avoid disaster. As Malenkov exclaimed at a May 27 Presidium meeting at which a draft resolution on the new course was discussed, "If we don't correct the situation now, catastrophe will come.... We must act quickly!"[81]

Two days before the arrival of the Ulbricht delegation in Moscow, Beria received a report from Major-General Mikhail Kaverznev, head of the inspectorate on security questions of the SCC, in which East Germany was criticized for coercive collectivization, insufficient attention to the private sector in the countryside, and the confiscation of ration cards from small entrepreneurs "who don't use wage labor." Meanwhile, the GDR leadership "still doesn't study the true causes of the flight of the refugees." They ignore "the gross distortions and extreme acts" by individual authorities, and the threats against small farmers and business owners, which is driving them to the West.[82]

All of the above critiques and implied remedies appeared in the New Course for the GDR adopted by the Presidium on June 2, 1953, "On measures to improve the political situation in the GDR." It was presented to Ulbricht and his colleagues over the next two days. On the first day of meetings, Germans were told the "accelerated construction of socialism was wrong," collective farms that had been created by coercion should be disbanded; limitations on small private capital should be relaxed; taxes on private enterprises should be reduced, and they should get the food ration cards previously denied them; the policy of favoring heavy over consumer industry should be reversed; and those who had been imprisoned without evidence should be released. In other words, there should be a more moderate approach to the construction of socialism, and a wholesale de-Stalinization of society.[83]

Soviet leaders reassured their German allies that "we have all made errors." Beria continued, "We are not making any kind of accusations." In recommending the new, more moderate course, Malenkov pointed out that even "Lenin had NEP," the New Economic Policy, a retreat from the accelerated construction of

---

[80] Elke Sherstianoi, "Vyzrevanie Politicheskogo Krizisa v GDR v 1953 Godu," *Novaia i Noveishaia Istoriia* 2 (2006): 52–53.

[81] Sherstianoi, "Vyzrevanie Politicheskogo Krizisa," 57.

[82] "Dokumenty Tsentralnogo Arkhiva FSB Rossii o Sobytiiakh 17 Iiunia 1953 g. v GDR," *Novaia I Noveishaia Istoriia* (February 2004): 73–82.

[83] Aksiutin, "Khrushchevskaia 'Ottepel,'" 40–41.

socialism often called "War Communism."[84] But still sensing German reluctance, Kaganovich reiterated the need for a reversal, a *perevorot*, or a turn around, not "merely reform," as the East Germans were suggesting. The Soviets also told their visitors to stop blaming foreigners for their problems.[85]

Upon their return home, the German leadership met from June 5 to June 9 to discuss how to adopt the new course imposed upon them in Moscow. Vladimir Semenov, newly appointed the first High Commissioner in the GDR, sat in on the meetings. The German leadership was so disappointed with the Soviet policy of slowing down the socialist transformation of the GDR that one asked, "Do we want socialism at all?" When Semenov was asked if publication of the new course could be delayed until June 25, he replied, "[I]n two weeks you may not have a state any more." The new course was made public on June 11. Meanwhile, during these German Presidium meetings, Semenov, Iudin, and Sokolovskii began sounding out German leaders about the advisability of removing Ulbricht from the leadership, given his resistance to reform and identification with Stalin's "old course." On June 16, the three sent a memorandum to the MFA recommending Ulbricht's removal.[86]

The same day, 100,000 workers took to the streets of East Berlin, joined by another 300,000 in the countryside, to protest the government's economic policies, first and foremost, rendering discussions of Ulbricht's ouster temporarily moot. On June 17, Soviet tanks began to restore order, resulting in the death of 200 German civilians and 18 Soviet soldiers. Ultimately, some 10,000 Germans would be arrested; 20 were sentenced to death.[87]

In performing the post mortem on the rebellion, the discourse of difference had its effect on Soviet interpretations. Instead of seeing the unrest as a vindication of Ulbricht's Stalinist policy, Soviet leaders realized just how vulnerable the GDR's political and economic system had become due to its economic orthodoxy and repressive politics. A compromise was reached whereby Moscow continued to support the New Course, but not very forcefully, while simultaneously, and relatedly, shifting to a policy of building socialism in the GDR, rather than trying to make it an attractive reunification partner in a neutral united Germany.

In the days following the military intervention, while accusing West Germans and the United States of fomenting unrest, there was much Soviet criticism of the East German leadership for having imposed higher labor rates in the first place, and not noticing the discontent that had provoked over the previous

---

[84] Filitov, "SSSR i GDR," 127–28.

[85] Harrison, *Driving the Soviets*, 29; and Kramer, "The Early Post-Stalin," 31.

[86] Kramer, "The Early Post-Stalin," 33; Harrison, *Driving the Soviets*, 34; and Boris L. Khavkin, "Berlinskoe Zharkoe Leto 1953 Goda," *Novaia i Noveishaia Istoriia* (April 2004): 172.

[87] Aksiutin, "Khrushchevskaia 'Ottepel,'" 42–43; and Kramer, "The Early Post-Stalin," 53–64.

month.[88] In a June 24 memorandum to Molotov, Semenov renewed his recommendation that Ulbricht be dismissed and that the New Course be rapidly implemented if further unrest was to be avoided.[89]

In a not too subtle, but still implicit, recognition of its overly exploitative economic relationship with the GDR, Moscow quickly increased economic aid to East Germany in a variety of ways. A week after the unrest, Moscow agreed to increase food and cotton supplies to East Germany.[90] Having the United States as its most significant Other in world politics entailed a need to compete with Washington, in this case in the supply of food to the GDR. On the first day the United States distributed food packages in West Berlin, July 27, 100,000 were given out, including, embarrassingly, to East German party members and officials. By August, 200,000 packages were being distributed daily. Despite an East German ban on receiving American food aid, by October, 5.5 million had been given out. In mid-July, Soviet officials in the GDR recommended Moscow counter with food aid of its own, the East German leadership having expressed anxiety that the United States was winning "the battle for the hearts and minds of the workers and peasants in the GDR."[91]

From August 20 to August 22, the German leadership met with their Soviet colleagues in Moscow. All East German debts to the Soviet Union were cancelled; Soviet occupation costs were lowered, and fixed at 5 percent of the GDR's budget; increased food and consumer good supplies were agreed; $2.5 billion in owed reparations were forgiven; 33 enterprises were restored to German control; and a large credit was offered. Grotewohl exclaimed at the meeting that it "is so much more than we had been expecting."[92]

In June 1956, preparing for the arrival of the GDR leadership, the Soviet Presidium, again in response to the dire economic situation in the GDR and the consequent mortifying flow of refugees, decided to increase aid again.[93] Khrushchev

---

[88] "Dokumenty Tsentralnogo Arkhiva FSB," 98; and Kramer, "Post-Stalin Succession," (Winter 1999): 49. It should be said that on June 17, Sokolovskii and Semenov sent a cable to Moscow reporting how the US radio station in West Berlin was "calling on rebels to subordinate themselves to the orders of Soviet authorities and not permit clashes with Soviet soldiers." Khavkin, "Berlinskoe Zharkoe Leto," 163. This recognition of US restraint was absent in Soviet public speeches and media.

[89] Mark Kramer, "The Early Post-Stalin Succession Struggle and Upheavals in East-Central Europe," Journal of Cold War Studies 1, no. 2 (Spring 1999): 8.

[90] Harrison, Driving the Soviets, 39.

[91] Mark Kramer, "The Early Post-Stalin Succession Struggle and Upheavals in East-Central Europe," Journal of Cold War Studies 1:3 (Fall 1999): 19–22.

[92] Harrison, Driving the Soviets, 41; Kramer, "Post-Stalin Succession," (Fall 1999), 21–22; and Khavkin, "Berlinskoe Zharkoe Leto," 174.

[93] In 1953, 270,000 East Germans fled westward; in 1954, 173,000; in 1955, 270,000; and in 1956, 316,000. In other words, more than one million East Germans left for the West in just four years. Harrison, Driving the Soviets, 72.

summarized: "Give the GDR everything they need—metal, raw materials, food, but not hard currency. Fill GDR factories with orders. Cut back our advisers and inspectors. Cut back the GDR army and our forces."[94] In cutting GDR's contribution to Soviet occupation costs in half, Soviet analysts cited the United States doing the same for the FRG earlier in the year.[95]

The unrest in East Berlin was also an occasion for Soviet leaders to confess their errors. Molotov admitted Soviet culpability for the unrest in East Germany at the July 2, 1953 CC meeting devoted to the removal of Beria from the Soviet party leadership. He observed that "over the last two to four years, more than half a million people have fled to western Germany, that is, from socialism to capitalism.... Industrialization was too rapid.... Besides that, they are paying the cost of our occupation and reparations. It was urgently necessary to correct this Leftist course, and we corrected it" with the introduction of the New Course.[96]

The Soviet Union adopted a middle course toward the GDR after the unrest in East Berlin. On the one hand, it did not support an abandonment of the New Course; on the other hand, it did not support the removal of Ulbricht in order to ensure the prompt and comprehensive implementation of those reforms. Instead, it supported the New Course with Ulbricht in command. On July 23, having received Moscow's support during a visit the first week of July, not only wasn't Ulbricht removed from power, but the two foremost proponents of the New Course, Rudolf Herrnstadt and Anton Ackermann, were ousted. Ulbricht, at the 4th party congress of the East German communist party in April 1954, dropped the "New Course" from the official discourse, and at its June 1955 CC Plenum, the party explicitly renounced it.[97]

By late 1955, the domestic situation in the GDR reminded Soviet observers of the run-up to June 1953. A new campaign against the church had been launched by the Ulbricht government, student demonstrations had broken out in response to compulsory military training, and refugee flows westward were continuing to grow.[98] During his July 1955 visit to the GDR, Khrushchev brought up the refugee issue, but the German solution of closing its borders with the West was not acceptable to Moscow; Moscow's solution of a more faithful implementation of the New Course recommended since June 1953 was not acceptable to Ulbricht and his colleagues.[99]

---

[94] Fursenko, *Arkhivy Kremlia Prezidium*, 140–44; and Harrison, *Driving the Soviets*, 74.
[95] Fursenko, *Arkhivy Kremlia Prezidium*, 316.
[96] RGANI f2 op1 d29, 49–50.
[97] Kramer, "Post-Stail Succession," (Fall 1999): 17, 29.
[98] Alexei M. Filitov, *Germanskii Vopros: Ot Raskola k Obedeneniiu* (Moscow: Mezhdunarodnye Otnosheniia, 1993), 169.
[99] Harrison, *Driving the Soviets*, 51.

Khrushchev's denunciation of Stalin's cult of personality and celebration of Soviet collective leadership at the Twentieth Party Congress in February 1956 inspired Ulbricht's colleagues to tell him that "he should examine his own cult of personality and put an end to it." After the removal of Rakosi in Hungary for not pursuing the New Course there, Karl Schirdewan, an East German Presidium member who, with Herrnstadt and Ackermann, had supported the New Course, told his colleagues that Ulbricht could share Rakosi's fate if he didn't implement the resolutions of the Twentieth Party Congress.[100]

The Soviet leadership was well aware of Ulbricht's resistance to reform. In a MFA Information Committee report to Khrushchev just prior to his July 1957 visit to East Germany, the domestic political situation in the GDR was described as "complicated. People continue to leave for West Germany. The GDR's population has declined by 1.2 million from 1951–6." And a record number left in 1956. Ivan Tugarinov, deputy head of the Information Committee, reported that the GDR's economy was inferior to the FRG's on all dimensions, if benefiting from Soviet aid.[101] Notwithstanding the gloomy outlook, Khrushchev supported Ulbricht during his visit, if not his enduring Stalinist views.

Yugoslavia: Undoing Stalin's Work

The rapprochement with Yugoslavia after Stalin's death was made possible by the replacement of the discourse of danger with the discourse of difference in Moscow. Recognition of difference made Yugoslavia an available ally; treatment of difference as danger had made Yugoslavia an enemy. Recognizing Yugoslavia once again as a socialist state had far-reaching consequences. So long as Yugoslavia was treated as a bourgeois or capitalist state, what Yugoslavia did at home, or in its foreign policy, had few implications for the Soviet Union's own socialist identity. But once Yugoslavia was understood as socialist, what Yugoslavia said and did as a socialist country became consequential, even dangerous. If Yugoslavia were socialist, then any Eastern European ally of the Soviet Union could defensibly adopt Yugoslavian policies, say, in economics, media, or politics. Still more alarming would be Soviets themselves citing the Yugoslav example to their more orthodox colleagues at home. This was the risk of difference, a risk Khrushchev, and most Soviet leaders, were willing to take after Stalin's death allowed societal understandings of socialism freer rein.

At first, Yugoslavia was understood as a bourgeois country with whom the Soviet Union should have normal interstate relations. In late May 1953 Mikhail

---

[100] Ibid., 68–69.
[101] RGANI f5 op30 d230, 215–21.

Zimianin, head of the 4th European Department of the MFA, delivered his report on Yugoslavia to Molotov, First Deputy Foreign Minister Andrei Gromyko, and his deputy, Valerian Zorin. After many pages of anti-Tito vitriol, Ziminanin nonetheless concluded, in consideration of the fact that Soviet foreign policy moderation was making anti-Sovietism less sustainable since Stalin's death, that "there are real preconditions for the normalization of relations between the Soviet Union and Yugoslavia as a bourgeois country." Zimianin couched the stakes in geopolitical terms: "One of the most important tasks of our foreign policy is . . . to use all possibilities to penetrate Yugoslavia with true information about the Soviet Union, to weaken American and English influence, and prevent the creation of an anti-Soviet strategic springboard in the Balkans."[102] On June 17, Moscow and Belgrade exchanged ambassadors for the first time in five years. Soviet tolerance of difference, combined with its own self-understanding as a great power in competition with the United States and the West, impelled Soviet leaders to re-evaluate their relationship with Belgrade.

One aspect of the relationship that deeply irritated Soviet officials was the appearance of any kind of criticism of the Soviet Union, or its brand of socialism, in the Yugoslavian press, or worse, in speeches given by Yugoslav officials. Again, this mattered only after the Soviets expanded their definition of socialism to include Yugoslavia, such that criticisms from Yugoslavia were coming from a state with whom the Soviet Union shared an identity. The stakes were high in the competition between Belgrade and Moscow to decide just who could claim to be a model of socialism.[103] Removing Soviet criticism of Yugoslavia and Tito from Soviet discourse required trips to the library to find books in which Yugoslavia or Tito were slandered and remove them from circulation.[104]

Yugoslavia's ambiguous identity led to some awkward situations. On his train ride to Belgrade to negotiate a modest trade agreement in 1954, a Ministry of Foreign Trade official, Vladimir Vinogradov, became anxious about how to address his Yugoslavian partners. "Should we call them Mister or Comrade?" They had not realized until then the political consequences of mis-identifying them, and the professional costs for them if they promoted Yugoslavs to socialist status without Moscow's approval. They "finally agreed that we would better wait until they addressed us."[105]

---

[102] Volokitina et al., *Vostochnaia Evropa v Dokumentakh Rossiiskikh Arkhivov, 1944–1953 gg. Tom II*, 906–13.

[103] See the reports from Soviet Ambassador Victor Valkov about his fruitless meetings with Yugoslav officials on this issue. Volokitina et al., *Sovetskii Faktor v Vostochnoi Evrope*, 812–15.

[104] RGANI f5 op16, d685, 51–59, 141; RGANI f5 op17, d490, 119; and RGANI f5 op16, d750, 155, 171, 307.

[105] Vladimir M. Vinogradov, *Diplomatiia: Liudi i Sobytiia iz Zapisok Posla* (Moscow: ROSSPEN, 1998), 24.

Official Soviet acknowledgement of Yugoslavia's socialist identity did in fact lead to confusion at home and abroad. At a May 1955 meeting of the Moscow party aktiv, Yekaterina Furtseva, the Moscow city committee's first secretary, reported party members expressing anxiety about accepting Yugoslavia's socialist credentials. In letters to the editor of *Krasnaia Zvezda*, the Red Army's official newspaper, readers asked for clarification about Yugoslavia's true identity: socialist or bourgeois?[106] Soviet ambassadors to Poland and China reported to Moscow of confusion in the press and at party meetings in those two countries, as well.[107]

By May 1955, the Soviet leadership had decided to send an official delegation to Belgrade to apologize and effect a rapprochement. Molotov led the opposition to any such reconciliation, invoking many elements from the discourse of danger. Most fundamentally, Molotov continued to think in black and white dichotomies. At a Presidium meeting one week before Khrushchev's trip to Yugoslavia, Molotov claimed that Yugoslavia was "on the path of bourgeois nationalism." Several days later, Voroshilov agreed with Molotov that the Yugoslavs were not Marxists or Leninists. Molotov demanded that his colleagues specify whether "Yugoslavia is bourgeois or proletarian." Rejecting the discourse of difference, Yugoslavia cannot be anywhere in between.[108] But the discourse of difference implied the opposite. "Who is not with us is against us" was replaced by "who is not against us is potentially with us." Yugoslavia fell into that new category. On May 23, just three days before the trip, the CPSU sent a telegram to all European communist parties suggesting they rescind the November 1948 Cominform condemnation of Yugoslavia.[109] A week after returning from Yugoslavia, there was a Presidium meeting held to discuss the results of the trip. Molotov alone objected to what had transpired there. He demanded that any references to Marxism-Leninism be removed from the official report of the trip since Yugoslavia is not a socialist country.

The battle between the two visions of the Soviet Union was played out in depth at the July 9–12, 1955 CC Plenum devoted to an assessment of the trip to Belgrade.[110] Opening the Plenum, Khrushchev declared that "we must think not only of organizing forces which firmly stand on our socialist positions, but . . . also those which cannot go with us to the end and can disagree with us on ideological questions."[111] The tolerance of difference is an ally multiplier. Presidium

---

[106] TsKhSD f5 op30 d90, 52, 67–71.

[107] TsKhSD f5 op30 d121, 86–87; and TsKhSD f5 op30 d116, 172.

[108] Fursenko, *Arkhivy Kremlia Prezidium*, 42–44. For the Presidium directives for the delegation to Yugoslavia, see RGANI f3 op8 d237, 146–64.

[109] RGANI f3 op10 d143, 24–27.

[110] For a detailed discussion of the plenum proceedings on the trip to Yugoslavia see Hopf, *Social Construction of International Politics*, 107–24.

[111] CC Plenum, July 9, 1955, morning session, 2.

member Nikolai Pervukhin, quoting from Lenin's essay on the dangers of Leftist extremism, observed that "people who still do not know [referring to Molotov and other defenders of Stalinist orthodoxy] that all boundaries... are mobile.... won't be helped by anything but long training and education...."[112]

The rapprochement with Yugoslavia was also made possible by the continuing Soviet understanding of itself as atop the hierarchy of socialist modernity, with all other socialist countries arrayed beneath it, albeit on the road to becoming the Soviet Union. Yugoslavia's version of socialism was fine, *for now, given its stage of development.* Anastas Mikoian argued that if Yugoslavia, or even China, were held to Soviet standards, the Soviet Union wouldn't have many socialist allies. Mikoian concluded that "it is one of the worst manifestations of great power chauvinism. Everything is ... allowed for us, but nothing is permitted others."[113]

Molotov rejected Yugoslavia's socialist credentials, arguing that its contention that a peaceful road to socialism was possible "ignore[d] class and the class struggle" and so was hardly socialist. Molotov pointed out that Yugoslavia had made strides, but backwards, on both collectivization of agriculture and centralized planning. Instead, Molotov suggested, Yugoslavia should be treated like Finland or India.[114] In February 1956, such a possibility of nonviolent transitions to socialism was officially proclaimed as Soviet doctrine at the Twentieth Party Congress in Khrushchev's report as general secretary.[115] Molotov further warned that granting Yugoslavia a socialist identity could set off dominoes all over eastern Europe, as each Soviet ally would see in Yugoslavia a possible road to communism for itself.[116]

Khrushchev and other supporters of a turn toward Yugoslavia effectively accused Molotov of abandoning Yugoslavia to the imperialists and, relatedly, of underestimating Soviet power. The latter was a very effective rhetorical weapon as it made Molotov look unpatriotic and unappreciative of the extent of socialist development in the Soviet Union. This was precisely what he had to recant in the pages of *Kommunist* in September of 1955. Khrushchev reminded the Plenum

---

[112] CC Plenum, July 11, 1955, evening session, 19.

[113] CC PLenum, July 11, 1955, morning session, 8.

[114] CC Plenum, July 9, 1955, evening session, 7–8. Reflective of its ambiguous identity, in the Bolshevik Revolution celebrations in November 1955, Yugoslavia was positioned between the countries of popular democracy and India, Indonesia, Austria, and Finland. The 1956 May Day slogans appeared in *Pravda* on April 9. Khrushchev was furious that Yugoslavia had been left between Eastern European socialist allies and Third World allies. After a fair amount of badgering, on April 11, *Pravda* printed an emended slogan for Yugoslavia granting it a socialist identity. Khrushchev, *Nikita Khrushchev*, 679–81.

[115] In further agreement with Tito, Khrushchev blamed Stalin, as well as Beria, for the rupture with Yugoslavia, at the congress.

[116] CC Plenum, July 9, 1955, morning session, 2.

that "now a struggle" is going on for Yugoslavia "between the United States and the Soviet Union, between US economic aid and Soviet."[117]

Bulganin listed Yugoslavia's strategic assets in some detail at the Plenum, citing "its important strategic position in southeastern Europe, with 16 million people," its 42 army divisions, making it the "strongest country in Europe." He then described its strategic importance in any war with NATO, as it "juts far to the east," and so could protect the Soviet flank. Khrushchev interrupted to observe that the United States would have to deploy 70 to 80 divisions to cover the area.[118] Even a neutral Yugoslavia would be a big gain, "but we hope for more," argued Aleksei Kirichenko, who that day had been promoted to full membership on the Presidium.[119] Here we see the importance of the Soviet great power identity, an identity not found in domestic discourses, but one daily generated in interaction with the United States and the West.

Soviet fears of Yugoslav deviation were mitigated by Soviet identity entailing an implicit Russian nation. While not as officially proclaimed as in the postwar Stalin era, the Russian nation remained central to Soviet understandings of themselves. This becomes obvious in discussions of Yugoslavia, a fellow Slavic country, a "little brother" abroad. In the lead editorial in *Pravda* that introduced the Soviet people to its leadership's upcoming trip to Yugoslavia, it referred to the "age-old friendship of the peoples of our country with the fraternal peoples of Yugoslavia."[120] At the July Plenum, Kaganovich referred to Yugoslavia as "a special state, close, and related/rodstvennoe to us. . . ."[121] Shepilov lamented the loss under Stalin of "the second biggest Slavic country after Poland."[122]

The Plenum had many admissions of Soviet errors in its previous treatment of Yugoslavia, including insensitivity to its national identity.[123] Khrushchev and others compared Yugoslavia to other Soviet socialist republics, like Ukraine, and argued that the same Leninist nationality policy used at home should have been, and should be, applied to Yugoslavia.[124] These ethnonational identity relations

---

[117] Ibid., 12.

[118] Not Ibid., 11–12.

[119] CC Plenum, July 12, 1955, morning session, 4.

[120] "For the Further Improvement of Soviet-Yugoslavian Relations and the Strengthening of Peace," *Pravda*, May 18, 1955: 1.

[121] CC Plenum, July 11, 1955, evening session, 13. "Rodstvennoe" has a meaning of family and blood relations.

[122] Ibid., 22.

[123] Molotov, on the other hand, at the June 8 Presidium meeting, had argued, contrary to the position of Khrushchev's delegation in Yugoslavia, that it wasn't Beria who was to blame for the rupture in relations with Belgrade, but rather Yugoslavian nationalism. Fursenko, *Arkhivy Kremlia Prezidium*, 53.

[124] CC Plenum, July 9, 1955, morning session, 18. Malenkov explained to the Moscow party aktiv after the Plenum that relations "between big and small nations," like the Soviet Union and Yugoslavia, should be just like relations between Moscow and republics at home. RTsKhIDNI, f83 op1 d12, 29.

concealed a hierarchy with the Soviet Union/Russia serving as the vanguard for the less-developed Yugoslavs who are still infected with bourgeois nationalism, and so need Moscow to substitute for the absent proletarian leadership in Belgrade.[125] In this regard, Mikoian compared Yugoslavia to the Soviet republics of Uzbekistan and Kazakhstan, both in need of Moscow's leadership.[126] Mikhail Suslov noted that it was Soviet duty to "return" Yugoslavia to the socialist camp.[127]

Even with the rapprochement with Yugoslavia, the Soviet leadership reserved itself the right to adhere to its own definition of socialism and criticize Yugoslavia for its deviations. Shepilov singled out three foundational elements that were not negotiable: the dictatorship of the proletariat; the leading role of the communist party in the world liberation movement; and continued differentiation between communist and social democratic parties.[128] The Soviet elite monitored Yugoslavia for dangerous deviance much as it did its own people at home. One of the more annoying and threatening Yugoslav "deviations" was its insistence that its "workers' councils" at factories were the means to do away with the state. This claim was most unwelcome because it was being made at the same time as Soviets were criticizing the "new class" of embourgeoisified party and state elites in the Soviet Union.[129]

Leading up to the Twentieth Party Congress, Suslov, Ponomarev, and Gromyko prepared a report for the Presidium "On certain results of the normalization of relations with Yugoslavia," summarizing all the benefits from the rapprochement. Most important was what was avoided: "Yugoslavia is no longer merging with the Western camp." Its domestic and foreign policies are getting closer to the socialist camp. Western economic pressure on Yugoslavia has been alleviated because of our "renewal of economic ties and cancellation of Yugoslavian debt." But all is not ideal. Yugoslavs still claim to have a dictatorship of the proletariat; that is, they claim to be as socialist as the Soviet Union. They insist on a Yugoslavian path to socialism, rather than a common one.[130] Yugoslavia declares itself to be neutral between the two blocs. There are anti-Soviet books on sale in Yugoslavia, and they sell books banned here, like those of Babel and Zoshchenko. The

---

[125] Needless to say, Tito and Yugoslavian communists are not going to put up with this subordinate position.

[126] CC Plenum, July 11, 1955, morning session, 4.

[127] CC Plenum, July 11, 1955, evening session, 29. Kaganovich accused Molotov of "a lack of faith in the power of the CPSU" during Presidium discussions on June 8. Fursenko, *Arkhivy Kremlia Prezidium*, 53.

[128] CC Plenum, July 11, 1955, evening session, 25.

[129] For Ambassador Valkov's report on this to Zimianin, AVPRF f144, op16 d740, 8–16.

[130] The authors could not know that the Twentieth Party Congress in February would implicitly endorse Yugoslavia's choice by authorizing multiple roads to socialism.

authors conclude that any differences should be discussed privately without public polemics.[131]

In preparing for Tito's three-week visit to the Soviet Union in June 1956, the Presidium met in late May. On the first day, Molotov argued for making Yugoslavia's inadequacies more prominent in discussions with its leaders in Moscow. Khrushchev responded by saying, "Molotov has maintained his old positions. It pains us that Molotov hasn't changed since the [July 1955] Plenum." The next day, the Presidium removed Molotov as foreign minister, replaced by Shepilov, just days before Tito's arrival.[132] On the other hand, after Tito's departure on June 22, the Presidium met to discuss Tito's visit, and it roundly criticized Bulganin for his June 5 toast to Tito in which he credited him with being a Leninist. It was such a serious ideological faux pas that the CC sent letters to foreign communist parties alerting them to such an identity being premature for Yugoslavia.[133]

On November 4, 1956, Khruschev met secretly with Tito on the island of Brioni, seeking Yugoslavian support for the imminent invasion of Hungary. Receiving it was understood as an important benefit from the rapprochement with Yugoslavia. Khrushchev's son remembers his father as returning pleasantly surprised with Tito's blessing of the intervention.[134] Not a week later, however, Tito gave a speech in Pula in which he criticized the Soviet decision to invade Hungary, the ill-advised Soviet support for Rakosi over the years, and the Soviet failure to realize that Stalinism is a systemic deviation from socialism, not just a product of Stalin's idiosyncratic personality.[135] The next day Khrushchev told the Yugoslavian ambassador in Moscow, Veljko Micunovic, that Yugoslavia was the new popular model in eastern Europe.[136] This was not said with joy.

Soviet relations with Yugoslavia continued to be riddled with areas of conflict. While appreciating that the rapprochement was a huge improvement over the hostility that prevailed under Stalin, Soviet leaders continued to be dissatisfied with Yugoslavia's ideological "progress." Moscow had to instruct its ambassador, Nikolai Firiubin, to tell the Yugoslav leadership about the continued presence of "anti-Soviet" literature in local bookstores. Tito explained the bookstores were just "selling excess inventory." At the February 14, 1957, CC Plenum, at which relations with Yugoslavia were discussed, Khrushchev said Tito wanted the Soviet Union to finance the construction of an aluminum plant, but "why

---

[131] Fursenko, *Arkhivy Kremlia*, 179–86.
[132] Molotov had been left off the Soviet delegation to Yugoslavia in June 1955.
[133] Fursenko, *Arkhivy Kremlia Prezidium*, 136–38, 145.
[134] Khrushchev, *Nikita Khruchev*, 200.
[135] Taubman, *Khrushchev*, 345.
[136] Micunovic, *Moscow Diary*, 159.

should we? They spit in our face." They want Mig-19 fighter jets. But why should we, "when Americans are strolling around the airport...." After a few more attacks on Yugoslavia, Khrushchev asked, "But, comrades, was it right that we have liquidated what we had previously?" Voices from the audience yelled out right. "We said Tito was a German spy. You would have to be insane to believe this." At Yugoslavia's last CC meeting, Firubin reports, there is neither support to "struggle against us," or to be friendly. And, Khrushchev continued, "Tito told me, and I believe him, ... that in the event of war, they will fight alongside the Soviet Union." So, at least the strategic value of Yugoslavia was secure.[137]

The Soviet choice to let difference reign in relations with Yugoslavia received further reinforcement at the June 1957 "anti-party" Plenum at which Molotov, Kaganovich, Voroshilov, and Shepilov "who joined them" were ousted from the Presidium. Molotov's continued opposition to rapprochement with Yugoslavia was brought up time and time again as evidence that Molotov was still a Stalinist, a prisoner of the discourse of danger. At the last session on the last day of the week-long Plenum, Khrushchev summed up the Stalinists' errors. "Molotov and Kaganovich attacked the position that the forms of transition to socialism can be different.... At the 10th anniversary of the victory over Germany, Molotov said the Yugoslavs are fascists. Comrade Molotov, if you are allowed in leadership, you will ruin your country; you will take it into isolation." The discourse of danger reduces the number of Soviet allies in the world. Khrushchev told the Plenum that Molotov "is a dogmatist, a hopeless, dried-up old man."[138]

China: Sowing the Seeds of the Sino-Soviet Split

Soviet identity relations with China underwent dramatic changes with the death of Stalin. As we recall from chapter 3, the orthodox Soviet Stalinist identity placed China on a lower rung on the ladder of socialist development and modernity. This had two different consequences. On the one hand, it permitted Chinese deviations from the Soviet model to be explained away as a developmental issue that the Chinese little brother, like other Soviet domestic republics, could overcome given the aid and tutelage of its elder brother in the Soviet Union. On the other hand, it smacked of paternalism and condescension.

Relations between China and the Soviet Union initially improved, as the Soviet Union admitted its errors in relations with China, mostly, but not only, to itself, and moved China up the hierarchy to an almost equal position in the socialist community. But by 1958, the Soviet and Chinese identities were clearly

[137] RGANI f2 op1 d219, 129–47.
[138] CC Plenum, June 28, 1957, 32.

heading in opposite directions: The Soviet Union was still committed to a de-Stalinized socialism, while China was recommitting itself to precisely the Stalinist understanding of socialism the Soviets had just rejected. The removal of Molotov from the Presidium in June 1957 could be seen as the beginning of the end of the Sino-Soviet alliance. As Westad observed, "The anti-party group was, in effect, Mao at home."[139]

The elevation of China to a position of near equality with the Soviet Union as the "center" and head of the socialist camp had serious consequences for identity relations between the two. In particular, once China had reached the status as the Soviet Union's single "Closest Other," any deviations on its part became the most serious challenges to the new Soviet identity. There cannot be two different models of socialism sharing the same identity as socialist leader. One had to give. But neither gave, and so the dissolution of the alliance ensued. As Kulik concluded, "Any deviation from [the Soviet model] was fraught with anti-socialist danger."[140]

Other scholars have argued that ideological differences, not material conflicts of interest or foreign policy differences over confronting the United States, caused the rupture in Sino-Soviet relations. I agree but go one step farther, in arguing that these "ideological" differences were not inter-elite disagreements over the meaning of socialism, but rather the result of a new Soviet identity emerging from Soviet society after Stalin's death.[141] To demonstrate the importance of this, I must skip ahead to Khrushchev's ouster in 1964, when many, including Mao, expected a restoration of the previously close alliance between Moscow and Beijing. The reason it did not happen, I would argue, is that the discourse of difference had far deeper roots, and had penetrated far more institutions, than merely Khrushchev's mind or team, and so imbued his successors, right up until Gorbachev, with a Soviet identity that was fundamentally incompatible with China's.

Soviet Fallibility

One of the first errors acknowledged and corrected by the new Soviet leadership was to end the stalemate in the Korean War. Not two weeks after Stalin's funeral, the Soviet Council of Ministers approved a resolution calling for an end to the

---

[139] Odd Arne Westad, Introduction to *Brothers in Arms: The Rise and Fall of the Sino-Soviet Alliance, 1945–1963*, ed. Odd Arne Westad (Stanford: Stanford University Press, 1998), 20.

[140] Kulik, *Sovetsko-Kitaiskii Raskol*, 49. Compare, for example, the split with China with continued Soviet toleration, albeit unenthusiastic, for Yugoslavia's many deviations from the Soviet model.

[141] Constantine Pleshakov, "Nikita Khrushchev and Sino-Soviet Relations," in Westad, ed., *Brothers in Arms* 226–45; Kulik, *Sovetsko-Kitaiskii Raskol*; and Luthi, *The Sino-Soviet Split*. Luthi's book is now the single best English-language volume on the Sino-Soviet split. Kulik's book, told from the perspective of a sophisticated cultural materialism, is the single best volume in Russian, and should be translated so that his arguments and evidence are given a broader audience.

war as soon as possible. On the same day, March 19, 1953, telegrams were sent to North Korea and China explaining that "it would be incorrect to continue the line on this question which has been heretofore followed. . . ." While it was not until after the Twentieth Party Congress, three years later, that China would use the opportunity of de-Stalinization in the Soviet Union to enumerate all of Stalin's many errors with regard to policy toward China, Mao let Soviet ambassador Pavel Iudin know what he thought about Soviet policy toward Korea. He said that in meetings with Stalin in Moscow in 1949–50 nothing was said about seizing South Korea. And then China was not consulted about Kim's plans and "there was a serious miscalculation in the Korean War about the supposed impossibility of the intervention of international forces on the side of South Korea."[142]

After Khrushchev's denunciation of Stalin at the Twentieth Party Congress, Mao revealed his assessment of Stalin on March 19, 1956, at the Chinese Communist Party (CCP) Politburo meeting called to discuss the Soviet congress. He crafted the 70:30 ratio of Stalin's good and bad conduct. As Luthi has summarized, all Stalin's mistakes were taken to be actions directed at Mao or China, and all his achievements concerned the orthodox Stalinist model of socialist development.[143] Two days later, Mao enumerated Stalin's errors to Ambassador Iudin. In 1926, he had exaggerated the revolutionary potential of the Kuomintang. In 1934–35, he had wrongly advised a popular front with the Kuomintang. In 1945, he had insisted the CCP make peace with Chiang Kai-shek. Mao continued, "In 1947, when our forces were gaining victories, Stalin insisted on concluding peace with Chiang." Mao also related his mistreatment during his visit to Moscow to meet Stalin. In his telling, Stalin refused to meet him and rejected signing a treaty with the PRC. "I was insulted and told them I will sit in the dacha." Finally, "Stalin insisted on control over the Changchun railroad, the naval base at Port Arthur, joint stock companies, and Manchuria and Sinkiang were turned into Soviet spheres of influence. . . ."[144] Later, Mao told Iudin, "had he always followed Stalin's advice, he would be dead already."[145]

---

[142] "New Evidence on Sino-Soviet Relations," *Cold War International History Project Bulletin* 6–7 (Winter 1995/1996): 80–84. As documented in chapter 3, Mao himself assured Kim in his May 1950 meeting with him in Beijing that the Americans wouldn't intervene.

[143] Luthi, *The Sino-Soviet Split*, 50; and Jian, *Mao's China*, 65.

[144] RGANI f5 op30 d163, 88–94; RGANI f5 op30 d163, 88–94. Mao repeated most of these charges to Tito during his visit to China in September 1956. "New Evidence on Sino-Soviet Relations," 149. The companies were transferred to Chinese control during Khrushchev's October 1954 visit to China. The "unilateral rights" in Sinkiang and Manchuria were renounced in May 1956. An official secret history of Sino-Soviet relations drafted in the MFA by Nikolai Fedorenko and Mikhail Kapitsa explained the closure of the joint stock companies as part of the "young China" maturing to the point of being able to run them alone. AVPRF f100 op48 d39, 9.

[145] Westad, *Brothers in Arms*, 15.

The Chinese leadership was never completely satisfied, even after Khrushchev reversed Stalin's policies on economic relations with China, and ramped up economic and military aid to unprecedented levels, that Soviet leaders really understood their previous errors. After his January 1957 trip to Moscow, Zhou Enlai reported to Mao that Soviet leaders "merely take a perfunctory attitude toward their mistakes. . . ." For example, "they denied their intervention in Poland was a mistake." Nevertheless, Zhou concluded that "Sino-Soviet relations are far better now than during Stalin's era. . . . We recognize a common threat; we can sit down to discuss issues equally; fraternal parties and states can discuss and argue with each other; and the majority of the Soviet people love China. . . ."[146]

Economic and Military Relations

After Stalin's death Sino-Soviet economic and military cooperation reached new heights. Between just 1953 and 1956, Moscow agreed to build 205 factories valued at $2 billion. Moscow sent 2,500 advisers to China, invited 10,000 Chinese students to the Soviet Union, and trained another 17,000 in China.[147] Much of the industrial materials and advanced technologies were on the Western embargo list, and so otherwise unattainable. Seventy per cent of China's foreign trade in the 1950s was with the Soviet Union.[148] According to Vladislav Zubok, Soviet aid to China from 1954 to 1959 amounted to seven percent of Soviet GDP, "a Soviet Marshall Plan."[149]

A May 1953 agreement upgraded Chinese fighters from MIG 15s to MIG 17s, replaced anti-aircraft guns with radar-guided Grom 2s, and sent more modern tanks.[150] Khrushchev's first major foreign trip was to China, from September 29 to October 16, 1954. Mao raised the issue of the Soviet Union supplying China with atomic weapons, but Khrushchev replied that China should concentrate on its economic development and rely on the Soviet nuclear umbrella. Khrushchev asked, "Is it really so little that we have a bomb? We are protecting you. In the event, we will strike for you."[151] In such a cavalier manner was a Soviet nuclear deterrent guarantee offered. He did, however, commit to giving China a

---

[146] "New Evidence on Sino-Soviet Relations," 153–54.

[147] Taubman, *Khrushchev*, 336. Eastern European allies built an additional 116 industrial plants. Kulik, *Sovetsko-Kitaiskii Raskol*, 163.

[148] Kulik, *Sovetsko-Kitaiskii Raskol*, 162–65.

[149] Vladislav Zubok, *The Soviet Union in the Cold War from Stalin to Gorbachev* (Durham, University of North Carolina Press, 2007), 111.

[150] Kulik, *Sovetsko-Kitaiskii Raskol*, 95.

[151] Dmitrii T. Shepilov, "Politicheskii Arkhiv XX Veka. Vospominaniia," *Voprosy Istorii* (October 1998): 28.

nuclear reactor for electricity generation. In April 1955, Moscow agreed to supply China with the equipment and technology to build a reactor and a cyclotron, including fissionable material, explicitly for peaceful purposes. Over the next few years, hundreds of Chinese were trained in nuclear physics at Dubna, the center of Soviet research in nuclear physics.[152]

In August 1957, Mikoian, during a trip to China, offered Soviet assistance in the development of an atomic weapon. On October 15, 1957, the Soviets agreed to deliver a prototype atomic weapon by 1959.[153] But the rift in identity relations intervened, as did Mao's peculiar take on nuclear warfare, which he publicly asserted during his last trip to the Soviet Union, in November 1957. Addressing the delegates of the world's communist parties, he said, "[I]f worse came to worst [in a nuclear war] and half of mankind died, the other half would remain, while imperialism would be razed to the ground and the world would become socialist."[154] Not unrelated, at this time, Mao gave the Soviet leadership a secret memorandum outlining, for the first time, China's opposition to the Soviet policy of peaceful coexistence.[155] While letting the remark pass at the time, Khrushchev and the rest of the Soviet leadership remembered it when they decided in August 1959 to deny China any further assistance in the development of a nuclear weapon.

The Soviet Union's Most Developed Younger Brother

While Stalin's successors immediately elevated China to the status of the "coleader" of the socialist camp, they could not avoid continually subordinating their ally on the ladder of modernity and socialist development. As Chinese material power grew and the Soviet Union admitted to a raft of errors in socialist construction and foreign policy, this subordination made the growing identity differences only that much more obvious. As Shepilov wrote some years later, "Because the Chinese revolution in 1956 was where the Soviet Union was in 1928, Khrushchev's continued slandering of Stalin undermined Chinese legitimacy...."[156]

At times, it really did appear as if Soviet leaders understood China as part of itself. For example, at his initial meeting with Mao in September 1954 in Beijing,

---

[152] Kulik, *Sovetsko-Kitaiskii Raskol*, 162–68; Holloway, *Stalin and the Bomb*, 355.

[153] Luthi, *The Sino-Soviet Split*, 74.

[154] Taubman, *Khrushchev*, 341. It should be noted that Mao had his counterparts in the United States. William F. Buckley wrote in 1962 that "if it is right that a single man be prepared to die for a just cause, it is right that an entire civilization be prepared to die for a just cause." "On Dead-Red," *National Review*, November 10, 1962.

[155] Luthi, *The Sino-Soviet Split*, 77.

[156] Shepilov, "Politicheskii Arkhiv XX Veka Vospominaniia," *Voprosy Istorii* (October 1998): 166.

Khrushchev told him, "[W]e are glad and proud of your great successes." Mao replied that these "successes are thanks to your selfless aid." Khrushchev argued that "one should not speak of 'selflessness' because strengthening China means strengthening our country, too."[157] In December 1955, Khrushchev explained to Burma's prime minister, U Nu, how to become an independent country. He said, "[W]ith friends like China, we have even greater possibilities to become more independent."[158] Only by understanding China and the Soviet Union as part of each other, or part of something superordinate, like the socialist community, could Khrushchev believe that increasing Soviet dependence on China actually increased Soviet independence, meaning vis-à-vis the rest of the non-socialist world.

The Soviet leadership frequently identified China as the "co-leader" of the socialist camp.[159] Khrushchev, during one of his frequent conflicts with Molotov at CC plena, attacked him for not acknowledging that China could "correct the CPSU in matters of Marxism-Leninism."[160] China was invited to the creation of the Warsaw Pact in May 1955 and, as under Stalin, was granted the leading role, at least for then, as vanguard of the national liberation movements of Asia. In fact, according to a July 1955 MFA Information Committee report, China was a paradigm for "popular-democratic revolution in a backward, semi-colonial, semi-feudal country, especially for the popular liberation movement of the East."[161]

But China was still just on its way to becoming the Soviet Union. Soviet analysts frequently noted the unstable nature of the Chinese revolution because of continuing class conflicts. Unlike in the Soviet Union, where antagonistic class relations had been eliminated, and so rendered socialism more secure, China was wracked by threats of "counter-revolution," penetration of the party and state apparatus with Kuomintang agents.[162] Soviet diplomats in China sent back a steady stream of reports attesting to the domestic political weakness of the Chinese revolution.[163]

The historian Anna Pankratova was part of the Khrushchev delegation to China in 1954. Upon her return, she gave a talk to the History Section of the Soviet Academy of Sciences, wherein she identified China as the most willing and grateful student of Moscow. She first placed the Soviet delegation atop the

---

[157] Dmitrii T. Shepilov, "Politicheskii Arkhiv XX Veka. Vospominaniia," *Voprosy Istorii* (September 1998), 25.

[158] TsKhSD f5 op30 d116, 230.

[159] For example, Molotov before the Supreme Soviet in February 1955, in *New Times*, no. 7, February 12, 1955, and Khrushchev at the CC Plenum, July 9, 1955, morning session, 17.

[160] CC Plenum, July 11, 1955, morning session, 18.

[161] AVPRF f100 op48 d127, 395.

[162] AVPRF f100 op48 d128, 91. Molotov underlined in blue pencil all the alarming parts of this report from the embassy in Beijing.

[163] For example, AVPRF f100 op48 dd 127 and 128.

hierarchy and at the center of it all, noting that "our Soviet delegation was given the first place among other foreign delegations and we were the center of attention for all visiting guests, to a great degree.... The Chinese are learning new things from all peoples, and especially from Soviet peoples.... Everywhere and always our meetings began with them thanking us for helping them to learn a new life, new art, etc.... The Soviet Union is our older brother, our friend, our teacher, we heard, read, and felt everywhere...."[164]

The Soviet leaders constantly cautioned moderation when advising Chinese colleagues on their development plans, not unlike the New Course recommended in eastern Europe. In May 1955, Gosplan and the CC Department on Economic Relations with People's Democracies commented on the second draft of China's five-year plan. The authors, Maksim Saburov and Igor Koval, remarked they had criticized the previous draft for excessively intensive growth rates, and for harsh treatment of local artisans who should "satisfy the needs of the countryside." While the CCP has admitted to alienating the middle peasants through forced collectivization and squeezing out private traders in the countryside, "the draft plan on cooperativization is too intense, can lead to the forced acceleration of the process, and violate the principle of voluntariness."[165] The Chinese continued to advocate a Stalinist model of development already abandoned in the Soviet Union. In July, contrary to Soviet advice, Mao criticized the slow pace of collectivization, declaring that "the road traversed by the Soviet Union is our model," despite Soviet advice not to follow it.[166] In October, the Chinese accelerated the nationalization of industry, again contrary to Soviet preferences.[167] At the August 27, 1956, Presidium discussion of China's second five-year plan, and the Soviet contribution to it, Soviet leaders were unanimous in declaring it "unrealistic." Mikoian noted that "they are very enamored of themselves," and Pervukhin recommended they redraft the plan.[168]

Mao, in conversation with Tito in September 1956, noted some improvement in Soviet attitudes toward the Soviet Union's little brother, but noted that "the shadow of the father-son relationship is not completely removed.... a patriarchal system is being toppled."[169] China was delighted with the Moscow Declaration on Soviet relations with socialist countries adopted during the turmoil in Hungary on October 31, 1956. Liu Shao-chi read a memo from Mao at the October 29 Presidium meeting in Moscow advocating the Soviet Union adopt the non-aligned

---

[164] "Nas Neobychaino Teplo i Serdechno Vstretili," *Istoricheskii Arkhiv* 2 (2008): 57–58.
[165] RGANI f3 op65 d385, 28–41.
[166] In January 1956, Mao announced a new plan for accelerated collectivization of the countryside.
[167] Luthi, *The Sino-Soviet Split*, 43.
[168] Fursenko, *Arkhivy Kremlia Prezidium*, 163–64.
[169] "New Evidence on Sino-Soviet Relations," 151.

movement's recently adopted principle of pancha shila in intrabloc affairs.[170] In January 1957, Mao predicted a rocky long-term relationship with a patronizing Soviet Union. He told provincial party officials that "wrangling will continue" between the two socialist powers. "Those in the Soviet Union who still want to practice big power chauvinism will invariably encounter difficulties.... With their steel, oil, and coal, they have become cocky.... [But] they have achieved nothing other than digging a few things out of the earth, turning them into steel, and manufacturing some planes and cars.... All we hope for now is to avoid major clashes.... Let these differences be dealt with in the future. Should they stick to the current path, one day we will have to expose everything."[171]

Identity relations, drifting apart since Stalin's death, pushed farther along by the Twentieth Party Congress, really accelerated in opposite directions with Mao's use of the Hundred Flowers Campaign to "unmask" opponents to orthodox Stalinism whom he could then repress with the "Anti-Rightist" campaign. At the very same time, Khrushchev's "unmasking" of the anti-party group led by Molotov guaranteed there would be no backsliding in the Stalinist, and Chinese, direction.[172] After events in Hungary, Mao claimed that "de-Stalinization is simply de-Marxification; it is revisionism."[173] This was the first time China had identified the Soviet Union's discourse of difference as a danger to socialism, a danger of bourgeois restoration. In May 1957, Mao kicked off the Hundred Flowers campaign for the masses. In just two weeks, the wave of popular criticism had reached the system itself, not just its idiosyncratic flaws. Instead of trying to rein it in, as Khrushchev had done in 1956, Mao decided he "wanted to catch big fish, and dig out poisonous weeds" once and for all. In June, he launched the counterattack known as the anti-Rightist campaign. And in the summer, explicitly repudiating the new Soviet discourse, he announced that as socialism got stronger, the class struggle only intensifies.[174]

The Developing World: Difference as Ally Multiplier

To Stalin's Soviet Union, the developing world was irrelevant at best, and dangerous at worst. This was so because the only reliable allies in the discourse of danger were those who were as identical to the Soviet Union as possible. There

---

[170] Jian, *Mao's China*, 150–55.
[171] "New Evidence on Sino-Soviet Relations," 152–53.
[172] Jian, *Mao's China*, 69.
[173] Luthi, *The Sino-Soviet Split*, 63.
[174] Ibid., 69–72. Significantly, Khrushchev had told Tito in June 1956 that one of Stalin's main errors was in believing in "the sharpening of class struggle under socialism." Micunovic, *Moscow Diary*, 62.

was just too much threatening variety among the Nehrus, Sukarnos, and Nassers of the newly independent states.

The discourse of difference changed all this; it created interests for the Soviet Union in states, regions, and leaders that were absent under Stalin. While most observers, including most scholars of Soviet foreign policy, associate domestic moderation in the Soviet Union with foreign policy moderation, exactly the opposite was the case with regard to the developing world. With Stalin's death there emerged a new arena of competition with the West with billions of people and entire continents involved. While the Cold War was indeed (thankfully) cold between the Soviet Union and the United States, the war was anything but cold in the developing world, where 20 million people died from 1945 to 1991 in wars and conflicts propagated by the United States and the Soviet Union. The combination of Soviet great power identity and recognition of difference proved to be very destructive for much of the globe.

In terms of how the Cold War played out, the post-Stalin toleration of difference had its greatest long-term effects on Soviet relations with China and on Soviet policy in the developing world, in particular, with regard to national liberation movements bent on gaining independence from colonial metropoles, or overthrowing more conservative regimes. The revolution in Hungary ended the further development of the effects of tolerated difference on eastern Europe. But the newly empowered discourse set Sino-Soviet relations onto a trajectory of discord and conflict, and launched a 30-year policy of Soviet "adventurism" in Asia, Africa, and Latin America.[175]

Perhaps the two signature events of the period from 1953 to 1958 were Khrushchev and Bulganin's month-long tour of India, Afghanistan, and Burma in November and December 1955, and Soviet support for Egypt during the November 1956 Suez crisis. The first signified the Soviet Union's entry into the decolonizing world as a developmental model and source of aid. The second captured the Soviet Union as great power competitor of the United States and the West in a new arena.

With few important exceptions, Soviet activities in the developing world started out slowly, and at a low level of commitment. Kwame Nkrumah, who would later become one of the Soviet Union's most progressive allies in Africa, invited the Soviet Union to send a delegation to mark Ghana's independence in March 1957. While the United States sent Vice-President Nixon, the Soviets sent

---

[175] Scholarship on Soviet foreign policy in the Third World for very good reason almost always treats the postwar Stalinist period in a few pages, while devoting hundreds to his successors. Elizabeth Valkenier, *The Soviet Union and the Third World* (New York: Praeger, 1983); Jerry Hough, *The Struggle for the Third World* (Washington, DC: The Brookings Institution Press, 1986); and Westad, *The Global Cold War*.

Ivan Benediktov, the Minister of State Farms. Beginning to compete with the West in the decolonizing world was confusing. Vladimir Vinogradov, a former Soviet trade official, recounts the story of establishing trade relations with Argentina in late 1954. Argentina had asked for a loan to cover its purchase of imports from the Soviet Union, but Moscow had never done this before. At a meeting chaired by Mikoian, they discussed what to charge for interest on the loan. Someone suggested no interest, since socialists are not interested in a profit. Mikoian rejected this idea, noting that Argentina would be politically uncomfortable with a gift. He asked, what do capitalists charge? The answer was four percent, so he suggested halving it, "but the rate must look like it has been calculated, so lets say 2.5% for five years." This became the standard Soviet interest rate for developing countries for many years.[176]

Khrushchev expressed the official Soviet rejection of continued binarization of the world into Us and Them, in India asking his audience, "[W]hy should we clarify the questions on which we don't agree? It is much more important to declare that upon which we fundamentally agree."[177] During the July 1955 Plenum debate on Yugoslavia, Mikoian, countering Molotov, laid out the logic for placing states along a continuum, rather than consigning them to either a black or white box. Mikoian noted, that by Molotov's reasoning, Iran, Pakistan, and India would all end up in the same "bourgeois" category.[178] Molotov's opposition to putting much stock in bourgeois nationalists came back to haunt him at the June 1957 Anti-Party Plenum after which he was demoted and sent to be the Soviet ambassador to the People's Republic of Mongolia. Mikoian reminded the plenum that "our comrades went to Burma and India, and undermined the influence of imperialist countries in Asia."[179]

Later at the same meeting, Mikoian made the serious charge of "leftwing infantilism" against Molotov, invoking Lenin's famous essay against Left sectarianism. Mikoian said, "[W]e shouldn't be fetishists or dogmatists. Why is the Afghan king worse than the Pakistani president? I would say he is better because he doesn't want to fall under the yoke of America and wants to be friends with us. Indeed the Pakistani president has joined the Baghdad Pact. This is a leftwing infantile disease; we cannot indulge the horse-trader who has assiduously wormed his way into society, but doesn't know how to behave there."[180] One critical difference that emerged from this deeper differentiation was the advice Soviets gave to the local communist parties in different countries. While local

---

[176] Vinogradov, *Diplomatiia*, 18–20.
[177] *Pravda*, 1, November 23, 1955.
[178] CC Plenum, July 11, 1955, morning session, 6.
[179] CC Plenum, June 24, 1957, 33.
[180] CC Plenum, June 25, 1957, 38.

Indian and Ghanaian communists, for example, were told to pursue "national democratic fronts," that is, form coalitions with the ruling nationalist bourgeoisie, communists elsewhere were not so constrained.[181]

As was the case with all other countries, the logic of hierarchy allowed the Soviet Union to tolerate difference more easily. If a country were lower on the rungs of modernity, and was becoming like the Soviet Union over time, deviations could be considered acceptable difference. Bulganin, for instance, placed India on such a developmental scale, telling his audience that it, like the Soviet Union in the past, "was faced with the problem of converting [its] country . . . into an advanced state with a developed national economy."[182]

Identities are always Selves understood in relationship to Others. The Soviet Union had a very particular Self by which it understood the decolonizing world. This was Central Asia. It was as if the Soviet Union had its own decolonizing world right within its borders. It was a region dominated by pre-modern, feudal, tribal, and religious vestiges, each an obstacle to socialism. But with the help of its vanguard in the Soviet Union, in Russia, in Moscow, this region, too, was moving toward socialism. From the Soviet perspective after Stalin's death, most of the world was a pre-modern expanse with the potential to move toward socialism, given Soviet aid and tutelage. The decolonizing world was another Central Asia, and, from the Soviet perspective, the Soviet Union had demonstrated that socialism could flourish there, too. This is critical to keep in mind, for it gave the Soviet Union confidence for 30 years that its development model could compete with the Western one from Ghana to India to Peru.

Reflecting the new Soviet identity of toleration for ambiguity, and continuua over dichotomies, was rejection of the dichotomous assigning of all decolonizing countries to either the socialist or capitalist camps. Instead, the Soviets developed a new "non-capitalist path of development" to characterize states that were neither socialist nor capitalist. Referring to the Central Asian experience, this path allowed for movement toward socialism without expropriating the bourgeoisie of their property, without a communist party at the vanguard of the revolution, and without a proletariat of any size. What was necessary, however, was the friendship and assistance of the Soviet Union. Moscow was the surrogate vanguard for the decolonizing world, and that role would prove very expensive in the years to come.

When the Soviet Peace Committee traveled to India in late March 1955, it brought along the movie *The Tajik People's Holiday* to show the other delegates,

---

[181] Apolon Davidson, Sergei Mazov and Georgii Tsypkin, *SSSR i Afrika* (Moscow: Institute of World History, 2002), 170–74.

[182] *New Times*, December 22, 1955, 8.

most of whom were from newly decolonized countries.[183] In reporting on his trip to India at a December 1956 CC meeting on literature, Alexander Korneichuk declared, "We all know what kind of influence Uzbekistan and Kazakhstan exert on India. When we [non-Central Asians] go, we get along well, but we don't talk especially. But when representatives of these republics go, they relate differently to them; they are surrounded...."[184]

The Soviet great power identity was invoked and assumed ever more frequently after Stalin's death. And it often entailed offering economic or military aid. In December 1955, while still in Afghanistan, Khrushchev cabled the Presidium members who were in Moscow, requesting that they approve an arms sale to Afghanistan he had negotiated. Molotov and Kaganovich opposed selling arms to this bourgeois feudal government. But Malenkov observed, "We should attract Afghanistan to our side." And Mikoian argued that "we will have to help some states if we wish to enter into more serious competition with the USA." This deft use of the "soft on imperialism" card against Molotov and Kaganovich resulted in a $100 million aid package being approved. Molotov remained consistent, opposing military aid to Egypt in January 1957 as well.[185]

One case in which Soviet great power competition with the United States resulted in less, not more, support for a national liberation movement was Algeria. In short, Soviet interests in being the vanguard of the world's national liberation movements were sacrificed to its interests in being a great power successfully competing against the United States in Europe. France, being a potential "ally" of Moscow against US plans, especially for Germany and the nuclearization of NATO, was granted unusual sufferance in Algeria. In a May 1956 meeting with French Prime Minister Guy Mollet in Moscow, the Soviet side agreed to a joint communique that said, "Soviet leaders understand the difficulties France is experiencing in Algeria and express the desire that the Algerian problem will be settled ... in the interests of both the French and Algerian people, since one cannot deny the historical ties between Algeria and France"—hardly a statement of support for the National Liberation Front (FLN) seeking Algerian independence. Even the French communist party, wanting to return to a coalition government in Paris, lobbied Moscow not to support the FLN, arguing it was an anti-communist tool of the United States and England in their intra-imperialist competition with France.[186]

The Soviets began to experience what would become an everyday occurrence for the ensuing 30 years of the Cold War: the unavoidable tradeoff

---

[183] TsKhSD f5 op17 d548, 63.
[184] RGANI f5 op36 d12, 128.
[185] Fursenko and Naftali, *Khrushchev's Cold War*, 81–82, 142.
[186] Evgeniia Obichkina, "Sovetskoe Rukovodstvo I Voina v Alzhire 1954–1962 gg.," *Novaia i Noveishaia Istoriia* (January 2000): 20–22.

between pursuing great power interests in the North and advancing revolutionary interests in the South. For example, in June 1956, Foreign Minister Shepilov experienced the displeasure of the Soviet Union's new Egyptian ally in Cairo. Shepilov was instructed to try to convince Nasser to agree to defer pressing for UN Security Council consideration of the Algerian question, "from the desire to not excessively aggravate our relations with France."[187]

The Israeli, British, and French invasion of Egypt in November 1956 enabled the Soviet Union to experience the risks and rewards of being a great power in competition with the West in the decolonizing world. The Soviet-Egyptian relationship started haltingly at best as Nasser continued to try to gain support and aid from Washington and Moscow simultaneously. The tenuousness and inconstancy of alliances in the post-colonial world would mark the Soviet (and American, to a lesser degree) experience there for the next three decades. In May 1955, Nasser told the Soviet ambassador in Egypt, Daniil Solod, that he feared closer ties with Moscow and the local communists. A month later, Nasser had the communist leadership arrested, and renewed his efforts to get weapons from the United States. Meanwhile the Soviets had been offering arms since April. Not until being frustrated by US temporizing did Nasser reach an arms supply agreement with the Soviet Union in September 1955, to be delivered through Czechoslovakia. Fearing Soviet arms would make Egypt more vulnerable, Nasser asked for Soviet support against any external threat. Khrushchev offered political and moral, but not military, support. In November 1955, the Presidium agreed to Egypt's request for 100 additional MiG fighter planes, while recognizing the risk of a Soviet commitment to Egypt.[188]

This alternation of waxing and waning desire for a closer relationship continued with Shepilov's offer to Nasser of a treaty of friendship and non-aggression in June 1956, while in Cairo negotiating the terms of the Soviet Union's pathbreaking $1.1 billion loan to build the Aswan Dam. Nasser rejected the treaty but accepted the money. On July 26, 1956, Egypt nationalized the Suez Canal. The Soviet Union consistently supported Egypt's right to nationalize the canal while simultaneously demanding that the international rights to navigation through the canal be maintained.[189] The Soviets advised Nasser accordingly.[190]

---

[187] RGANI f3 op14 d35, 332–333. Not coincidentally, the Algerian brief was handled by the MFA's 1st European Department. Obichkina, "Sovetskoe Rukovodstvo," 23.

[188] Fursenko and Naftali, *Khrushchev's Cold War*, 64–78.

[189] Mikhail M. Narinskii, "Sovetskii Soiuz I Suetskii Krizis 1956 Goda," *Novaia i Noveishaia Istoriia* (April 2004): 55; and Fursenko and Naftali, *Khrushchev's Cold War*, 98.

[190] RGANI f3 op 14 d47, 62–65. In the August 1956 instructions from the Presidium to the Shepilov delegation heading to London for the great power conference on Suez, Shepilov was told to "defend Egyptian interests and ... freedom of passage.... Don't allow the Soviet Union to be depicted as if it is ignoring the interests of England and France.... The Soviet Union fully appreciates the importance of Suez ... especially England as a naval island power...." RGANI f3 op14 d49, 12–21.

Throughout the crisis Soviet leaders recognized that the United States had a different position on Suez than its French and British allies. But for public purposes, the Soviets pretended as if Moscow and the newly independent states in the Middle East were alone against an imperialist front. For example, the deputy minister of foreign affairs, Vladimir Semenov, assured the Egyptian ambassador in Moscow, Mohammed al-Kuni, that the "US follows a somewhat different line on Suez" than other Western powers.[191] At the August Suez conference in London, Shepilov assured Dulles that Moscow and Washington might find a way out of the crisis together.[192] On November 28, during negotiations over a withdrawal from Egypt after the cease-fire, Khrushchev told the French ambassador in Moscow that France had to withdraw now, saying, "the US is against you."[193] But on November 2, three days into the war, Shepilov told the Syrian foreign minister that "the main director is the USA."[194]

As the London conference produced no results, Khrushchev resorted to some public deterrent threats, declaring at an August reception in the Rumanian embassy in Moscow, "The Arab peoples won't stand alone if war breaks out." He went on to suggest that Soviet volunteers, including his son Sergei, might go to Egypt to help fight.[195] In another threat, this time in a letter from Bulganin to Prime Ministers Eden and Mollet, the Soviet Union's great power identity was invoked. The September 10 letter said, in part, that "as a great power, the USSR is interested in maintaining peace, and cannot be indifferent to this question." The latter, in diplomatic parlance, is a deterrent threat.[196] At the conclusion of the Anti-Party Plenum, Khrushchev declared that Suez had demonstrated that "we can deter imperialist aggressors."[197]

On October 30, 1956, the Israeli invasion of Egypt began, soon joined by British and French forces. In the event, the Soviet Union behaved very cautiously at first. Nasser's requests that the Soviet Union send fighter pilots were simply ignored. Soviet ambassador Evgenii Kiselev was instructed on the 31st to respond to Nasser's requests for volunteers by saying, absurdly, that the Presidium was in discussions with the governments of its Central Asian republics.[198] On November 3, the Soviet Union refused Nasser's request that the Soviet Navy be sent to help Egypt.[199]

---

[191] Narinskii, "Sovetskii Soiuz i Suetskii Krizis," 58.
[192] Fursenko and Naftali, *Khrushchev's Cold War*, 99.
[193] Narinskii, "Sovetskii Soiuz i Suetskii Krizis," 66.
[194] Ibid., 62.
[195] Ibid., 105.
[196] Narinskii, "Sovetskii Soiuz i Suetskii Krizis," 59.
[197] CC Plenum, June 28, 1957, 32.
[198] On December 9, TASS pronounced the question of volunteers moot, since "the aggressors have withdrawn." Narinskii, "Sovetskii Soiuz i Suetskii Krizis," 66.
[199] Fursenko and Naftali, *Khrushchev's Cold War*, 127; and Narinskii, "Sovetskii Soiuz i Suetskii Krizis," 63–65.

Finally on November 6, the Soviet Union issued a coercive threat that its leadership would remember for some time.[200] On that day, Bulganin sent a letter to Eisenhower proposing a joint military intervention under UN aegis. He also made veiled nuclear threats to Britain and France to accept a cease-fire and withdraw, or else.[201] A cease-fire was voted for in the UN General Assembly the same day. The Soviet elite apparently learned from Suez that its compellent threats worked. Khrushchev told the Yugoslavian ambassador that the ceasefire was "the direct result" of Soviet warnings.[202] Mikoian and other Soviet leaders reported to the June 1957 Anti-Party Plenum that "showing their teeth had achieved the end of the war" in Suez.[203]

The United States: The Soviet Union's Most Significant Other

Identity relations between the United States and the Soviet Union are a special case, in several respects. They are mostly the product of interaction at the interstate level, where two very conflictual identity relations are reproduced on a daily basis: great power competitors and ideological enemies. This is not to say that the United States is absent in Soviet domestic discourse; far from it, as we saw in chapter 4. But, unlike the other elements of Soviet identity, class, modernity, hierarchy, orthodoxy, the Russian nation, and so forth, which are primarily constructed internally, in reference to events and realities situated in the Soviet Union itself, the US element of Soviet identity is significantly constructed in Soviet external relations with the United States, as well as at home. This external focus of Soviet identification with, but mostly against, the United States, as great power and ideological competitor, already predisposes US-Soviet identity relations, and foreign relations, in a hostile direction. As a real and potential enemy abroad, domestic identifications with the United States within the Soviet Union, as we have seen, can be easily construed within the elite discourse as dangerous deviation from the Soviet model, including even bourgeois degeneration and counter-revolutionary attitudes toward socialism. The United States, by treating

---

[200] For example, at the June 1957 Anti-Party Plenum, Mikoian reminded his audience that "we found the power both to keep Hungary and threaten the imperialists that if they don't end the war in Egypt we will use missiles against them. Everyone admits we resolved the fate of Egypt." June 24, 1957, 36. The United States was similarly impressed with its own success. Having overthrown the Arbenz government in Guatemala in 1954, many, especially in the CIA, thought that the Bay of Pigs operation in April 1961 would go off in the same manner.

[201] Ibid., 65.

[202] Taubman, *Khrushchev*, 359.

[203] June 24, 1957, 33.

the Soviet Union as the other superpower, and as a global challenger, helped Soviet leaders understand the Soviet Union as precisely that: the other great power locked in a bipolar competition for global ideological supremacy.

While the United States as ideological competitor, and the Soviet Union as its necessary opponent, are widely and broadly distributed throughout Soviet domestic discourses, the Soviet Union as a great power is not. In fact, Soviet great power identity is located exclusively in the highest reaches of Soviet foreign policy-making, especially in the Ministry of Foreign Affairs, but also in Presidium and CC Plenum discussions of foreign relations.

Unlike in Stalin's times, when comparisons with the United States had to conclude in a statement of Soviet superiority, the more realistic view of the Soviet Union entailed comparing itself with the United States as a kind of challenge, an aspirational level of material achievement. Mikoian, for example, criticizing a draft of a new political economy textbook, noted that "in a number of cases, Soviet achievements are depicted in a glorifying tone insufficiently backed up by the necessary facts. So, for example, on page 372, it says that 'in the Soviet Union *in all areas* of industry the mechanization of production has reached a level *unseen* under capitalism.'" He concludes by forgiving the authors for having written "in conditions difficult for creative work," that is, under Stalin.[204]

Immediate De-Stalinization

As Zubkova has observed, "[T]he contours of a new foreign policy course appeared immediately after the death of Stalin."[205] Less than two weeks after Stalin's burial, Malenkov made an encouraging public statement to the effect that there were no issues between the United States and the Soviet Union that couldn't be solved by negotiations. Oleg Troianovskii recalls that Molotov told him in April 1953 that "an important new stage of Soviet foreign policy was beginning when we will try to achieve the removal of tensions with the West."[206] A string of resolutions of thorny conflicts ensued: the Korean War armistice in June 1953; the Geneva Accords on Vietnam in July 1954; the Austrian state treaty in May 1955; normalization of relations with Yugoslavia in June 1955; the Four Power summit in Geneva in June 1955; and the establishment of diplomatic relations

---

[204] RGANI f5 op30 d51, 44 (emphasis in original).

[205] Elena Iu. Zubkova, "Malenkov i Khrushchev: Lichnyi Faktor v Politike Poslestalinskogo Rukovodstva," *Otechestvennaia Istoriia* 4 (1995): 113.

[206] Oleg Troianovskii, *Cherez Gody I Rasstoianiia: Istoriia Odnoi Semi* (Moscow: Vagrius, 1997), 170. On September 28, 1953, the Soviet Union proposed a summit with France, Britain, China, and the United States. All but the Chinese foreign ministers met in Berlin from January 25 to February 2, 1954, and agreed to meet in Geneva, with the Chinese, in July.

with Germany in September 1955. As Zubok summarized, "[J]ust days after Stalin's death, Soviet foreign policy changed on the Korean War, Yugoslavia, Greece, and Turkey."[207]

A More Secure Soviet Union

As was elaborated in the previous chapter, the newly empowered discourse of difference entailed an understanding of the Soviet Union as fundamentally more secure than was admitted under Stalinist orthodoxy. The gravest threat ever to Soviet security, the German invasion of World War II, had ended victoriously; the Soviet people had not rebelled against socialism; and the Soviet Union had ended the US atomic monopoly. Stalin's death, therefore, allowed for an immediate re-evaluation of relations with the United States, from the standpoint of a more secure Soviet Union.

By the pathologic of nuclear deterrence, Malenkov's March 12, 1954, declaration that a nuclear war would destroy global civilization was a dramatic statement of fundamental Soviet security, in that its nuclear deterrent was sufficiently strong so as to promise a devastating counter-strike if the United States were rash enough to use its nuclear weapons on Soviet territory.[208] A less explicit way of saying that war was no longer inevitable between the United States and the Soviet Union was Khrushchev's formulation at the Twentieth Party Congress in February 1956, in which he publicly declared that war between socialist and imperialist states "was no longer a fatalistic inevitability," because the USSR was stronger and able to deter such a war, and Western publics were more powerful in being able to constrain their elites who might be interested in taking fatal risks. The replacement of "capitalist encirclement" with a "zone of peace" at the congress spoke to the Soviet sense of much greater security than in years past.

As might be expected, those Soviet leaders who remained carriers of the discourse of danger resisted Khrushchev's understanding of war. Kaganovich, at a January 30, 1956, Presidium meeting called to discuss the general secretary's report to the congress, objected to "a number of risky propositions in the report." In particular, "on the principled question of the inevitability of war, the conscious will of the people cannot nullify the objective laws..." of capitalism causing war.[209]

Arguments also erupted over whether Khrushchev should authorize multiple, peaceful, and parliamentary paths to socialism. Such a formulation not

---

[207] Zubok and Pleshakov, *Inside the Kremlin's Cold War*, 155.
[208] Malenkov was forced to recant this position in January 1955, but Khrushchev adopted it as his own at the Twentieth Party Congress in February 1956, and at the July 1955 summit with Eisenhower, both he, and especially Zhukov, repeatedly intimated an acceptance of mutually assured destruction.
[209] Fursenko, *Arkhivy Kremlia Prezidium*, 88.

only projected the discourse of difference from Soviet society onto the entire globe, but also reflected a new Soviet confidence in socialism's ultimate triumph by force of example, not arms. Kaganovich objected, saying that "we must say we are for the revolutionary path of struggle." Molotov joined in, insisting, "[W]e shouldn't speak of a parliamentary path to socialism without criticizing Laborites and Socialists.... This is not a path to socialism in England, Norway, or Sweden." Mikoian countered, "We only push the masses away when we only assert: 'We will come and cut you all down.'" Suslov added that insisting on civil war was "sectarianism." Shepilov, Kirichenko, and Khrushchev all piled on Kaganovich, who ultimately conceded, "[W]e have no fundamental disagreements." The language remained unchanged.[210]

In fact, only from the perspective of minimal nuclear deterrence was the Soviet homeland secure from US nuclear attack. At Stalin's death the Soviet Union had only 120 atomic bombs, none of which were deliverable to the United States.[211] In 1953, the United States had 1,200 deliverable bombs; by 1955, 2,300—probably 10 times Soviet levels. By 1960, the United States had 5,500 nuclear warheads, two-thirds of them gravity bombs. And they had the bombers to deliver them on Soviet targets. In June 1955, the United States deployed the first of hundreds of B-52 intercontinental strategic bombers. The United States had been relying on over 1,100 B-47 strategic bombers. The first Soviet Tu-95 entered service in 1955 but was extremely vulnerable to air defenses because of its slow and low cruising profile.[212] The United States had clear strategic nuclear superiority.[213]

Soviet confidence in the absolute security afforded by nuclear weapons was reflected in the cancellation of Stalin's plans for a large blue water navy to counter US naval assets around the world. In November 1955, Stalin's plans to build four aircraft carriers were abandoned; the navy was reduced in size from 600,000 to 500,000 sailors by 1957; and 375 ships were mothballed.[214]

A more secure Soviet Union also made Soviet cuts in conventional forces thinkable, especially if nuclear weapons, if only those scheduled for future

---

[210] Ibid., 88–93.

[211] Taubman, *Khrushchev*, 347.

[212] Holloway, *Stalin and the Bomb*, 322–29.

[213] The first test of a Soviet "super bomb," or a hydrogen device of potentially unlimited yield, was successful in November 1955. Its 1.6 megaton (MT) yield compared to the US tests of 10 and 15 MT in October 1952 and February 1954, respectively. Matthew Evangelista, "'Why Keep Such an Army?': Khrushchev's Troop Reductions," Cold War International History Project, Working Paper 19 (Washington, DC: Woodrow Wilson Center for Scholars, December 1997), 28. Despite the launch of Sputnik in October 1957 and the panic it spawned in the West about Soviet ICBM capabilities, Moscow didn't deploy functional ICBMs until the 1960s. Why deploy IRBMs in Cuba in 1962 if one had a usable strategic missile force? Taubman, *Khrushchev*, 378–79.

[214] Fursenko and Naftali, *Khrushchev's Cold War*, 77; and Zubok, "The Soviet Union," 127.

production, gave the USSR strategic invulnerability. In May 1955, the Soviets in effect made a proposal that accepted most of what the United States had proposed just months before. Moscow agreed to a limit of one to 1.5 million men under arms in Europe for both the United States and the Soviet Union, a plan for eliminating nuclear weapons, including multiple kinds of heretofore rejected on-site inspections, and a demand to close all foreign military bases, but without linking this issue to the rest of the package, as it was unacceptable to the United States, which had foreign military personnel based all over the world.[215] Soviet armed forces had peaked in 1953 at 5.4 million and had been reduced by 600,000 by 1955, although without any Soviet announcement. The resulting conventional balance in Europe was the most favorable the United States and NATO had experienced until that time, because while the United States reduced its army from 1.5 million to 850,000 from 1953 to 1961, its numbers in Europe actually increased from 350,000 to 400,000; the West German Bundeswehr was created with another 500,000 soldiers; and the United States deployed tactical nuclear weapons with its ground forces in Europe, which numbered 3,000 by 1960. In August 1955, Moscow announced an additional unilateral cut of 640,000 men, although only 340,000 were actually discharged, leaving Soviet armed forces of 4.4 million by January 1956.[216] In May 1956, the Soviets announced another unilateral cut, this time of 1.2 million men.[217]

Along with US opposition, significant arms control foundered on Soviet fears that comprehensive US surveillance of Soviet military capabilities would reveal just how weak the Soviet Union really was, relative to the United States and the West. Khrushchev was appalled at Bulganin's willingness to consider Eisenhower's "Open Skies" proposal at the Geneva summit. Not only would it reveal Soviet weakness to US aviation, but the inability of the Soviet Union to even

---

[215] Evangelista, "Why Keep Such an Army?" 2–3. Expressing the logic of what would become the heart of confidence-building measures in the 1991 Conventional Forces in Europe Agreement, Bulganin explained to the visiting Indian prime minister Jawaharlal Nehru that foreign inspectors at airfields, ports, railroads and major roads were useful because "no war can begin without the redeployment of forces." Given the inspectors, no such "concentration of forces could go undetected," in effect, supplying an early warning of hostile intentions and attack. RGANI f5 op30 d116, 83.

[216] Evangelista, "Why Keep Such an Army?," 4, 28; and Vladislav Zubok, "The Case of Divided Germany, 1953–1964," in *Nikita Khrushchev*, ed., William Taubman, Sergei Khrushchev, and Abbott Gleason (New Haven: Yale University Press, 2000), 287.

[217] Evangelista, "Why Keep Such an Army?" 5. Even after these announced cuts, and after the intervention in Hungary in November 1956, Khrushchev confided to Micunovic that "Soviet armed forces in East Germany alone were stronger than what NATO had at its disposal at the moment in all Europe." Micunovic, *Moscow Diary*, 156.

conduct aerial surveillance over the United States would be humiliating.[218] Khrushchev told Zhukov in Geneva that whoever has more power "is more interested in intelligence" and told Eisenhower at Geneva that "in our eyes, [Open Skies] is a very transparent espionage device.... You could hardly expect us to take this seriously."[219]

On April 13, 1957, the Presidium discussed a new draft disarmament proposal generated within the MFA. Khrushchev opened the discussion by calling Gromyko's proposals "insufficient." Khrushchev instead suggested lower numbers, to perhaps one million, and more on-site inspection. Molotov tried to link the question of conventional arms control to a ban on nuclear weapons, a position already discussed and rejected for its unacceptability to the United States. Khrushchev countered, concluding that "if nothing has changed, as Molotov says, then there is nothing to discuss.... But colossal changes have occurred.... The US has reduced its armed forces. If an opponent makes real concessions, we shouldn't be thick-skulled. To link atomic [and conventional] weapons now means no forward movement." The Presidium sent the draft back to Gromyko, Konev, and Sokolovskii to work on in light of the discussion.[220]

A more secure and stronger Soviet Union also implied a less coercive approach to the external world. It must be stressed that there is no objectively logical connection between a state getting stronger and acting more circumspectly in world affairs. Quite the contrary, most realist accounts of world politics would predict exactly the opposite. But Soviet understandings of itself as more secure, both at home and in the world, meant a repudiation of the kinds of practices that had earlier been associated with weakness and vulnerability, to wit, coercion, repression, and ultimata. Bulganin made these connections explicit at the antiparty plenum of June 1957: "Since the death of Stalin, the international situation has fundamentally changed in our favor.... Our country has gotten stronger. It has become a great power.... In the years before Stalin's death we stood on the brink of war with the Western powers and the US.... In northern Europe, we had settled relations with Sweden, Norway, and Finland, but these relations were constructed on the principle of force and the jackboot."[221]

A key change adopted by Stalin's successors was to abandon thinking of the Soviet Union as some besieged citadel of socialism subjected to "capitalist encirclement."

---

[218] Khrushchev, *Nikita Khruchev*, 155. What was more humiliating was that the United States didn't need any "open skies" agreement to conduct aerial surveillance. While Khrushchev was toasting US independence at the Moscow embassy for only the second time, on the Fourth of July in 1956, the United States made its first U-2 reconnaissance flights across Soviet airspace. The Soviets sent an official note of protest five days later. Fursenko and Naftali, *Khrushchev's Cold War*, 93.

[219] Fursenko and Naftali, *Khrushchev's Cold War*, 48.

[220] Fursenko, *Arkhivy Kremlia Prezidium*, 249–51.

[221] CC Plenum, June 24, 1957, 46.

Instead, as Mikoian argued in his comments on a new draft textbook on political economy in May 1954, "Can we really speak of capitalist encirclement now that the Soviet Union borders on friendly countries of people's democracy and in the East with China?" He continued, "[I]s it correct to speak of an economic blockade of the socialist camp, when we have a world market?"[222]

It is quite interesting that the Soviet leadership concluded the Soviet Union and socialism were both more secure while simultaneously realizing that the United States was far stronger and economically healthier than ever acknowledged under Stalin. For example, Mikoian, who was the first Soviet leader to utter critical words about Stalin at the Twentieth Party Congress, did so by belittling Stalin's arguments in *Economic Problems of Socialism in the USSR*, saying that "the volume of production will decline in the US, England, and France" after the war.[223] I think this demonstrates several points. First, a minimal nuclear deterrent is acceptable for strategic invulnerability. Second, security is not entirely material, but also a toleration of difference and fallibility, such that deviations and making errors are not signs of fatal flaws in the project, but rather of strength in being able to entertain different ways of being socialist, as well as being able to learn from errors. This is just what Ehrenburg had in mind.

Identifying the United States as one's significant other, especially in material terms, and claiming that one will equal and surpass it in the production of the good life for the population both reflects confidence in the Soviet project and also creates a very high standard against which the Soviet elite and the Soviet people would measure the achievements of the Soviet project, and socialism, more generally. After Khrushchev declared at the Twentieth Party Congress that socialism was already built in the Soviet Union, and they were now building communism, a retiree in Kharkov wrote to the Central Committee: "When a worker in our city lives better than the average worker in any capitalist country, and the average worker in the countryside better than the average American or Dutch farmer, then we will correctly assert that we have built socialism...."[224]

Daily Soviet diplomatic practices abroad changed, too, as a consequence of realizing the Soviet Union was not fundamentally in danger of dissolving upon contact with the outside world. Delegations of Soviet writers and journalists to the UN in New York as late as 1955 reported that Soviet diplomats were like "hermit crabs" afraid of any contact with anyone outside the embassy—for good reason, if we can imagine what any "denunciation" of such contacts with the Western enemy would have meant in Stalinist times. With Shepilov's replacement of Molotov as foreign minister in June 1956, constraints on interaction

---

[222] RGANI f5 op30 d51, 42.
[223] Aksiutin, "Novoe o XX Sezde KPSS," 110.
[224] Pyzhikov, "Problema Kulta Lichnosti," 53.

with foreigners abroad were loosened, enabling a much greater flow of disparate information to be available to Soviet diplomats.[225] Even if such impressions rarely made it into official memoranda sent to Moscow, tens of thousands of Soviets would return home with understandings of the outside world quite at variance with the memos they prudently edited. While recognizing the huge change from Stalin's times, we must not exaggerate. There was less fear of contagion from the West, but still fear. Of 37 graduates of the International Relations Institute of the MFA in 1956, only five were sent to work at the UN, and these five were all veterans of the Great Patriotic War. It was feared that the UN was a hotbed of foreign intelligence recruiters.[226]

A Fallible Soviet Union

Often in private among themselves, Soviet leaders confessed their past mistakes.[227] But there were notable admissions to foreign leaders, too. Marshal Zhukov, at the Geneva summit in July 1955, listened to Eisenhower explain why the Soviet Union seemed threatening to the West, citing the Greek civil war, blockade of Berlin, the revolution in China, and the Korean War. Zhukov first said that in his opinion there is no sense in digging up the past. But he allowed "that in the past both sides made mistakes." But, he added, one must look to the future.[228]

In March 1956, Khrushchev explained to the Danish prime minister, Hans Christian Hansen, that the birth of NATO had been the result of a "big military psychosis" that "we also gave a pretext for." But "we will prove our peacefulness and thereby loosen up NATO. We will unilaterally reduce our armed forces and then it will be hard for you to maintain NATO in front of your public opinion."[229]

At home, those in favor of self-criticism argued that it was a sign of strength to be able to find faults with socialism, and correct them. Khrushchev expressed the same logic with regard to Soviet foreign policy. Speaking with the Yugoslavian ambassador, Micunovic, in April 1956, Khrushchev, musing about the Twentieth Party Congress, told him that "capitalists will realize that we are strong since we

---

[225] At the anti-party plenum, Mikoian attacked Molotov for "not travelling anywhere and not allowing anyone else to travel anywhere. Our country suffered from this, not having necessary contacts and connections with the masses." CC Plenum, June 25, 1957, 41.

[226] Boris L. Kolokolov, *Professiia: Diplomat* (Moscow: Mezhdunarodnye Otnosheniia, 1998), 13.

[227] For example, in a February 9, 1956, Presidium discussion of Khrushchev's upcoming secret speech, Saburov observed that Stalin's mistakes "were not inadequacies, as Kaganovich says, but crimes. We lost a lot due to his stupid policies in the Finnish War, Korean War, and Berlin. . . ." Fursenko, *Arkhivy Kremlia Prezidium*, 102.

[228] G. K. Besedy and I. D. Zhukova, "Eizenkhauera na Zhenevskom Soveshchanii 1955 g.," *Novaia i Noveishaia Istoriia* (May 1999): 106.

[229] RGANI f5 op30 d163, 33.

are able to break with Stalin in this decisive way; anyone who is weak wouldn't undertake anything like this."[230] This is a clear illustration of the close connection between domestic understandings of the Soviet Union as secure enough to tolerate discussions of fallibility and foreign policy change.

There was no greater outpouring of self-criticism of Soviet foreign policy than at the June 1957 anti-party plenum. Khruschev and his allies catalogued a host of foreign policy blunders under Stalin, albeit to justify Molotov's removal from party leadership. Nevertheless, a new public record of Soviet fallibility was established in the arena of foreign affairs, one that condemned the previous strategy of consigning all those who were not allies to the enemy camp.

Khrushchev declared,

> Our party couldn't have achieved success in the struggle for peace and security had we not dethroned and abandoned the policy of turning the screw, the main inspirer of which was comrade Molotov.[231] Remember the sad results this policy brought. The rupture of friendly relations with Turkey and Iran, our neighbors. This was literally stupid. We helped American imperialism with out incorrect policy toward Turkey.... We wrote Turkey a note in which we abrogated the treaty of friendship. Why? Because you will not give us the Dardanelles. Listen, only a drunkard could have written this.... What did we do in Iran? We introduced our armed forces and began to act like masters there.... We poisoned the feelings of the Persians.... With our shortsighted policy, we pushed Turkey and Iran into the embrace of the United States, Britain, and the Baghdad Pact.

Khrushchev continued, identifying the Korean War as a mistake, as it had "aggravated the international situation to the extreme.... Essentially the international policy of Stalin is the policy of Molotov. Although, one must say that Stalin was much smarter and more flexible." What Molotov failed to recognize was that "establishing broad contacts with the leaders of capitalist countries has won new supporters of the Soviet Union among millions of people of all countries."[232] The Soviet Union was wrong to isolate itself; it is strong and attractive enough to interact in the world with confidence.

---

[230] Micunovic, *Moscow Diary*, 27.

[231] Of course, there is no evidence at all that Khrushchev, or any of Molotov's other accusers, ever opposed Stalin's foreign policy choices after the war.

[232] CC Plenum, June 28, 1957, 35–66. At the July 1955 CC Plenum, Khrushchev had blurted out, "We started the Korean War. Everyone knows we did." Mikoian added, "Everyone but our own people." The latter was edited out of even the transcript for internal circulation. Taubman, *Khrushchev*, 268.

Stalin's successors quickly realized the need to establish, or re-establish, scholarly and research institutions that could provide them with information about the outside world that Stalin had not deemed necessary. One example of such research was a long memo prepared by the founder of the Institute of World Economics and International Relations (IMEMO), Anushavan A. Arzumanian, for Khrushchev in March 1954. He criticized those who had not recognized the complexity of American foreign policy-making, those who adopt a "simplified, vulgarized, and undifferentiated approach to" US domestic politics; it was not an imperialist monolith. These writers only disinform readers by, for example, claiming the "struggle between Eisenhower and McCarthy, and Truman and McCarthy was just for show," or the argument that there are no differences between Taft and Eisenhower.

While the interests of the biggest monopolies dominate, and they do want "world domination, economic and military hegemony," they are "all the same against excessive risk." The really crazy ones, "the clearly adventuristic, putschist" ones who are for preventive war, fortunately, do not dominate. Moreover, there is a third group, of "the more moderate, less militaristic bourgeoisie" that is " more inclined toward peaceful relations and trade with" socialist countries. These are former "FDR co-workers."[233] But the most important element of American foreign policy missing in Soviet analyses, according to Arzumanian, was the "tradition of isolationism which contradicts the policy of unlimited global expansion." In fact, "the very word isolationism is as if banned from our press," he said. Although the economic roots of isolationism are attenuated, world markets are less important for the United States than for other capitalist countries. "Average enterprises are far less tied to foreign markets, especially beyond the Western Hemisphere" than the dominant monopolies. Moreover, the military industrial complex isn't a mass phenomenon, either. "Only 100 companies got 62% of all the military orders during the Korean War." Isolationism is also favored by geography, the United States sitting behind two oceans, "without strong neighbors." Arzumanian noted that under Eishenhower, the US "defense budget has decreased, and the armed forces have been reduced from 3.5 to 3 million men." Arzumanian concluded that the "Soviet peace policy" is especially important in influencing the balance of power within US foreign policy circles.[234]

While we don't know how this memo was received, it certainly provides much evidence to support elite Soviet arguments for a policy of restraint with regard to the United States, recognizing that Soviet behavior can influence American policy in the world.

[233] Franklyn Griffiths, "The Sources of American Conduct," *International Security* 9, no. 2 (Fall 1984): 3–50 is relevant here.
[234] RGANI f5 op30 d75, 27–49.

Conclusions

There was a revolution in Soviet foreign policy after Stalin's death. It was made possible by the empowerment of a new Soviet identity the central feature of which was an understanding of socialism that permitted variety and did not demand the strictest adherence to the Soviet model. This alternative discourse of difference had been maintained in society during the postwar Stalin years, often in official Soviet institutions. This change in Soviet identity had profound effects in Eastern Europe, where Stalinist regimes had been in power for years and had adopted Stalinist policies and practices, most often at the behest of Moscow. This had included the arrest, imprisonment, and execution of many thousands of communists, just as Moscow had ordered. Moscow was now recommending that "new courses" be adopted in the entire socialist community, a reversal of Stalinization, a liberalization of domestic life. In some cases, this meant the return to power of those who had been repressed, and had even been awaiting execution, as in the case of Gomulka. The limits of the toleration of difference were breached in Hungary, but even in this case, the Soviet leadership still preferred a government led by Kadar, who had been repressed by the Stalinist Rakosi, to any return to more orthodox times. The toleration of difference also meant that a rapprochement with Yugoslavia became possible.

Soviet foreign policy in the developing world began to change dramatically after Stalin's death. Instead of the Stalinist dichotomization of the developing world, represented by Molotov, into capitalists and communists, the new Soviet identity permitted an understanding of the decolonizing world as a vast sea of gray. Bourgeois nationalist leaders need not be socialist to be potential allies of the Soviet Union. A vast new arena of competition between the Soviet Union and the United States had opened up. Since the Soviet Union understood itself through its own experiences of non-capitalist development in Central Asia, Moscow had ready-made expectations for how poor, semi-feudal, dependent former colonies could make their way toward socialism.

In recognizing difference, it was understood that another state did not have to be identical in order to be a reliable friend or ally. The default had changed. Just by not being an enemy, one could potentially be a friend. This was as true in the case of Yugoslavia as it was in the case of India.

This new Soviet confidence that difference was possible, if not always desirable, was supported by old elements from the discourse of Stalin's times: hierarchy, modernity, and the Russian nation. These three items were consensual parts of both societal and elite discourse about the Soviet Union. With the Soviet Union atop the socialist hierarchy, as the most modern and developed socialist state, it could plausibly see all other socialist states as if they were on the road to becoming the Soviet Union. This was reassuring, as any deviations were just teething problems, or issues that could be attributed to the stage of development. This was certainly how eastern Europe and China were understood. And the rapprochement with Yugoslavia was further facilitated by the Soviet recognition of Yugoslavs as little Slavic brothers, like Ukrainians. Still more obvious was that the decolonizing world was near the bottom of a long developmental ladder, and so was accorded much more forbearance by Moscow in its policies and practices.

The new Soviet identity was also one of greater security, confidence, and self-assurance. If you are in a world where everyone is against you who is not with you, you are in a world of capitalist encirclement, and Africa, Asia, and Latin America are just full of imperialist hirelings. But toleration of difference made the Soviet Union much more secure, as only committed enemies of the Soviet Union were judged as threats. Meanwhile, having won the war against Nazi Germany, advanced far on the road to recovery, and tested an atomic and hydrogen bomb, the Soviet Union could feel secure about the socialist project at home, as well. This new level of security also allowed the Soviet Union to admit its previous errors. In so doing, it was able to adopt policies that in the past had been rejected.

Relations with the United States and the West benefited from this more secure Soviet Union. The new Soviet commitment to détente, unilateral arms reductions, and reversals of antagonistic policies in places like Austria and Korea, all were made possible by a new Soviet identity that included a higher level of security. On the other hand, interaction with the United States and the West daily reinforced a Soviet great power identity that was inherently competitive.

6

Conclusions

After a brief summary of the findings of the last four chapters, I will discuss the implications of those findings for the development of IR theory and Cold War historiography.

Summary

We began by establishing some kind of Stalinist baseline for how Soviet identity was understood after World War II. After an initial period of a year or so of hesitation and uncertainty, the discourse of danger became the official Soviet identity. It contained several very consequential elements. First, it understood the Soviet Union and the socialist project at home as vulnerable to bourgeois degeneration and even subversion. This fear was directly tied to the threat posed by the West, especially the United States. But the threat was not only, or even so much, a military threat, as it was a constitutive one. The Soviet project was threatened by the mere existence of an attractive capitalist alternative in the West. Recognizing this, the last years of Stalin's rule were marked by extraordinary efforts to quarantine the Soviet population from contacts with the West. The official discourse's concern about the effects of the West on its population was consistent with its infantilization of the Soviet people. They were understood as vulnerable children who were susceptible to the misleading attractions of the bourgeois West.

The societal discourses of Soviet identity repudiated these aspects of the official project. They, first and foremost, denied that the Soviet project was in much, if any danger. Victory in the war against Hitler's fascism had demonstrated the strength of socialism and the Soviet population's support for that system. Confidence in the fundamental security of socialism allowed the Soviet public to freely criticize the system's flaws and shortcomings, while the official discourse maintained its commitment to infallibility.

Societal discourses also had a broad and deep identification with the West, especially Europe, but including the United States, as well. And this identification was indeed threatening to the official discourse, which tolerated no deviation whatsoever from complete and total commitment to the idealized socialist project. Finally, these challenging discourses rejected characterizing the Soviet people as immature, necessitating the tutelage and discipline of the party and state. Societal discourses in general welcomed a bigger private sphere in which being oneself could be pursued without fear of official sanction for not being Soviet enough. And as far as being Soviet, societal understandings of what it meant fell along a broad continuum, rather than into a narrow dichotomy. This meant that much conduct officially repressed as anti-Soviet by the regime was understood by the population as perfectly consistent with being a good Soviet citizen.

There were also areas of agreement between the official and societal discourses under Stalin. The Soviet Union was a center of modernity atop a hierarchy of modern development. Russia was the center of the Soviet Union, as Moscow was the center of Russia. Cities were centers; rural areas were peripheries. Places like Central Asia and Siberia were underdeveloped, pre-modern peripheries that relied on their Russian/Muscovite vanguard to advance them into the twentieth century. The second shared understanding was the implicit acceptance of the Russian nation as the Soviet nation. While of course non-Russians did not accept this understanding of Soviet identity, the size of the Russian and Ukrainian and Belarussian populations, combined with Russified elites, made the implicit Russian nation a taken for granted feature of Soviet identity. Some Russians, moreover, went far beyond what the official discourse permitted, in their anti-Semitic attacks on Jews, for example.

These societal discourses had institutional homes that protected them from complete suppression. The Writers' Union, the editorial boards of numerous publications, university departments and research institutes all carved out some space within which alternative understandings of Soviet identity could persist. This helps to account for the substance of the new Soviet identity that appears in official circles after Stalin's death.

But before we talk about that, we need to see if the elements of Soviet identity enumerated above manifest themselves in the discussions of the Soviet foreign policy elite under Stalin. The first test of societal constructivism's hypotheses occurs in chapter 3. If we find that the elements of Soviet identity identified in the texts explored in chapter 2 figure in how the Soviet foreign policy elite understands other countries in the world, and its interests in them, then we can be confident that domestic discourses of national identity do in fact inform the foreign relations of states. The evidence strongly supports the main hypothesis. Elements of Soviet identity at home appear to inform many different Soviet relationships with other states, and very frequently.

It is revealing that during the period of more ambiguous Soviet identity in the months after the war, Soviet foreign policy in the period is also rather restrained and halting. The United States and West are not the totalized enemy they would shortly become in Soviet understanding. Only after the Soviet Union begins to fear for the security of socialism at home do the United States and the West become that most dangerous Other.

The effects of the discourse of danger are probably most clearly and comprehensively manifested in Soviet relations with eastern Europe. Two factors account for this. First, as socialist countries, they are some of the Soviet Union's very closest Others, in that deviations there are especially dangerous to Soviet self-understanding. And second, the discourse of danger permitted no deviation from the idealized socialist reality officially promulgated at home. Therefore, the domestic political and social orders in eastern Europe were increasingly becoming replicas of the Soviet model. This even concerned the timing and character of Eastern European political repression. For example, recall that official anti-Semitism in Eastern Europe was criticized by Soviet leaders, at least until they themselves had launched their "affair" against Soviet cosmopolitans. Moscow controlled the content of Eastern European show trials and affairs so that the "correct" enemies/Others would be identified as threats.

With the creation of the Cominform in September 1947, the Soviet Union created yet another institution designed to promote uniformity among its socialist allies. No more "national roads" to socialism would be permitted, let alone encouraged. Finally, the United States policy Soviets regarded as most dangerous, the Marshall Plan, speaks to how the discourse of danger implied Soviet interests, and threats to those interests. The lure of US capital and the corrosive effect of a Western presence on the ground in Eastern Europe frightened Soviet leaders, who themselves already feared the Western effects on returning POWs. That the Marshall Plan could result in the reversal of the socialist choices made in Eastern Europe was axiomatic to Soviet decisionmakers because the discourse of danger predicted precisely that outcome.

The excommunication of Tito's Yugoslavia from the ranks of socialist countries repeated the domestic pattern of exemplary punishment that the Soviet party and state repeatedly used against deviants at home. Choosing Yugoslavia as the deviant in the bloc sent shock waves through the socialist world because Tito's Yugoslavia had theretofore been hailed as the most advanced in the construction of socialism in Eastern Europe. It was like singling out Aleksandr Fadeev's *Young Guard* for condemnation, despite the novel already receiving a Stalin Prize and Fadeev being a famous Soviet writer in general. Other Eastern European leaders quickly searched through their own policy choices to make sure no "Yugoslavian deviations" lurked there. This was precisely how Moscow wished it to work.

There is a massively important non-event that the discourse of danger explains well: no Soviet interests in anti-colonial revolutions in the Third World.

Given that the Soviet Union was locked in a bipolar struggle with the United States for global influence, most scholars and policy-makers would expect Moscow to compete with the West in the decolonizing world. But this did not occur because the discourse of danger made potential Soviet allies—the bourgeois nationalist leaders of newly independent countries and national liberation movements—dangerous deviants from Soviet socialist ideals. From the Soviet point of view, these leaders were unreliable and unworthy of Soviet support. At best, they were neutral; at worst, they were imperialist hirelings.

In terms of relations with China, the period of domestic ambiguity in the Soviet Union accords with Moscow's hesitant approach to supporting Mao against the Kuomintang. But once the polarization of relations with the United States had occurred, Soviet support for the Chinese communists and the Red Army was very robust. Having established formal relations with the PRC, China came to be understood by Moscow according to the hierarchy of modernity that was shared by both official and societal discourses of Soviet identity. By subordinating China to developing status and consigning it the role of revolutionary exemplar only in underdeveloped parts of the world, Moscow was sowing the seeds of future discord after Stalin's death.

It would be a mistake to credit domestic discourses of Soviet identity with the responsibility for defining Soviet relations with the United States. Of course, the Soviet Union's most dangerous Other was the imperialist United States. But that identity relationship would have only the most indeterminate of implications. What appears to have governed the daily calculations of how to behave with regard to the West was the Soviet Union's great power identity, one that was absent in domestic discourse, but ubiquitous in foreign policy elite discussions of Soviet relations with the imperialist West, especially the United States. As will be taken up below, this production of state identity through interstate interaction is consistent with the expectations of systemic constructivists and highlights potential limits to the universal applicability of societal constructivism.

Stalin's death provides an opportunity to assess whether elements of the repressed societal discourses of identity end up in the official discourse thereafter. They do, to a significant degree. Elements of societal discourse made themselves felt immediately after Stalin's death. That discourse's understanding of the Soviet Union and its socialist project as fundamentally secure at home and from imperialism was adopted as part of the official discourse, allowing for a much broader definition of socialism. What was previously considered dangerous deviance, such as writings, speeches, or conversations that criticized mistakes by the state and party, were now officially treated as evidence of Soviet strength, not as evidence of socialism under threat.

From the theoretical point of view it is important that Beria became the earliest and most enthusiastic proponent of the discourse of difference. He clearly was not some closet liberal waiting for Stalin's death. His assumption of the role as the party elite's greatest liberal, however, demonstrates the power of societal discourse. Why else adopt the discourse, if it did not have some political advantages, or resonate among the public? And Beria's colleagues on the Politburo thought precisely this way about it, fearing Beria's policy positions were designed to garner public support for himself in the ongoing and ensuing leadership struggle. He was arrested and shot. But, demonstrating the structural aspects of societal constructivism, the discourse of difference did not die with Beria. It was adopted, first by Malenkov, and finally by Khrushchev and the ruling elite in general. Societal discourses have power of their own, even if their translation into official policy requires political elites to adopt them, believe them, be socialized into them, or simply manipulate them for political purposes.

One area of continued agreement between Soviet elites and society was the placement of the Soviet Union atop a hierarchy of modernity. This hierarchical arrangement of Moscow helped reinforce the centrality of Russia, and the Russian nation, to a large part of the Soviet population. Official discourse remained supranational, but the daily practices of the Soviet state and party continued to favor the Russian nation and the Russian Orthodox Church, at the expense of non-Russians, and non-Orthodox.

Societal discourse, despite its many gains within the official view of Soviet identity, still continued to struggle to expand the boundaries of permissible difference, of what counted as socialism and being Soviet. One area of constant friction was not just the continued, but the deepening, societal identification with the West and the United States. While violently and brutally suppressed under Stalin, appreciating the West was hardly encouraged by Soviet leaders after his death, either.

The Twentieth Party Congress was the apogee of the Thaw, or the toleration of difference. There was some backsliding after the Hungarian revolution, but never a return to the discourse of danger. The removal of Molotov, Kaganovich, and Voroshilov from the Soviet leadership in June 1957 was a high-level official repudiation of the discourse of danger, and any return to Stalinism.

The death of Stalin was marked by the partial replacement of the discourse of danger with the discourse of difference. The effects on Soviet foreign relations from this newly empowered discourse were no less revolutionary than on Soviet domestic life. The two core elements of this new understanding of what it meant to be the Soviet Union were toleration of deviation from the previously proclaimed Soviet ideal and increased recognition that the Soviet Union and socialism in the Soviet Union were far more secure than the discourse of danger allowed.

The consequences were most dramatic in Eastern Europe. Since all these allies, as we saw in chapter 3, competed to be more Stalinist than Stalin, the creeping repudiation of Stalinism in Moscow left many Eastern European communists politically vulnerable. As we have seen, figures like Gomulka and Nagy and Kadar made comebacks from prison and even likely execution. Once more moderate approaches to socialism were tolerated, it became thinkable to permit national roads to socialism, or at least roads to socialism whose details are determined by local context, not Moscow's model. Such expectations were still more aroused by the rapprochement between Moscow and Belgrade. Tito and Titoism become the new alternative socialist model in Eastern Europe, to Moscow's chagrin.

The permissible boundary of the "new course" in Eastern Europe was established in Hungary in November 1956 with the Soviet decision to use military force to suppress Hungary's revolution. But even in this instance, the Soviet leadership chose to bring Kadar to power, rather than restore the Stalinist Rakosi and his colleagues. Only Molotov and his few fellow defenders of the discourse of danger preferred Rakosi. Molotov also opposed the rapprochement with Yugoslavia, arguing, accurately in the case of Hungary and Poland, it turned out, that recognizing Titoism as socialism would only inspire other Eastern Europeans to re-imagine socialism in ways incompatible with Soviet interests.

The discourse of difference initially resulted in improved relations between the Soviet Union and China because Moscow admitted its previous errors under Stalin and tried to address Chinese resentment at being subordinated in the Soviet hierarchy of modernity and socialism. But toleration of difference only worked so long as China was not committed to the discourse of danger that the Soviet Union was rejecting. But ultimately the Thaw ran into the Great Leap Forward, and the Sino-Soviet split began. Soviet and Chinese identities were heading in two different directions, especially after Khrushchev's secret speech at the Twentieth Party Congress denouncing Stalin. Meanwhile, Mao was turning toward the Stalinist model for China. The contradiction soon became too acute for the relationship to bear since both understood themselves to be models of socialist development. But both could not be.

While the discourse of difference ended up losing the Soviet Union its most important strategic ally of the Cold War, China, it also provided Moscow with dozens of new potential allies in the decolonizing world. By abandoning the discourse of danger's axiom—who is not with us is against us—and replacing it with another—who is not against us might be with us—the discourse of difference made dozens of bourgeois nationalist leaders in the decolonizing world suddenly available as Soviet allies and created interests all around the world for the Soviet Union that did not exist under Stalin. By abandoning another dichotomy—either capitalist or socialist—and replacing it with the "noncapitalist path of development," Soviets could understand countries like India, Egypt, and Afghanistan in ways precluded by the previous discourse of danger.

Those countries were now on their way to becoming socialist—eventually. Moreover, Moscow could look to its own Soviet experience for appropriate analogies. Central Asia had been what the Third World was now: an undeveloped rural periphery, beset with religious traditions and feudal social relations. But the Soviet Union had made these areas socialist by providing the proletarian vanguard these areas lacked. So too could Moscow perform this role for the decolonizing world.

The discourse of difference did not turn the United States from a foe into a friend of the Soviet Union. But Soviet understanding of itself as fundamentally more secure did allow for a change in Soviet policy toward the United States and the West. It was characterized by more moderation and unilateral efforts to wind down the arms race to some degree. Instead of situating itself within capitalist encirclement, as in the days of Stalin, the Soviet Union espoused the idea of a "zone of peace" around its borders, which of course would be impossible if Moscow were to continue to treat Turkey, Iran, and Afghanistan, for example, as imperialists or imperialist lackeys. The United States was clearly the Soviet Union's most significant Other in world politics. Through interacting with the United States, the Soviet Union's great power identity was reproduced and reinforced on a daily basis. This meant a necessarily competitive, if not hostile, relationship with Washington. But it also meant that the Soviet Union was locked into a continual comparison with the United States on every dimension—political, military, and economic, the last of which would become the most vulnerable part of Soviet identity in years to come.

Theoretical Implications

To the extent that bringing society back into social constructivism has produced convincing explanations for many Soviet relationships from 1945 to 1958, it points to the need for IR theorists to pay more attention to how societies construe themselves. There has been no lack of attention by IR scholars to the domestic level of analysis. Liberals, whether as neoliberal institutionalists studying political economy, or as democratic peace researchers sketching out the presumed special relationships among democratic regimes, privilege the domestic level of analysis in their work. But societal constructivism suggests a different, structural and discursive, approach to operationalizing the idea of the domestic. We should be paying attention to discourses of national identity, and their institutional sites of creation, production, and reproduction, if we wish to understand the identity relations among states. Moreover, if we want to speculate about what a change in regime would mean in a particular state, we would benefit by knowing what alternative discourses of national identity are available for the new leadership. For example, had US and Western intelligence paid more attention to the widespread dissemination of cassette recordings of Ayatollah Khomeini's thoughts in Iranian society, perhaps the kind of regime that replaced the Shah would not have been so surprising. On a more contemporaneous note, expectations about future Chinese-US relations could be grounded in an investigation of the various societal discourses of Chinese national identity that are now competing in Chinese society.

Of course a systemic theory cannot be built out of domestic discourses of national identity. But a mid-range theory of a state's relationships with many states, groups and categories of states, and social movements in the world may be theorized productively by adding domestically generated identities to the analysis. So, here, for example, it was possible to explain broad swaths of Soviet relationships with the outside world, in particular with Eastern Europe and the decolonizing world. So long as other states are categorized or typed in general ways, an identity relationship is formed that may include the entire decolonized world or European socialist allies, as demonstrated in the Soviet case. Narrower relationships, like dyads between two countries, may also be explained by identity relations. Such was the case with the Soviet Union and China, for example.

Societal constructivism, while less general than systemic theories, is far more general than theories that rely upon individual leaders or elites. In this sense it sits between these two extremes. And for good reason, as the case of the post-Stalinist Soviet leadership shows, the discourse of difference was picked up by, or reflected in, no less a Stalinist sociopath as Beria at one point, and then a majority of the Soviet leadership shortly thereafter. Societal discourses of national identity have proved to be the appropriate unit of analysis for generating broad, mid-range, medium-term statements about a state's foreign relations. Societal discourses of identity have legs that allow their generalizability to transcend any particular regime or leader in power, and affect succeeding decision makers.

I might add that the Soviet case is not an easy one for societal constructivism, or for any approach that claims society has a role in determining foreign policy outcomes. There is not much evidence, during the Thaw, still less so under postwar Stalinism, of a free press or representative institutions that could transmit societal preferences to the Soviet leadership. But that is not the model of politics entertained by societal constructivism in the first place. Instead, it privileges intersubjective structures of identity, or discourses, that infuse what members of society and the political elite think about themselves, their country, its meaning in the world. This is not necessarily done consciously and certainly need not be an object of political interest. Instead, it provides the taken-for-granted content of a state's and society's self-understandings.

The analysis here has also shown the benefits for constructivists in including institutions in their analyses of how identities get carried across time, even in the face of official opposition and repression. It is important to see how discursive elements find a home in social collectivities which are sometimes even protected by the state. Perhaps the most striking examples are the state committees on Religious Cults and the Russian Orthodox Church. In an avowedly atheist state and in the face of daily attacks by committed party activists, these two institutions continued to do their officially authorized work: protect the formal rights of believers. This institutional support, albeit limited, helps explain the durability of religious beliefs and communities in the Soviet Union, such that they are a continuous part of societal discourses of national identity.

The evidence in this book has established the empirical link between societal discourses of identity and the predominant official discourse, in that the post-1953 elite discourse was suffused with elements of societal discourse previously repressed. But a second crucial link has also been established: the one between the official discourse and foreign relations with other states. In fact, identities do imply interests in other states, as constructivists have hypothesized for 20 years. There was vindication for this proposition under Stalin, in that the discourse of danger definitely was reflected in relations with Eastern Europe and the West, and in Soviet reaction to presumably the most innocuous of US Cold War programs, the Marshall Plan. But the most convincing evidence for the connection came after Stalin's death, for we had the opportunity to trace elements of societal discourse in their appearance in the new post-Stalinist discourse of difference propagated by the state and party elite. And these new elements helped account for titanic changes in Soviet foreign relations: with Eastern European allies, with Yugoslavia, with China, and with the decolonizing world.

Notice that I omit here relations with the United States. This is because that relationship was governed far more fundamentally by the great power identity generated in Soviet interactions with the United States than by the identities generated in Soviet society. This is a very important confirmation of one of the central hypotheses of systemic constructivism, viz., that identities are constructed in interstate interaction, not at home. Of course, the true answer, as this book shows, is that a state's identity is constructed both at home and abroad, not in one site or the other.

We might speculate about what this anomaly means for societal constructivism as a theory of relations among states. First, to its credit, it still helps us understand relations between the United States and the Soviet Union, although not its fundamental character. But I would suggest that being able to explain why the decolonizing world became an arena of bloody competition between the two countries after Stalin, but not before, is no small contribution to our understanding of great power relations. That said, it is worth suggesting some limits, or boundary conditions, for societal constructivism.

First, we might infer from the US-Soviet case here that relations among great powers are always going to be significantly defined by the fact that they interact on a daily basis on matters that concern the balance of power between them in the world. Moreover, these interactions are likely to be deeply institutionalized in foreign and defense ministries, whose discourse will then significantly inform whatever deliberations occur on these great power relations among political elites.

Second, it could also be the case that societal constructivism is historically bounded. It is probably a post eighteenth century phenomenon. Prior to the American and French revolutions, political elites were as likely to be transnational dynastic elites as "national" ones. Their discourses of identity were as likely to be about the identities they shared with other dynastic elites as they were about the identities they shared with their own peoples. If this is the case, then we should not expect societal constructivism to have much to say about interstate relations so characterized.[1]

On the other hand, it could be that the US-Soviet relationship is itself an artifact of the postwar discourse of decolonization. While prior to World War II, it was not uncommon for domestic publics to relish their state's imperial identity, sing drinking songs about it, consume it in textbooks, and devour novels glorifying it, after World War II, neither Soviet nor US publics consumed imperialist or colonialist identities for their countries. Far from it. This could help account for why a Soviet great power identity is absent from mass public texts after the war, and perhaps makes systemic constructivism's boundary conditions more constraining than we might expect. If mass publics valorized colonialism and imperialism for much of the nineteenth and twentieth centuries, then societal constructivism could well explain great power relations quite adequately.

The findings of this book also shed light on the relationship between power, security, and foreign policy. One might think, as realists do, that a more powerful and secure Soviet Union would imply a more aggressive foreign policy, or at least one that challenged the status quo more vigorously than before. But the evidence here is ambiguous. Soviet understandings of the Soviet Union as more secure, both at home and in the world, meant a repudiation of the kinds of practices that had earlier been associated with weakness and vulnerability, to wit, coercion, repression, and ultimata. This was especially true vis-à-vis its socialist allies in Eastern Europe, but also the "capitalist" countries on its borders—Iran and Turkey. The one area in which greater Soviet security resulted in a more vigorous foreign policy was in the decolonizing world. Meanwhile, Soviet insecurity and sense of vulnerability resulted in an extremely brutal foreign policy in Eastern Europe: the forced Stalinization of the bloc. On the other hand, as

---

[1] I thank Jennifer Mitzen for raising this possibility.

noted, it prevented Moscow from having much interest in the decolonizing world.

As Mastny puts it, "not only an aggressive but also an accommodating foreign posture can be a product of internal insecurity."[2] What appears to figure into whether insecurity and vulnerability, or security and strength, result in a more aggressive foreign policy is how these factors interact with the predominant discourse of identity in the state.

There has also been a literature that associates domestic liberalization with foreign policy moderation. In the Soviet case, it was argued that liberalization at home, understood as less repression and more consumer goods, implied a Soviet need for a quiet international environment so the people could benefit from trade and investment, and spend less on the military industrial complex.[3] Another group of scholars, like Etel Solingen, argue that liberalization creates domestic interest groups in favor of cooperation with the external world, and so a more moderate foreign policy follows.[4] On the other hand, other scholars have pointed out that liberalization, from an authoritarian to a democratic direction, increases the probability that that state will be involved in a war.[5]

The evidence here shows the effects of liberalization are indeterminate, because they depend on the identity relations of the state with others in the international system. For example, the discourse of difference moderated Soviet foreign policy toward Eastern Europe and the West, but resulted in a much more active foreign policy in the decolonizing world.

Cold War Historiography

As I promised in the introduction, this is not a book aimed at challenging other scholars' interpretations of the Cold War or particular events, but rather an effort to show how societal constructivism can offer a compelling account of many of those events and Soviet relations with the world in general. That said, the findings here do speak to some of the eternal questions about the Cold War. Who started it? Was it inevitable?[6]

As we know there are traditionalists, revisionists, and post-revisionists in the world of Cold War scholarship. In short, traditionalists blame the Soviet Union or Stalin; the revisionists blame the United States or capitalism; and the last blame

---

[2] Mastny, *The Cold War*, 6.
[3] Melvyn P. Leffler, *For the Soul of Mankind* (New York: Hill and Wang, 2007), 147.
[4] Etel Solingen, *Regional Orders at Century's Dawn* (Princeton: Princeton University Press, 1998).
[5] Edward D. Mansfield and Jack L. Snyder, *Electing to Fight* (Cambridge: MIT Press, 2005).
[6] The other eternal question, "How did it end?" will be answered in a subsequent volume.

both sides more or less equally. I think the evidence presented here supports the post-revisionist view more strongly than the rest. The Cold War gets off the ground in 1947 because of a discourse of danger taking hold in Moscow. While it was primarily a product of domestic fears, some of those fears, such as nationalist separatism in the Western reaches of the Soviet Union and expressed preferences for capitalism among the masses and party elites, were not dampened by the United States and Britain supplying weapons and materiel to resistance fighters in the Soviet Union, especially the Baltic republics and western Ukraine.

It is hard to exaggerate the level of Soviet insecurity. The fact that the most benign of US Cold War policies, the Marshall Plan, was the Western action that set off the Stalinization of Eastern Europe demonstrates the intense fear Moscow had of US economic power and political attractiveness. In this sense, the United States and the West's mere existence was a threat to the Soviet Union, because it always represented an alternative to the Soviet system.[7] The question of responsibility for the Cold War, then, rests on one's judgment about the manipulability of insecurity in the Soviet Union after the war. Historians have mixed views on whether Stalin deliberately exaggerated Soviet insecurity so as to impose repressive measures at home, or whether the Soviet ruling elite genuinely feared for the stability of socialism in the Soviet Union, and hence engaged in repression. The argument in this book generally favors the latter interpretation because the discourse of danger appears to be partly animated by the real dangers at home faced by the Soviet regime. Of course, Stalin goes on to play the insecurity card for years thereafter.

It should be said that most historians stress Stalin's sense of personal insecurity, rather than Soviet insecurity more generally.[8] My theoretical approach, on the other hand, stresses the structural quality of Soviet insecurity at home, that is, the shared sense of insecurity by the elite in general. If so, Stalin might have been sufficient, but not necessary, for the level of insecurity experienced by the Soviet Union after the war. The discourse of danger, rather than Stalin himself, helps explain the timing of the onset of the Cold War. Given the discourse's fear of any deviation from the Soviet model of socialism, Eastern European eagerness to sign on to the Marshall Plan was understood as especially threatening to

---

[7] It should be added that US identity was constituted by the Soviet Union, as well. Civil rights, progressive taxation, rights to unionize, and other more liberal social and economic policies can be usefully understood as being partial products of the competition with the socialist aspirations represented by the Soviet Union. It is worth pondering the consequences of the Soviet Union's demise in 1991 on US identity, in particular, on its accelerating inequalities in income distribution, continuing de-unionization of the work force, and the revival of the gilded age of Wild West capitalism, in general. I thank Matthew Evangelista for asking me to consider these issues.

[8] For example, Mastny, *The Cold War*.

the Soviet Union. It demonstrated that the level of Sovietization imposed on these countries up until then was insufficient to ensure their reliability as Soviet satellites.

The Cold War was not inevitable only insofar as no event involving human agency is inevitable. But the often deadly and dangerous conflict between the United States and the Soviet Union was certainly overdetermined, in the sense that many variables pointed toward the outcome. The combination of the Stalinization of Eastern Europe and the Western commitment to democratic capitalism in those countries made the Cold War highly probable. In fact, the oxymoronic deal made by Stalin and Roosevelt at Yalta that Eastern European states would be "free and friendly to the Soviet Union" sowed the seeds of the Cold War. But the Cold War was not inevitable, even if it was extraordinarily hard to avert. Had the discourse of difference won out in Moscow, Stalinization of Eastern European regimes would have been avoided. On the US side, had US politicians explained to the American people during and after World War II that the Soviet Union had won the war in the East, and so was entitled to a certain level of control over its western frontier, mass popular hostility toward the Soviet Union in the United States might have been averted. Maybe.

On the other hand, many factors pointed to a Cold War. The first was the strategic vacuum in the center of Europe. With Germany crushed, and the French and British economies on the ropes, the United States and Soviet Union sat astride the center of Europe. From a realist point of view, neither could let the other fill that void. So, they both did, and hence the conflict was almost a geopolitical certainty. Moreover, the security dilemma between the two powers was also geographically reinforced. Had the United States been a European power, the security dilemma would have been acute enough, in that neither side could be sure of the pacific intentions of the other. But one geostrategic feature made the security dilemma still more acute was that the United States was situated in North America, an ocean away from the main strategic prize.

This meant that the United States deployed long-range bombers, maintained and expanded a blue-water navy, and stationed troops and aircraft, nuclear-capable aircraft at that, at dozens, if not hundreds, of foreign military bases circling the Soviet Union. All this was plausibly necessary to deter and fight a war against the Soviet Union. But it simultaneously signaled to the Soviet Union the United States' aggressive intentions, as many of these weapons systems could be easily used offensively, as well as defensively.

The Cold War was also made nearly inevitable by the fact that both the United States and the Soviet Union were possessed with universalist ideologies: liberalism and communism, respectively. American elites were not just convinced, but took it as natural that the entire globe would become like the United States. Any deviations from capitalism or liberalism were understood as the products of communist interference or of lower levels of economic and political development.[9] On the Soviet side, as we have seen, especially after the death of Stalin, the Soviet foreign policy elite saw it as scientifically and objectively the case that all peoples aspired to become socialist. Any deviations were understood as the machinations of imperialists or colonialists or their lackeys and as evidence of a lower level of economic and political development. What is more, the "non-capitalist path of development" for most of the world had already showed its merit in Soviet Central Asia, and so it was obvious that any "backward" people could become the Soviet Union. When two universalist ideologies meet, conflict is hard to avoid.

If I may foreshadow the end of the Cold War, what caused it to end? The evidence here offers a preliminary and simple answer: the mere existence of the United States and the West. The fear Soviets had of exposure to the West—its mass culture, quality of daily life, economic achievements, and political freedoms—was well-founded. Throughout the dozen years of this study, the attraction of the West manifested itself at all levels of Soviet society, from state farm peasants to party elites in Moscow. The critical point here is that all the West had to do was be the West—that is, carry on in its normal way, economically, politically, and culturally. The West's greatest power in the Cold War was itself, not its weaponry. While military capabilities might have been necessary to deter Soviet military adventures, although none were given serious consideration by Soviet elites in this period at least, an attractive alternative to the Soviet model was also necessary. And the West provided it. One of George Kennan's least noted sections in his "long telegram" of 1946 was his warning that the United States, in confronting the Soviet Union, not become like it. This was good advice against becoming a garrison state, but also in arming the United States with the kind of power that would win the Cold War, too.

---

[9] On the American propensity to project its own idealized model onto the rest of the world, see Louis Hartz, *The Liberal Tradition in America* (New York: Harcourt, Brace, and World, 1955); Robert A. Packenham, *Liberal America and the Third World* (Princeton: Princeton University Press, 1973); and D. Michael Shafer, *Deadly Paradigms* (Princeton: Princeton University Press, 1988).

REFERENCES

Abebe, Ermias. "The Horn, the Cold War, and Documents from the Former East-Bloc: An Ethiopian View," *Cold War International History Project Bulletin* 8–9 (1996/1997): 40–45.

Acharya, Amitav. "How Ideas Spread: Whose Norms Matter?" *International Organization* 58 (2004): 239–75.

Adams, Jan S. "Russia's Gas Diplomacy," *Problems of Post-Communism* 49, no. 3 (May/June 2002): 14–22.

Adibekov, Grant M. *Kominform i Poslevoennaia Evropa, 1947–1956* (Moscow: Rossiia Molodaia, 1994).

Adler, Emmanuel, and Michael Barnett. "Security Communities in Theoretical Perspective." In *Security Communities*, ed. Emanuel Adler and Michael Barnett (Cambridge: Cambridge University Press, 1998), 3–28.

Afiani, V. U. "Ideologicheskie Komissii TsK KPSS (1958–1964) v Mekhanizme Upravleniia Kulturoi." In *Ideologicheskie Kommissii TsK KPSS, 1958–1964 gg, Dokumenty* (Moscow: ROSSPEN, 2000), 23–29.

Aksenov, Iurii S. "Poslevoennyi Stalinizm: Udar po Intelligentsii," *Kentavr* (October-December 1991): 80–99.

Aksiutin, Iurii V. "Pochemu Stalin Dalneishemu Sotrudnichsestvu s Soiuznikami Posle Pobedy Prepochel Konfrontatsiiu s Nimi?" In *Kholodnaia Voina: Novye Podkhody, Novye Dokumenty,* ed. M. M. Narinskii (Moscow: Institute of General History, 1995), 48–63.

———. "Novoe o XX Sezde KPSS," *Otechestvennaia Istoriia* 2 (1998): 108–23.

———. "Popular Responses to Khrushchev." In *Nikita Khrushchev*, ed. William Taubman, Sergei Khrushchev, and Abbott Gleason (New Haven: Yale University Press, 2000), 177–208.

———. "Khrushchevskaia "Ottepel" i Obshchestvennye Nastroeniia." In *SSSR v 1953–1964* (Moscow: ROSSPEN, 2004).

Aksiutin, Iurii V., and Aleksandr V. Pyzhikov. "O Podgotovke Zakrytogo Doklada N. S. Khrushcheva XX Sezdu KPSS v Svete Novykh Dokumentov," *Novaia i Noveisshaia Istoriia* 2 (2002): 107–17.

Alekseeva, Liudmila M. *Istoriia Inakomysliia v SSSR* (Vilnius: Vest, 1992).

Alexeyeva, Ludmilla, and Paul Goldberg. *The Thaw Generation: Coming of Age in the Post-Stalin Era* (Boston: Little, Brown and Company, 1990).

Allilueva, Svetlana. *Twenty Letters to a Friend* (New York: Harper & Row, 1967).

Allison, Roy. "Subregional Cooperation and Security in the CIS." In *Building Security in the New States of Eurasia: Subregional Cooperation in the Former Soviet Space*, ed. Renata Dwan and Oleksandr Pavliuk (Armonk: M.E. Sharpe, 2000), 149–76.

Althusser, Louis. *For Marx* (New York: Pantheon, 1969).

References

Anderson, Kirill M, ed. *Kremlevskii Kinoteatr, 1928–1953: Dokumenty* (Moscow: ROSSPEN, 2005).

Anderson, Richard D. Jr. *Public Politics in an Authoritarian State: Making Foreign Policy During the Brezhnev Years* (Ithaca: Cornell University Press, 1993).

Andrew, Christopher, and Vasili Mitrokhin. *The Sword and the Shield: The Mitrokhin Archive and the Secret History of the KGB* (New York: Basic Books, 1999).

Anno, Tadashi. "Nihonjinron and Russkaia Ideia: Transformation of Japanese and Russian Nationalism in the Postwar Era and Beyond." In *Japan and Russia: The Tortuous Path to Normalization, 1949–1999*, ed. Gilbert Rozman (New York: St. Martin's Press, 2000), 329–56.

Arbatov, Georgi. *The System: An Insider's Life in Soviet Politics* (New York: Times Books, 1992).

Artizov, Andrei, and Oleg Naumov, eds. *Vlast i Khudozhestvennaia Intelligentsiia: Dokumenty TsK RKP(b)-VKP(b), VChK-OGPU-NKVD, o Kulturnoi Politike, 1917–1953 gg.* (Moscow: Demokratiia, 1999).

Babichenko, Denis L. *Pisateli I Tsenzory: Sovetskaia Literatura 1940-x Godov pod Politicheskim Kontrolem TsK* (Moscow: Rossiia Molodaia, 1994).

Babichenko, Denis L., ed. *Literaturnyi Front: Istoriia Politicheskoi Tsenzury, 1932–1946 gg. Sbornik Dokumentov* (Moscow: Entsiklopediia Rossiiskikh Dereven, 1994).

Baev, Pavel. "Russian Policies and Non-Policies Toward Subregional Projects Around its Borders." In *Building Security in the New States of Eurasia: Subregional Cooperation in the Former Soviet Space*, ed. Renata Dwan and Oleksandr Pavliuk (Armonk: M. E. Sharpe, 2000), 119–47.

Bajanov, Evgueni. "Assessing the Politics of the Korean War, 1949–1951," *Cold War International History Project Bulletin* 6–7 (Winter 1995/1996): 54–91.

Barker, Adele Marie. "The Culture Factory: Theorizing the Popular in the Old and New Russia." In *Consuming Russia: Popular Culture, Sex, and Society Since Gorbachev*, ed. Adele Marie Barker (Durham: Duke University Press, 1999), 12–45.

Barnett, Michael. "The Israeli Identity and the Peace Process: Re/creating the Un/thinkable." In *Identity and Foreign Policy in the Middle East*, ed. Shibley Telhami and Michael Barnett (Ithaca: Cornell University Press, 2002), 58–87.

Baron, Samuel H. *Bloody Saturday in the Soviet Union: Novocherkassk, 1962* (Stanford: Stanford University Press, 2001).

Barsukov, Nikolai A. "XX Sezd v Retrospektive Khrushcheva," *Otechestvennaia Istoriia* 6 (1996): 169–77.

Baskakov, Vladimir. "'Serebrianyi Vek' Sovetskogo Kino." In *Kinematograf Ottepeli: Dokumenty i Svidetelstva* (Moscow: Materik, 1998), 178–87.

Baudin, Antoine. "'Why is Soviet Painting Hidden from Us?' Zhdanov Art and its International Relations and Fallout, 1947–53." In *Socialist Realism Without Shores*, ed. Thomas Lahusen and Evgeny Dobrenko (Durham: Duke University Press, 1997), 227–56.

Beda, Anatolii M. *Sovetskaia Politicheskaia Kultura Cherez Prismu MVD: Ot "Moskovskogo Patriotizma" k Idee "Bolshogo Otechestva," 1946–1958* (Moscow: Mosgorarkhiv, 2002).

Bell, Bowyer. "Assassination in International Politics," *International Studies Quarterly* 16, no. 1 (March 1972): 59–82.

Bennett, Andrew. *Condemned to Repetition? The Rise, Fall, and Reprise of Soviet-Russian Military Interventionism, 1973–1996* (Cambridge: MIT Press, 1999).

Berger, Peter L., and Thomas Luckmann. *The Social Construction of Reality* (New York: Anchor, 1966).

Berger, Thomas U. *Cultures of Antimilitarism: National Security in Germany and Japan* (Baltimore: Johns Hopkins University Press, 1998).

Besedy, G. K., and I. D. Zhukova. "Eizenkhauera na Zhenevskom Soveshchanii 1955 g.," *Novaia i Noveishaia Istoriia* (May 1999): 98–114.

Blitstein, Peter A. "Nation-Building or Russification? Obligatory Russian Instruction in the Soviet Non-Russian School, 1938–1953." In *A State of Nations: Empire and Nation-Making in the Age of Lenin and Stalin*, ed. Ronald Grigor Suny and Terry Martin (Oxford: Oxford University Press, 2001), 253–74.

Blium, A. V., ed. *Tsenzura v Sovetskom Soiuze: 1917–1991* (Moscow: ROSSPEN, 2004).
Block, Fred L. *The Origins of International Economic Disorder* (Berkeley: University of California Press, 1977).
Bloom, William. *Personal Identity, National Identity and International Relations* (Cambridge: Cambridge University Press, 1990).
Blum, Douglas W. "The Soviet Foreign Policy Belief System: Beliefs, Politics, and Foreign Policy Outcomes," *International Studies Quarterly* 37, no. 3 (1993): 373–94.
———. "Domestic Politics and Russia's Caspian Policy," *Post-Soviet Affairs* 14, no. 2 (1998): 137–64.
Bokarev, Iurii P. "Eshche Raz ob Otnoshenii SSSR k Planu Marshalla," *Otechestvennaia Istoriia* 1 (2005): 86–97.
Boobbyer, Philip. *Conscience, Dissent and Reform in Soviet Russia* (London: Routledge 2005).
Bordiugov, Gennadii, and Gennadi Matveev, eds. *SSSR-Polsha: Mekhanizmy Podchinennia, 1944–1949 gg.* (Moscow: AIRO-XX, 1995).
Borev, Iurii. *Istoriia Gosudarstva Sovetskogo v Predaniiakh I Anekdotakh* (Moscow: RIPOL, 1995).
Boterbloem, Kees. *The Life and Times of Andrei Zhdanov, 1896–1948* (Montreal: McGill-Queen's University Press, 2004).
Brandenberger, David. *National Bolshevism: Stalinist Mass Culture and the Formation of Modern Russian National Identity* (Cambridge: Harvard University Press, 2002).
———. "Stalin's Last Crime? Recent Scholarship on Postwar Soviet Antisemitism And the Doctor's Plot," *Kritika: Explorations in Russian and Eurasian History* 6, no. 1 (Winter 2005): 187–204.
Breslauer, George W. *Khrushchev and Brezhnev as Leaders* (London: Allen and Unwin, 1982).
Brooks, Jeffrey. *Thank You, Comrade Stalin! Soviet Public Culture from Revolution to Cold War* (Princeton: Princeton University Press, 2000).
Brutents, Karen. *Tridtsat Let na Staroi Ploshchadi* (Moscow: Mezhdunarodnye Otnosheniia, 1998).
Brysk, Alison, Craig Parsons, and Wayne Sandholtz. "After Empire: National Identity and Post Colonial Families of Nations," *European Journal of International Relations* 8, no. 2 (2002): 267–305.
Bukharin, Nikolai. "Otnosheniia mezhdu Sovetskim Soiuzom I Polskoi Narodnoi Respublikoi (1944–1989 gg.)," *Voprosy Istorii* (October 2007): 100–10.
Bukkvoll, Tor. "Arming the Ayatollahs: Economic Lobbies in Russia's Iran Policy," *Problems of Post-Communism* 49, no. 6 (November/December 2002): 29–41.
Bukovansky, Mlada. "The Altered State and the State of Nature: The French Revolution and International Politics," *Review of International Studies* 25, no. 2 (1999): 197–216.
Bystrova, Nina E. "Obrazovanie Vostochnogo Bloka," *Otechestvennaia Istoriia* (June 2005): 38–55.
Castillo, Greg,."Peoples at an Exhibition: Soviet Architecture and the National Question." In *Socialist Realism Without Shores*, ed. Thomas Lahusen and Evgeny Dobrenko (Durham: Duke University Press, 1997), 91–119.
Cederman, Lars-Erik, and Christopher Daase. "Endogenizing Corporate Identities: The Next Step in Constructivist IR Theory," *European Journal of International Relations* 9, no. 1 (2003): 5–35.
Chafetz, Glenn. "The Struggle for a National Identity in Post-Soviet Russia," *Political Science Quarterly* 111, no. 4 (1996–97): 661–88.
Chavez, Leo. *Covering Immigration* (Los Angeles: University of California Press, 2001).
Checkel, Jeffrey T. *Ideas and International Political Change: Soviet/Russian Behavior and the End of the Cold War* (New Haven: Yale University Press, 1997).
———. "Norms, Institutions, and National Identity in Contemporary Europe," *International Studies Quarterly* 43, no. 1 (1999): 83–114.
———. "Why Comply? Social Learning and European Identity Change," *International Organization* 55, no. 3 (2001): 553–88.
Cherniaev, Anatolii S. *Moia Zhizn i Moe Vremia* (Moscow: Mezhdunarodnye Otnosheniia, 1995).

Chernyaev, Anatoly S. *My Six Years with Gorbachev* (University Park: Pennsylvania State University, 2000).

Chesnova, L. V. "Iu. I. Polianksii I Biologiia v Leningradskom Universitete (20-60-e Gody)." In *Repressirovannaia Nauka*, vol. 1, ed. M.G. Iaroshevskii (Leningrad: Nauka, 1991), 212–22.

Christie, Ian. "Canons and Careers: The Director in Soviet Cinema." In *Stalinism and Soviet Cinema*, ed. Richard Taylor and Derek Spring (London: Routledge, 1993), 142–70.

Chuev, Felix. *Molotov Remembers: Inside Kremlin Politics* (Chicago: I. R. Dee, 1993).

Chukovsky, Kornei. *Diary, 1901–1969* (New Haven: Yale University Press, 2005).

Chumachenko, Tatiana A. *Church and State in Soviet Russia: Russian Orthodoxy from World War II to the Khrushchev Years* (Armonk, New York: M. E. Sharpe, 2002).

Clark, Katerina. *The Soviet Novel: History as Ritual*, 3rd ed. (Bloomington: Indiana University Press, 2000).

Condee, Nancy. "Cultural Codes of the Thaw." In *Nikita Khrushchev*, ed. William Taubman, Sergei Khruschev, and Abbott Gleason (New Haven: Yale University Press, 2000), 160–76.

Cortell, Andrew P., and James W. Davis Jr. "Understanding the Domestic Impact of International Norms: A Research Agenda," *International Studies Review* 2, no. 1 (2000): 65–87.

Craig, Campbell, and Sergey Radchenko. *The Atomic Bomb and the Origins of the Cold War* (New Haven: Yale University Press, 2008).

Crankshaw, Edward. *Russia without Stalin* (New York: Viking Press, 1956).

Danilov, Aleksandr A., and Aleksandr V. Pyzhikov. *Rozhdenie Sverkhderzhavy: SSSR v Pervye Poslevoennye Gody* (Moscow: ROSSPEN, 2001).

Davidson, Apolon, Sergei Mazov, and Georgii Tsypkin. *SSSR I Afrika* (Moscow: Institute of World History, 2002).

Deutsch, Karl. *Political Community and the North Atlantic Area* (Princeton: Princeton University Press, 1957).

Dimitrov, Georgi. *The Diary of Georgi Dimitrov, 1933–1949* (New Haven: Yale University Press, 2003).

Djilas, Milovan. *Conversations with Stalin* (New York: Harcourt, Brace & World, 1962).

Dobrenko, Evgenii. *Metafora Vlasti: Literatura Stalinskoi Epokhi v Istoricheskom Osvshchenii* (Munich: Verlag Otto Sagner, 1993).

Dobson, Miriam. "POWs and Purge Victims," *The Slavonic and East European Review* 86, no. 2 (April 2008): 328–45.

"Dokumenty Tsentralnogo Arkhiva FSB Rossii o Sobytiiakh 17 Iiunia 1953 g. v GDR," *Novaia I Noveishaia Istoriia* (February 2004): 73–124.

Dostal, M. Iu. "Zapis Besedy A.A. Zhdanova s Organizatorami Kongressa Uchenykh-Slavistov, Mart 1948 g.," *Istoricheskii Arkhiv* 5 (2001): 3–13.

Doty, Roxanne Lynne. "Aporia: A Critical Exploration of the Agent-Structure Problematique in International Relations Theory," *European Journal of International Relations* 3, no. 3 (1997): 365–92.

Dunham, Vera S. *In Stalin's Time: Middleclass Values in Soviet Fiction* (Durham: Duke University Press, 1990).

"Dve Besedy I.V. Stalina s Generalnym Sekretarem Organizatsii Obedinennykh Natsii TrygveLie," *Novaia i Noveishaia Istoriia* (January 2001): 104–16.

Eckstein, Harry. "Case Study and Theory in Political Science." In *Handbook of Political Science*, vol. 7, ed. Fred L. Greenstein and Nelson W. Polsby (Reading, MA: Addison-Wesley, 1975), 79–137.

Egorova, Nataliia I. "'Iranskii Krizis' 1945–1946gg. Po Rassekrechennym Arkhivnym Dokumentam," *Novaia i Noveishaia Istoriia* 3 (1994): 24–42.

———. "Stalin's Foreign Policy and the Cominform, 1947–53." In *The Soviet Union and Europe in the Cold War, 1943–53*, ed. Francesca Gori and Silvio Pons (New York: St. Martin's Press, 1996), 197–207.

Ehrenburg, Ilya. "Zashchitniki Kultury," *Novoe Vremia* 46 (1947): 5–10.

———. *Post-War Years, 1945–1954*, trans. Tatiana Shebunina (Cleveland: The World Publishing Company, 1967).

Eimermacher, Karl. "Partiinoe upravlenie kulturnoi i formy ee samoorganizatsii (1953–1964/67)." In *Kultura I Vlast ot Stalina do Gorbacheva: Ideologicheskie Komissii TsK KPSS 1958–1964. Dokumenty* (Moscow: ROSSPEN, 2000), 5–22.

Ekedahl, Carolyn McGiffert, and Melvin A. Goodman. *The Wars of Eduard Shevardnadze*, 2d ed. (Washington, DC: Brassey's, 2001).

English, Robert D. *Russia and the Idea of the West: Gorbachev, Intellectuals, and the End of the Cold War* (New York: Columbia University Press, 2000).

Ermolaev, Herman. *Censorship in Soviet Literature: 1917–1991* (Lanham, MD: Rowman & Littlefield, 1997).

Esakov, Vladimir D. "Novoe o Sessii VasKhNiL 1948 Goda." In *Repressirovannaia Nauka*, vol. II, ed. M. G. Iaroshevskii, (Sankt-Peterburg: Nauka, 1994), 57–75.

Esakov, Vladimir D., and Elena S. Levina. *Stalinskie 'Sudy Chesti:' Delo 'KR,'* (Moscow: Nauka, 2005).

Evangelista, Matthew. *Innovation and the Arms Race* (Ithaca: Cornell University Press, 1988).

———. "'Why Keep Such an Army?': Khrushchev's Troop Reductions." Cold War International History Project, Working Paper 19 (Washington, DC: Woodrow Wilson Center for Scholars, December 1997).

———. *Unarmed Forces: The Transnational Movement to End the Cold War* (Ithaca: Cornell University Press, 1999).

Farrell, Theo. "Transnational Norms and Military Development: Constructing Ireland's Professional Army," *European Journal of International Relations* 7, no. 1 (March 2001): 63–102.

Fearon, James. "Bargaining, Enforcement, and International Cooperation," *International Organization* 52, no. 3 (Spring 1998): 269–305.

Ferguson, Yale, and Richard Mansbach. *Polities: Authority, Identities, and Change* (Columbia: University of South Carolina Press, 1996).

Filitov, Alexei M. *Germanskii Vopros: Ot Raskola k Obedeneniiu* (Moscow: Mezhdunarodnye Otnosheniia, 1993).

———. "The Soviet Administrators and Their German 'Friends.'" In *The Establishment of Communist Regimes in Eastern Europe, 1944–1949*, ed. Norman Naimark and Leonid Gibianskii (Boulder: Westview Press, 1997), 111–22.

———. "SSSR I GDR: God 1953-i," *Voprosy Istorii* (July 2000): 123–35.

Filitov, Alexei, and T. V. Domracheva. "Sovetskaia Politika v Germanskom Voprose (1953–1955 gg.)." In *Kholodnaia Voina* (Moscow: Russian Academy of Sciences, Institute of General History, 1995), 240–57.

Finnemore, Martha. *National Interests in International Society* (Ithaca: Cornell University Press, 1996).

Finnemore, Martha, and Kathryn Sikkink. "International Norm Dynamics and Political Change," *International Organization* 52, no. 4 (Autumn 1998): 887–917.

Florini, Ann. "The Evolution of International Norms," *International Studies Quarterly* 40, no. 3 (1996): 363–89.

Foucault, Michel. *Discipline and Punish: The Birth of Prisons* (New York: Vintage 1979).

Frankel, Edith Rogovin. *Novy Mir: A Case Study in the Politics of Literature, 1952–1958* (Cambridge: Cambridge University Press, 1981).

Franklin, Simon, and Emma Widdis. *National Identity in Russian Culture* (Cambridge: Cambridge University Press, 2004).

Fraser, Nancy. "Women, Welfare, and the Politics of Need Interpretation," *Hypatia: A Journal of Feminist Philosophy* 2, no. 1 (1987): 103–21.

Frederking, Brian. "Constructing Post-Cold War Collective Security," *American Political Science Review* 97, no. 3 (2003): 363–78.

Friedberg, Maurice. *A Decade of Euphoria: Western Literature in Post-Stalin Russia* (Bloomington: Indiana University Press, 1977).

Fursenko, Aleksandr A., ed. *Arkhivy Kremlia. Prezidium TsK KPSS 1954–1964*, vol. 1 (Moscow: ROSSPEN, 2003).

———. *Arkhivy Kremlia. Prezidium TsK KPSS 1954–1964*, vol. 2 (Moscow: ROSSPEN, 2006).
Fursenko, Aleksandr, and Timothy Naftali. *"One Hell of a Gamble:" Khrushchev, Castro, and Kennedy, 1958–1964* (New York: W. W. Norton, 1997).
———. *Khrushchev's Cold War* (New York: W. W. Norton 2006).
Gaddis, John Lewis. *We Now Know: Rethinking Cold War History* (Oxford: Oxford University Press, 1997).
Gaiduk, Ilya V. *Confronting Vietnam: Soviet Policy toward the Indochina Conflict, 1954–1963* (Stanford: Stanford University Press, 2003).
Garrard, John Gordon, and Carol Garrad. *Inside the Soviet Writers' Union* (London: Tauris, 1990).
Garthoff, Raymond L. "Some Observations on Using Soviet Archives," *Diplomatic History* 21, no. 2 (1997): 243–57.
———. *A Journey through the Cold War: A Memoir of Containment and Coexistence* (Washington, DC: Brookings Institution Press, 2001).
Gati, Charles. *Failed Illusions: Moscow, Washington, Budapest, and the 1956 Hungarian Revolt* (Palo Alto: Stanford University Press, 2006).
Geertz, Clifford. *The Interpretation of Cultures* (New York: Basic, 1973).
George, Alexander L. "Case Studies and Theory Development: The Method of Structured, Focused Comparison." In *Diplomatic History: New Approaches*, ed. Paul Gordon Lauren (New York: Free Press, 1979).
———. "The Causal Nexus Between Cognitive Beliefs and Decision-Making Behavior: The 'Operational Code' Belief System." In *Psychological Models in International Politics*, ed. Lawrence S. Falkowski (Boulder: Westview Press, 1979), 95–124.
George, Alexander L., and Andrew Bennett. *Case Studies and Theory Development in the Social Sciences* (Cambridge: MIT, 2005).
George, Alexander L., and Timothy J. McKeown. "Case Studies and Theories of Organizational Decision Making," *Advances in Information Processing in Organizations* 2 (1985): 21–58.
Gerring, John. *Case Study Research: Principles and Practices* (New York: Cambridge University Press, 2007), 21–58.
Gibianskii, Leonid Ia. "Problemy Mezhdunarodno-Politicheskogo Strukturirovaniia Vostochnoi Evropy v Period Formirovaniia Sovetskogo Bloka v 1940-e Gody." In *Kholodnaia Voina: Novye Podkhody, Novye Dokumenty*, ed. M. M. Narinskii (Moscow: Institute of General History, 1995), 99–126.
———. "Kominform v Deistvii. 1947–1948 gg. Po Arkhivnym Dokumentam," *Novaia i Noveishaia Istoriia* 1 (1996): 149–70.
———. "Kominform v Deistvii. 1947–1948 gg. Po Arkhivnym Dokumentam," *Novaia i Noveishaia Istoriia* 2 (1996): 157–72.
———. "Na Poroge Pervogo Raskola v 'Sotsialisticheskom Lagere,'" *Istoricheskii Arkhiv* 4 (1997): 90–122.
———. "N. S. Khrushchev, I. Broz Tito i Vengerskii Krizis 1956 g.," *Novaia i Noveishaia Istoriia* (January 1999): 10–29.
Gibianskii, Leonid Ia., ed. "Sekretnaia Sovetsko-Iugoslavskaia Perepiska 1948 Goda," *Voprosy Istorii* 4 (1992): 119–36.
———. "Sekretnaia Sovetsko-Iugoslavskaia Perepiska 1948 Goda," *Voprosy Istorii* 6 (1992): 158–72.
———. "Sekretnaia Sovetsko-Iugoslavskaia Perepiska 1948 Goda," *Voprosy Istorii* 10 (1992): 141–60.
———. "Kak Voznik Kominform. Po Novym Arkhivnym Materialam," *Novaia i Noveishaia Istoriia* 4 (1993): 131–52.
———. "Poslednii Vizit I. Broza Tito k I.V. Stalinu," *Istoricheskii Arkhiv* 2 (1993):16–35.
Giddens, Anthony. *Modernity and Self-Identity* (Stanford: Stanford University Press, 1991).
Gigolaev, German. "Sovetsko-Italianskie Otnosheniia 1953–1956 Godov," *Novaia i Noveishaia Istoriia* (March 2008): 22–34.
Ginetsinskaia, T. A. "Biofak Leningradskogo Universiteta Posle Sessii VASKhNiL." In *Repressirovannaia Nauka*, vol. I, ed. M. G. Iaroshevskii (Leningrad: Nauka, 1991), 114–25.

Goban-Klas, Tomasz, and Pal Kolsto. "East European Mass Media: The Soviet Role." In *The Soviet Union in Eastern Europe, 1945–89*, ed. Odd Arne Westad, Sven Holtsmark, and Iver B. Neumann (London: St. Martin's Press, 1994), 110–36.

Goldberg, Anatol. *Ilya Ehrenburg: Writing, Politics, and the Art of Survival* (London: Weidenfeld and Nicolson, 1984).

Goldgeier, James M. *Leadership Style and Soviet Foreign Policy* (Baltimore: Johns Hopkins University Press, 1994).

———. *Not Whether But When: The U.S. Decision to Enlarge NATO* (Washington, DC: Brookings Institution Press, 1999).

Goncharov, Sergei N., John W. Lewis, and Xue Litai, *Uncertain Partners: Stalin, Mao, and the Korean War* (Stanford: Stanford University Press, 1993).

Gorlizki, Yoram. "Party Revivalism and the Death of Stalin," *Slavic Review* 54, no. 1 (Spring 1995): 1–22.

———. "Stalin's Cabinet: The Politburo and Decision Making in the Post-war Years," *Europe-Asia Studies* 53, no. 2 (2001): 291–312.

Gorlizki, Yoram, and Oleg Khlevniuk. *Cold Peace: Stalin and the Soviet Ruling Circle, 1945–1953* (New York: Oxford University Press, 2004).

Van Goudoever, Albert P. *The Limits of Destalinization in the Soviet Union* (London: Croom Helm, 1986).

Graffy, Julian. "Cinema." In *Russian Cultural Studies: An Introduction*, ed. Catriona Kelly and David Shepherd (Oxford: Oxford University Press, 1998), 165–91.

Granville, Johanna. "In the Line of Fire: The Soviet Crackdown on Hungary, 1956–58," *The Carl Beck Papers in Russian and East European Studies* 1307 (December 1998).

Griffiths, Franklyn. "The Sources of American Conduct," *International Security* 9, no. 2 (Fall 1984): 3–50.

Grinevskii, Oleg. *Tainy Sovetskoi Diplomatii* (Moscow: Izd-vo Vagrius, 2000).

Gromov, Evgenii. *Stalin: Vlast i Iskusstvo* (Moscow: Respublika, 1998).

Grose, Peter. *Operation Rollback* (Boston: Houghton Mifflin, 2000).

Gunther, Hans. "Wise Father Stalin and his Family in Soviet Cinema." In *Socialist Realism Without Shores*, ed. Thomas Lahusen and Evgeny Dobrenko (Durham: Duke University Press, 1997), 178–90.

Habermas, Juergen. "Replik auf Einwande." In *Vorstudien und Ergaenzungen zur Theorie des kommunikativen Handelns* (Frankfurt am Main: Suhrkamp, 1995).

Hahn, Werner G. *Postwar Soviet Politics: The Fall of Zhdanov and the Defeat of Moderation, 1946–1953* (Ithaca: Cornell University Press, 1982).

Hall, Peter A. *Governing the Economy* (Cambridge, UK: Polity Press, 1986).

Hall, Rodney Bruce. *National Collective Identity: Social Constructs and International Systems* (New York: Columbia University Press, 1999).

Hall, Stuart. "Who Needs Identity?" Introduction to *Questions of Cultural Identity*, ed. Stuart Hall and Paul du Gay (London: Sage, 1996), 1–17.

Harrison, Hope M. *Driving the Soviets Up the Wall* (Princeton: Princeton University Press, 2003).

Hart, Allen J. et al. "Differential Response in the Human Amygdala to Racial Outgroup vs. Ingroup Face Stimuli," *NeuroReport* 11, no. 11 (August 2000): 2351–55.

Hartz, Louis. *The Liberal Tradition in America* (New York: Harcourt, Brace, and World, 1955).

Hasenclever, Andreas, Peter Mayer, and Volker Rittberger. *Theories of International Regimes* (Cambridge: Cambridge University Press, 1998).

Haslam, Jonathan. "Russian Archival Revelations and Our Understanding of the Cold War," *Diplomatic History* 21, no. 2 (1997): 217–28.

"Head of the Soviet Foreign Ministry's Far Eastern Department, Mikhail Zimyanin, on Sino-Soviet Relations, September 15, 1959." In *Brothers in Arms: The Rise and Fall of the Sino-Soviet Alliance, 1945–1963*, ed. Odd Arne Westad (Stanford: Stanford University Press, 1998), 356–60.

Heinzig, Dieter. *The Soviet Union and Communist China, 1945–1950: The Arduous Road to the Alliance* (Armonk, NY: M. E. Sharpe, 2004).

Heller, Leonid. "A World of Prettiness: Socialist Realism between Modernism and Postmodernism." In *Socialist Realism Without Shores*, ed. Thomas Lahusen and Evgeny Dobrenko (Durham: Duke University Press, 1997), 51–75.
Holloway, David. *Stalin and the Bomb* (New Haven: Yale University Press, 1994).
Hopf, Ted. *Peripheral Visions: Deterrence Theory and American Foreign Policy in the Third World, 1965–1990* (Ann Arbor: University of Michigan Press, 1994).
———. *Social Construction of International Politics: Identities and Foreign Policies, Moscow, 1955 and 1999* (Ithaca: Cornell University Press, 2002).
———. "The Logic of Habit in International Relations," *European Journal of International Relations* 16, no. 4 (December 2010): 539–61.
Hough, Jerry. *The Struggle for the Third World* (Washington, DC: The Brookings Institution Press, 1986).
Hurrell, Andrew. "An Emerging Security Community in South America?" In *Security Communities*, ed. Emanuel Adler and Michael Barnett (Cambridge: Cambridge University Press, 1998), 228–64.
Iakovlev, Aleksandr N., ed. *Reabilitatsiia: Politicheskie Protsessy 30-50-x godov* (Moscow: Izdatelstvo Politicheskoi Literatury, 1991).
———. *Reabilitatsiia: Kak eto Bylo. Dokumenty Prezidiuma TsK KPSS i Drugie Materialy*, vol. I (Moscow: Mezhdunarodnyi Fond "Demokratiia," 2000).
———. *Reabilitatsiia: Kak eto Bylo. Fevral 1956—Nachalo 80-x Godov*, vol. II (Moscow: Mezhdunarodnyi Fond "Demokratiia," 2003).
Iaroshevskii, M. G. "Stalinizm I Sudby Sovetskoi Nauki." In *Repressirovannaia Nauka*, vol. I, ed. M. G. Iaroshevskii (Leningrad: Nauka, 1991), 9–34.
Ideologicheskie Kommissii TsK KPSS, 1958–1964: Dokumenty (Moscow: ROSSPEN, 2000).
Ikenberry, G. John, David A. Lake, and Michael Mastanduno, eds. *The State and American Foreign Economic Policy* (Ithaca: Cornell University Press, 1988).
Inayatullah, Naeem, and David L. Blaney. "Knowing Encounters: Beyond Parochialism in International Relations Theory." In *The Return of Culture and Identity to IR Theory*, ed. Yosef Lapid and Friedrich Kratochwil (Boulder: Lynne Rienner, 1996), 65–84.
"'International Affairs' During Thaws, Confrontations, Perestroika, the Transition to Strategic Partnership and Other Changes in Foreign Policy" (1994): 75–92.
Islamov, Tofik M., and Tatiana A. Pokivailova. "SSR I Transilvanskii Vopros (1945–1946 gg.)," *Voprosy Istorii* 12 (2004): 26–40.
Jenson, Jan. "Gender and Reproduction: Or, Babies and the State," *Studies in Political Economy* 20, no. 1 (1986): 9–46.
Jian, Chen. *Mao's China and the Cold War* (Chapel Hill: University of North Carolina Press, 2001).
Jones, Polly. "From the Secret Speech to the Burial of Stalin: Real and Ideal Responses to de-Stalinization." In *The Dilemmas of De-Stalinization*, ed. Polly Jones (London: Routledge 2006), 41–63.
Jonson, Lena. "The Foreign Policy Debate in Russia: In Search of a National Interest," *Nationalities Papers* 22, no. 1 (1994): 175–94.
———. "Russia and Central Asia." In *Central Asian Security: The New International Context*, ed. Roy Allison and Lena Johnson (Washington, DC: Brookings Institution, 2001), 95–126.
Jun, Niu. "The Origins of the Sino-Soviet Alliance." In *Brothers in Arms: The Rise and Fall of the Sino-Soviet Alliance, 1945–1963*, ed. Odd Arne Westad (Stanford: Stanford University Press, 1998), 47–89.
Kaganovich, Lazar. *Pamiatnye Zapiski* (Moscow: Vagrius, 1996).
"Kak Reshalis 'Voprosy Vengrii,'" *Istoricheskii Arkhiv* (February 1996): 73–104.
"Kak Reshalis 'Voprosy Vengrii,'" *Istoricheskii Arkhiv* (March 1996): 87–121.
Kallinikova, V. D., and V. Ia. Brodskii. "*Delo 'KR.'*" In *Repressirovannaia Nauka*, vol. II, ed. M. G. Iaroshevskii (Sankt Peterburg: Nauka, 1994), 113–20.
Katzenstein, Peter J. *Cultural Norms and National Security: Police and Military in Postwar Japan* (Ithaca: Cornell University Press, 1996).

———. "Alternative Perspectives on National Security." Introduction to *The Culture of National Security: Norms and Identity in World Politics* (New York: Columbia University Press, 1996), 1–32.
Kaverin, Veniamin A. *Literator: Dnevniki i Pisma* (Moscow: Sovetskii Pisatel, 1988).
———. *Epilog* (Moscow: Moskovskii Rabochii, 1989).
Keck, Margaret, and Kathryn Sikkink. *Activists Beyond Borders: Advocacy Networks in International Relations* (Ithaca: Cornell University Press, 1998).
Kenez, Peter. *Cinema and Soviet Society, 1917–1953* (Cambridge: Cambridge University Press, 1992).
Kenez, Peter, and David Shepherd. "'Revolutionary' Models for High Literature: Resisting Poetics." In *Russian Cultural Studies: An Introduction*, ed. Catroina Kelly and David Shepherd (Oxford: Oxford University Press, 1998), 21–55.
Keohane, Robert O. "International Institutions: Two Approaches," *International Studies Quarterly* 32 (1988): 379–96.
———. *International Institutions and State Power* (Boulder: Westview Press, 1989).
Khavkin, Boris L. "Berlinskoe Zharkoe Leto 1953 Goda," *Novaia i Noveishaia Istoriia* (April 2004): 159–74.
Khrushchev, Sergei N. *Nikita Khrushchev and the Creation of a Superpower* (University Park: Pennsylvania State University Press, 2000).
Kier, Elizabeth. *Imagining War* (Princeton: Princeton University Press 1997).
Kirshner, Lev A., and Svetlana A. Prokhvailova, eds. *Svet i Teni "Velikogo Desiatiletiia:" N. S. Khrushchev I ego Vremia* (Leningrad: Lenizdat, 1989).
Kiselev, A. S. ed. *Moskva Poslevoennaia 1945/47* (Moscow: MOSGOARKhIV, 2000).
Klotz, Audie. "Norms Reconstituting Interests: Global Racial Equality and US Sanctions Against South Africa," *International Organization* 49, no. 3 (1995): 451–78.
Knight, Amy. *Beria: Stalin's First Lieutenant* (Princeton: Princeton University Press, 1993).
Kochkin, Nikolai V. "SSSR, Angliia, SshA I 'Turetskii Krizis' 1945–1947 gg.," *Novaia i Noveishaia Istoriia* 3 (2002): 58–77.
Kojevnikov, Alexei. "Rituals of Stalinist Culture at Work: Science and the Games of Intraparty Democracy circa 1948," *Russian Review* 57, no. 1 (January 1998): 25–52.
Kolchinskii. "Vzgliad iz Rektorata na Biologiiu v Leningradskom Universitete." In *Repressirovannaia Nauka*, vol II., ed. M. G. Iaroshevskii (Sankt Peterburg: Nauka, 1994), 169–75.
———. "Trudnye Gody Nauki Glazami Odnogo Fiziologa." In *Repressirovannaia Nauka*, vol. II, ed. M. G. Iaroshevskii (Sankt Peterburg: Nauka, 1994), 176–86.
Kolokolov, Boris L. *Professiia: Diplomat* (Moscow: Mezhdunarodnye Otnosheniia, 1998).
Kolsto, Pal. *Political Construction Sites: Nation-building in Russia and the Post-Soviet States* (Boulder: Westview Press, 2000).
———. "Ethnicity and Subregional Relations: The Role of the Russian Diasporas." In *Building Security in the New States of Eurasia: Subregional Cooperation in the Former Soviet Space*, Renata Dwan and Oleksandr Pavliuk (Armonk: M. E. Sharpe, 2000), 201–26.
Kornblatt, Judith Deutsch. "Christianity, Antisemitism, Nationalism: Russian Orthodoxy in a Reborn Orthodox Russia." In *Consuming Russia: Popular Culture, Sex, and Society Since Gorbachev*, ed. Adele Marie Barker (Durham: Duke University Press, 1999), 414–36.
Kornienko, Georgii M. *Kholodnaia Voina: Svidetelstvo ee Uchastnika* (Moscow: Mezhdunarodnye otnosheniia, 1994).
Kostyrchenko, Gennadii. *Gosudarstvennyi Antisemitizm v SSSR, 1938–1953: Dokumenty* (Moscow: Materik, 2005).
Kowert, Paul, and Jeffrey Legro. "Norms, Identity, and their Limits: A Theoretical Reprise." In *The Culture of National Security: Norms and Identity in World Politics*, ed. Peter J. Katzenstein (New York: Columbia University Press, 1996), 451–97.
Kozhevnikov, Aleksei B. "Uchenyi i Gosudarstvo: Fenomen Kapitsy." In *Nauka I Vlast*, ed. A. P. Ogurtsov and B. G. Iudin (Moscow: Akademiia Nauk SSSR, 1990), 161–87.
Kozlov, Vladimir A. *Mass Uprisings in the USSR: Protest and Rebellion in the Post-Stalin Years* (Armonk: M. E. Sharpe, 2002).

Kozlov, Vladimir. A., ed. *Neizvestnaia Rossiia: XX Vek*, vol. II (Moscow: Istoricheskoe Nasledie, 1992).
Kozlov, Vladimir A., and Sergei V. Mironenko, eds. *Kramola: Inakomyslie v SSSR pri Khrushcheve i Brezhneve, 1953-1982 gg.* (Moscow: Materik, 2005).
Kramer, Mark. "New Evidence on Soviet Decision-Making and the 1956 Polish and Hungarian Crises," *Cold War International History Project Bulletin* 8-9 (1996/1997): 358-84.
———. "The Soviet Union and the 1956 Crises in Hungary and Poland," *Journal of Contemporary History* 33, no. 2 (1998): 163-214.
———. "The Early Post-Stalin Succession Struggle and Upheavals in East-Central Europe," *Journal of Cold War Studies* 1, no. 1 (Winter 1999): 3-55.
———. "The Early Post-Stalin Succession Struggle and Upheavals in East-Central Europe," *Journal of Cold War Studies* 1, no. 2 (Spring 1999): 3-38.
———. "The Early Post-Stalin Succession Struggle and Upheavals in East-Central Europe," *Journal of Cold War Studies* 1, no. 3 (Fall 1999): 3-66.
Kratochwil, Friedrich V. "Constructing a New Orthodoxy? Wendt's 'Social Theory of International Politics' and the Constructivist Challenge," *Millennium* 29. no. 1 (2000): 73-102.
Krementsov, Nikolai. *Stalinist Science* (Princeton: Princeton University Press, 1997).
Kriuchkov, Vladimir. *Lichnoe Dela. Chast Pervaia* (Moscow: Olimp, 1996).
Kulik, Boris T. *Sovetsko-Kitaiskii Raskol: Prichiny i Posledstviia* (Moscow: Institut Dal'nego Vostoka RAN, 2000).
———. "O Knige A.M. Ledovskogo 'SSSR I Stalin v Sudbakh Kitaia,'" *Novaia I Noveishaia Istoriia* 5 (2001): 194-205.
Kultura I Vlast ot Stalina do Gorbacheva. Apparat TsK KPSS I Kultura 1953-1957. Dokumenty (Moscow: ROSSPEN, 2001).
Kumanev, Georgii A. *Ryadom So Stalinym: Otkrovennye Svidetelstva* (Moscow, 1999).
Kvitsinskii, Iulii A. *Vremia i Sluchai: Zametki Profesionala* (Moscow, 1999).
Kynin, Georgii P., and Johan P. Laufer. "Vvedenie: Politika SSSR po Germanskomu Voprosu (9 maia 1945 g.—3 oktiabria 1946 g.)." In *SSSR I Germanskii Vopros*, vol. II (Moscow: Mezhdunarodnye Otnosheniia, 2000), 11-87.
———. "Vvedenie: Politika SSSR po Germanskomu Voprosu (6 oktiabria 1946 g.—15 iiuniia 1948 g.)." In *SSSR I Germanskii Vopros*, vol. III (Moscow: Mezhdunarodnye Otnosheniia, 2003), 13-84.
Laffey, Mark, and Jutta Weldes. "Beyond Belief: Ideas and Symbolic Technologies in the Study of International Relations," *European Journal of International Relations* 3, no. 2 (1997): 193-237.
Lahusen, Thomas. *How Life Writes the Book: Real Socialism and Socialist Realism in Stalin's Russia* (Ithaca: Cornell University Press, 1997).
Lake, David A. "The New Sovereignty in International Relations," *International Studies Review* 5, no. 3 (2003): 303-24.
Lakshin, Vladimir. *Novy Mir vo Vremena Khrushcheva* (Moscow: Knizhnaia Palata, 1991).
Larsen, Susan. "In Search of an Audience: The New Russian Cinema of Reconciliation." In *Consuming Russia: Popular Culture, Sex, and Society Since Gorbachev*, ed. Adele Marie Barker (Durham: Duke University Press, 1999), 192-216.
Latysh, M. V. "'Doktrina Brezhneva' i 'Prazhskaia Vesna' 1968 goda." In *Sovetskaia Vneshniaia Politika v Gody "Kholodnoi Voiny," (1945-1985)*, ed. L. N. Nezhinskii (Moscow: Mezhdunarotnosheniia, 1995), 303-33.
Lawton, Anna. "The Ghost that Does Return: Exorcising Stalin." In *Stalinism and Soviet Cinema*, ed. Taylor Richard and Derek Spring (London: Routledge, 1993), 186-200.
Ledovskii, Andrei M. "Na Diplomaticheskom Rabote v Kitae v 1942-1952 gg.," *Novaia I Noveishaia Istoriia* 6 (1993): 102-32.
———. "Peregovory I.V. Stalina s Mao Tszedunom v Dekabre 1949-Fevrale 1950 g. Novye Arkhivnye Dokumenty," *Novaia I Noveishaia Istoriia* 1 (1997): 23-47.
———. "Stenogrammy Peregovorov I.V. Stalina s Czhou Enlaem v Avguste-Sentiabre 1952 g.," *Novaia I Noveishaia Istoriia* 2 (1997): 69-86.

———. "12 Sovetov I.V. Stalina Rukovodstvu Kompartii Kitaia," *Novaia Noveishaia Istoriia* 2 (2004): 125–39.
———. "Stalin, Mao Tszedun i Koreiskaia Voina 1950–1953 Godov," *Novaia i Noveishaia Istoriia* 5 (2005): 79–113.
Leffler, Melvyn P. *For the Soul of Mankind* (New York: Hill and Wang, 2007).
Levina, Elena S. *Vavilov, Lysenko, Timofeev-Resovskii Biologiia v SSSR: Istoriia i Istoriografiia* (Moscow: AIRO-XX, 1995).
Light, Margot. "Post-Soviet Russian Foreign Policy: The First Decade." In *Contemporary Russian Politics: A Reader*, ed. Archie Brown (New York: Oxford, 2001), 419–28.
"Liu Shaoqi's Report to the CPSU CC Politburo, July 4, 1949." In *Brothers in Arms: The Rise and Fall of the Sino-Soviet Alliance, 1945–1963*, ed. Odd Arne Westad (Stanford: Stanford University Press, 1998), 301–13.
Loth, Wilfried. "Stalin's Plans for Post-War Germany." In *The Soviet Union and Europe in the Cold War, 1943–53*, ed. Francesaca Gori and Silvio Pons (New York: St. Martin's Press, 1996), 23–36.
Lotman, Iurii M., and Boris A. Uspenskii. "Binary Models in the Dynamics of Russian Culture to the End of the Eighteenth Century." In *The Semiotics of Russian Cultural History*, ed. Alexander D. and Alice Stone Nakhimosvsky (Ithaca: Cornell University Press, 1985), 30–66.
Lovell, Stephen. *Summerfolk: A History of the Dacha, 1710–2000* (Ithaca: Cornell University Press, 2003).
Lovell, Stephen, and Rosalind Marsh. "*Culture and Crisis: The Intelligentsia and Literature after 1953.*" In *Russian Cultural Studies*, ed. Catriona Kelly and David Shepherd (Oxford: Oxford University Press, 1998), 56–84.
Lukes, Igor. "The Czech Road to Communism." In *The Establishment of Communist Regimes in Eastern Europe 1944–1949*, ed. Normal Naimark and Leonid Gibianskii (Boulder: Westview Press, 1997), 243–65.
Luthi, Lorenz. *The Sino-Soviet Split: Cold War in the Communist World* (Princeton: Princeton University Press, 2008).
MacDonogh, Giles. *After the Reich: The Brutal History of the Allied Occupation* (New York: Basic Books, 2007).
Maher, Kristen Hill. "Who Has a Right to Rights." In *Globalization and Human Rights*, ed. Alison Brysk (Berkeley: University of California Press, 2002), 26–36.
Malcolm, Neil. "Russian Foreign Policy Decision-Making." In *Russian Foreign Policy since 1990*, ed. Peter Shearman (Boulder: Westview, 1995), 3–27.
"'Malin' Notes on the Crises in Hungary and Poland, 1956," *Cold War International History Project Bulletin* 8–9 (1996/1997): 385–410.
Mansfield, Edward D., and Jack L. Snyder. *Electing to Fight* (Cambridge: MIT Press, 2005).
Mansourov, Alexandre Y. "Stalin, Mao, Kim, and China's Decision to Enter the Korean War, September 16–October 15, 1950: New Evidence from the Russian Archives," *Cold War International History Project Bulletin* Issues 6–7 (Winter 1995/1996): 94–119.
March, James G., and John P. Olsen. "The Institutional Dynamics of International Political Orders," *International Organization* 52, no. 4 (1998): 943–69.
Marchuk, N.I . "Voina v Afganistane: 'Internatsionalizm' v Deistvii ili Vooruzhennaia Agressiia?" In *Sovetskaia Vneshniaia Politika v Gody "Kholodnoi Voiny" (1945–1985)*, ed. L. N. Nezhinskii (Moscow: Mezhdunar otnosheniia, 1995), 453–79.
Mariamov, Grigorii B. *Kremlevskii Tsenzor: Stalin Smotrit Kino* (Moscow: Kinotsentr, 1992).
Marx, Karl, and Friedrich Engels. *The German Ideology* (London: Lawrence and Wishart, 1965).
Mastny, Vojtech. *The Cold War and Soviet Insecurity* (New York: Oxford University Press, 1996).
Matz, Johan. *Constructing a Post-Soviet International Political Reality: Russian Foreign Policy Towards the Newly Independent States, 1990–95* (Uppsala: Acta Universitatis Upsaliensis, 2001).
McAlister, Melani. *Epic Encounters: Culture, Media, and U.S. Interests in the Middle East Since 1945* (Berkeley: University of California Press, 2001).
McSweeney, Bill. *Security, Identity, and Interests: A Sociology of International Relations* (Cambridge: Cambridge University Press, 1999).

Medvedev, Roi. *Neizvestnyi Andropov: Politcheskaia Biografiia Iuriia Andropova* (Moscow: Prava Cheloveka, 1999).
Medvedev, Zh. *Istorik I Vremia: 20-50-e Gody XX Veka A.M. Pankratova* (Moscow: MOSGO-RARKHhIV, 2000).
"Memorandum of Conversation, East German official with Soviet Ambassador to Ethiopia Ratanov, Addis Ababa, 6 December 1977," *Cold War International History Project Bulletin* 8–9 (1996/1997): 82–83.
Mendelson, Sarah E. *Changing Course: Ideas, Politics, and the Soviet Withdrawal from Afghanistan* (Princeton: Princeton University Press, 1999).
Menshikov, Mikhail A. *S Vintovkoi I Vo Frake* (Moscow: Mezhdunarodnye Otnosheniia, 1996).
Micunovic, Veljko. *Moscow Diary* (New York: Doubelday, 1980).
Mikoyan, Anastas. *Tak Bylo: Razmyshleniia o Minuvshem* (Moscow: Vagrius, 1999).
Milliken, Jennifer. "The Study of Discourse in International Relations: A Critique of Research and Methods," *European Journal of International Relations* 5, no. 2 (1999): 225–54.
Milner, Helen V. *Interests, Institutions, and Information: Domestic Politics and International Relations* (Princeton: Princeton University Press, 1997).
———. "Rationalizing Politics: The Emerging Synthesis of International, American, and Comparative Politics," *International Organization* 52, no. 4 (1998): 759–86.
Mitrokhin, Nikolai. *Russkaia Partiia: Dvizhenie Russkikh Natsionalistov v SSSR 1953–1985 gody* (Moscow: Novoe Literaturnoe Obozrenie, 2003).
Mitzen, Jennifer. "Ontological Security in World Politics," *European Journal of International Relations* 12, no. 3 (2006): 341–70.
Mlechin, Leonid. *MID: Ministry Inostrannykh Del, Romantiki i Tsiniki* (Moscow: TSentrpoligraf, 2001).
Moravcsik, Andrew. "Taking Preferences Seriously: A Liberal Theory of International Politics." *International Organization* 51, no. 4 (1997): 513–53.
"More New Evidence on the Cold War in Asia," *Cold War International History Project Bulletin* 8–9 (1996/1997): 220–69.
Morgenthau, Hans. *Politics Among Nations* (New York: Knopf, 1967).
Muller, Friedemann. "Energy Development and Transport Network Cooperation in Central Asia and the South Caucasus." In *Building Security in the New States of Eurasia: Subregional Cooperation in the Former Soviet Space*, ed. Ranata Dwan and Oleksandr Pavliuk (Armonk: M. E. Sharpe, 2000), 177–200.
Murashko, Galina P., and Albina F. Noskova. "Repressii—Instrument Podavleniia Politicheskoi Oppozitsii." In *Moskva i Vostochnaia Evropa. Stanovlenie politicheskikh rezhimov sovetskogo tipa (1949–1953).*, ed. Tatiana V. Volokitina et al. (Moscow: ROSSPEN, 2002), 426–94.
———. "Repressii Kak Element Vnutripartiinoi Borby Za Vlast'." In *Moskva i Vostochnaia Evropa. Stanovlenie politicheskikh rezhimov sovetskogo tipa (1949–1953). Ocherki istorii*, ed. Tatiana V. Volokitina et al. (Moscow: ROSSPEN, 2002), 495–591.
———. "Institut Sovetskikh Sovetnikov v Stranakh Regiona: Tseli, Zadachi, Rezultaty." In *Moskva i Vostochnaia Evropa. Stanovlenie politicheskikh rezhimov sovetskogo tipa (1949–1953). Ocherki istorii*, ed. Tatiana V. Volokitina et al. (Moscow: ROSSPEN, 2002), 592–655.
———. "Sovetskii faktor v poslevoennoi Vostochnoi evrope (1945–1948)." In *Sovetskaia Vneshniaia Politika v Gody "Kholodnoi Voiny" (1945–1985)*, ed. L. N. Nezhinskii (Moscow: Mezhdunar otnosheniii, 1995), 69–114.
———. "Sovetskoe Rukovodstvo i Politicheskie Protsessy T. Kostova i L. Raika." In *Stalinskoe Desiatiletie Kholodnoi Voiny: Fakty i Gipotezy*, ed. I. V. Gaiduk, N. I. Yegorova, and A. O. Chubarian, (Moscow: Nauka, 1999), 23–35.
Musatov, V. L. "SSSR I Vengerskie Sobytiia 1956 g.," *Novaia i Noveishaia Istoriia* (January 1993): 3–22.
Naimark, Norman M. *The Russians in Germany: A History of the Soviet Zone of Occupation, 1945–1949* (Cambridge: Belknap Press of Harvard University Press, 1995).

———. "The Soviets and the Christian Democrats: the Challenge of a 'Bourgeois' Party in Eastern Germany, 1945–9." In *The Soviet Union and Europe in the Cold War, 1943–53*, ed. Francesca Gori and Silvio Pons (New York: St. Martin's Press, 1996), 37–56.

Narinskii, Mikhail M. "SSSR I Plan Marshalla," *Novaia i Noveishaia Istoriia* 2 (1993): 11–19.

———. "I. V. Stalin i Moriz Torez. Zapis Besedy v Kremle, 1947 g.," *Istoricheskii Arkhiv* 1 (1996): 4–26.

———. "The Soviet Union and the Berlin Crisis, 1948–9." In *The Soviet Union and Europe in the Cold War, 1943–53*, ed. Francesca Gori and Silvio Pons (New York: St. Martin's Press, 1996), 57–75.

———. "Sovetskii Soiuz I Suetskii Krizis 1956 Goda," *Novaia i Noveishaia Istoriia* (April 2004): 54–66.

"Nas Neobychaino Teplo i Serdechno Vstretili," *Istoricheskii Arkhiv* 2 (2008): 53–69.

"'Nasha liniia Takaia' Dokumenty o vstreche IV Stalina s rukovoditeliami SEPG. Ian-fev 1947g.," *Istoricheskii Arkhiv* 4 (1994): 22–44.

Nation, R. Craig. "A Balkan Union? Southeastern Europe in Soviet Security Policy, 1944–8." In *The Soviet Union and Europe in the Cold War, 1943–53*, ed. Francesca Gori and Silvio Pons (New York: St. Martin's Press, 1996), 125–43.

Naumov, Vladimir P. "Byl li Zagovor Berii? Novye Dokumenty of Sobytiiakh 1953 g.," *Novaia I Noveishaia Istoriia* 5 (1998): 17–39.

——— "Repression and Rehabilitation." In *Nikita Khrushchev*, ed. William Taubman, Sergei Khrushchev, and Abbott Gleason (New Haven: Yale University Press, 2000), 85–112.

Nepomnyashchy, Catharine Theimer. "Markets, Mirrors, and Mayhem: Aleksandra Marinina and the Rise of the New Russian Detektiv." In *Consuming Russia: Popular Culture, Sex, and Society Since Gorbachev*, ed. Adele Marie Barker (Durham: Duke University Press, 1999), 161–91.

Neumann, Iver B. "Self and Other in International Relations." *European Journal of International Relations* 2, no. 2 (1996): 139–74.

"New Evidence on the Korean War," *Cold War International History Project Bulletin* 6–7 (Winter 1995/1996): 30–125.

"New Evidence on Sino-Soviet Relations," *Cold War International History Project Bulletin* 6–7 (Winter 1995/1996): 148–207.

North, Douglass C. "The New Institutional Economics," *Journal of Institutional and Theoretical Economics* 142 (1986): 230–37.

Novikov, Nikolai V. *Vospominaniia Diplomata* (Moscow: Politizdat, 1989).

"'Nuzhno Idti k Sotsializmu ne Priamo, a Zigzagami:' Zapis Besedy I.V. Stalina s Rukovoditeliami SEPG. Dekabr 1948 g.." *Istoricheskii Arkhiv* 5 (2002): 3–26.

Obichkina, Evgeniia. "Sovetskoe Rukovodstvo I Voina v Alzhire 1954–1962 gg.," *Novaia i Noveishaia Istoriia* (January 2000): 19–30.

Olcott, Anthony. *Russian Pulp: The Detektiv and the Russian Way of Crime* (Lanham, MD: Rowman & Littlefield, 2001).

Olcott, Martha Brill, Anders Aslund, and Sherman W. Garnett. *Getting It Wrong: Regional Cooperation and the Commonwealth of Independent States* (Washington, DC: Carnegie Endowment for International Peace, 1999).

Orekhov, A. M.. "Sobytiia 1956 goda v Polshe i Krizis Polsko-Sovetskikh Otoshei." In *Sovetskaia Vneshniaia Politika v Gody "Kholodnoi Voiny," (1945–1985)*, ed. L. N. Nezhinskii (Moscow: Mezhdunar Otnosheniia, 1995), 217–40.

Orloff, Ann Shola. "Motherhood, Work, and Welfare in the United States, Britain, Canada, and Australia." In *State/Culture: State-Formation after the Cultural Turn*, ed. George Steinmetz (Ithaca: Cornell University Press, 1999), 321–54.

Orlov, Iurii. *Opasnye Mysli* (Moscow: Argumenty i Fakty, 1992).

Orlova, Raisa, and Lev Kopelev. *Myi Zhili v Moskve* (Moscow: Kniga, 1990).

Ostrom, Elinor. "An Agenda for the Study of Institutions," *Public Choice* 48 (1986): 3–25.

Packenham, Robert A. *Liberal America and the Third World* (Princeton: Princeton University Press, 1973).

Pain, Emil A. "Contagious Ethnic Conflicts and Border Disputes Along Russia's Southern Flank." In *Russia, the Caucasus, and Central Asia: The 21st Century Security Environment*, ed. Rajan Menon, Yuri E. Fedorov, and Ghia Nodia (Armonk: M. E. Sharpe, 1999), 177–202.

Parrish, Scott. "The Marshall Plan, Soviet-American Relations, and the Division of Europe." In *The Establishment of Communist Regimes in Eastern Europe, 1944–1949*, ed. Norman Naimark and Leonid Gibianskii (Boulder: Westview Press, 1997), 267–90.

Parthe, Kathleen. "The Empire Strikes Back: How Right-Wing Nationalists Tried to Recapture Russian Literature," *Nationalities Papers* 24, no. 4 (1996): 601–24.

Pavliuk, Oleksandr. "GUUAM: The Maturing of a Political Grouping into Economic Cooperation." In *Building Security in the New States of Eurasia: Subregional Cooperation in the Former Soviet Space*, ed. Renata Dwan and Oleksandr Pavliuk (Armonk: M. E. Sharpe, 2000), 33–56.

Paznyak, Vyachaslau. "The Customs Union of Five and the Russia-Belarus Union." In *Building Security in the New States of Eurasia: Subregional Cooperation in the Former Soviet Space*, ed. Renata Dwan and Oleksandr Pavliuk (Armonk: M. E. Sharpe, 2000), 57–85.

Pechatnov, Vladimir O., and Vladislav M. Zubok. "The Allies are pressing on you to break your will." Cold War International History Project Working Paper (Washington, DC: Wilson Center, 1999).

Perovic, Jeronim. "The Tito-Stalin Split," *Journal of Cold War Studies* 9, no. 2 (Spring 2007): 32–63.

Perrie, Maureen. *The Cult of Ivan the Terrible in Stalin's Russia* (Hampshire: Palgrave, 2001).

Pike, David. *The Politics of Culture in Soviet-Occupied Germany, 1945–1949* (Stanford: Stanford University Press, 1992).

———. "Censorship in Soviet-Occupied Germany." In *The Establishment of Communist Regimes in Eastern Europe, 1944–1949*, ed. Norman Naimark and Leonid Gibianskii (Boulder: Westview Press, 1997), 217–41.

Pikhoia, Rudolf G., *Sovetskii Soiuz: Istoriia Vlasti, 1945–1991* (Novosibirsk: Sibirskii Khonograf, 2000).

"Plenum TsK KPSS. Iiun 1957 goda. Stenograficheskii otchet," *Istoricheskii Arkhiv* 3 (1993): 5–94.

"Plenum TsK KPSS. Oktyabr 1964 goda. Stenofraficheskii otchet," *Istoricheskii Arkhiv* 1 (1993): 6–19.

Pleshakov, Constantine. "Nikita Khrushchev and Sino-Soviet Relations." In *Brothers in Arms: The Rise and Fall of the Sino-Soviet Alliance, 1945–1963*, ed. Odd Arne Westad (Stanford: Stanford University Press, 1998), 226–45.

Pokivailova, Tatiana A. "Moskva i Ustanovlenie monopolii Kompartii na Informatsiiu na Rubezhe 40-50-x godov." In *Moskva i Vostochnaia Evropa. Stanovlenie politicheskikh rezhimov sovetskogo tipa (1949–1953). Ocherki istorii*, ed. Tatiana V. Volokitina et al. (Moscow: ROSSPEN, 2002), 305–425.

Pollock, Ethan. *Stalin and the Soviet Science Wars* (Princeton: Princeton University Press, 2006).

Pomfret, Richard. "Trade Initiatives in Central Asia: The Economic Cooperation Organization and the Central Asian Economic Community." In *Building Security in the New States of Eurasia: Subregional Cooperation in the Former Soviet Space*, ed. Renata Dwan and Oleksandr Pavliuk (Armonk: M. E. Sharpe, 2000), 11–32.

Pons, Silvio. "A Challenge Let Drop: Soviet Foreign Policy, the Cominform and the Italian Communist Party, 1947–8." In *The Soviet Union and Europe in the Cold War, 1943–53*, ed. Francesca Gori and Silvio Pons (New York: St. Martin's Press, 1996), 246–63.

———. "Stalin, Togliatti, and the Origins of the Cold War in Europe," *Journal of Cold War Studies* 3, no. 2 (Spring 2001): 3–27.

"Posledniaia 'Antipartiinaia' Gruppa. Stenograficheskii otchet iiunskogo (1957 g.) plenuma TsK KPSS," *Istoricheskii Arkhiv* 4 (1993): 4–82.

"Posledniaia 'Antipartiinaia' Gruppa," *Istoricheskii Arkhiv* 2 (1994): 4–88.

"Posledniaia 'Antipartiinaia' Gruppa. Stenograficheskii otchet iiunskogo (1957 g.) plenuma TsK KPSS," *Istoricheskii Arkhiv* 3 (1993): 5–94.

"Posledniaia 'Antipartiinaia' Gruppa. Stenograficheskii otchet iiunskogo (1957 g.) plenuma TsK KPSS," *Istoricheskii Arkhiv* 4 (1993): 4–82.

"Posledniaia 'Antipartiinaia' Gruppa," *Istoricheskii Arkhiv* 1 (1994): 4–77.
"Posledniaia 'Antipartiinaia' Gruppa," *Istoricheskii Arkhiv* 2(1994): 4–88.
Poulantzas, Nicos. *Political Power and Social Classes* (London: New Left Books, 1975).
Pouliot, Vincent. "The Logic of Practicality," *International Organization* 62, no. 2 (2008): 257–88.
Prados, John. *Safe for Democracy: The Secret Wars of the CIA* (Chicago: Ivan R. Dee, 2006).
Price, Richard. "Reversing the Gun Sights: Transnational Civil Society Targets Land Mines," *International Organization* 52, no. 3 (1998): 613–44.
Primakov, Evgenii. *Gody v Bolshoi Politike* (Moscow: Kollektsiia Sovershenno Sekretno, 1999).
Prizel, Ilya. *National Identity and Foreign Policy: Nationalism and Leadership in Poland, Russia, and Ukraine* (Cambridge: Cambridge University Press, 1998).
Procacci, Giuliano ed. *The Cominform: Minutes ot the Three Conferences, 1947/1948/1949* (Milan: Fondazione Giangiacomo Feltrinelli, 1994).
Prozumenshchikov, M. Y. "The Sino-Indian Conflict, the Cuban Missile Crisis, and the Sino-Soviet Split, October 1962: New Evidence from the Russian Archives," *Cold War International History Project Bulletin* 8–9 (1996/1997): 251–57.
Pyzhikov, Aleksandr V. *Khrushchevskaia 'Ottepel,' 1953–1946* (Moscow: OLMA-PRESS, 2002).
———. "Problema Kulta Lichnosti v Gody Khrushchevskoi Ottepeli," *Voprosy Istorii* 4 (2003): 47–57.
Radchenko, Sergei. *Two Suns in the Heavens: Sino-Soviet Struggle for Supremacy* (Stanford: Stanford University Press, 2009).
Rakhmanin, Oleg B. "Vzaimootnosheniia I.V. Stalina I Mao Tszeduna Glazami Ochevidtsa," *Novaia i Noveishaia Istoriia* 1 (1998): 78–91.
Rakosi, Matiash. "'Videl, kak voznikaet kult lichnosti'," *Istoricheskii Arkhiv* (January 1997): 111–40.
Rakosi, Matiash. "Liudiam Svoistvenno Oshibatsia," *Istoricheskii Arkhiv* (January 1999): 3–84.
Rapoport, Yakov. *The Doctors' Plot of 1953* (Cambridge: Harvard University Press, 1991).
"*Record of Conversation, Chervonenko and Zhou Enlai, June 25, 1961.*" In *Brothers in Arms: The Rise and Fall of the Sino-Soviet Alliance, 1945–1963*, ed. Odd Arne Wedstad (Stanford: Stanford University Press, 1998), 369–74.
"Record of Conversation, Stalin and Mao Zedong, December 16, 1949." In *Brothers in Arms: The Rise and Fall of the Sino-Soviet Alliance, 1945–1963*, ed. Odd Arne Westad (Stanford: Stanford University Press, 1998), 314–18.
"Record of Conversation, Stalin and Mao Zedong, January 22, 1950." In *Brothers in Arms: The Rise and Fall of the Sino-Soviet Alliance, 1945–1963*, ed. Odd Arne Westad (Stanford: Stanford University Press, 1998), 323–29.
"Record of Conversation, Stalin and Zhou Enlai, September 19, 1952." in *Brothers in Arms: The Rise and Fall of the Sino-Soviet Alliance, 1945–1963*, ed. Odd Arne Westad (Stanford: Stanford University Press, 1998), 329–35.
"Records of Meetings of CPSU and CCP Delegations, Moscow, July 5–20, 1963." In *Brothers in Arms: The Rise and Fall of the Sino-Soviet Alliance, 1945–1963*, ed. Odd Arne Westad (Stanford: Stanford University Press, 1998), 376–90.
Reus-Smit, Christian. "The Constitutional Structure of International Society and the Nature of Fundamental Institutions," *International Organization* 51, no. 4 (1997): 555–90.
Richter, James. *Khrushchev's Double Bind: International Pressures and Domestic Coalition Politics* (Baltimore: Johns Hopkins University Press, 1994).
———. "Russian Foreign Policy and the Politics of Russian Identity." In *The Sources of Russian Foreign Policy after the Cold War*, ed. Celeste A. Wallander (Boulder: Westview, 1996), 69–94.
Risse, Thomas. "Let's Argue!: Communicative Action in World Politics," *International Organization* 54, no. 1 (2000): 1–39.
———. "Constructivism and International Institutions: Toward Conversations Across Paradigms." In *Political Science: The State of the Discipline*, ed. Ira Katznelson and Helen Milner (New York: Norton, 2002), 597–623.

Risse, Thomas, and Kathryn Sikkink. "The Socialization of International Human Rights Norms into Domestic Practices." In *The Power of Human Rights*, ed. Thomas Risse, Stephen C. Ropp, and Kathryn Sikkink (Cambridge: Cambridge University Press, 1999).

Rodovich, Iurii V. "O 'Note Stalina' ot 10 Marta 1952 g. Po Germanskomu Voprosu," *Novaia i Noveishaia Istoriia* 5 (2002): 63-79.

Ro'i, Yaacov. *Islam in the Soviet Union: From the Second World War to Gorbachev* (New York: Columbia University Press, 2000).

Rorty, Richard. *Philosophy and the Mirror of Nature* (Princeton: Princeton University Press, 1979).

Rossiiskii Illiuzion (Moscow: Materik, 2003).

Rubenstein, Joshua. *Tangled Loyalties: The Life and Times of Ilya Ehrenburg* (New York: Basic, 1996).

Ruggie, John G. "What Makes the World Hang Together?" *International Organization* 52, no. 4 (1998): 870-84.

Sakharov, Andrei D. "Pismo Prezidentu Akademii Nauk, SSSR," *Znamia* 3, no. 2 (1990).

Saveliev, Aleksandr V. "Nomenklaturnaia Borba Vokrug Zhurnala 'Voprosy Istorii' v 1954-1957 Godakh." *Otechestvennaia Istoriia* 10 (2003): 148-62.

Schutz, Alfred. *Collected Papers* (The Hague: M. Nijhoff, 1973).

Selunskaya, Valeriya, and Maria Zezina. "Documentary Film—A Soviet Source for Soviet Historians." In *Stalinism and Soviet Cinema*, ed. Richard Taylor and Derek Spring (London: Routledge, 1993), 171-85.

Semichastnyi, Vladimir. *Bespokoinoe Serdtse* (Moscow: Vagrius, 2002).

Shafer, D. Michael. *Deadly Paradigms* (Princeton: Princeton University Press, 1988).

Shakhnazarov, Georgii. *Tsena Svobody: Reformatsiia Gorbacheva Glazami ego Pomoshchnika* (Moscow: Rossika/Zevs, 1993).

———. *S Vozhdiami i Bez Nikh* (Moscow: Vagrius, 2001).

Shepilov, Dmitrii T. "Politicheskii Arkhiv XX Veka. Vospominaniia," Voprosy Istorii (March 1998): 3-24.

———. "Politicheskii Arkhiv XX Veka. Vospominaniia," Voprosy Istorii (May 1998): 3-27.

———. "Politicheskii Arkhiv XX Veka. Vospominaniia," Voprosy Istorii (June 1998): 3-45.

———. "Politicheskii Arkhiv XX Veka. Vospominaniia," Voprosy Istorii (August 1998): 3-31.

———. "Politicheskii Arkhiv XX Veka. Vospominaniia," Voprosy Istorii (September 1998): 3-33.

———. "Politicheskii Arkhiv XX Veka. Vospominaniia," Voprosy Istorii (October 1998): 3-31.

Shepsle, Kenneth A. "Institutional Equilibrium and Equilibrium Institutions." In *Political Science: The Science of Politics*, ed. Herbert Weisburg (New York: Agathon, 1986), 51-82.

Sherstianoi, Elke. "Vyzrevanie Politicheskogo Krizisa v GDR v 1953 Godu," *Novaia i Noveishaia Istoriia* 2 (2006): 34-57.

Shkarovskii, Mikhail V. *Russkaia Pravoslavnaia Tserkov i Sovetskoe Gosudarstvo v 1943-1964 Godakh. Ot "Peremiriia" k Novoi Voine* (Saint Petersburg: DEAN+ADIA-M, 1995).

———. *Russkaia Pravoslavnaia Tserkov pri Staline I Khrushcheve* (Moscow: Graal, 1999).

Shulman, Marshall D. *Stalin's Foreign Policy Reappraised* (Cambridge: Harvard University Press, 1963).

Sidorova, L. A. "'Vorposy Istorii' Akademika A. M. Pankrotovoi." In *Istorik I Vremia: 20-50-e Gody XX Veka A.M. Pankratova*, ed. Zh. V. Medvedeva (Moscow: MOSGORARKHhIV, 2000), 76-85.

Sikkink, Kathryn. *Ideas and Institutions: Developmentalism in Brazil and Argentina* (Ithaca: Cornell University Press, 1991).

———. "Human Rights, Principled Issue-Networks, and Sovereignty in Latin America," *International Organization* 47, no. 3 (1993): 411-41.

Simon, Herbert A. *Administrative Behavior* (New York: Macmillan, 1947).

Simonov, Konstantin. *Glazami Cheloveka Moego Pokoleniia: Razmyshleniia o I. V. Staline* (Moscow: Kniga, 1990).

Slezkine, Yuri. *Arctic Mirrors: Russia and the Small Peoples of the North* (Ithaca: Cornell University Press, 1994).

Smith, Kathleen E. "Gulag Survivors and Thaw Policies." Unpublished manuscript, 2006.
Smith, Rogers M. *Stories of Peoplehood: The Politics and Morals of Political Membership* (Cambridge: Cambridge University Press, 2003).
Smith, Steve. "Wendt's World." *Review of International Studies* 26, no. 1 (2000): 151–63.
Snyder, Jack. "The Gorbachev Revolution: A Waning of Soviet Expansionism?" *International Security* 12, no. 3 (1987/1988).
Solingen, Etel. *Regional Orders at Century's Dawn* (Princeton: Princeton University Press, 1998).
"The Soviet Union and Afghanistan, 1978–1989: Documents from the Russian and East German Archives," *Cold War International History Project Bulletin* 8–9 (1996/1997): 133–84.
Spar, Debora. *The Cooperative Edge: The Internal Politics of International Cartels* (Ithaca: Cornell University Press 1994).
SSSR I Germanskii Vopros, vol. II (Moscow: Mezhdunarodnye Otnosheniia, 2000).
SSSR I Germanskii Vopros, vol. III (Moscow: Mezhdunarodnye Otnosheniia, 2003).
"SSSR: Narody i Sudby," *Voennye Arkhivy Rossii* 1 (1993): 246–70.
"SSSR i Polsha: Oktiabr 1956-go," Istoricheskii Arkhiv (May-June 1996): 178–91.
Stalin, Joseph. "Speech Delivered by J. V. Stalin at a Meeting of the Voters of the Stalin Electoral District, Moscow, February 9, 1946." In *Speeches Delivered at Meetings of Voters of the Stalin Electoral District, Moscow* (Moscow: Foreign Languages Publishing House, 1950), 19–44.
Steege, Paul. "Holding on in Berlin: March 1948 and SED Efforts to Control the Soviet Zone," *Central European History* 38, no. 3 (September 2005): 417–49.
Steinmetz, George. *Regulating the Social: The Welfare State and Local Politics in Imperial Germany* (Princeton: Princeton University Press, 1997).
Sternthal, Susanne. *Gorbachev's Reforms: De-Stalinization through Demilitarization* (Westport: Praeger, 1997).
Stites, Richard. *Russian Popular Culture: Entertainment and Society since 1990* (Cambridge: Cambridge University Press, 1992).
———. "Introduction: Russia's Holy War." In *Culture and Entertainment in Wartime Russia*, ed. Richard Stites (Bloomington: Indiana University Press, 1995), 1–8.
Stivers, William. "The Incomplete Blockade: Soviet Zone Supply of West Berlin, 1948–49," *Diplomatic History* 21, no. 4 (Fall 1997): 569–602.
Suganami, Hidemi. "On Wendt's Philosophy: A Critique," *Review of International Studies* 28, no. 1 (2002): 23–37.
Swayze, Harold. *Political Control of Literature in the USSR, 1946–1959* (Cambridge: Harvard University Press, 1962).
Taliaferro, Jeffrey W., Steven E. Lobell, and Norrin M. Ripsman. "Neoclassical Realism, the State, and Foreign Policy." Introduction to *Neoclassical Realism, the State, and Foreign Policy* (Cambridge: Cambridge University Press, 2009), 1–41.
Tannenwald, Nina. "The Nuclear Taboo: The United States and the Normal Basis of Nuclear Non-Use," *International Organization* 53, no. 3 (1999): 433–68.
Taras, Raymond. "Gomulka's 'Rightist-Nationalist Deviation,' The Postwar Jewish Communists, and the Stalinist Reaction in Poland, 1945–1950," *Nationalities Papers* 22, no. 1 (1994): 111–27.
Taubman, William. "Khrushchev vs. Mao: A Preliminary Sketch of the Role of Personality in the Sino-Soviet Split," *Cold War International History Project Bulletin* 8–9 (1996/1997): 243–48.
———. *Khrushchev: The Man and His Era* (New York: W. W. Norton, 2003).
"Telegram, Stalin to Mao Zedong, April 20, 1948." In *Brothers in Arms: The Rise and Fall of the Sino-Soviet Alliance, 1945–1963*, ed. Odd Arne Westad (Stanford: Stanford University Press, 1998), 298–99.
Tikhvinskii, S. L. "Perepiska I. V. Stalina s Mao Tszedunom v Ianvare 1949 g.," *Novaia I Noveishaia Istoriia* 4–5 (1994): 132–40.
Tolchanova, Tamara, and Mikhail Lozhnikov, ed. *I Primknuvshii k nim Shepilov* (Moscow: Zvonnitsa-MG, 1998).
Tolz, Vera. "Conflicting 'Homeland Myths' and Nation-State Building in Postcommunist Russia," *Slavic Review* 57, no. 2 (Summer 1998): 267–94.

---. "'Cultural Bosses' as Patrons and Clients: The Functioning of the Soviet Creative Unions in the Postwar Period," *Contemporary European History* 11, no. 1 (2002): 87–105.
Toranska, Teresa. *"Them:" Stalin's Polish Puppets* (New York: Harper & Row, 1987).
"Transcript, Meeting of East German leader Erich Honecker and Soviet leader Leonid Brezhnev, Crimea, USSR, 25 July 1978," *Cold War International History Project Bulletin* 8–9 (1996/1997): 122–23.
Tri Vizita A. Ia. *Vyshinskogo v Bukharest, 1944–1946: Dokumenty Rossiiskikh Arkhivov* (Moscow: ROSSPEN, 1998).
Troianovskii, Oleg. *Cherez Gody I Rasstoianiia: Istoriia Odnoi Semi* (Moscow: Vagrius, 1997).
Turner, Jonathan. *A Theory of Social Interaction* (Stanford: Stanford University Press, 1988).
Turovskaya, Maya. "Soviet Films of the Cold War." In *Stalinism and Soviet Cinema*, ed. Richard Taylor and Derek Spring (London: Routledge, 1993), 131–41.
Ulunian, Artiom A. "The Soviet Union and 'the Greek Question,' 1946–53: Problems and Appraisals." In *The Soviet Union and Europe in the Cold War, 1943–53*, ed. Francesca Gori and Silvio Pons (New York: St. Martin's Press, 1996), 144–60.
---. "Gretsiia i Turtsiia: Vzgliad iz apparata TsK VKP(b)KPSS, 1946–1958." In *Stalin i Kholodnaia Voina*, ed. A. O. Chubarian (Moscow: In-t vseobshchei istorii RAN, 1997), 23–43.
Urban, Michael. "The Politics of Identity in Russia's Postcommunist Transition: The Nation Against Itself," *Slavic Review* 53, no. 3 (Fall 1994): 733–65.
"USSR/Russia—Egypt: 50 Years of Cooperation," *International Affairs* (October 1993): 83–100.
Valkenier, Elizabeth. *The Soviet Union and the Third World* (New York: Praeger, 1983).
Volkov, Fedor D. *Vlzet i Padenie Stalina* (Moscow: Spektr, 1992).
"Vengriia, Aprel-Oktiabr 1956 goda. Informatsiia Iu V Andropova," AI Mikoiana, i MA Suslova iz Budapeshta. Istoricheskii Arkhiv (April 1993), 103–42.
"Vengriia, Oktiabr-Noiabr 1956 goda," Istoricheskii Arkhiv (May 1993): 132–60.
"Vengriia, Noiabr 1956—Avgust 1957," Istoricheskii Arkhivi (June 1993): 130–44.
Vinogradov, Vladimir M. *Diplomatiia: Liudi i Sobytiia iz Zapisok Posla* (Moscow: ROSSPEN, 1998).
"'Volnodumstvo' v MGU: Dokumentalnoe Povestvovanie po Protokola. 1951–1959 gg.," *Istochnik* 3 (2002): 84–96.
Volobuev, Pavel V. "Istoriia Otvechaet ne na Vse Vorposy." In *Nauka i Vlast: Vospominaniia Uchenykh-Gumanitariev i Obshchestvovedov*, ed. G. B. Starushenko (Moscow: Nauka, 2001), 106–30.
Volokitina, Tatiana V. "Stalin i Smena Strategicheskogo Kursa Kremlia v Kontse 40-x Godov: ot Kompromissov k Konfrontatsii." In *Stalinskoe Desiatiletie Kholodnoi Voiny: Fakty i Gipotezy*, ed. I. V. Gaiduk, N. I. Yegorova and A. O. Chubarian (Moscow: Nauka, 1999), 10–22.
---. "Nakanune: Novye Realii v mezhdunarodnykh Otnosheniiakh na kontinente v kontse 40-x godov i Otvet Moskvy." In *Moskva i Vostochnaia Evropa. Stanovlenie politicheskikh rezhimov sovetskogo tipa (1949–1953), Ocherki istorii*, ed. Tatiana V. Volokitina et al. (Moscow: ROSSPEN, 2002), 27–60.
---. "Istochniki Formirovaniia Partiino-Gosudarstvennoi nomenklatury—Novogo Praviashchego Sloia." In *Moskva i Vostochnaia Evropa. Stanovlenie politicheskikh rezhimov sovetskogo tipa (1949–1953) Ocherki istorii*, ed. Tatiana P. Volokitina et al. (Moscow: ROSSPEN, 2002), 100–233.
---. "Oformlenie i Funktsionirovanie novogo Mekhanizma Gosudarstvennoi Vlasti." In *Moskva i Vostochnaia Evropa. Stanovlenie politicheskikh rezhimov sovetskogo tipa (1949–1953). Ocherki istorii*, ed. Tatiana V. Volokitina et al. (Moscow: ROSSPEN, 2002), 234–302.
Volokitina, Tatiana V., Galina P. Murashko, and Albina F. Noshova. "K Chitateliu." In *Moskva i Vostochnaia Evropa. Stanovlenie politicheskikh rezhimov sovetskogo tipa (1949–1953). Ocherki istorii*, ed. Tatiana V. Volokitina et al. (Moscow: ROSSPEN, 2002), 3–26.
Volokitina, Tatiana V. et al., eds., *Vostochnaia Evropa v Dokumentakh Rossiiskikh Arkhivov, 1944–1953 gg.*, Tom I, 1944–48 (Moscow: Sibirskii Khronograf, 1997).

———. *Vostochnaia Evropa v Dokumentakh Rossiiskikh Arkhivov, 1944–1953 gg.*, Tom II, 1949–1953 (Moscow: Sibirskii Khronograf, 1998).

———. *Moskva i Vostochnaia Evropa. Stanovlenie politicheskikh rezhimov sovetskogo tipa (1949–1953). Ocherki istorii* (Moscow: ROSSPEN, 2002).

———. *Sovetskii Faktor v Vostochnoi Evrope, 1944–1953*, vol. 2, 1949–1953 (Moscow: ROSSPEN, 2002).

Vorontsov, Aleksandr V. "'Okazat Voennuiu Pomoshch Koreiskim Tovarishcham,'" *Istochnik* 1 (1996): 123–36.

———. "Kak Prinimalos Reshenie o Vvode 'Kitaiskikh Dobrovoltsev' v Koreiu v 1950 g.," *Novaia i Noveishaia Istoriia* 2 (1998): 13–21.

Vorotnikov, Vitalii I. *A Bylo Eto Tak. Iz Dnevnika Chlena Politbiuro TsK KPSS* (Moscow: Sovet veteranov knigoizdaniia/SI-MAR, 1995).

Vorotnikov, Vitalii I. *Takoe Vot Pokolenie* (Moscow: Print-Servis, 1999).

Vtoroi Vsesouznyi Syezd Sovetskikh Pisatelei: 15–26 Dekabria 1954 goda, Stenograficheskii Otchet (Moscow, 1956).

Walt, Stephen M. *The Origins of Alliances* (Ithaca: Cornell University Press 1987).

Waltz, Kenneth. "Evaluating Theories," *American Political Science Review* 91, no. 4 (1997): 913–17.

Weathersby, Kathryn. "Sovetskie Tseli v Koree, 1945–1950." In *Kholodnaia Voina: Novye Podkhody, Novye Dokumenty*, ed. M. M. Narinskii (Moscow: Institute of General History, 1995), 315–33.

———. "New Russian Documents on the Korean War," *Cold War International History Project Bulletin* 6–7 (Winter 1995/1996): 30–84.

———. "Stalin, Mao, and the End of the Korean War." In *Brothers in Arms: The Rise and Fall of the Sino-Soviet Alliance, 1945–1963*, ed. Odd Arne Westad (Stanford: Stanford University Press, 1998), 90–116.

Weiner, Amir. *Making Sense of the War: The Second World War and the Fate of the Bolshevik Revolution* (Princeton: Princeton University Press, 2001).

Weinerman, Eli. "The Polemics between Moscow and Central Asians on the Decline of Central Asia and Tsarist Russia's Role in the History of the Region," *Slavic and East European Review* 71, no. 3 (July 1993): 428–81.

Weldes, Jutta. *Constructing National Interests: The United States and the Cuban Missile Crisis* (Minneapolis: University of Minnesota Press, 1999).

Weldes, Jutta et al., eds. *Cultures of Insecurity: States, Communities and the Production of Danger* (Minneapolis: University of Minnesota Press, 1999).

Wendt, Alexander. "Levels of Analysis vs. Agents and Structures: Part III," *Review of International Studies* 18 (1991): 181–85.

———. "Anarchy is What States Make of It," *International Organization* 46, no. 2 (1992): 391–425.

———. "Collective Identity Formation and the International State," *American Political Science Review* 88, no. 2 (1994): 384–96.

———. *Social Theory of International Politics* (Cambridge: Cambridge University Press, 1999).

Westad, Odd Arne. "Concerning the Situation in `A': New Russian Evidence on the Soviet Intervention in Afghanistan," *Cold War International History Project Bulletin* 8–9 (1996/1997): 128–32.

———. "Moscow and the Angolan Crisis, 1974–1976: A New Pattern of Intervention," *Cold War International History Project Bulletin* 8–9 (1996/1997): 21–32.

———. Introduction to *Brothers in Arms: The Rise and Fall of the Sino-Soviet Alliance, 1945–1963*, ed. Odd Arne Westad (Stanford: Stanford University Press, 1998), 1–46.

———. *The Global Cold War: Third World Interventions and the Making of Our Times* (Cambridge: Cambridge University Press, 2005).

Widdis, Emma. "Russia as Space." In *National Identity in Russian Culture*, ed. Simon Franklin and Emma Widdis (Cambridge: Cambridge University Press, 2004), 30–50.

Wilson, Jeanne L. "Strategic Partners: Russian-Chinese Relations and the July 2001 Friendship Treaty," *Problems of Post-Communism* 49, no. 3 (May/June 2002): 3–13.

Wishnick, Elizabeth. *Mending Fences: The Evolution of Moscow's China Policy from Brezhnev to Yeltsin* (London: University of Washington Press, 2001).

Wohlforth, William. *The Elusive Balance: Power and Perceptions during the Cold War* (Ithaca: Cornell University Press, 1993).

Yazhborovskaia, I. S. "Vovlechenie Polshi v Stalinskuiu Blokovuiu Politiju: Problemy i Metody Davleniia na Plskoe Rukovodstvo. 1940-e gody." In *Stalin i Kholodnaia Voina*, ed. A. O. Chubarian (Moscow: In-t vseobshchei istorii RAN, 1997), 84–101.

Yegorova, N. I. "NATO i Evropeiskaia Bezopasnost: Vospriiatie Sovetskogo Rukovodstva." In *Stalin i Kholodnaia Voina*, ed. A. O. Chubarian (Moscow: Institutvseobshchei istorii RAN, 1997), 291–314.

———. "Evropeiskaia Bezopasnost i 'Ugroza' NATO v Otsenkakh Stalinskogo Rukovodstva." In *Stalinskoe Desiatiletie Kholodnoi Voiny: Fakty i Gipotezy*, ed. I. V. Gaiduk, N. I. Yegorova, and A.O. Chubarian (Moscow: Nauka, 1999), 56–78.

Yeltsin, Boris. *The Struggle for Russia* (New York: Times Books, 1994).

Yurchak, Alexei. "Gagarin and the Rave Kids: Transforming Power, Identity, and Aesthetics in Post-Soviet Nightlife." In Consuming Russia: *Popular Culture, Sex, and Society Since Gorbachev*, ed. Adele Marie Barker (Durham: Duke University Press, 1999), 76–109.

———. *Everything was Forever, Until it was No More: The Last Soviet Generation* (Princeton: Princeton University Press 2006).

"Za Sovetami v Kreml: Zapis Besedy I. V. Stalina s Rukovoditeliami SEPG. Mart 1948 g.," *Istoricheskii Arkhiv* 2 (2002): 3–27.

"Zakrytoe Pismo TsK VKP(b)—O Dele Professorov Kliuevoi i Roskina," *Kentavr*, no. 2 (1994): 65–69.

Zehfuss, Maja. "Constructivism and Identity: A Dangerous Liaison," *European Journal of International Relations* 7, no. 3 (2001): 315–48.

Zezina, Mariia R. *Sovetskaia Khudozhestvennaia Intelligentsiia I Vlast v 1950-e-60-e Gody* (Moscow: Dialog-MGU, 1999).

Zhang, Shu Guang. *Economic Cold War: America's Embargo against China and the Sino-Soviet Alliance, 1949–1963* (Washington, DC: Woodrow Wilson Center Press, 2001).

Zhelitski, Bela. "Nazrevanie Obshchestvennogo nedovolstva I Politicheskogo Krizisa v Vengrii v Pervoi Polovine 50-x godov." In *Vengriia 1956 goda: Ocherki Istorii Krizisa*, ed. Bela Zhelitski, T. M. Islamov, and Iu. S. Novopashin (Moscow: Nauka, 1993), 13–49.

———. "Budapesht—Moskva: god 1956-I." In *Sovetskaia Vneshniaia Politika v Gody "Kholodnoi Voiny (1945–1985),"* ed. L. N. Nezhinskii (Moscow: Mezhdunar otnosheniia, 1995), 241–82.

———. "Postwar Hungary, 1944–1946." In *The Establishment of Communist Regimes in Eastern Europe, 1944–1949*, ed. Norman Naimark and Leonid Gibianskii (Boulder: Westview Press, 1997), 73–92.

———. "Tragicheskaia Sudba Laslo Raika. Vengriia 1949g," *Novaia i Noveishaia Istoriia* 2 (2001): 125–38.

———. "Arest Raika. Smena Kontseptsii 'Dela'," *Novaia i Noveishaia Istoriia* 3 (2001): 166–86.

———. "Imre Nad," *Voprosy Istorii* (August 2006): 50–77.

Zhihua, Shen. "Sino-Soviet Relations and the Origins of the Korean War: Stalin's Strategic Goals in the Far East," *Journal of Cold War Studies* 2, no. 2 (Spring 2000): 44–68.

Zhukov, Iu. N. "Borba za Vlast v Rukovodstve SSSR v 1945–1952 godakh," *Voprosy Istorii* 1 (1995): 23–39.

Zhukov, Iurii. *Stalin: Tainy Vlasti* (Moscow: Vagrius, 2005).

Zimmerman, William. *The Russian People and Foreign Policy: Russian Elite and Mass Perspectives, 1993–2000* (Princeton: Princeton University Press, 2002).

Zubarevich, Natalia V., and Yuri E. Fedorov. "Russian-Southern Economic Interaction: Partners or Competitors." In *Russia, the Caucasus, and Central Asia: The 21st Century Security Environment*, ed. Rajan Menon, Yuri E. Fedorov and Ghia Nodia (Armonk: M. E. Sharpe, 1999), 119–44.

Zubkova, Elena Iu. *Obshchestvo i Reformy: 1945–1964* (Moscow: Rossiia Molodaia, 1993).

———. "Malenkov i Khrushchev: Lichnyi Faktor v Politike Poslestalinskogo Rukovodstva," *Otechestvennaia Istoriia* 4 (1995): 103–15.

———. *Russia After the War: Hopes, Illusions, and Disappointments, 1945–1957* (Armonk: M. E. Sharpe, 1998).

———. "Mir Mnenii Sovetskogo Cheloveka. 1945–1948 Gody," *Otechestvennaia Istoriia* 3 (1998): 25–39.

———. "Mir Mnenii Sovetskogo Cheloveka. 1945–1948 gg.," *Otechestvennaia Istoriia* 4 (1998): 99–108.

———. "Stalin i Obshchestvennoe Mnenie v SSSR, 1945–1953." In *Stalinskoe Desiatiletie Kholodnoi Voiny: Fakty i Gipotezy*, ed. I. V. Gaiduk, N. I. Yegorova and A. O. Chubarian (Moscow: Nauka, 1999), 151–70.

———. "The Rivalry with Malenkov." In *Nikita Khrushchev*, ed. William Taubman, Sergei Khrushchev, and Abbott Gleason (New Haven: Yale University Press, 2000), 67–84.

———. "Sovetskii Faktor v Baltiiskom Regione: Kadrovaia Politika kak Mekhanizm Sovetizatsii, (1944–1947 gg.)." In *Stalin. Stalinizm. Sovetskoe Obshchestvo*, ed. G. Sh. Sagateian, B. S. Ilizarov and O. V. Khlevniuk (Moscow: Zvezdopad, 2000), 194–211.

———. "Fenomen "Mestnogo Natsionalizma: 'stonskoe Delo' 1949–1952 Godov v Kontekste Sovetizatsii Baltii," *Otechestvennaia Istoriia* (May 2001): 89–102.

———. "'Lesnye Bratia' v Pribaltike: Voina Posle Voiny," *Otechestvennaia Istoriia* (February 2007): 74–90.

Zubok, Vladislav. "The Case of Divided Germany, 1953–1964." In *Nikita Khrushchev*, ed. William Taubman, Sergei Khrushchev, and Abbott Gleason (New Haven: Yale University Press, 2000), 275–300.

———. *The Soviet Union in the Cold War from Stalin to Gorbachev* (Durham, University of North Carolina Press, 2007).

———. *A Failed Empire: The Soviet Union in the Cold War from Stalin to Gorbachev* (Chapel Hill: University of North Carolina Press, 2009).

Zubok, Vladislav, and Constantine Pleshakov. *Inside the Kremlin's Cold War* (Cambridge: Harvard University Press, 1996).

INDEX

Abakumov, Viktor, 95, 146
Abramov, Fedor
   "People of the Kolkhoz Countryside," 152
Abrasimov, Petr, 214n68
Acheson, Dean, 127
Ackermann, Anton, 220, 221
Adenauer, Konrad, 116
Admiral Ushakov, 51
Afghanistan, 5, 236, 237, 239, 259, 260
Ageev, V., 187
Agranenko, Zakhar
   We are Together, 187
Akhmatova, Anna, 39, 69, 84, 111, 117, 154, 179n146
Albania, 81, 106
   central committee, 108
   Stalinization, 87–88
   Yugoslav relations, 106, 107, 108, 136
Aleksandrov, Georgii, 40, 49, 51, 53, 107, 111, 179, 194
Alexeyeva, Ludmilla, 54, 170
Algeria, 131, 239–40
Aliger, Margarita, 183, 187, 189, 191
al-Kuni, Mohammed, 241
Allied Control Commission (ACC), 140, 141
Allies, 132n281, 136
All-Union Economic Exhibition, 158n60
Althusser, Louis, 19
Angola, 12
anti-racism, 9n3
anti-Semitism,
   Eastern Europe, 256
   Moscow, 212n54
   Russian nation, 159–62
   Soviet Union, 33, 51, 53, 54–55, 78, 93, 133, 158, 176, 180
Argentina
   economic development, 22
   trade relations, 237

Aristov, Averky, 210
Armenia, 50, 164n88
atomic bombs
   Japan, 7
   Soviet Union, 114, 245
   United States, 134, 135, 136
Auezov, Mukhtar, 151, 163, 164
Auschwitz (concentration camp), 116
Azerbaijan, 82, 146, 168
Azhaev, Vasilii
   Far from Moscow, 34, 65

Babel, Isaac, 179, 226
Babochkin, Boris, 53
Baghdad Pact, 237, 250
Balkyrs, 164
Baranov, L. S., 105
Barnet, Boris
   Secret Agent's Feat, 38
Belarus, 42, 47, 54, 144, 159, 162, 163, 165, 194
   population, 255
Belgrade, Serbia, 3, 4, 81
   Cominform, 86
   Operation Whirlwind, 2094
   relationship with Albania, 107
   relationship with Soviet Union, 199, 222–23, 225n123, 126, 259
Belkin, M. I., 91
Benedek, Dr., 94
Benes, Edvard, 97
Bergen-Belsen (concentration camp), 116
Beria, Lavrentii, 37, 192, 217
   arrest, 148n13, 150, 160, 220
   attacks on Rakosi, 200
   Banana Affair, 31
   freeing of prisoners in labor camps and penal colonies, 144, 149
   funeral speech, 145
   Gomulka trial, 87n68

Beria, Lavrentii (*continued*)
   investigation of Doctors' Plot, 152, 159
   19th Party Congress, 50
   post-Stalin, 5, 22, 56, 143–46, 148, 152, 159, 162, 257–58, 261
   proposed redirecting investments, 148
   rupture with Yugoslavia, 4, 224n115, 225n123
   treatment of prisoners, 150
Berlin, Germany, 66, 199
   airlift, 4
   blockade, 4, 109n159, 111, 135, 140, 141, 248, 249
   closing of border, 215
   East, 213, 218, 220
   elections, 113, 114
   food packages, 141n325, 219
   protests, 218
   Soviet march into, 115
   summit in 1953, 243n206
   unrest, 220
   West, 135, 141n325, 219
Berman, Adolph, 89n73
Berman, Jakub, 86, 89n75, 94, 100, 105, 212n54
Bernadotte, Folke, 133
Bevin, Ernest, 140
Bierut, Bolesław, 76, 80, 87, 94, 95, 100, 104, 105, 211, 212
"Bibliography of Russian Literature," 85
The Big Life (film), 39, 65, 69, 183
Bizonia, 140
Blaney, David L., 14
Bodrov, M. F., 105
Bolshakov, Ivan, 34, 37, 51
Bolshoi Theater, 52, 124
Brandenberger, David, 48, 51, 158–59
Brazil, 12, 22
British Broadcasting Company (BBC), 61
Brussels Pact, 3, 139
Brzezinski, Zbigniew
   Unity and Disunity in the Soviet Bloc, 73n1
Bubennov, Mikhail, 161, 162
Buchenwald (concentration camp), 115, 116
Budapest, Hungary
   communist parties, 77
   elections, 74
   Mikoian visit, 203
   Soviet relations, 85, 90, 94, 101, 104, 200, 206, 208
      armed forces in, 202, 204–5, 207
   writers, 155
Bukharin, Nikolai, 179, 201
Bulganin, Nikolai, 56, 85, 146, 152, 153, 157, 191, 206, 207, 210, 225, 227, 236, 238, 241, 242, 246, 247
Bulgaria, 71, 74, 75, 77, 99
   armed forces, 82, 100n117,
   constitution, 106
   political criminals, 90
   rejected Stalin's order to merge with Yugoslavia, 109
   Soviet grain for Greek resistance, 81
   Soviet relations, 92, 105, 108, 110
   treaty with Hungary, 107, 108
   treaty with Yugoslavia, 136
   Western influence, 88
Bulgarian Communist Party, 73
Burma, 5, 233, 236, 237
Bush, George W., 19
Byrnes, James, 137, 138

camps, concentration. *See* concentration camps
camps, labor. *See* labor camps
camps, prison. *See* prison camps
capitalist encirclement, 244, 247–48, 253, 260
capitalists, 64, 167, 252, 267
   Czechoslovakia, 208
   East Germany, 216
   humane, 187
   right of, 85
   Poland, 86
   Russia, 76
   Soviet Union, 237, 249, 259
   United States, 135, 139
   West, 98, 153, 156, 189, 254
   Yugoslavia, 221
capitalist countries/states, 5, 89, 150, 158, 181, 249, 250, 251, 263
Catholics, 57, 77, 86
   Lithuanian, 47
   Poland, 87, 211
   Russia, 59, 95, 215
Catroux, Georges, 131
Central Asia, 44, 65, 168, 255
   Muslim clergy, 167
   socialism, 238
   Soviet Union relations, 50, 124, 164, 177, 238, 241, 252, 260, 267
   writers, 164
Changchun, China, 119, 125, 230
Charles University, 101
Chechens, 164
Checkel, Jeffrey T., 15
Chekhov, Anton, 55
Cherniaev, Anatolii, 173, 193
Chervenkov, Vulko, 92
Chiang, Kai-shek, 118, 230
China
   Great Leap Forward, 4, 6, 199, 259
   Korean War, 118, 126–30
   Kuomintang, 117, 118, 119, 121, 122, 125, 230, 233, 257
   People's Liberation Army (PLA), 119, 121, 122, 127
   Politburo, 230

Index

socialism, China, 124, 229, 233, 259
Soviet Union's relations with. *See* Sino-Soviet relations
Treaty of Friendship and Cooperation, 4
US relations with. *See* Sino-American relations
See also Changchun; Chiang, Kai-shek; Harbin; Kim, Jong Il; Mao, Zedong; Nanking; Port Arthur; Quiqihaer; Shaoqi, Liu
Chinese Communist Party (CCP), 117, 119–20, 121, 122–23, 230, 234
Christian Democratic Union (CDU), 114
Chuikov, Vasilii, 216
Chukhrai, Grigorii
    The Forty-First, 174
Chukovsky, Kornei, 146n9, 156, 168
Churchill, Winston, 80, 114n191, 137
Clark, Katerina, 66, 67, 69
Clementis, Vladimir, 93, 104, 132
Cominform, 3, 82, 84, 85, 86, 97, 98, 103, 105, 106, 108n160, 110, 122, 136, 223, 256
Communist International (Comintern), 3, 75. *See also* Cominform
concentration camps, 31, 75, 100, 115, 116, 144, 150, 160, 187. *See also* Auschwitz; Bergen-Belsen; Buchenwald; Dachau; Sachsenhausen
Congress of Criminology, 91
Congress of Engineers, 91
Congress of Veterinarians, 91
Congress on Forestry, 91
constructivism, 15
    definition, 6–7, 8n1, 9
    norm-centric, 14–16
    societal, 5, 6, 8, 9, 10, 11, 13, 14, 16–17, 29, 47, 72, 196, 255, 257, 258, 260–62, 263, 264
        and institutions, 20–23
        international politics, 23
        and liberalism, 17–20
        sources and methods, 23–28
        (*see also specific location, e.g.,* Eastern Europe)
    systemic, 8, 10–14, 16, 257, 262, 263
        international politics, 10, 11
    theoretical implications, 260–64
    weak, 15
cosmopolitanism, 50n68, 58, 89n75, 159, 161n75, 256
    anti-, 33, 50, 54, 63, 89, 94, 107, 132, 161n73, 162
Council of Foreign Ministers (CFM), 99, 141
    London meeting, 73, 137, 140
    Moscow meeting, 114
    New York meeting, 132
    Paris meeting, 138

Couve de Murville, Maurice Jacques, 113
"cultural match," 15
Czechoslovakia, 71, 74n8
    Allied treaty, 136
    armed forces, 90
    Central Committee, 93
        Information Department, 103
    coup, 97, 109n159
    Israel relations, 132–33
    letter against Tito, 110
    Politburo, 110
    political criminals, 90
    servility before the West, 88
    Slansky Affair, 92–95
    socialism, 85, 93
    Soviet Union relations, 79, 84, 85, 92–93, 97, 103–4, 108, 208, 240
    spies, 103–4
    Stalin's 70th birthday, 101
    treaty with Poland, 77
    US relations, 97
    Yugoslavia relations, 110
    See also Charles University; Prague

Dachau (concentration camp), 116
Dele bylo v Penkove/It Happened in Penkov, 172
détente, 5, 199, 253
Dimitrov, Georgi, 73, 75, 92, 99, 107, 108, 109n150, 123n232, 136
Djilas, Milovan, 67, 107, 123n232, 136
Dolgorukii, Iurii, 48
domestic policy
    choices, 19n52
    See also specific country, e.g., Yugoslavia
Dubinin, Nikolai, 157
Dudintsev, Vladimir, 183, 184, 185n168, 186, 187n174, 191, 192
    Not by Bread Alone, 154, 175, 188–89
Dunham, Vera, 66
Dymshits, Alexander, 117

East Berlin, Germany, 213, 218, 220
Eastern Europe
    allies, 73, 75, 78, 83, 85, 90, 91, 96, 98, 100, 101, 102, 106, 107, 108, 109n166, 110, 128n262, 134, 135, 198, 231n147, 258, 262, 263
    anti-Semitism, 78, 256
    communists, 74, 75, 76, 79, 90, 99, 100, 103, 105, 198, 259
    constitutions, 116
    fear of United States, 136
    and Germany, 136–42
    marriages banned, 61
    New Course, 198, 201, 202, 203, 204, 211, 234, 259
    relationship with Hungary, 236, 259

Eastern Europe (*continued*)
  relationship with Soviet Union, 70–76, 83, 111–12, 198, 210, 212, 221, 234, 252, 253, 256, 261, 264, 266
  relationship with United States, 136–42, 199, 256
  relationship with Yugoslavia, 110–11, 224, 225, 227, 259
  socialism, 87, 90, 111, 128, 256
  societal constructivism, 6, 28
  Stalinization, 3, 72–73, 83–108, 112, 115, 123, 136, 137, 139, 142, 199, 252, 262, 263, 265, 266
    de-, 4, 5, 30, 144, 145–46, 164, 196, 197, 200, 202, 206, 211, 212, 213, 215, 217, 230, 235, 243–44
    re-, 182, 203, 210
East Germany, 217
  emigration, 219n93
  socialism, 216, 217–18, 254
  Soviet relations, 5, 73, 78, 85, 100, 111–17, 141, 213, 218, 220
    armed forces in, 138, 246n217
    economic aid, 219
    land reform legislation, 102–3
    New Course, 216, 217, 218, 219, 220–21
    Stalin advised not to join Cominform, 136
  US relations, 219
Egypt, 8, 133
  invasion of, 82, 207n37, 240–41, 242n200
  Soviet relations, 239, 240–41, 259
  Suez crisis, 236
Ehrenburg, Ilya, 55, 176–77, 179n146, 183, 188–89, 190, 191, 248
  Second Day, 56
  The Storm, 33
  The Thaw, 150n27, 155, 171, 173, 174
  visit to the United States, 63
Eisenhower, Dwight D., 185, 242, 244n208, 246–47, 249, 251
Eisenstein, Sergei
  Ivan the Terrible, Part One, 60
  Ivan the Terrible II, 39, 60, 135
endogenization, 22
Enlai, Zhou, 123n230, 123n232, 125n241, 130, 133, 136, 231
Ermilov, Vladimir, 34
European Recovery Plan (ERP), 3, 96, 97, 139
  See also Marshall Plan

Fadeev, Aleksandr, 62, 68, 189
  general secretary of the Union of Writers, 33, 151, 161, 171
  meeting with Stalin, 65
  memo to Khrushchev and Malenkov, 171
  Molodaia Gvardiia (*Young Guard*), 67, 69, 179, 256

The Rout, 55
  suicide, 146n9, 179, 180
The Fall of Berlin, 34, 66
Far East, 65, 83, 119, 124, 128
Farkas, Mikhail, 94
Farkash, Mihaly, 202, 203, 203, 204n22, 209
Fearon, James, 14
Federenko, Nikolai, 124
Feltrinelli, Giorgio, 184n163, 188
Ferents, Nad, 79
Finland, 167, 224, 247. *See also* Helsinki
Finnemore, 15
Firiubin, Nikolai, 227
Formosa, 122, 124
France
  Francophone Africa, 10

Gaddis, John Lewis, 127n250
Games of the Underground World, 84
Gamzatov, Rasul, 49
Gang, Gao, 123
Gati, Charles, 206
Geneva, Switzerland, 4, 243, 247
  summit, 201, 246, 249
Geneva Accords, 4, 243
Gerasimov, Sergei, 53, 155
Germany, 4, 48, 266
  alliances, 79
  Academy of Sciences, 117
  Christian Democratic Union (CDU), 114
  Eastern Europe relations, 137–42
  films, 37, 64, 117
  foreign plays, 117
  Liberal Democratic Party (LDP), 114
  Nazi, 84, 171, 253
  rapes, 102, 114
  Social Democratic Party (SDP), 76, 114
  socialism, 117, 218, 220
  Soviet Union relations, 80, 83, 90, 96, 112, 113, 115, 131, 134, 215–21, 228, 239, 244
    Four Power agreements, 112, 119, 141, 243
  Soviet Union-US relations, 136–42
  victimization of Slavics, 77
  Weimar Republic constitution, 116
  See also Berlin; concentration camps; East Germany; Nazis; Stuttgart; West Berlin; West Germany
Gero, Erno, 203, 204, 205, 209, 210
Ghana, 236, 238
Gheorgiu-Dej, Gheorge, 76n13, 78, 80n33, 103, 104
Gibianskii, Leonid, 74n6, 106, 109
Goban-Klas, Tomasz, 89
Gomulka, Wladyslaw, 75, 77, 82, 84, 86, 89, 94, 100, 103, 110, 211, 213–15, 259
Gomulka Affair, 87, 93n93, 104, 252

Goncharov, Ivan, 161
  Fregat Pallada, 54n91
Gorbachev, Boris, 193n197, 202, 229
Gorbatov, Boris, 62
Gordov, Lieutenant General, 42
Gorkii, Maksim, 49
Gorky Institute of World Literature, 181n154
Gosplan, 137, 234
Gottwald, Klement, 77, 93, 97, 103, 104, 128
Great Britain, 12, 79, 73, 207
  Bizonia, 140
  Czechoslovia relations, 97
  economic conditions, 266
  Germany relations, 138
  Greece relations, 96
  invasion of Egypt, 240, 241
  Khrushchev's visit, 155
  Korean War, 128
  Soviet Union relations, 141, 157
  Suez crisis, 241
  Turkey relations, 96
  writers, 154
  See also Bergen-Belsen; British Boradcasting Company; Churchill, Winston
Great Leap Forward, 4, 6, 199, 259
Greece, 82
  civil war, 109, 249
  communists, 81, 82
  Democratic Army of, 81
  partisans, 107
  resistance, 81
  Soviet foreign policy, 244
  US military support, 3, 96, 108, 133, 136
Grigorian, V. G., 88
Gromyko, Andrei, 122, 126, 132, 133, 222, 226, 247
Grossman, Vasilii
  "For a Just Cause," 68
  For a Just Cause, 151
Grotewolhl, Otto, 78, 116, 138, 219
Gunther, Hans, 66

Habermas, Juergen, 20
Hall, Peter A., 17
Hansen, Hans Christian, 249
Harbin, China, 119
Harvard University, 49, 96
Hegedus, Andras, 201, 203, 210
Heifits, Iosif
  Big Family, 169
  The Rumiantsev Affair, 169
Helsinki, Finland, 91
Hemingway, Ernest
  Old Man and the Sea, 155
Herrnstadt, Rudolf, 220, 221
Higher Party School, 101
Hiroshima, Japan, 7, 134

historiography, 264–67
Hitler, Adolf, 29, 80, 81, 187, 254
  anti-Hitler underground, 86
Hobbesian world, 11, 12
Ho Chi Minh, 5, 123, 131
Hollywood, CA, 33, 188
Horthy, 94
Horthyites, 209
Hoxa, Enver, 87, 88n69
human rights, 23n62
  See also International Congress of Jurists on Human Rights
Hungary, 90
  Allied Control Commission (ACC), 74
  Bourgeois Democratic Party, 74
  Central Committee, 85
  invasion of, 178, 182–93, 198, 199–211, 227
  National Peasants Party, 74
  New Course, 221
  occupation army, 102
  Politburo, 201, 202, 203, 204
  political criminals, 90
  rebellion, 5, 84
  Smallholders Party, 74
  socialism, 201, 204, 209
  Soviet Union relations, 28, 79, 84, 92, 105, 110, 176
  spies, 93
  Western influence, 88
  See also Budapest; Rajk Affair

Iashin, Alexander, 192
  Levers, 190
Iceland, 82, 141
Ilyichev, Ivan, 216
Ilyichev, Leonid, 34
Inayatullah, Naeem, 14
India, 194n203
  art exhibitions, 155
  communists, 238
  film industry, 34
  relationship with China, 127
  relationship with Soviet Union, 5, 6, 224, 236, 237, 238–39, 252, 259
Indochina, 131
Indonesia, 82, 132, 224n114
Ingush, 164
Inner Mongolia, 121
Inostrannaia Literatura/Foreign Literature, 155
Institute of Marx, Engels, and Lenin, 48
Institute of Oriental Studies, 181n154
Institute of Physical Chemistry, 52
Institute of Theoretical and Experimental Physics, 181
Institute of World Economics and International Relations (IMEMO), 251
Institute of World Literatures, 163

International Congress of Jurists on Human Rights, 91
International Congress of Meteorologists, 91
International Exhibit of Philately, 91
International Organization of Health Care, 91
international politics, 16–17, 19, 20n56
    societal constructivism, 23
    systemic constructivism, 10, 11
International Relations Institute, 249
international relation (IR) theory, 17
    constructivist, 23
    reductionist, 14
Iran, 81–82, 237, 250, 260, 261, 263
Iraq, 61n122, 82n43
Israel, 10, 20, 58, 89n75
    invasion of Egypt, 207n37, 240, 241
    recognition as state, 132–33
    Ukrainian relations, 59
Italian Communist Party (PCI), 98, 100
Italian Socialist Party, 135
Italy
    communist party, 98, 107, 188
    film festival, 155
    rightist deviationism, 110n170
    socialism, 98
    Soviet Union relations, 99
    Tito's plan for attack, 108n156
Iudin, Pavel, 105, 122n226, 216, 218, 230
Izvestiia, 34, 55, 63

Japan, 34, 80, 125, 126, 129, 134, 137, 138
    film industry, 34
    surrender, 119
    See also Hiroshima; Nagasaki
Jewish Anti-Fascist Committee, 51, 52n77
Jews, 50n68, 53, 54, 58, 132
    Eastern European leaders, 94
    Hungarian, 94
    Institute of Physical Chemistry, 52
    massacre at Babi Yar, 33
    Polish, 212n54
    purge of, 52
    Rumanian, 79
    Russian, 47, 165, 255
    Soviet, 51, 55–56, 95, 159–60, 163
    Ukrainian, 59
    writers, 161
    See also anti-Semitism
Jones, Polly, 181

Kachmarek, Bishop, 211
Kadar, Janos, 201n6, 202–3, 204, 205, 206, 207, 208, 209, 210, 252, 259
Kaganovich, Lazar, 152, 153, 182, 191, 192, 201, 204n20, 205, 206, 207, 210, 218, 225, 226n137, 228, 239, 244, 245, 249n227, 258

Kalmyks, 164
Kamenev, Lev, 177, 179
Kantian world, 11, 12
Karachaevtsy, 164, 165
Kardelj, Edvard, 107, 110, 123n232, 136
Kaunas, Lithuania, 182
Kazakevich, Emmanuil, 187, 188, 189
    A House on the Square, 190n184
Kazakstan, 56, 194, 226, 239
Kennan, George, 130, 267
Khikmet, Nazym
    But Was that Ivan Ivanovich?, 185, 190
Khomeini, Ayatollah, 261
Khrushchev, Nikita, 6, 25, 28, 40nn30–31, 144, 145, 146, 148n13, 150–51, 157, 162, 171, 174, 182n158, 185, 186, 191–94, 205–7, 242, 245, 246
    agricultural reforms, 156
    Arzumanian's memo for, 251
    Baptist bimonthly approval of, 166
    Belgrade visited by, 4
    CC Plenum
        July 1955, 250n232
    de-Stalinization speech, 143, 152, 164n88, 180, 221, 230, 250
    East German relations and, 247n217
    Egypt relations and, 240, 241
    Eisenhower's meetings with, 247
    GDR visited by, 220
    Germany relations and, 219–20
    Great Britain visited by, 155
    Hansen's meeting with, 249
    India, Burma, and Afghanistan visited by, 5, 236–37, 239
    July 9–12, 1955 CC Plenum, 223
    July 14, 1956 communication with Micunovic, 213
    labor disputes, 160
    Micunovic's meeting with, 249
    NATO, 249
    "On the Cult of Personality and its Consequences," 177–78
    ouster of, 229
    Poland relations and, 212, 214
    Presidium, 56, 143, 148n15, 209–11
        February 9, 1956, 249n227
        April 13, 1957, 247
    reduction of Soviet troops, 148
    Sheplov's opposition of, 182n158
    Sino-Soviet relations and, 230n144, 231, 232–35, 259
    societal constructivism, 258
    Stalin's birthday party, 124
    Twentieth Party Congress, 202, 203, 224–25, 230, 244, 248, 249
    U-2 incident and, 247n218
    US relations and, 247

UW Plenum meeting in May 1957, 188–89, 194
Yugoslavia relations and, 224–25, 227–28
Zhukov meetings with, 247
Khutsiev, Marlen
Spring on Zarechnaia Street, 169
Kiev, Ukraine, 46n51, 52, 65, 176
anti-religion, 167
synagogue attendance, 160
Kim, Jong Il, 118, 127
Kirichenko, Alexei, 163, 225, 245
Kirov, Soviet Union, 40, 179
Kiselev, Evgenii, 92, 201, 202n14, 241
Kliszko, Zenon, 100
Kliueva, Nina, 61, 62
Kliueva-Roskin affair, 36
Kochetov, Vsevolod, 107, 111, 194
Zhurbiny, 54
Kolman, Arnost, 101
Komsomolskaia Pravda, 53, 55, 145n2
Konchalovskaia, Natalia P., 162
Koptiaeva, Antonina
Ivan Ivanovich, 33
Korea, 118, 136, 199, 230, 253
See also North Korea; South Korea
Korean Peoples' Army (KPA), 129, 130
Korean War, 4, 72, 83, 126–30, 136, 142, 229, 230, 243, 244, 250, 251
Korneichuk, Aleksandr, 185, 239
Koshevoi, Oleg, 67
Kostov, Traicho, 92, 93, 107, 123n232
Koval, Igor, 234
Kovalev, Ivan, 120, 124, 135
Krasnaia Zvezda, 26, 223, 249
Kremlin, 5, 49, 81, 99, 124, 146n9, 190, 212, 214
Kruglov, Sergei, 42–43, 160
Kruzhkov, V. S., 164, 165, 167, 168
Kuban Cossacks, 34
Kultura and Zhizn (*Culture and Life*), 35
Kutuzov, General, 115
Kuznetsov, Aleksei, 51
Kyrgystan, 164

labor camps, 106, 144, 149, 176n137, 187, 190n184
See also prison camps
lakirovanie (varnishing), 45, 68, 193
Lavrentiev, Anatolii, 109
Lebedev, Viktor, 86, 87, 89, 94
Lenin, Vladimir, 76, 78, 109–10, 151, 152, 163, 183
dangers of Leftist extremism, 224, 237
imperialism theory, 80, 135
New Economic Policy, 217
"Out with the Non-Party Writers!", 33
party literature, 171
tolerance for dissent, 177–78
See also Marxism-Leninism

Leningrad, Russia, 36, 47, 65, 180
artistic intelligentsia, 187n176
Writer's Union, 69, 154, 169, 181n154, 194
Leningrad (journal), 35, 39, 59, 65, 67, 69, 183
Leningrad Affair, 138, 146
Leningrad Library Institute, 195
Leningrad University, 182
Lenin Library, 170
Lenin Museum, 145n2
Lenin Prizes, 146, 187n174
Leonov, Leonid, 162
Russian Forest, 34, 173
Liberal Democratic Party (LDP), 114
liberalism, 163, 266
societal constructivism and, 17–20
state as institutional resource, 21
Likharev, Boris, 59
Literaturnaia Gazeta (*LG*), 26, 34, 36, 49, 145, 183, 194
Literaturnaia Moskva (*Literary Moscow*), 188, 189, 194
Lithuania, 162, 182, 215
Catholics, 47
language, 163
See also Kaunas
Lockean world, 11, 12
Loga-Sowinski, Ignacy, 100
Lozovsky, Solomon, 138
Luka, Laszlo, 100, 103
Lysenko, Trofim, 36–37, 64, 157
Lysenkoism, 37, 87, 117, 157

Malenkov, Georgi, 51, 56, 59, 135, 143, 144, 145, 157, 192, 210, 217, 225n134, 258
Afghanistan relations, 239
anti-Khrushchev, 191
budget, 148
Fadeev memo, 171
Hungarian relations, 200, 206, 209
India, Burma, and Afghanistan tour, 5
memo to Stalin, 62
nuclear warfare, 244
US-Soviet relations, 243
Malik, Iakob, 130, 133
Mao, Zedong, 6, 29, 145
assessment of Stalin, 230
Great Leap Forward, 4, 6
Hundred Flowers Campaign, 235
Korean War, 125–30
Moscow visit, 124, 131
nuclear warfare, 232
Sino-Soviet relations, 117, 119, 120–30, 229–35, 257, 259
Stalin's negotiations, 95, 118, 120–30, 135
Tito's conversations, 234

Marshall, George, 3, 96, 113n183, 119, 132, 139
   Moscow visit, 137n304
Marshall Plan, 3, 5, 71, 91, 95, 96, 97, 98, 107, 135, 139, 140
   Soviet, 231
   Soviets against, 256, 262, 265
Marxism-Leninism, 49, 78, 175, 223, 233
Masaryk, Tomas, 97
Mastny, Vojtech, 111, 142, 264
McSweeney, Bill, 13
Meditsinskii Rabochii, 55
Melnikov, L. G., 160, 163
Menshikov, Mikhail, 31
Meyerhold, Vsevolod, 179
   Mandat, 190
Michurin, Vladimir, 37n21
Michurinist doctrine, 37
Middle East, 20, 132, 241
migration policy, 19n52
Mikhalkov, Sergei V., 162
   First-Class Chauffeur/Shofer Ponevole, 186
Mikhoels, Solomon, 52, 133, 150, 159
Mikoian, Anastas, 139, 143, 152, 153, 157–58, 239, 245
   anti-party plenum, 249n225
   Argentina relations, 237
   atomic weapon assistance to China, 232
   criticism of political economy textbook, 243, 248
   Hungary relations, 203–8, 209
   Khrushchev supporter, 191
   Korean War, 250n232
   meetings with Mao, 120–21, 124, 125
   Sino-Soviet relations, 120–21, 124, 125, 232, 234
   Stalin's Banana Affair, 31
   Stalin's birthday, 146
   Suez Canal, 242
   Yugoslavia relations, 224, 226
Mikolayczyk, Stanislaw, 77
Milk Congress, 91
Minc, Hilary, 86, 87, 94, 100
Mingrelian Affair, 50, 150, 152
Mollet, Guy, 239, 241
Molotov, Viacheslav, 3, 24, 37, 62, 63, 72, 74, 77, 80, 81, 84, 86, 87, 89n74, 99, 108, 110, 149, 152–53, 176, 192, 201, 203, 205, 206, 207, 210–11, 245
   Afghani relations, 239
   anti-party group, 143, 201n8, 204n20, 235, 249n225, 250
   anti-Semitism, 159
   Berlin border, 215
   chair of Presidium, 179–80
   complaints against Ulbricht, 216, 219
   eastern Germany land reform, 112
   foreign policy, 243, 248–50, 252
   French relations, 113, 131
   GDR relations, 216–17, 220
   Hungarian relations, 140, 259
   Mao's visit, 124–25
   Nazi concentration camps, 115
   nuclear warfare, 247
   ouster, 182, 191, 229, 258
   Paris trip, 96–97
   Rumanian relations, 113n180
   Sino-Soviet relations, 233
   Stalin's funeral speech, 145
   UN trusteeships, 132
   US-Soviet relations, 119, 134, 137–39
   Yugoslavia relations, 98, 222–24, 225n123, 226n127, 227–28, 237
   ZIS-110 limousines, 148
Mongolia, 118, 121, 237
   See also Inner Mongolia; Outer Mongolia
Montezuma, 14
Moravcsik, Andrew, 17–18
Moscow, Soviet Union, 3, 25
   Writers' Union, 179, 194
   See also Cominform; Higher Party School; Soviet Union
Moscow Declaration, 208, 234
Moscow Museum of New Western Art, 61
Moscow State University
   Institute of Physics, 37
Mosfilm, 187
Moslems, 57, 166
Munnich, Ferenc, 208, 209
Muradeli, Vano
   The Great Friendship, 110

Nagasaki, Japan, 7, 134
Nagy, Ferenc, 102
Nagy, Imre, 200, 201–2, 204–7, 208, 209, 259
Naimark, Norman, 112
Nanking, China, 122
Nasser, Gamal Abdel, 199, 236, 240, 241
national liberation movements (NLMs), 5, 82, 121, 131, 233, 236, 239, 257
National Peasants Party, 74
NATO. *See* North Atlantic Treaty Organization
Nazis, 84, 100, 171, 253
   cartoons, 53
   See also concentration camps
Nehru, Jawaharlal, 6
Nekrasov's Craft, 156
Nelson, Horatio, 51
Nenni, Pietro, 135
Nevskii, Aleksandr, 50
New Course, 252
   Eastern Europe, 198, 201, 202, 203, 204, 211, 234, 259
   East Germany, 216, 217, 218, 219, 220–21

Index

Hungary, 221
   Poland, 211, 214
Nixon, Richard M., 236
Nkrumah, Kwame, 236
North Atlantic Treaty Organization (NATO), 3, 141–42, 225, 239, 246, 249
North Korea, 118, 126–30, 230
Nosek, Vaclav, 104
Novikov, Nikolai, 138
Novoe Vremia/New Times, 63
Novyi Mir/New World, 22, 32, 68, 150, 152, 161, 170, 179, 188, 193n197, 194
nuclear aircraft, 266
nuclear arms, 148, 231, 232, 242, 245–47
   control, 12, 244, 245, 248
nuclear physics, 232
nuclear reactors, 232

The Oath, 66
Ochab, Edward, 87n68, 212, 213, 214
Oktiabr, 40, 172
Omelchenko, Konstantin, 53
Operation Whirlwind, 207, 209, 210
Orlov, Iurii, 181, 214n69
Orlova, Raisa, 175
Outer Mongolia, 118, 121
Ovechkin, Valentin, 176
   "On the Brink," 152

Palestine, 56, 132, 133
Panferov, Fedor, 161
   "O cherepakh i cherepushkakh,"
   "On Turtles and Small Brains," 40
Panova, Vera
   Kruzhilikha, 32
   Span of Time, 172–73
Paris, France
   Congress of Criminology, 91
   government, 239
   Marshall Plan, 3, 96–97
   Molotov's visit, 96, 138
   theaters, 158
Pasternak, Boris, 179, 180n150, 190, 192, 195
   Doctor Zhivago, 183, 184–85, 188
Pasternak, Yevgeny, 188
Patolichev, Nikolai, 163
Pauker, Anna, 100
Paustovsky, Konstantin, 175, 183, 194
People's Liberation Army (PLA), 119, 121, 122, 127
People's Republic of China. *See* China
People's Republic of Mongolia. *See* Mongolia
Petrosian, A., 163
Petrushevskii, General, 100n117
Piech, Wilhelm, 112, 114n190, 115, 116, 138, 142
Pilniak, Boris, 190
Pishevari, Said Jafar, 82

Pleshakov, Constantine, 80
Poland, 5
   Academy of Sciences, 212n55
   Allies, 136, 138
   anti-Russian nationalism, 86
   border, 114
   Central Committee, 87, 213, 215
      Press Department, 89
   Joint Committee, 94
   New Course, 211, 214
   Politburo, 212n54, 213
   religion, 95
   riots, 203
   socialism, 76–77, 84, 211, 215
   Soviet Union relations, 28, 71, 75, 76–77, 79, 84, 85–89, 95, 100, 103–4, 108, 138, 182, 184, 185, 189, 194n203, 199–215, 223, 225, 231, 259
   See also Warsaw; Warsaw Pact; Warsaw University
Polevoi, Boris, 154, 184, 185
Polianskii, Ivan, 59, 160, 166
Polikarpov, Dmitrii, 40, 162, 183, 185, 186n169, 187
Polish Workers' Party, 73n2, 75, 86
Polotskii, Vladimir, 50
Pomerantsev, Alexander, 154, 155, 172, 184, 192, 212
   "On Sincerity in Literature," 170
Ponomarenko, Panteleimon K., 194, 212nn54–55, 214
Ponomarev, Boris, 104, 145, 188, 226
Port Arthur, China, 95, 118, 122, 124, 125, 230
Pospelov, Petr N., 145, 152, 154, 158, 163, 164, 170, 184, 185, 191, 193, 212
Poulantzas, Nicos, 21
Prague, Czechoslovakia, 77, 91, 93, 95, 97, 103, 104, 132–33.
   See also Charles University
Pravda, 26, 36, 50, 145, 157n55, 160, 163, 225
   Doctors' Plot, 53
   editorial, April 1952, 68
   Ehrenburg letter, 55
   May Day 1956 slogans, 224n114
   "On the Brink," 152
   PRC recognition, 122
   Soviet Declaration, 207
   Stalin's death, 146
   Stalin's editorial, 73n3
   Stalin's reply to Churchill's Fulton, Missouri speech, 80
Pravda Ukraina, 160
prison camps, 179, 180, 186
"Professors' Affair," 61–62
Pudovkin, Vsevolod
   Admiral Nakhimov, 69
   Return of Vasilii Bortnikov, 169
Pushkin, Georgii M., 49, 105

Pushkin Museum, 145, 155
Pushkin Theater, 187
Pyrev, Ivan, 53, 187, 196
　Tale of the Siberian Land, 65

Quiqihaer, China, 119

Raizman, Iuli, 54
Rajk, Laszlo, 74, 83, 87, 91, 94, 100, 204
Rajk Affair, 92–93, 104, 202
Rakosi, Matias
　attacks by Beria, 200
　clique, 210
　disavowal of New Course, 201–2, 204, 221
　Khrushchev's speech, 212
　letter from Stalin, 83
　in Moscow, 100
　ousting, 209, 221
　prisoner of war, 100
　resignation as prime minister, 200
　Soviet Union relations, 74, 84, 90, 91–92, 105, 110, 201–5, 209, 211, 227, 252, 259
　spreading kompromat, 103–4
　Stalin's birthday celebration, 101
Rapoport, Iosif, 157
Rapoport, Yakov, 55
Red Army, 40, 76, 84, 86, 88, 102, 110, 113n180, 115, 150, 174, 190n184, 223, 257
relationality, 8
Revai, Jozsef, 85, 94
Rhee, Syngman, 127n250
Rhodesia, 12
Richter, Stanislav, 195
Ripka, Hubert, 80
Riurikov, Boris, 183, 186, 188, 194, 195
Rokk, Marika
　Girl of My Dreams, 38, 64
Rokossovsky, Konstantin, 87, 90, 105, 214
Romm, Mikhail, 53, 187, 196
Roosevelt, Franklin D., 114n191, 131, 137, 266
Roshal, Grigorii, 54
Roshchin, Nikolai, 122
Roskin, Grigorii, 61, 62
　See also Kliueva-Roskin affair
Rorty, Richard, 13n26
Ruggie, John G., 15
Rumania, 76n13, 78–79, 91, 105
　expelled from party, 90
　Politburo, 110
　Red Army, 113n180
　Soviet liberation, 100
　Soviet relations, 103, 104, 110
Rumiantsev, Alexei, 145, 162, 165, 166, 167, 168, 171n119, 184, 193
Russian nation, 30, 43–45, 47–56, 60, 61, 62, 70, 77, 78, 83, 95, 225, 242, 252, 258
　anti-Semitism, 159–62
　foreign relations, 196
　and non-Russian nations, 162–65
　Orthodoxy, 57–59, 147, 165–68
　Poland against, 86
　Soviet, 158–65, 255
　　Muscovite Center, 168–69
　　writers, 194
Russian Orthodox Church, 45, 57–58, 60, 158, 165–68, 258, 262
　State Council for russian Orthodox Church Affairs, 38
Rybalchenko, Major General, 42
Rykov, Alexei, 179

Saburov, Maksim, 191, 234, 249n227
Sachsenhausen (concentration camp), 115, 116
Saint-Saens, Camille
　Samson and Delilah, 52
Savchenko, Igor, 53, 173
Saveliev, Aleksandr, 193
Schirdewan, Karl, 221
Schumann, Robert, 195
Semenov, Vladimir, 133n289, 141, 216, 218, 219, 241
Semushkin, Tikhon, 161
Serov, Ivan, 113, 115
Shakespeare, William, 63, 190
Shaoqi, Liu, 119n209, 121, 124n233, 139n313, 234
Shatalin, N. N., 160
Shelepin, Aleksandr, 145
Shepilov, Dimitrii, 38n25, 62, 63, 68, 78, 145, 153, 160, 163, 182, 184, 185, 192, 193, 207, 208, 210, 212n55, 225, 226, 227, 228, 232, 240, 241, 245, 248
Sholokhov, Mikhail, 49, 162
　Quiet Don, 55
Shkarovskii, Mikhail, 168
Shveitser, Mikhail
　Sasha Vstupaet v Zhizn/Sasha Embarks on Life, 187
　Tugoi Uzel/Tight Knot, 187
Shvernik, Nikolai, 153
Shtykov, Terentii, 126–27
Sikkink, Kathryn, 22
Silin, Mikhail A., 101, 103
Simonov, Konstantin, 33, 34, 62, 154–55, 191
　Chuzhaia Ten (*Someone Else's Shadow*), 31
　condemnation of Zhdanov's 1946 CC Resolutions, 179, 183, 184–86
　defended Dudintsev, 188–89
　editor of *Novyi Mir*, 32, 151, 161, 171, 179, 188
　rejection of Pasternak's *Doctor Zhivago*, 188
　removal as editor of *Literaturnaia Gazeta*, 145

Index

Sinkiang, China, 121, 125, 230
Sino-American Relations, 70–71, 232n154, 261
   Taiwan invasion, 118, 122, 127–28, 129, 130
   US-China détente. *See* détente
Sino-Soviet relations, 117–19, 257, 261
   alliance, 120–25
   Khrushchev and, 230n144, 231, 232–35, 259
   Mao and, 117, 119, 120–30, 229–35, 257, 259
   split, 228–35
      economic and military relations, 231–32
      Taiwan invasion, 118, 122, 127–28, 129, 130
      Treaty of Friendship and Alliance, 118
      Treaty of Friendship and Cooperation, 4
      Treaty of Friendship, Cooperation, and Mutual Assistance, 125
      United States, 229
   See also Chiang, Kai-shek; Kim, Jong Il; Mao, Zedong; Shaoqi, Liu
Slansky, Rudolf, 93, 95, 103, 104
Slansky Affair, 92–93, 95
Smallholders Party, 74
Smith, Rogers, 16
Smith, Walter, 133n289
Smirnov, A. A., 115, 140, 162
Smirnov, N., 185
Snechkus, Antanas, 215
Social Democratic Party (SDP), 114
social identities, 7, 8–10, 17, 18, 19, 20
socialism, 64, 98, 107, 120
   Central Asia, 238
   China, 124, 229, 233, 259
   Czechoslovakia, 85, 93
   Eastern Europe, 87, 90, 111, 128, 256
   East Germany, 216, 217–18, 254
   Germany, 117, 218, 220
   Hungary, 201, 204, 209
   Poland, 76–77, 84, 211, 215
   Soviet Union, 3, 6, 41, 42, 84, 88, 95, 116, 131, 142, 146, 147, 149, 152, 158, 167, 169, 170, 171, 175, 177–78, 180, 181, 188, 189, 198–99, 201, 221, 222, 227, 228, 229, 233, 235, 238, 242, 244–45, 247, 248, 249, 252, 254, 256, 257, 258, 259, 265
   Vietnam, 131
   Yugoslavia, 4, 110, 201, 222, 224, 226, 259
Socialist United Party, 73n2
Socialist Workers' Party, 73n2
societal constructivism. *See* constructivism, societal
Sofronov, Anatolii, 161, 162
Sokolovskii, Marshal Vasilii, 113, 133n289, 140, 141, 155, 218, 219n88, 247
Solingen, Etel, 264
South Africa
   Hobbesian world, 12
South Korea, 118, 127, 129, 230

Sovetskaia Etnografia, 26, 169
Soviet Union, 3, 25
   Academy of Sciences, 36, 37, 48, 51, 233
   Institute of Ethnography, 169
      (see also *Sovetskaia Etnografiia*)
   Institute of Philosophy, 158
   Algeria relations, 239
   atomic weapon assistance to China, 232
   Bolshevik Revolution, 33, 48, 63, 67, 79, 80, 154n36, 172, 224n114
   Central Committee (CC), 36, 39, 41, 56, 58, 87, 102, 103, 105, 150, 153, 158, 163, 165–66, 167, 177, 180, 191, 203, 248
      anti-Semitism, 52, 53n86
      Culture Department, 35, 155, 162, 171n119, 176, 183, 192, 194–95
      Department of Relations with the International Communist Movement, 99
      Department on Economic Relations with People's Democracies, 234
      Department on Ties with Foreign Communist Parties, 188
      editorial boards, 35
      films, 37, 65, 69, 174, 183
      Foreign Policy Department (CC FPD), 75n9, 84, 85n55, 88, 93, 99, 101, 104, 105, 106, 107, 109
      Ideology Department, 35, 145
      International Information Department (CC IID), 75, 77
      Jewish writers, 52
      literature, 185, 239
      plays, 176
      Plenum, 143, 148n15, 150, 186, 190, 243
         agriculture, September 1953, 152, 156
         Belgrade trip assessment, July 9–12, 1955, 223
         Beria removal, July 2, 1953, 150, 220
         industry, July 1955, 157
         Khrushchev, July 9, 1955, 233, 250n232
         New Course, June 1955, 220
         October 1952, 191, 215
         Yugoslavia, February 14, 1957, 227
         Yugoslavia, July 11, 1955, 224
      Propaganda and Agitation (Agitprop) Department, 34, 37, 40, 49, 51, 55, 57, 58, 62, 88, 166, 167, 192
      Kultura and Zhizn (Culture and Life), 35
      Resolutions
         April 5, 1956, 181
         Muradeli's opera, 110
         1946, 179, 183, 185, 187, 188, 189n183
         1948, 179, 188, 189n183
         Novyi Mir, 151
         "On Big Inadequacies in Scientific-Atheistic Propaganda and Measures for its Improvement," 167

Soviet Union (*continued*)
    "On Restructuring Literary and Arts Organizations," April 1932, 40
    "On the Anti-Marxist Ideological Positions of the Leadership of the Polish Workers' Party," 86
    "On the Cult of Personality and its Consequences," 177
    "On the Journals *Zvezda* and *Leningrad*," 65, 67, 69, 117, 183
    purging biology and agronomy of Lysenkoism, 157n55
    reduce taxes, 148
    religious revivals, 167
    Russian Orthodox Church, 166
    Science and Culture Department, 40n30, 156, 161, 164, 169, 193
    Science and Higher Education Department, 52
    "Table of the Dynamics of the Quantitative Representation of Bureaucrats of Jewish Origin in the Soviet Nomenklatura in 1945–52," 53
Central Statistical Administration, 193
Chinese relations. *See* Sino-Soviet relations
Chinese revolution, 232, 233
Control Commission (SCC), 216, 217
Council of Ministers, 42, 61, 68, 92, 93, 105, 229
Cuba, 245n213
culture market, 37–38
de-Stalinization, 4, 5, 30, 144, 145–46, 164n88, 196, 197, 198, 200, 202, 206, 210, 211, 212, 213, 215, 217, 229, 230, 235, 243–44
détente. *See* détente
East German relations, 111–17
Egypt relations, 240
famines, 29, 34, 42
film industry, 33–34
foreign policy
    before the Cold War, 1945–47, 73–83
    East Germany, 111–17
    excommunication of Yugoslavia in 1948, 106–11, 256
    Four Power agreements, 112, 119, 141, 243
    Korean War, 126–30
    Stalinization of Eastern Europe, 1947–53, 83–105
    third world, 131–33
    United States, 133–42, 257, 260–67
        fear of a new war, 134–36
        Germany and Eastern Europe, 136–42
    See also Sino-Soviet relations; Soviet Union: Thaw
Hungarian invasion, 182–93, 198, 207n37, 227
honor courts, 62

hydrogen bombs, 253
Interior Ministry, 104
    Special Commission, 39
Khrushchev's de-Stalinization speech, 143, 152, 164n88, 180, 221, 230, 250
Korean War, 126–30
Kremlin, 5, 49, 81, 99, 124, 146n9, 190, 212, 214
Main Administration for Preserving State and Military Secrets in the Press (Glavlit), 35, 53, 151, 193n197
Mao's visit, 124–25
Marxism-Leninism,, 49, 78, 175, 223, 233
Ministry of State Security (MGB), 52, 56, 78, 85, 90, 91, 93, 94, 95, 101, 103, 104, 150, 152
"On the nationalistic manifestations of certain workers of the Jewish Antifascist Committee," 51
modern project, 64–66
Politburo, 6, 58, 86, 87, 94, 97, 99, 104, 105, 107, 126, 129, 145, 258
protector against Germany, 84
"real" dangers, 41–43
recognition of the state of Israel, 132
religion, 38–39, 57–59
    (*see also* State Council for Russian Orthodox Church Affairs;
socialism, 3, 6, 41, 42, 84, 88, 95, 116, 131, 142, 146, 147, 149, 152, 158, 167, 169, 170, 171, 175, 177–78, 180, 181, 188, 189, 198–99, 201, 221, 222, 227, 228, 229, 233, 235, 238, 242, 244–45, 247, 248, 249, 252, 254, 256, 257, 258, 259, 265
State Council on the Affairs of Religious Cults)
Special Commission for Studying Materials on the Mass Repressions from 1935–40, 152
Sputnik program, 245n213
State Council for Russian Orthodox Church Affairs, 38, 57, 58, 165, 166, 167, 168
State Council on the Affairs of Religious Cults (CARC), 22, 38, 57, 58, 59, 160, 166, 262
Suez Crisis, 207n37, 236, 241–42
televisions, 30n2
Thaw, 143–97
    fallibility of, 152–53
    discourse of danger meets discourse of difference, 146–47
    external others, 153–58
    Hungarian invasion, 182–93, 198, 207n37, 227
    implications for foreign policy, 196–97
    institutions and identities, 192–96
    more private space, 169–71
    more secure, 148–51

Muscovite Center, 168–69
new Soviet class, 174–77
Russian Orthodox Church, 165–68
Soviet Russian Nation, 158–65
  anti-Semitism, 159–62
  and non-Russian nations, 162–65
Yugoslavia relations,
  excommunication in 1948, 106–11, 256
See also Kirov
Spychalski, Marian, 100, 104, 211, 214n69
Stalin, Josef, 4, 22
  Banana Affair, 31
  Czechoslovakian relations, 79, 80
  death, 4, 5, 26, 27, 29, 32, 35, 47, 61, 77, 87,
    95, 99, 118, 142, 143–47, 152, 156,
    157, 158, 159, 161, 163, 170n116,
    173, 182, 190, 192, 195, 197, 198, 199,
    200, 211, 215, 221, 222, 228, 229, 231,
    235, 236, 238, 239, 243, 244, 245, 247,
    252, 255, 257–58, 262, 267
  Economic Problems of Socialism in the USSR,
    148, 158, 248
  foreign policy, 72–42
    Chinese relations, 117–19
      Alliance, 120–25
    East German exception, 111–17
    excommunication of Yugoslavia in 1948,
      106–11
    irrelevant third world, 131–33
    Korean War, 612–30
    Stalinization of Eastern Europe, 1947–53,
      83–105
    tolerance of difference, 73–83
  last meeting with Tito, 79
  "On Rightist Deviation," 85
Stalinism, 227
  anti-, 200
  de-Stalinization, 4, 5, 30, 144, 145–46,
    164n88, 196, 197, 198, 200, 202, 206,
    210, 211, 212, 213, 215, 217, 229,
    230, 235, 243–44
  postwar, 29–71, 144, 178
    cinema, 33–34
    creative unions, 35
    culture market, 37–38
    defending rights of religious believers,
      38–39
    discursive elements and danger, 66–70,
      258–59
    editorial boards, 35
    institution, 35, 143, 182, 235, 261
    predominant discourse of Soviet identity,
      43–56
      Soviet relations with other states, 70–71
    "real" dangers, 41–43
    religion, 57–58
    scientific intelligentsia, 36–37

uncertainty, 1945–47, 39–41
Western Other, 59–64, 96
Stalin Prizes, 32, 68, 107, 146
State Council on Religious Cults, 22
Stites, Richard, 40
Stuttgart, Germany, 138
Suez Canal, 240
Suez Crisis, 207n37, 236, 241–42
Sun Valley Serenade, 64
Supreme Soviet, 34, 99, 114, 148, 149, 150, 159,
  180, 193, 233n159
Surkov, Aleksei, 34, 161, 162, 168,
  172, 185
okSuslov, Mikhail, 62, 77–78, 84, 145,
  203, 206, 208, 245
  anti-religion, 58
  anti-Semitism, 94
  Bolshoi Theater stoppage, 52
  Polish relations, 105
  Hungarian relations, 77, 207
  Khrushchev ally, 191
  letter from Ehrenburg, 56
  memo to Stalin, 51
  visit to Hungary, 202–3, 205
  Yugoslav relations, 109, 110, 226
Suvorov, General, 115
Svoboda, Tsena, 104
Syria, 82, 241

Taiwan, 118, 122, 127–28, 129, 130
The Tajik People's Holiday, 238
Tarasov, P., 155, 164, 169
Tashkent, Uzbekistan, 51, 54, 55, 155, 160
Tatars, 49, 164, 168, 180n148
Tendriakov, Vladimir
  *Sasha Vstupaet v Zhizn/Sasha Embarks on
    Life*, 187
  Tugoi Uzel/Tight Knot, 187
Thaw
  abroad, 198–253
    developing world, 235–42
    Germany, 215–21
    Hungary, 199–211
    Poland, 211–15
    United States, 242–51
    Yugoslavia, 221–28
  Soviet Union, 143–97
    fallibility of, 152–53
    discourse of danger meets discourse of
      difference, 146–47
    external others, 153–58
    Hungarian invasion, 182–93, 198, 207n37,
      227
    implications for foreign policy, 196–97
    institutions and identities, 192–96
    more private space, 169–71
    more secure, 148–51

Thaw (continued)
	Muscovite Center, 168–69
	new Soviet class, 174–77
	Russian Orthodox Church, 165–68
	Soviet Russian Nation, 158–65
		anti-Semitism, 159–62
		and non-Russian nations, 162–65
Thorez, Maurice, 98, 99, 100
Tikhomirov, M.
	Voprosy Istorii, 61
Tito, Josip Broz, 87
	Balkans relations, 77
	China relations, 234
	civil war, 98
	excommunication, 5, 106–11, 256
	Krushchev meeting, June 1956, 235n174
	Krushchev meeting for Operation Whirlwind, 209
	Khrushchev's apology, 4, 224n115
	lasting meeting with Stalin, 79
	overthrow and assassination, 3
	socialism, 259
	Soviet Union relations, 92, 222, 226
	visit to China, 230n144
	visit to Soviet Union, 227–28
	See also Slansky Affair
Titoism, 4, 91, 259
Tiulpanov, Sergei, 102n129, 113, 114, 115, 117
Tiurin, V. N., 176
Togliatti, Palmiro, 98, 100, 135
Traktoristy, 68
Trieste, 15n36, 106
Troepolskii, Gabriil
	"From the Notes of an Agronomist," 152
Trotsky, Leon, 184n164
Trotskyism, 68, 91, 105, 153, 184, 186
Trud, 55
Truman, Harry S., 127, 130, 134, 139, 251
	Administration, 96, 137
Truman Doctrine, 3, 5, 96
Turkey, 96
	Soviet relations, 244, 250, 260, 263
	US aid, 134, 136
	US military support, 3
Turkmenistan, 164, 168, 171
Tvardovsky, Aleksandr, 150, 170, 174, 183, 184, 187, 192, 194
	"Terkin in the Other World," 151
	Za daliu dal, 190

Ukraine, 42, 47, 78, 144, 159, 160–61, 162, 253, 265
	anti-Jewish pogroms, 54
	authors, 60
	Jews, 58–59
	literature, 50
	nationality policy, 163
	population, 255
	writers, 169, 185
	See also Kiev
Ulbricht, Walter, 112, 115, 116, 117, 138, 210, 211, 216–17, 218–19, 220–21
Union of Writers (UW), 22, 33, 154, 175, 184
	See also Writers' Union (or better to just put cites from WU under here?)
	14th Plenum, 161
	2nd Congress, 171
	Plenum meeting, 188
	Third Plenum, 194
United Nations (UN), 81, 242
	Security Council (UNSC), 125, 128, 129, 130, 240
United States, 8, 61, 131
	agriculture, 156–57
	Algeria relations, 239
	Bizonia, 140
	Eastern Europe relations, 98
	East Germany, 218
	Ehrenburg visits, 63
	Francophone Africa relations, 10
	Geneva summit, 201
	Germany relations, 219–20
	Ghana delegation, 236–37
	Hungary relations, 209
	Jews, 53
	Korea War, 126–30
	Middle East relations, 20, 20n54
	national identity, 25
	occupation policy, 115–16
	Poland relations, 75, 86, 105
	racism, 9n3
	Soviet Union relations, 6, 42–43, 70, 73, 79, 81, 84, 95–96, 122, 133–42, 199, 236, 242–52, 253, 256–58, 260–67
		fear of a new war, 80, 82, 118, 119, 134–36, 153, 254
		Germany and Eastern Europe, 136–42
		Lend-Lease suspension, 137
		Suez Crisis, 207n37, 236, 241–42
	Yalta Conference, 121, 124
	Yugoslavia relations, 83, 222, 225
US Congress, 61n132
Uzbekistan, 50, 51, 155, 226, 239
	See also Teshkent

Valdescu-Rakoas, G., 91
Valkov, Victor, 222n103, 226n129
Vandenburg Resolution, 135
Varga, Evgenii
	Changes in the Economy of Capitalism as a Result of the Second World War, 64
Vas, Zoltan, 94
Vietnam, 4, 5, 123, 243
	socialism, 131
Vinogradov, Vladimir, 222, 237
Voice of America, 61, 201

Index

Volobuev, P. V., 193
Volokitina, Tatiana V., 74n6, 101, 111
Voprosy Istorii/Questions of History, 61, 164, 193
Voroshilov, Kliment, 58, 74, 146, 150, 152, 182, 191, 204n30, 205–6, 207, 223, 228, 258
Vyshinsky, Andrei, 92, 94, 99n112, 112, 124, 127

Waltz, Kenneth, 10, 11
Warsaw, Poland, 86, 89, 105, 212, 213
Warsaw Pact, 207, 208, 214, 233
Warsaw University, 212n55
Weiner, Amir, 54
Weldes, Jutta, 16–17
Wendt, Alexander, 10, 11, 12, 13, 14, 17
Westad, Odd Arne, 229
West Berlin, Germany, 135, 141n324, 219
West Germany, 138, 140, 141, 142, 202, 216, 217, 218, 220, 221, 246
West European Union (WEU), 111, 140, 141
World War II, 4, 28, 29, 33, 57, 64, 80, 100, 117, 178, 213, 244, 254, 263, 266
World War III, 128, 130, 134, 135
writers, 31, 35, 38, 39, 40, 62, 67, 151, 160, 164, 170, 179, 251
   American, 63
   British, 154
   critical of Rakosi, 202
   foreign, 59, 195
   Hungarian, 155
   Jewish, 33, 52, 161
   Kazakh, 163
   Mexican, 155
   Moscow, 188n181
   Muscovite, 168
   Russian, 161n75, 168n107
   Soviet, 49, 65, 145, 151, 154, 161, 162, 163, 189, 190, 191, 194, 256
   to the UN, 248
   supporting suppression of Hungary, 183
   Ukrainian, 169, 185
   See also Leningrad Writers' Union; Union of Writers; Writers' Union; *specific individual authors, e.g., Simonov, Konstantin*
Writers' Union (WU), 146n9, 152, 154, 161, 162, 171, 185, 190, 196, 255
   Leningrad, 69, 154, 169, 194
   Moscow, 179, 194
   Polish, 212
   2nd Congress, 161, 168, 169, 171, 172, 174, 176, 193
   See also *Literaturnaia Gazeta*; *The Moscow Literator*

Yalta Conference, 113, 114n191, 121, 124, 126, 137, 266
Young Men's Christian Associations, 88
Yudin, Pavel, 230
Yugoslavia
   Bulgaria treaty, 136
   Central Committee, 228
   condemned for nationalist deviations, 84
   domestic policy, 108, 109
   economy, 79
   excommunication, 4, 106–11, 199, 256
   Israel relations, 132
   Politburo, 108, 109
   socialism, 3, 4, 6, 110, 198, 201, 204, 222, 224, 226, 259
   Soviet-Yugoslav split, 6, 28, 106–11
   Soviet Union relations, 4, 71, 72, 77, 79, 83, 120, 136, 198, 209, 210, 213, 221–28, 229n140, 237, 242, 243, 244, 249, 256, 262
   rapprochement, 252, 253, 259
   writers, 168n107, 202

Zabolotskii, Nikolai, 179, 190
Zakhariades, Nikos, 109
Zambrowski, Roman, 86, 94, 100, 212n54
Zhdanov, Andrei, 32, 69, 73, 78, 80, 99
   CC Resolutions of 1946, 179, 184
   criticism of *Ivan the Terrible II*, 60
   denunciation of Zoshchenko, 154
   Jewish literature, 52
   letter to Thorez, 98
   memo from Aleksandrov, 40
   servility, 62
   speech at opening of the Cominform, 106–7
   Stalin Prizes, 68
Zhdanov, Iurii, 52
Zhdanovschina, 32n7, 39, 65
Zhebrak, Anton, 157
Zhemchuzhinaia, Polina, 159
Zhuiovich, Sreten, 109
Zhukov, Georgii, 42, 138, 180, 191, 207, 208, 210, 244n208, 247, 249
Zimianin, Mikhail, 163, 211, 214n69, 222, 226n129
Zinoviev, Grigorii, 177, 179, 186
Znamia, 61, 170, 173
Zorin, Leonid, 184, 192
   Alpatov, 176
   Guests, 172, 176, 183, 185
Zorin, Valerian, 91, 222
Zoshchenko, Mikhail, 39, 65, 84, 111, 117, 154, 155, 179, 226
   "Partisan Stories," 32
Zubkova, Elena, 42, 57, 144, 243
Zubok, Vladislav M., 80, 110n170, 231, 244